TASTE

TASTE

THE STORY OF BRITAIN
THROUGH ITS COOKING

Kate Colquhoun

BLOOMSBURY

Published by Bloomsbury USA, New York
Distributed to the trade by Holtzbrinck Publishers

All papers used by Bloomsbury USA are natural, recyclable products made from wood
grown in well-managed forests. The manufacturing processes conform to the environmental
regulations of the country of origin.

LIBRARY OF CONGRESS CATALOGING-IN-PUBLICATION DATA HAS BEEN APPLIED FOR

ISBN-10 1-59691-410-6
ISBN-13 978-1-59691-410-0

First U.S. Edition 2007

1 3 5 7 9 10 8 6 4 2

Typeset by Hewer Text UK Ltd, Edinburgh
Printed in the United States of America by Quebecor World Fairfield

for
Freddie and Billy
Iain and Sally

Cookery means the knowledge of Medea and of Circe and of Helen and of the Queen of Sheba. It means the knowledge of all herbs and fruits and balms and spices, and all that is healing and sweet in the fields and groves and savoury in meats. It means carefulness and inventiveness and willingness and readiness of appliances. It means the economy of your grandmothers and the science of the modern chemist; it means much testing and no wasting; it means English thoroughness and French art and Arabian hospitality; and, in fine, it means that you are to be perfectly and always ladies – loaf givers.

– JOHN RUSKIN

Contents

Author's Note

The story of Britain's culinary past can be unfolded from letters, diaries, manuscript collections and household accounts, paintings and drawings, poems and plays, as well as from published records, cookbooks and even novels. From the sixteenth century onwards, as Britain's printed cookbook tradition began to flourish, literally hundreds of these books – tiny little things that smell of cinnamon or vast multi-volume tomes – appeared, and many find their way into the pages that follow. What they do not describe is the endless watercarting, the scrubbing with sand, the chapped hands (though there are recipes for ointments), chimneys that will not draw, spits that shed their loads, guttering candles in the kitchen gloom or the uphill struggle to keep things fresh and vermin-free. The life behind the ideas.

Recipes peddle dreams as well as reality, and few printed recipes appeared at the vanguard of change. Even ostensibly ground-breaking collections scooped up and ordered a process of change that was ongoing – so that we have to be wary of using them as a way of absolutely dating changes in culinary techniques and tastes. Some writers, including Elizabeth David, have suggested that until the mass media changed the speed of communication printed books lagged thirty to forty years behind culinary practice. My own view is that there is a certain fluidity about historical fashion; we can absolutely date the first printed recipe (to have survived) for a certain dish, but in reality – as with changes in fashions for clothes, furniture, decoration, the fine arts, architecture and the like – the old and the new often marched happily hand in hand.

Recipes, from the time of the Romans until the turn of the twentieth century, were known as *receipts*, a lovely word which, for the sake of clarity only, I have modernised to *recipe* throughout.

I have consciously quoted all weights and measures, spelling and dates as I have found them in their original sources because it seems to me that this is the point about history: you take it as you find it, which is rarely all neat and orderly. In any case, the standardisation of weights was a tenuous business in Britain until well into the nineteenth century, so that a British pint is quite different from an American (or old English) one. Spelling was an equally fluid business. The change from the Julian to the Gregorian calendar in 1752 should not present problems since I have again given all dates in their original form.

List of Illustrations

IMAGES IN THE TEXT

ENDPAPERS

PROLOGUE

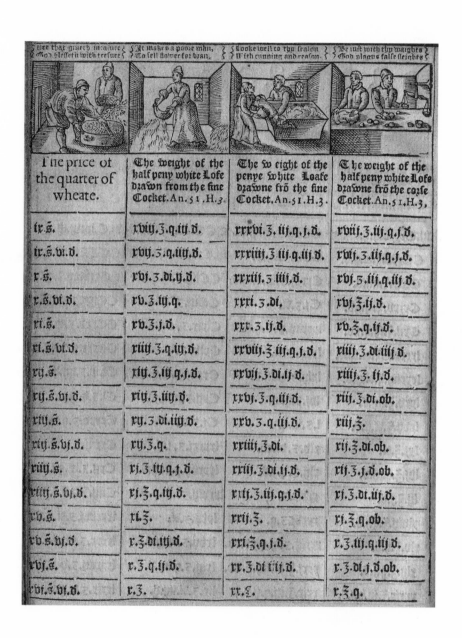

'The Assize of Bread newly corrected and enlarged from 12d the quarter of wheat into 3 pound + 6d the quarter. London 1600.'

The Staff of Life

Acorns were good till bread was found
— FRANCIS BACON

In 1782 Carl-Philip Moritz, a German visitor to London, enthused that

> the slices of bread and butter given to you with tea are as thin as poppy-
> leaves, but there is a way of roasting slices of buttered bread before the
> fire which is incomparable. One slice after another is taken and held to
> the fire with a fork until the butter is melted, then the following one will
> be always laid upon it so that the butter soaks through the whole pile of
> slices. This is called 'toast'.

Moritz luxuriated in this novel way of enjoying the most basic of all
foods in the Western diet: bread. In the same decade George Biggins –
one of the amateur experimenters of the 1760s known as the Lunar
Men and, coincidentally, the inventor of the coffee percolator – gave up
his place in a hot-air balloon in deference to an overweight actress who
took with her a picnic of chicken legs and bread rolls. Why was their
food recorded? Why is it important to us to know what people ate?

Well before the arrival of the Romans in Britain, bread formed the
cornerstone of 'companionship' (literally: 'with bread') and therefore
of society. With ale, it was the first foodstuff to be regulated in England
by law, in 1266. Without bread, the peasants revolted. In the Middle
Ages, bread was for some a basic of death as well as of life – at funerals,
paupers might be hired to take upon themselves the sins of the
deceased in order to rescue them from purgatory; these sin-eaters
sat by the corpse eating bread and salt with, occasionally, a tankard
of ale.

Bread was politics, but it was also such an ordinary daily detail that although it was essential, it was – for those who had it, at least – broadly overlooked. Its first written recipe did not appear in print until 1615, and the first full collection of bread recipes came almost two centuries after that. In general, its production, in common with other fundamental (if complicated) techniques like how to roast over an open fire, was taken entirely for granted. The processes were obvious, timeless, unchanging. Everyone, it seemed, just *knew* how to do it.

What Gervase Markham showed in 1615 in his collection of culinary and medical recipes called *The English Huswife* was that bread-making was not quite as easy as falling off a log. In fact, in the days before pre-processed and packaged foods, making anything at all was a wearying and labour-intensive graft. Unlike any of his predecessors, Markham took nothing for granted. Among recipes for curing the plague, for whitening teeth and for erasing freckles, there it is for the first time: a detailed essay on baking.

Markham's book was something of a best-seller in a world waking up to the printed word and craving instruction as well as erudition. But how did we get to this first proper recipe for a loaf of bread, and why was there a continuing demand for recipe collections in Britain? What did the earliest kitchens look like as they thrilled to the smell of a new batch emerging from the courtyard oven, and what kind of foods were eaten with this most basic of all Western staples?

Though fleeting, temporary and perishable, cookery plays such a powerfully symbolic role in our lives that they provide us with a valuable common language. We seem as a society to be unable to stop talking about food and the way we cook it. Has this always been so? Have we always known how to bake bread, raise pies, stuff a goose, skin an eel or freeze ice cream? As an island nation laced with stream, river and loch, why do we eat so little fish? Has our culinary use of vegetables always been narrow? Can the story of our foods and how we have chosen to cook and present them really tell us who we have been: is the kitchen the crucible of our domestic history? Are we, in our postmodern world, really so different from the invading Romans of the first century or the strutting imperial nabobs of the eighteenth?

To search for the answers, we have to go back to the beginning . . .

PREHISTORY

A woman crushing grain: before the introduction of the rotary quern, preparing grain for bread and pottage was back-breaking work.

1

The Kittiwake at Danebury

Most of the tribes in the interior do not grow corn but live
on milk and meat, and wear skins

— JULIUS CAESAR

In the middle of the nineteenth century a mighty storm battered the Orkney coast, washing away an ordinary dune to reveal a prehistoric kitchen midden, or rubbish dump, some 16 feet high. Oyster shells were discovered as well as the horns of ox and deer, and then a number of small stone houses emerged, remarkably preserved. These were the dwellings of some of the earliest inhabitants of the shores of the Bay of Skaill, evidence of the lives of people dating back to 3200 BC, sophisticated village houses containing rooms with square central hearths and filled with stone furniture including beds, benches, tables, dressers and boxes for food storage. A small stone cup still stood on one side of a hearth; there were stone mortars for pounding, large square blocks for breaking bones or splitting shellfish open, rough hatchets, circular flakes of stone sharpened for cutting, and crude vessels that showed evidence of use over a strong fire. Five millennia after its construction, one of the earliest British kitchens had been discovered.

During the same century, as industrialisation raged alongside a new passion for collection and classification, many more extraordinary objects rose to the surfaces of bogs and were pulled from land that had lain untouched for thousands of years. Some were finely wrought cooking utensils so beautiful in their craftsmanship and practicality that to look at them is to telescope the centuries, bringing us face to face with the culinary practices of our Bronze Age forebears. Among the oldest was the Dunaverney Flesh Hook lifted from a bog north of Ballymoney, County Antrim in 1829. A 4-foot-long wooden and cast-bronze pole with sharp prongs designed to haul large pieces of meat from a boiler, it is gloriously adorned with bronze models of a pair of ravens and a family of swans. When first crafted in the tenth century BC, this must have been a prized possession.

Downstream from London's Chelsea Bridge, as it began to rise from its construction site during the 1850s, the so-called Battersea Cauldron was dislodged from its muddy prison to rise to the surface of the Thames. Emerging into the modern world from that of the late eighth century BC, this splendid object was fashioned from seven sheets of carefully curved bronze riveted together to make a feasting vessel almost 2 feet wide. Its creation had required labour and skill; in its own day, the cauldron had proclaimed the wealth, power and social status of its owner.

In the absence of all written records, these kinds of archaeological discoveries allow us to piece together the history of our earliest cooking practices, offering us glimpses of the sorts of foods that were available, the ways in which they were cooked and the manner in which they were eaten.

Millennia before even Skara Brae, early humans acquired one of the very few things that set them apart from all other animals: fire. Now they could keep warm and begin to cook in the most rudimentary of ways, breaking down the fibres of meat to make it easier to digest and chew. And so the story is endlessly repeated: once human beings could rely on fire and on food, they could begin to civilise and to settle, to form societies, develop religions and, ultimately, learn to tame the technology of fire, driving it to higher and higher temperatures through the Stone, Bronze and Iron ages.

Around 4000 BC, Continental Neolithic farmers began to arrive in Britain, domesticating animals and cultivating patchworks of land using primitive ox-drawn ploughs with wooden shares, swapping the old hunter-gatherer lifestyle for settlement. The earliest cultivated wheats were known as *emmer* and *einkorn*, both with tough ears that held on so tightly to their grain that they had to be toasted to loosen them; barley was also sown, though rye and oats appeared only as weeds among the crops. Once parched, the ears were threshed, winnowed and pounded to a rough flour using the ancient saddle quern, a bow-shaped stone with a rolling-pin-shaped grinder. The effort was enormous, and the bread, cooked on hot stones, was so gritty and dry that teeth were universally worn to stumps. In fact, early cereals were so gluten-light that they were far more effectively cooked in porridges – like the ones found preserved in the bellies of ancient bodies discovered in bogs – soupy stews made of bruised corns boiled with water or milk in a crude earthenware pot until they swelled and thickened. When crops failed, dried wild beans, acorns, beech mast, chestnuts or – in remote coastal settlements like Skara Brae – ground fish bones stood in for cultivated grain.

Bronze Age peoples piled glowing coals over inverted clay pots to form primitive ovens which trapped the steam from cooking bread dough, making it lighter and more palatable than before. Separately, primitive ales were made from naturally fermenting grains, and perhaps their yeasty barm was at first simply used to flavour doughs, a practice that – quite by chance – led to the discovery of the airy magic of yeast in baking. Honey was the sweetest known taste, delightfully softening these dry early breads.

By the Iron Age, a hardier wheat – spelt – had been discovered, able to survive winter sowing so that corn was available for a greater part of the year. In about 400 BC the invention of the rotary quern – made up of a static lower stone sandwiched to an upper twin by a wooden axle that passed through holes in both their centres – began to transform the drudgery of grinding: the top stone could be rotated by a handle, speeding up the whole back-breaking process. Surplus oats, beans and wheat were now stored in specially built granaries on stilts like the one at Danebury Hill Fort in Hampshire, or in deep, sealed pits like those found at the lake villages of Meare and Glastonbury. There the carbon dioxide released by the grains killed off any lurking bacteria, and the crust that formed around the edges and bottom kept the pits dry. So successful were these early British farmers that the first-century Greek geographer Strabo recorded that they produced enough corn to export.

The Battersea Cauldron would have been used to boil large sides of meat that were hauled out when cooked by strong arms plying flesh hooks like rakes. Uniquely in Britain and Ireland, meat was also boiled in pits lined with stones or wood in which water was heated using fired stones. Great mounds of discarded boiling stones have been found in Cornwall and County Cork, and we know that it took about twenty minutes to bring the water to a lazy boil. Then the meat, wrapped in straw, leaves or fragrant herbs, was lowered in. It took around three and a half hours to cook ten pounds of mutton – about the same time that it would take in an oven today.

But as cereals became central to the early diet and because boiling meat leached its salts, people began to crave salt for the first time. In Cheshire it was mined, and along the British coastline it was worked with evaporation techniques learned from Central Europe. Soon its magical ability to preserve meat was discovered. We know from Strabo that the practical, belligerent Celts of the last millennium BC prized their bacon and salt meat, trading it widely.

These Celtic tribesmen had brought new technology and ideas with them from the Continent: iron ploughs, fortified settlements, highly wrought weapons, brightly dyed cloth, tattoos, woad and chased jewellery that satisfied their lust for warfare and their love of display. They cleared more land for cultivation, decreasing the forests and multiplying the settlements. They kept small Celtic shorthorn cattle, straggly sheep, goats and small horses or ponies in corrals and used their dung to re-fertilise the land.

In Wales, the east of Scotland and the north-west, the population was scattered, but in the south and south-west distinctive settlements contained several families in round huts which – by about 800 BC – were being transformed into defended hill forts such as Harrow Hill in Sussex and Ram's Hill in Berkshire. At Danebury, with its defensive earthwork rings, circular timber buildings had central fires for cooking and some rudimentary, separate clay ovens. In settlements like these, small metal cauldrons became more common, jars began to develop necks, urns were fashioned in barrel shapes, and plain cooking bowls were made of earthenware and bronze.

The hearth was the connecting point, a place to congregate and to share food, literally the *focus* of communal life. The Greek historian Diodorus wrote that Celts sat on the floor on animal skins or straw, though other Classical writers also described their rudimentary wooden tables. Food for the family was prepared and cooked here at the centre of the hut, and in the very largest houses, firedogs were developed to hold the spits used for roasting meat. The paraphernalia of hospitality began to assume a symbolic role, and prized silver, shale and amber vessels were even enshrined in burial mounds.

Classified by the Romans as 'drinkers of milk', the barbarian Celts probably happened upon butter by accident as milk bumped and churned around in a skin bag while being transported. Whisked up with sticks or shaken in a skin, flavoured with garlic or herbs and preserved with salt, butter was common to all cold-climate Northern Europeans, an effective way of preserving the milk from cows, sheep and goats. In Ireland and Scotland, bog butters – rich, creamy fats pushed into decorated wooden containers or wrapped in skins – are relatively common archaeological finds. The bogs themselves were a kind of 'black butter melting and opening underfoot' – dark, cool, airless and perfect for hiding and preserving valuable winter stores.

The Celts also prized cheeses, made from naturally souring milk easily coagulated with the rennet enzyme found in the stomachs of sucking calves and lambs or with nettle or thistle juice. High-protein soft curds could be smoked, salted or flavoured with berries, nuts, honey or herbs like wood sorrel, myrtle or mint. It was an ancient practice: the Beaker People of 1800 BC had used perforated clay bowls to drain the whey from curd to make hard, long-lasting cheeses.

The easily perishable nature of food means that archaeology offers us only a narrow window on our ancestors' habits. But from rare archaeo-botanical remains, we do know that the Celts foraged for Britain's abundant wild, seasonal foods: laver and carrageen seaweeds on the coast, rock samphire and sea kale or scurvy-grass not unlike asparagus. Fungi grew in the woods, and wild vetches and herbs made porridges more tasty. Early mustard has been discovered at Bronze Age sites in Cornwall; there were sour crab apples, burdock, nettle, dandelions, clover, wild celery and garlic, the bitter pungency of tansy and the pep of native mint, as well as a wild spinach high in calcium called 'fat-hen' or 'goosefoot' and, startlingly, even native coriander. Elder and hazelnuts were both high in nutritious fats, and at the Glastonbury Iron Age site, hundreds of sloe stones were identified, as well as the remains of raspberries, blackberries, cornel cherries, strawberries, dewberries and hawthorn. The remains of eggshells with charcoal show that nests were plundered and their contents cooked in embers. The landscape was a living larder; life often depended on it.

Wild foods aside, it was meat – wrote the learned ancient Greek Athenaeus – that took central place in the Celts' diet. From the scarcity of archaeological evidence, it seems that our deep-grained aversion to horse meat was shared by our distant ancestors, but butchered bone remains reveal that sheep, cows and goats were mostly slaughtered once their wool and milk were past their best and the animals had been used for breeding. Then the carcasses were stripped clean, their bones were smashed for their marrow and their skulls cracked apart to get at their brains. Rough-backed pigs were valuable and economical, foraging at the edges of forests and rooting out food for themselves until they were fat enough for slaughter. The evidence for eating small animals like voles and hedgehogs is, unsurprisingly, sparse.

Along the coasts and on inland waters, fish were caught in nets and baskets made from skins, hair and vegetable fibres, and occasionally on lines with bronze hooks or by using tridents with deer-antler or metal points. Few fish bones have survived, but we do have evidence of conger, bream, shark, skate, wrasse, ray, eel, haddock, limpets and other shellfish, most of which would have been impaled on sticks and set over glowing fires to cook. Birds like duck, swan, quail, pigeon, teal, blackcock, red grouse, plover, corncrake and heron were also eaten and, especially in Ireland, goshawks, guillemots and barnacle geese. Indeed, the Roman Emperor Julius Caesar recorded that the barbarians loved to eat goose flesh, keeping chickens, recently introduced from India, for their eggs alone. Songbirds, buzzards, kites, kestrels, ravens and even crows supplemented the cooking pot, and at the Danebury Iron Age fort a kittiwake's bones were unearthed – perhaps an early culinary luxury brought up from the coast with a load of salt. To drink there was water, milk and warming mead, the ancestor of all fermented drinks, made from honey and water, herbs and fruit. Pytheas the Greek explorer recorded that the Celts brewed too, spreading out their barley until it sprouted, baking and crushing the malt into a watery wort and leaving it to ferment. Celtic beer, according to Dioscorides, the Greek philosopher, was the cause of many a miserable hangover.

On the cusp of the final century BC the Belgae, most sophisticated of all Iron Age peoples, migrated en masse from the Seine and the Rhineland, introducing cauldron chains, tripods and wider iron ploughshares that could turn even heavy soils. They formed a highly developed society with a ruling élite sporting heavy gold torques, armbands of twisted and ribbed gold, coiled gold-wire earrings, chains, necklaces and brooches, plucking unwanted hair with tweezers, and importing perfume in tiny flasks from Arabia and Persia. They also transformed cooking equipment and pottery, fashioning bowls with the use of a wheel and producing fine drinking cups and elegant, flat plates with ridged edges which suggest that the stews and porridges of earlier generations must now have been joined by drier foods.

In 55 BC Caesar wrote that the land of Britain was 'thickly studded with homesteads . . . the cattle very numerous' and that the Belgae were rearing hares, fowl and geese. Trade with the Continent was flourishing: in return for silver, lead and tin the wealthiest Britons imported their fashionable utensils from the Gauls in north-eastern France, as well as olive oil from Roman Italy and Spain, figs and luxurious glass. Amphorae of wine arrived from Italy, Germany, Greece and Spain, drunk – contrary to the Roman practice – undiluted, earning the Britons a reputation for drunkenness. All the evidence suggests that, on the margins of the Roman Empire, settled life and cooking were becoming, relatively, rather fine. Peopled by red-headed barbarians with large limbs and unbroken spirits, Britain was an island of marshes, mountains and rivers, lush southern pasture and rugged northern uplands. But it was on the verge of invasion and conquest, and its society was about to change beyond recognition.

ROMAN BRITAIN

A piece of the Vindolanda fragments, written around AD 100 on wafer-thin 'postcards' of wood. This birthday invitation from Claudia Severa to the wife of commander Cerialis makes the Romans in Britain just a little less remote.

2

Conspicuous Culinary Consumption

The man with whom I do not dine is a barbarian to me
— GRAFFITO FROM POMPEII

In AD 43, lured by precious metals, pearls, cattle and slaves, driven by their ungovernable appetite for conquest and by the unpopular Emperor Claudius' desire for glory, the Romans finally succeeded in their invasion of southern Britain. Within a year they had pressed as far north as the Trent, Severn and Dee, establishing colonies first at Colchester, then at Gloucester and London, bringing their strange foods with them. When Boudicca sacked Camulodunum (Colchester) in AD 60, her warriors burned not only the grand new buildings there but the bowls of dried dates, olives, figs and raspberries inside them.

Within thirty-five years, the Celts in the south had become submissive enough, according to the historian Tacitus, for Governor Agricola to begin a process of Romanisation: building temples, central squares and houses, and educating chiefs' sons, teaching them Latin and law and employing them in public administration. As small towns sprouted marketplaces and stone buildings, larger colonies established forums and ambitious young men began to adopt the toga. In élite families at least, the first generation born under Roman rule was soon beguiled by all things new, powerful and civilised, 'led into the demoralising temptations of arcades, baths and sumptuous banquets'.

Rome was, literally, the world's greatest marketplace, sucking in produce from the furthest edges of its Empire, and its cuisine was as sophisticated and complex as its aqueducts and local government. Roman cooking used wine rather than milk, and oil instead of butter, and it was robustly flavoured with sharp herbs and strong, expensive spices trailing exotic resonances. At their most intense, these flavours could enrage the palate: Plautus wrote as early as the second century BC about cooks whose seasonings were like 'screech owls to eat the entrails out of living guests'.

As Roman society became wealthier and outward display was linked with political and social power, food was no longer simply about sustenance; demand for Asian spices was one essential part of a growing demand for the exotic. Livy wrote that banquets had become elaborate and extravagant around 187 BC, when 'the cook, who up to that time had been employed as a slave of low price became dear: what had been nothing but a metier was elevated to an art'; in his view, the new art of cooking heralded the decline of the Empire. So excessive was Rome's appetite for conspicuous consumption that the first sumptuary laws attempted to regulate it. Both the *Lex Orchia* and the *Lex Fannia* restricted not only the kind of clothes people of different ranks could wear but the number of allowable dishes to three at dinner and five at a celebration; shellfish and 'strange birds from another world' were prohibited and, under a later law, the *Lex Aemilia*, stuffed dormice were banned.

As the cult of the kitchen emerged, Pliny complained that cooks had begun to cost more than horses. Satirists like Juvenal, famous for characterising the mindless activities of the Romans as 'panem et circenses', also ridiculed wealthy gourmandism: the infamous 6-pound mullet bought by Crispinus for 6,000 *sesterces* and the decadent solitary patron dining on seven courses of swollen goose livers, oversized capons and baskets of truffles while the poor gathered outside. Writing of greedy emperors and their frequent emetics, Suetonius recorded a notorious feast given by the Emperor Vitellius, the centrepiece of which was a dish called 'The Shield of Minerva', made of edible exotica from the corners of the Empire: pike livers, pheasant and peacock brains, flamingo tongues and lamprey milt. Food had become an expression not only of power and of excess but of cruelty.

The most biting of all satires about feasting and nouveau-riche culinary spectacle was written by Petronius in *Trimalchio's Feast*, a first-century denunciation of lurid debauch at which the table was piled with a crescendo of dishes: live fish in peppered wine, hen's milk, mushroom spawn, a boar stuffed with sausages made to look like raw guts, eggs made of pastry filled with tiny woodland warblers called figpeckers, a hare made to look like Pegasus, sows' nipples and vulvas (the Romans adored the sexual parts of animals), dormice rolled in honey and poppy seeds, pastry thrushes, and quinces stuck with thorns – all disguise and farcical theatre.

Yet within these distortions lurked a nugget of truth about the place of cooking in Roman society. If the elaborate foods recorded in the satires were not the norm, good food – however simple – was considered a mark of civility, so that a graffito in Pompeii declared, 'The man with whom I do not dine is a barbarian to me'. Pliny the Younger entertained with relative simplicity, teasing a friend for failing to turn up for dinner with a list of what he had missed: 'a lettuce (each), three snails, two eggs, porridge, with *mulsum* [a sweet wine sauce] and snow (yes, I must count the snow right away because it melted on the plate), olives, beetroot, gourds, bulbs and a thousand other things no less enviable . . . such is my generosity . . . But you chose to go to someone else's and what did you get? Oysters, sow's wombs, sea urchins and dancing girls from Cadiz?!' Similarly, Martial delighted in lettuce, boiled eggs and tuna fish to start, main dishes of sausage and green cabbage or bacon with pale beans, and desserts of Syrian pears, roasted chestnuts, hot chickpeas and warm lupins.

The earliest Roman prose works in the form of the farming hand-books of Cato, Columella and Varro also celebrated frugal foods, revering olive oil, cakes with honey, seasoned olives and preserved fruits or vegetables. From these writers we learn of a paste of celery tops and coriander and of garlic pounded into hard balls of cheese with a little oil, vinegar and salt – each quite perfect eaten with bread in the rustic shade at midday, a far cry from the baked udders and spiced fish pastes of surfeited Rome.

The invaders must have seemed incomprehensibly alien to the conquered Britons, but as Roman civilisation began to take root, so did the many new crops and herbs they brought from southern climates. In our rich, moist soil, new varieties of carrot and cabbage thrived beside parsnips, turnips, endive, celery, lettuce, alexanders, cucumber, marrow, asparagus, onions and leeks. Along with pepper and ginger from the East the Romans brought many of the aromatic herbs we now take for granted: fennel, rocket, parsley, borage, dill, chervil, spearmint, aniseed, hyssop, rosemary, sage, sweet marjoram, thyme and the peppery watercress so favoured by emperors for its apparent encouragement of bold decisions.

Some believe that the routes of the imperial army through the south of England can be traced by following the white blossom of the wild cherry trees, distant descendants of the saplings that sprang up wherever the soldiers spat out stones as they marched. It may be true, for the Romans nurtured their orchards, improving native stocks by grafting and planting new varieties of plums, apples, damsons, the vine and the sweet cherry. With all these and more, the Romans began to transform the very taste of the country they had occupied.

In parallel, Roman practices transformed the treatment of livestock, improving sheep and cattle through selective breeding and feeding them on roots and beans. Few creatures fell outside the focus of their sophisticated husbandry: imported fallow deer were kept in enclosed parks and rabbits in *leporia* from where the young were either cut from the womb or taken newborn to the kitchen. Young cock chickens were 'caponised', or neutered, to fatten them for the table without sacrificing egg-laying hens; dormice were raised in pottery vessels called *gliraria*, fed on acorns and chestnuts until they were plump enough to roast on a spit; snails were fattened on milk and spelt wheat until they could not get back into their shells. Columella recorded that thrushes were reared on millet and on figs pre-chewed by slaves; the remains of aviaries were found at the Roman villa of Fishbourne, where it seems likely that wild ducks were also fattened for the cook's knife. Dovecots, or *columbaria*, were widespread, providing a rich source of winter meat; guinea fowl and pheasants were introduced along with peacocks, whose flesh was so tough that it could only be minced into rissoles. Even fish were bred in pools called *vivaria*, and edible frogs' bones have been found at Roman sites in York and Silchester.

In the fields, the Romans cultivated rye and oats alongside wheat and barley and erected corn-drying furnaces so efficient that Britain soon became the granary of the Empire, the tedium of grinding grain reduced by new donkey and water mills. Yet, vital as it was to everyone as a daily staple, Romano-British bread has vanished from the record and no remains have been discovered. Only the restaurant preserved at Pompeii gives us a clue, listing fourteen different types, each uniquely flavoured or shaped: the richer you were, the whiter your bread and the more likely it was to have a crusting of poppy, anise, celery or caraway seed.

At the extreme edge of governable Britain, the 75 miles of Hadrian's Wall stretched out from the Tyne to the Solway Firth, up to 10 feet thick and 20 feet high with forts strung out along it, the largest undertaking of the Empire. From the observation post at Vindolanda in the South Tyne valley the oldest ink documents yet uncovered in Northern Europe have been discovered, fragile letters from soldiers and their families written on wafer-thin wooden tablets the size of postcards. In one, Claudia Severa, wife of Commander Cerialis, invites her sister to celebrate her birthday, and in another a soldier sends thanks for a gift of fifty oysters which, to judge from the heaps of discarded shells found on military sites across Britain, were something of a favourite, transported even to remote inland locations in amphorae of salt water.

The Vindolanda fragments mention a wide variety of foods: roe-deer venison, goat's meat, pigs' trotters, hams, radishes, honey and even pepper; there is an account for large quantities of Celtic ale, a small detail mentioning napkins, and a long list of provisions including semolina, lentils, chickens, eggs, olives, plums, beans and barley for brewing. Many were the fancy goods finding their way along a network of new roads linking remote areas for the first time: luxury vintage Massic wine; cooking vinegar called *acetum*, which was drunk heavily diluted by soldiers on the march; and *liquamen*, a universal fishy condiment. The soldiers were sent baskets for bread, cups for eggs and a variety of dishes, side plates and platters which they stored carefully in chests. The fragments offer us glimpses of a novel, distinct cuisine never before seen in Britain.

In the bleak north, in Wales and among the poorest peasants, where Roman influence remained weak, tribalism and its subsistence tradition of boiling and of porridges continued largely uninterrupted, and the days remained dominated by anxiety over crops, weather and the health of livestock. Here cooking still centred – as it had done for centuries – around a single pot, the staples of peas, beans, root vegetables, fruit and cereals supplemented by occasional wild game or fish and perhaps a pig. But further south, in the new, rich towns like Silchester, Colchester, London or Verulamium (St Albans), Roman theatres, baths, markets and bars had begun to cater to a fast-growing urban population and a money-based economy. Rows of narrow timber-framed, mud-brick buildings displayed the diverse wares of vegetable sellers, bakers, potters, florists, spicers, wine and olive-oil vendors, while in butchers' shops freshly slaughtered cows and pigs were hung to tenderise.

Near the public baths, the forum and the city gates, a range of restaurants, inns and snack bars appeared. For poorer families and slaves who had no cooking facilities in their tenements, known as *insulae*, there were steaming cookshops where, among a somewhat dubious clientele, they could order warmed wines spiced with honey, hot water spiced with pepper, or wine in its rough, raw state, heavily diluted. Here they could buy sourdough, honeyed cheesecakes, roasted cows' vulvas, dried hogs' cheeks, salted hams, goose-liver pâtés, chickpeas, lettuce and perhaps cooked larks and thrushes. The philosopher Macrobius wrote of eggs and onions displayed in jars of water to make them appear larger, and Seneca complained of the noise from street sellers touting pancakes, sausages and confectionery. These were the new foods tickling the tastebuds of newly urbanising Britons.

Roman breakfasts were taken at sunrise – simple meals of bread and fruit – and the midday meal was also likely to be a mere snack of leftovers or of bread and vegetables, eggs or cheese. But dinner, or *cena*, taken at twilight, was abundant, often in the form of a *convivium*, or dinner party, that oiled the wheels of commerce, politics and friendship.

Marvellously known as *promulsis*, or promises, light dishes designed to tempt the appetite came first – such as olives, tripe, cucumbers, lettuce, mushrooms, snails or asparagus. Then the first course, or *primae mensae*, of intensely symbolic sacrificial meat, rissoles, sausages or mixtures of fish and meat together with highly flavoured sauces. The *secundae mensae* of shellfish, fruit, nuts, flaky cheesecakes, fritters, honeyed custards or pastries often sprinkled with pepper closed the meal, but an optional *symposium* might also follow during which serious drinking, witty conversation and debate or music and dancing were applauded as was the grandest of all Italian wines, *Falernian*.

As stability and prosperity grew in southern Britain during the second century after the invasion, country villas like those discovered at Chedworth, Rudston, Aldborough and Fishbourne were built by rich families and retiring soldiers anxious to proclaim their refinement. They were sumptuous, the smartest of them constructed with under-heated mosaic floors and separate baths; bluish-green glass glinted at the windows; plaster walls were colourfully painted with columns, garlands of fruit, flowers or vegetables; fountains played in gorgeous courtyards; and peas, roots, herbs and salads were cultivated in large kitchen gardens.

In villas like these British cooking was vitalised. Stoves using charcoal for its intense and controllable heat were built to waist height in the centre of the main room so that cooking could be done standing up, and occasionally there were separate kitchens with earthen floors and small windows. At Fishbourne there was a separate masonry bread oven, a domed structure that required skilful firing with seasoned wood to make the flames plume up and around the curved sides until the bricks glowed white and a little flour thrown in sparked in the heat. At just the right moment, the trained cook (probably a slave) raked out the ashes, swabbed the oven floor clean with a damp roll of cloth, and placed the proved dough inside before closing it up tight. Each such oven had its own temperament and its own secrets; each one took some getting to know.

In such small kitchens cauldrons hung from ornate chains alongside new equipment like frying pans, known as *patellae*, some with folding handles so that they could also be used in the oven and some with deep moulded rings to equalise the heat across the base. A first-century cook at Faversham in Kent used a bronze pan with a beautifully ornamented handle and a relief of Medusa's head in the centre, and a pan used in the kitchens of Orickwillow in Cambridge sported an exquisitely crafted image of the god Bacchus.

The Romans introduced the three-legged cauldron, shallow two-handled dishes called *patinae* and portable pottery ovens that could be brought to the table to keep dishes hot. Iron knives had wood, bone or bronze handles, and cooks used ladles, spatulas, sifters, skewers, meat hooks, cleavers and pottery sieves. But if clay cooking pots and curd strainers were so cheap that they could be thrown away when they soured, metal cauldrons were lovingly mended and patched, so that the Roman Britons Exsuperius and Oconea fulminated against thieves who had purloined theirs on curse tablets found at Aqua Sulis (Bath). *Mortaria* – heavy mixing bowls with pouring spouts, rims for gripping and often with grit baked into the bottom – were equally indispensable, used for grinding flesh, herbs and spices with a pestle into fine pastes to make sausages, dumplings and forcemeats – the kind of foods that could be eaten with one hand.

For as Celtic manners became Romanised male diners (women were never present at formal dinner parties and were more likely to sit at domestic meals on straight-backed chairs or stools) would recline on three wooden couches set around a low table in the dining room, or *triclinium*, three to each bench and all swathed in large white napkins brought from home in order to carry away any choice leftovers. It was rumoured that the greatest gourmets trained themselves to bear food that was still intensely hot in order to beat their fellow guests to the tastiest dishes. More commonly a dog might salvage bits of food or bone customarily thrown to the floor, itself sometimes decorated with mosaic images of discarded bones, fish heads, pips and cores.

A passing glance around the Roman galleries of London's British Museum brings the stylised domestic world of Roman Britain to life with its collections of impressive tablewares made from chased silver or bronze; of scrolled, coloured glassware; of imported red Samian pottery with its relief decoration of animals, birds and gods; or of black-slip cups imported from the Moselle region encouraging bibulation ('enjoy me!'). By the second century there were sixteen known active glassmakers in London, and home-grown industries were developing to keep pace with demand, with fine white pottery flourishing in the Nene Valley and imitation Samian ware in the hands of Oxford artisans. The Romans delighted in ingenuity: folding spoons were designed with sliding collars to lock them open and small animal heads to act as hooks and prevent them slipping into dishes; sets of long-handled spoons, carefully fashioned from bone, pewter or silver, had pointed ends to hook out shellfish; and pocket knives folded away for handy carriage.

So much we know about the kinds of food admired in Roman society and how they were eaten. But there is one more vital document offering more than a mere glimpse of the labour-intensive, highly flavoured Roman cookery that gradually became less foreign to Britons as the invaders' habits inevitably percolated down and into their lives. It is the earliest surviving cookery manuscript in the Western world, a collection of 459 recipes compiled some time during the first century and known as the *De re coquinaria* by Apicius.

Apicius was a name synonymous with gastronomy – he could have been any one of several recorded gourmets with that name, each with a reputation for decadent eating, each fixated on culinary inventiveness. Fittingly, the first word of each of his culinary instructions gives us the noun that we use to this day, for *recipe* was the Latin word for 'take':

> Take and pluck the flamingo, wash, truss and put it in a saucepan: add water, dill and a little vinegar. Halfway through the cooking make a bouquet of leek and coriander and let it cook with the bird. When it is nearly done, add defrutum to give it colour. Put in a mortar pepper, caraway, coriander, asafoetida root, mint, rue – pound. Moisten with vinegar, add Jericho dates, pour over some of the cooking liquor. Put in the same saucepan. Thicken with flour. Pour the sauce over the bird and serve. The same recipe can be used for parrot.

Clearly there were few, if any, British kitchens that could lay their hands either on a flamingo or a parrot, but with its lack of quantities, sparse method, omission of temperatures or cooking times, the stewing of the meat with herbs and roots and, finally, the separate preparation of a thickened peppery-sweet sauce, Apicius' recipe for flamingo is typical of his collection.

Apicius relied on a small handful of basic flavourings: pepper and lovage (similar to sharp celery leaves), Roman fish sauce, or liquamen, olive oil, honey, vinegar, wine, cumin, bitter rue and coriander. And as commonly as we turn to garlic, he reached for asafoetida, a strong-smelling gum taken from the root of a plant related to the giant fennel (called 'hing' in Indian cooking today). But his recipes are less for broths and porridges than for specialised dishes, carefully made using the choicest ingredients: teats of sows about to farrow, tongues and brains of songbirds, goose livers, cockscombs, thyroids, udders, tes-ticles and sweetbreads – he even included a recipe for a tortoise and one for baked dormouse stuffed with minced pork, pepper, pine nuts, asafoetida and liquamen. These were artful creations showing a marked preference for small, tender pieces of meat from hare, pork, kid and lamb rather than beef, and most of them called for mincing or pounding the meat with spices before shaping it for frying into rissoles or simmering in a broth. Sausages were also made from meat pastes or forcemeats stuffed into cleaned animal guts and either hung up in the smoke of the rafters to cure, or boiled and served with a hot mustard sauce – easily made by grinding mustard seeds with vinegar or grape must and, sometimes, honey.

Apicius' pounded-up dishes contain baffling medleys of ingredients such as fillets of fish, chicken meat, figpeckers and the cooked breasts of turtle doves, all minutely chopped and bound into a smooth mixture with egg before being cooking in an oiled pan and serving with a sauce of pepper, lovage, liquamen, wine and a syrupy reduction of wine called *passum*. Perhaps unnecessarily he added as an aside that the cook could also add 'whatever good things you can think of'. He also recommended an intricate terrine of layered belly pork with peas, brains, sausages, leeks and pine kernels, all pressed into a mould, cooked slowly and offered with a sauce of hard-boiled egg whites pounded with liquamen and spices.

Sauces like these were the ambassadors of Roman cooks' skills, and most aimed at a particularly desirable, discordant alliance of the sweet mixed with the bitter and the sour, using brine, vinegar or the juice of sour crab apples or unripe grapes – known as *verjuice* – with honey or wines reduced to thick, sweet syrups.* Strong herbs like tansy, pennyroyal and fenugreek were pounded with handfuls of toasted pine kernels or almonds along with dates or raisins, the paste made liquid with the addition of wine, stock or oil. Mustard, garlic, horse-radish and – always – pepper were used liberally, and to thicken sauces Apicius used breadcrumbs, eggs, crumbled pastry, rice imported from India or a wheat starch known as *amulum*, designing his creations not only to complement but sometimes to disguise a dish: we can almost hear him chuckle as he takes a well-salted liver and makes it taste exactly like a fish.

Romano-British cooks also prepared far simpler dishes for their households: perhaps meat roasted plain in an oven, sprinkled with plenty of salt and served with honey; a boiled ham with dried figs and bay leaves; a sucking pig stuffed and boiled, or a dish something like an omelette, prepared with eggs and lettuce. There are very few recipes in Apicius for the cabbages and roots that were probably already con-sidered inappropriate for fine dining, but he used leeks widely in his sauces, was particularly fond of aniseedy fennel and cautioned against overcooking asparagus. We know too that the Romans prized fish highly. At the Roman port of Lincoln the remains of salmon, halibut, eel, garfish, conger and carp have been found, and along the Thames Estuary the remains of eel, perch, pike and roach as well as mackerel, cod, herring, plaice and flounder. Judging by the recipes of the *De re coquinaria*, we may assume that fish pulled from British waters were mostly grilled or boiled and served with a green-and-peppery or a sweet-and-sour sauce.

Winter stores were still crucial, and salt remained the great magician, so valuable that it could form a part of a man's pay or taxes – his *salary* – so important that an inadequate man would be labelled 'not worth his salt'. Cooks preoccupied with sweetening salt meat for the table regularly boiled it first in milk and then, repeatedly, in water to make it palatable. Or they used honey to preserve meat and fruits,

---

* Even the classical sources disagree on the reduction of each type, but, broadly speaking, *caroenum* was boiled to between half and two-thirds of its original volume, *defrutum* to about a third and *sapa* to a thick, sweet syrup. Passum and mulsum were very sweet wine sauces made from reduced young wine with the addition of honey.

particularly quinces. Sugar, in minute quantities, was imported into the Empire, but it had not yet been introduced to the kitchen, remaining emphatically medical, considered the most perfectly 'balanced' of any ingredient.

This concept of balance profoundly influenced the way in which all Roman food was prepared, a philosophy of health propounded by Galen, a doctor who believed in cooking as a cure and whose late first-century study *On the Properties of Foodstuffs* was of such fundamental importance that its rippling influence would extend undiminished into the Middle Ages and beyond. Aimed at the wealthy and itself based on a more ancient Hippocratic tradition, Galen's dietetic rules categorised foods according to their effect on the body's four 'humours': blood, phlegm and black and yellow bile – or melancholy and choler, as these last were also called. The humours were in turn influenced by heat, cold, wetness and dryness and by the elements earth, air, fire and water. The secret of perfect health was to keep everything in harmony and symmetry, and food could assist in this. Too much phlegm caused indigestion – cold and wet by nature, it could be 'tempered' by foods that were classified as hot and dry: any of the spices but particularly pepper and wine.

Because the humoural properties of the body were influenced by age, the seasons, climate, weather and even the location of your house, Galen's principles of balance as applied to cooking could become extraordinarily complex. Every dish became, in effect, a remedy and a prophylactic against disease caused by disequilibrium. Even the choice of cooking medium was important, so that frying in oil moderated the wet and cold properties of fish, and blended sauces were used fundamentally to alter the equipoise of a dish and, by extension, its diner. Like an artist searching for the perfect colour, part of the point of grinding multiple ingredients together was to create an 'ideal' compound. No wonder Roman cooks could be so highly paid; millennia before our own insistence on a 'balanced diet', food preparation was considered by them to be not just an art but a science – a matter of life and death for some.

Liquamen

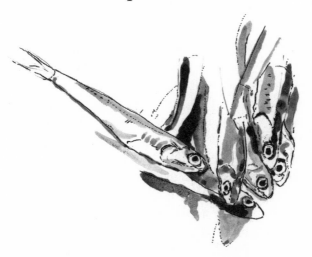

Rome's taste for pungent flavours was typified by its favourite condiment, liquamen – or *garum* or *muria*, as it was also called – a murky-
brown, salty relish made from fermented fish. Liquamen enhanced the
taste of other foods and, sharing the putrid whiff of asafoetida,
distinguished Roman cuisine more than any other ingredient. It was
used liberally in recipes and added to salads, meats or seafood as
frequently as we might turn to ketchup: Worcestershire sauce, which
has a little asafoetida and much anchovy essence, or the Asian fish
sauces *num pla* and *nuc nam* are probably the closest we come today to
a taste anything like it.

The *Geoponica* contain several recipes for fish sauces, including one
in which 'the entrails of fish are thrown into a vessel and salted. Take
small fish either atherinae or small red mullet or sprats or anchovy or
any other small fish and salt all this together and leave to dry in the sun,
shaking it frequently. When it has become dry from the heat extract the
garum from it as follows: take a long fine meshed basket and strain it.'

Oily, fatty fish were best, and Apicius chose to use fiendishly
expensive red-mullet livers, but large sea fish were pricey: Diocletian's

price edict of AD 310 rated the best quality at 16 *denarii* a pint, or about a third of an artisan's daily wage, and sea fish in general were at least double the cost of freshwater varieties. For those with smaller purses, a far cheaper and quicker alternative was needed: Pliny suggested using only fish that were unfit for any other purpose, and another cheap method was to put useless small fish in a brine salty enough to float an egg – the mixture was then boiled slowly until the liquid had reduced to a syrup, softened with a little reduced wine, and flavoured with oregano before being strained and served clear.

Other cooks used the entrails of mackerel or the inferior Mediterranean tuna fish, or shellfish including sea urchins, and Apicius also gave a recipe for a particularly rank version using gills, intestines and fish blood saturated with a pickle of salt, vinegar, parsley, wine and sweet herbs, all left in the sun to ferment and mature for up to three months before being strained and bottled. The remaining brine-preserved guts had a further value all their own when ground into a paste called *alec* that could be used as a less expensive alternative to liquamen, or even as a medicine.

Liquamen could be modified to one's own particular taste by diluting it with water, wine or vinegar, when it would be called, variously, *hydrogarum, oenogarum or oxygarum*. But recipes were limited only by the maker's imagination, and families might have their own particular method handed down through generations and closely guarded. Demand for liquamen was so high that its manufacture was the only large-scale factory industry in the ancient world, and almost every major port in Italy had its own distinct blend. Wherever it was made, the smell of fishy fermentation oozed through the sun-warmed markets and the backstreets, the olive orchards and the bath houses, mingling with the rising dust, joined by the stench from the *murex* factories that extracted royal purple dyes from spiny shellfish, each inviting and distracting the neighbourhood cats. Sometimes liquamen's stench would reach such heights that even the local governors could stand it no longer and production would be temporarily suspended.

This most famous of Roman sauces was exported throughout the Empire: to soldiers in Britain hunched under grey autumnal skies or shivering in the forts of the north and to expats in the new colonies craving a taste redolent of home. Varieties from Pompeii and even Leptis Magna in modern-day Libya were particularly famous, though from discarded containers we know that the Romans in York imported theirs from a maker called Postumus and that the veterans at Colchester preferred theirs straight from Urbicius' factory. For any of them, cooking without liquamen was simply unthinkable.

THE RAIDER CENTURIES

A Saxon cook. Much of the cooking for feasts took place outside and most meat was still boiled or roasted in large quantities; this slim cook looks barely up to the task.

3

An Art in Peril

Empty then stood
The best of houses, and for no brief space

— BEOWULF

By AD 367, raiders had already begun to make incursions into Britain from across the North Sea, followed by Scottish Picts and Irish Gaels taking advantage of the Romans' withdrawal of troops back into their crumbling Empire. Gildas recorded an appeal to Aetius in around AD 446 known as 'The Groans of the Britons', a complaint that 'the barbarians drive us into the sea, the sea drives us into the barbarians; between these two means of death we are either killed or drowned.' But such cries for protection were ignored; the Britons were left to their fate. The aromas of fish sauces, warm honey, sharp vinegar and spices were soon dispersed by the violence of a new generation of invaders, and Roman traditions and practices declined and disappeared. Villas and towns were abandoned, and public temples, rituals and civic administration began to fall away along with the market buildings and the forums. In the country, the harvests went unmanaged, orchards became overgrown, and carrots, parsnips and fennel ran to seed. Sanitation systems that would not be matched until the nineteenth century retreated into the mud. It was the age of collapse.

Throughout the fifth century, Saxon barbarians poured into Britain, and, riven by attacks, the island became a race of warriors and peasants; there was no longer time to savour food, let alone elevate cooking to an art. Separate kitchens and waist-height hearths soon reverted to fires at floor level. With conflict came a return to butter and ale, to a monotonous diet, and to cycles of famine and hunger.

Then, as the seventh-century Jarrow monk Bede recorded, a broadly feudal system gradually developed with the great timbered hall of Scandinavian tradition at its heart. There the noble *ealdormen* and *thegns* sat feasting while the fire burned in the centre of the hall and birds flew in and out through the open ends of the building, sheltered momentarily from the ravaging storms outside. Here the most favoured warriors also slept. In just such a 'mead hall' as that found at Yeavering in Northumberland sat King Hrothgar in the eighth-century epic poem *Beowulf*. Eighty, perhaps a hundred feet long, these halls were the centres of courtly custom and heroism where warriors, seated by rank, pledged support to their lords and where feasts sealed the bonds of fealty:

> Then in the beer hall were benches made ready
> For the Greatish heroes . . . they sat them down
> And a beer-tane served them; bore in his hands
> The patterned ale-cup, pouring the mead
> While the scop's sweet singing was heard in the hall
> There was joy of heroes, a host at ease . . .

It was a world of the chanting bard, of heavy men sitting upright on benches around temporary trestles, of the glint and glimmer of jewels. Feasts offered a period of rest and respite from the hammer-blows of battle, twilight hours when the clear note of the harp erased the sounds of slaughter, a shared society of warrior nobility founded on order and coherence whose culinary emblem was the boar, meadow-fattened and spit-roasted.

At the long tables with their lord at one end, the men shared wooden or clay plates and used their own sharp-pointed knives for spearing meat or spoons of metal, bone, horn or, more usually, wood – *spon*, the Old English word for 'spoon', means simply 'splinter of wood'. Blood-stained swords were put aside in favour of hard drinking: of cider, ale or mead from horns, leather beakers, pottery mugs or fine conical glass vessels imported from the Rhineland from about the fifth century, decorated with trails of glass threads and coloured green or brown, sometimes nacreous as pearls. Such fine drinking horns caught the candlelight as they were raised, shared and passed, and their fragility was revered: chequerboard millefiori glass was unearthed from the seventh-century Sutton Hoo ship burial, and from the excavated Taplow Barrow emerged foot-long, green-glass claw beakers and 2-litre drinking vessels with silver-gilt rims made from vast ox horns.

Outside the powerful, male-dominated world of the hall, foodstuffs were no longer imported, once again arriving only with the seasons or produced by the poor in small communities. Deprivation rather than perpetual feasting was the norm, and much of the population was undernourished and dependent on food that could be foraged: the Old English word *steorfan* had not yet evolved into the word for 'starvation'; it simply meant 'to die'.

It is frustrating that the detail of cooking virtually disappears from sight in this period; if not quite dark, these are centuries veiled in silence. So rare are written records that we leap on the few survivors, including the rare *Leechdoms*, or manuscripts of *wortcunning* – magic herbals that brought together both charms and plant remedies. These contain laxatives and purges, gout waters of crow leek, cumin and laurel, and eye balms made of strawberry plants steeped in sweetened wine. They show that the mortar was still used to work ingredients into pastes, that liquids were reduced to concentrate flavours, and that butter and salt were used to season cooked vegetables and pulses. Oil and butter were both used for deep-frying fish, ingredients were strained by wringing them out in a cloth, and eggs were made into omelettes flavoured with herbs like sorrel and sage along with the basic spices of pepper, coriander and mustard. It was a world full of superstition and spirits in which wild basil was gathered while holding an oak leaf to ward off evil, where coriander was used to speed labour, and where elves were kept at bay with a mixture of bitter herbs, leek, garlic, fennel, butter and mutton fat.

In most homes, small cauldrons, or *cytel*, were hung by chains or from a pole suspended on upright forks over hearths that once again filled small houses with sinus-inflaming smoke. In these cauldrons simmered a semi-permanent stock or soup of water, root vegetables, herbs and small pieces of meat; larger pieces might be wrapped in a cloth bag to be boiled in the same liquid, perhaps held down with a block of wood. Separate starchy fillers were made with grains or dried legumes, such as pease pudding stuffed into a pig's intestine and boiled nutritious *frumenty*, a gelatinous porridge of cleaned wheat grains crushed and soaked in water until they swelled and softened. According to the skill and resources of the cook, gruels like this might be flavoured with leeks, bone marrow, dried beans or peas: they comforted empty stomachs and partially relieved the saltiness of preserved meat.

One early *Leechdom* provides a rare recipe for an Anglo-Saxon pottage of barley meal, stewing together shredded radish, herbs and salt in quantities of rich butter as a cure for lung complaints. Another shows that stews could be quite refined in the quest to restore an invalid's health, poaching chicken in wine, adding walnut oil and pulping it all into a liquid that could be eaten without chewing. Small details about life also emerge from the pages of the vocabulary that Aelfric – Archbishop of Canterbury from AD 995 – wrote to teach monastic novices to read Latin. Set out as a *colloquy*, or dialogue, with several people including a baker, a ploughman, a shepherd, a hunter, a fisherman and a merchant, this text lists the objects each used in his work. Aelfric's baker emphasises the importance of grain to the daily diet, claiming that 'without my skill every table seems empty and without bread all food is turned to loathing. I gladden the heart of men, I strengthen folk and because of this the little children will not shun me.'

Bread was the staple of the diet of the poor, growing coarser, darker and drier as it descended the social scale, and rye bread sat in the belly like a stone. By today's standards, vast quantities of bread were eaten: 4 pounds a day for the poor of all ages according to the canonised Bishop of Metz in his eighth-century Rule of Chrodegang. It was so much the staff of life that Old English words vibrate with its importance: the lord – *hlaford* – was literally the bread guardian or bread-winner; the lady – *hlafdige* – was the bread-maker; and dependents – *hlafaeta* – were the bread-eaters.

In the wetter, colder north, oats developed into a regular crop, and flat cakes would be baked on a griddle in the floor-level hearth. Further south, many households still used inverted pots for baking, though some had their own small clay or turf oven and others shared a larger, communal wood-fired one. While waterwheels were becoming increasingly widespread, the daily grind of hand-milling at home still took up a considerable amount of time and energy. Despite arms aching from the milling, grain meal had to be sieved through several layers of cloth to clean and refine it: the more bran that was removed, the whiter and more palatable the bread (but the less there was of it). Hands chapped from the cold stirred and kneaded flour and water together in a wooden trough in the yard, adding ale barm or a piece of sourdough kept from a previous batch as the wind whipped aprons around legs. The oven was fired while the dough proved, and the bread was put in to cook for an hour or so; when it was done, meat might be left to bake in the remaining heat. We know from the Anglo-Saxon vocabularies that honey dumplings were also baked and that crumpets were made from a thick, yeasted batter dolloped on to a hot, flat pan and cooked until the air bubbles rose, making holes at the top.

In honour of Eastre, goddess of spring and of the dawn, bread dough could be studded with dried fruits and baked into small loaves that, as Christianity spread, began to be marked with a cross by monks: the earliest form of hot-cross bun. Precious, sensuous foods, they were bound up with hope for good harvests and abundant summers, and they must have been eagerly awaited, filling the senses with keen anticipation as they were taken hot from the oven or coated in honey. Later in the year, bread would be left to soak in the juice of wild berries, the original summer pudding.

Throughout the spring and summer, women made cheeses and butter (both are Old English words and both appear in Aelfric's vocabulary) from goats', cows' or ewes' cream, glowing deep yellow in the spring from the rich early grasses. Buttermilk did not keep, so it must have been drunk immediately, but cheese could be smoked or, like butter, heavily salted for the unproductive months: as Aelfric's salter says, '. . . you would lose all your butter and cheese were I not at hand to protect it for you'. Vegetable plots were planted with plenty of woody, purplish carrots, as well as leeks, garlic and herbs like rue and the Roman fennel that quickly naturalised in Britain, all to add savour to the pottage. Children may have been sent out to collect wild roots like radish – Bald's *Leechbook* of the tenth century suggested that a radish eaten at night protected men from incessant female chatter – as well as burdock and rape from field edges or wild nettles and watercress from hedgerows and riverbanks. Hardy peas and beans were dried for winter storage; tough cabbages were sown for the winter, and an early form of kale grew so splendidly in the cold months that the Old English word for February was *Sproutkele*. In Wales, leeks and cabbage already formed the basis of the national dish, *cawl*.

Both Aelfric's vocabulary and the *Leechdoms* list edible meats including pig, goat, deer, hare, pigeon, chicken, swan, duck and goose.* Since everyone hunted, there was no particular social cachet attached to different meats – though roasting clearly required quantities of wood – but the fact that our modern words *beef, veal* and *mutton* are Norman rather than Anglo-Saxon suggests that the mass of Anglo-Saxon society kept these animals primarily for their wool, skins and working ability rather than for the table.

The pig (itself an Old English word), on the other hand, was so important that it headed Aelfric's list of animals. Most households would have had one or two long-snouted, razor-backed, bristly pigs, putting them to forage in the woods, fattening them throughout the summer on the leavings of barley brew and whey from the cheese press. With Martinmas (11 November) came slaughter, and the geese also fell under the knife, plump now from picking at the fallen grains in harvested cornfields. Only breeding stocks were left to replenish the herds in spring. It was a time of surfeit during which most of the pork would be preserved in a fever of bleeding, rendering, salting and sausage-making, while offcuts of fatty skin might have been crisped in the fire for the children to snap between their teeth.

Economical in every respect, there was hardly a part of the pig that could not be turned to account. Its fine white guts were cut into lengths, squeezed empty and thoroughly washed for use as sausage casings or for boiled puddings, a practice still widely followed among primitive peoples and mentioned in the Rule of Chrodegang. The pig's

---

* Oddly, given their ability to breed in quantity, Roman rabbits do not appear to have survived, and there is no evidence of rabbits in England after their departure until the Normans reintroduced them.

organs, including the heart, lungs and liver, were eaten fresh or chopped with fats and herbs to make sausages or puddings bulked with oatmeal like the ancient Scottish haggis – a term that may have derived from *hagga*, a Viking word meaning to 'hack'. The blood could be mixed with oatmeal and lard to make black puddings, the bones split for their marrow; brains and tongues might be used in stews, and fats were rendered down for cooking or for use as rubbing ointments or grease for the plough.

Large sides of bacon, known as flitches, were submerged in a pickle, or souse, of brine made from salt bought from peddlers' carts as they trundled across the country between salt-producing towns like Nantwich, Sandwich, Northwich and Droitwich. Alternatively, the flitches were rubbed with dry salt and set on clean straw, turned and re-salted every few days until they were ready to be hung in the rafters to dry or cure in the smoke of the chimney. So vital were salt-preserved foods that the ninth-century Welsh Prince Hywel Dda ruled that should a couple divorce, the woman could claim cheese or meat still in its brine while the man owned any cured or smoked provisions already hanging on hooks. These were among cottagers' most valuable possessions; without them, they might not survive the winters.

But it was religion, not magic, that would have the most far-reaching effect on Anglo-Saxon eating and cooking. By the close of the sixth century, Christianity was developing in parallel with secular feudal society, bringing with it new commands. Dominating Church thinking, the Rule of St Benedict, originally formulated in Italy early in the fifth century, insisted that monks should give up meat and alcohol and that their meals – taken only twice, at midday and in the evening between vespers and compline – should contain only two cooked dishes.

Christianity brought with it the concept of gluttony as a sin and of abstinence and fasting as symbolic assertions of faith. Surviving predominantly on a poor man's diet of bread, seasonal fruits, vegetables and herbs, monks took pride in their productive gardens, and as monasteries expanded so, famously, did horticulture. Fine herbs and aromatics were grown for medicinal as much as culinary use, while leeks, onions and garlic took their place in the vegetable enclosures known as *leac-tun* or *wort-tun*. Orchards of plums, pears, medlars, quinces, mulberries, walnuts (a new introduction taking its name from *wealh*, meaning 'foreign lands') were improved by grafting: Aelfric also listed, astonishingly, the peach, and by Domesday there were as many as thirty vineyards in the south of England, the monastery at Ely so rich in them that it was known as the Isle des Vignes.

St Benedict ruled that only the sick could indulge in the 'flesh of quadrupeds', but the monks were quick to interpret this as excluding birds and fish so that fishponds known as *stews* and ornamental dovecotes for pigeons (known as stockdoves) gained currency in monastery grounds, each providing a constant supply of allowable flesh. Bede saw the irony that although the Church espoused the maxim that 'he that eateth often lyveth a beastly life', it was the monks who were re-stimulating the art of gastronomy. Rising out of the hush of the post-Roman centuries, his rare voice tells us that even cells designed for prayer had been converted into places for the forbidden delights of feasting, drinking and talking. As the monks grew rich and fat, their skilful cooks increasingly circumvented the spirit if not the letter of the holy rules so that by the beginning of the eleventh century St Anselm was cursing what he considered to be the clergy's immoderate eating, their dishes of 'chicken spiced with pepper and cumin'.

As Christianity spread, fasting also began to form part of the culinary rhythm of every week, observed by rich and poor alike on Fridays (in memory of the Crucifixion), Wednesdays (the day that Judas pocketed his bag of silver) and Saturdays (Sabbath's eve). According to Aethelred around 1009, it was the law to fast on bread, herbs and water for the three days before Michaelmas, and there were also four Ember days, the eves of every significant saint's day, and all of Advent and Lent – days on which every household was expected to abstain not only from meat but from other animal products including dairy. Unless you were excused from fasting by virtue of your age or health, the reality was that religion ensured that meat was off the menu for a significant portion of the year.

The poorest may have hardly noticed the difference, but for the rest the culinary gap was filled by fish. Aelfric's fisherman speaks of his nets, hooks and baits, of baskets of firm-fleshed eels that could survive several days out of water, and of river fish including pike, minnows, trout, perch, roach and eel-like lamprey. From the sea came herring, turbot and salmon, porpoise and sturgeon, plaice, whiting, flounder, cod, lobster, crab, oysters and other shellfish. But it was the herring, easy to salt and cure, that topped Aelfric's list of sea fish, the great shoals off the east coast that had drawn Viking raids during the eighth century making them cheap and widely available. Only the most courageous fishermen braved hostile seas to hunt whale for its flesh, bones and fat and for its tongue, which was served as a delicacy on fine tables; from the tenth century, salted whale known as *craspois* came instead from Rouen for the tables of the rich, arriving in sufficient quantity for Aethelred to tax it at London Bridge.

With Alfred the Great, the first monarch to style himself King of all England in the mid-ninth century, a period of relative peace and stability returned. The Danes continued to attack and to settle along the east coast, but elsewhere the acreage of cultivated land increased, forests shrank, and rich nobles began to build large manor houses with clay ovens in their yards and to reserve wild game for themselves. Hunting with expensive hawks or packs of hounds became the privilege of the few, reducing the amount of meat available to the poor and symbolically confirming the status of the wealthy. Wine, oil and some spices began to be imported again from the Continent.

If in small houses it was the women who toiled over their bread, brewing, vegetables and animals, in the great kitchens of noble or monastic houses only men had the strength to lift the enormous equipment. The Old English word for 'cook', *cok*, is a masculine noun, the earliest sign of a division between the professional, male, cook and the domestic female that would be marked throughout later history. Although Aelfric's short list of kitchen equipment bespeaks no high degree of gastronomic refinement – indeed, the majority of our modern culinary words derive emphatically from Latin or French rather than Old English – his cook worked in a large kitchen that was already hierarchical with its master cook, under-cooks, waferers, scullions and boys for turning spits and running errands.

As such kitchens multiplied, what began as a dribble of new ingredients and a fancy for culinary indulgence slowly become a flood and a passion. A whole new world of scents and tastes was about to burst once more across our frontiers, bringing with it textures and techniques whose influence would ripple across the centuries into our own. As if the earth sensed the upheavals in store, AD 1065 drew to a close with violent winds which destroyed churches, halls and ancient trees. In April of the following year, Halley's Comet blazed across the skies; in September the Normans, having long harboured ambitions for expansion, invaded Britain with force, and by sunset on the 26th the Battle of Hastings had run its course. On Christmas Day 1066 the French conqueror William was crowned in Westminster Abbey. The stage was set for one of the greatest culinary renaissances in the history of Britain.

MEDIEVAL BRITAIN

Eating in hall; note the buffet or cupboard to hold wine and water for hand-washing. The cloth is neatly draped, the great salt is set at the lord's table, and a stack of neatly cut trenchers is prepared by the pantler and passed on his knife. The rest of the hall appears to be eating four to a 'messe', or platter, some with their hands and others with spoons. Musicians entertain their lord.

4

'Newe Conceytes'

Cookes with theire newe conceytes, choppynge,
stampynge and gryndynge
Many new curries alle day they ar contryvynge
— JOHN RUSSELL

The momentous events of 1066 changed not only the politics and the language of Britain but the very face of authority as close-cropped, clean-shaven Normans replaced long-haired, bearded Saxon lords. The historical record also alters dramatically – it begins to hum with voices and flash with illustrations of daily life. Images of cooks and of cooking now burst from needlework, tapestries and the pages of illuminated manuscripts. In the Bayeux Tapestry, an epic embroidered frieze of plunging horses and butchered bodies, we see William the Conqueror feasting with sophisticated order and ceremonial before the battle, while the margin text explains, 'here the meat is cooked and here the servers serve it, here the feast was made, and here the bishop blessed the food and drink.' Cooks with long knives and precariously long-toed boots strain against the weight of an enormous cauldron, dress meat – flesh, as it was known – add sauces and organise the details of presentation; small birds and rabbits are carried on spits to the table to be eaten from shared bowls, and a servant on bended knee ritually presents food to his King and bishop.

This was to be a period of astonishing culinary connoisseurship. From the start, Norman cooks were valued so highly that by 1086 two royal master-cooks – Walter in Essex and Tezelin in Surrey – were being given manorial lands for their culinary services, Walter's descendants becoming the King's official turnspits. With a new Anglo-Norman language to grapple with, Alexander Neckam produced a new vocabulary, *De utensilibus*, but unlike Aelfric before him, Neckam began with the kitchen, describing its large preparation table, its tripods, pestles and mortars, frying pans, eel spears, fish baskets and leather vessels for wine. Cooks hung their cloths on poles to keep them from the mice, and the head cook was so elevated that he had his own apartment for preparing condiments. There were separate sinks for viscera and offal, ladles for basting, hatchets, hooks and sharpened knives, saucepans and cauldrons, gridirons and kettles for cooking lamprey – the fish venerated by medieval gourmets, a surfeit of which supposedly killed Henry I in 1135, sparking a new civil war.

Neckam takes us right into the warmth of a high-class kitchen in the twelfth century, but he gives us more than a list of equipment, recommending cumin sauce for stewed ham, mentioning three kinds of sausage (*andulyes, saucistres and pudingis*) and giving fine directions for roasting pork with a little salt to make its rind really crunchy. In a separate work on horticulture called *De naturis rerum*, he catalogued an expanding range of tasty culinary herbs including parsley, fennel, coriander, sage, savory, hyssop, mint, sorrel, thyme, saffron, dittany, smallage, pellitory, lettuce, garden cress and the strong-smelling rue also used to treat snakebite and poor eyesight. Rosemary would arrive in the 1340s with Queen Philippa, but pumpkins, cucumbers and spinach-like orache were now cultivated in kitchen gardens, and we can assume that turnips and woody carrots known as *skirrets* were grown, though oddly they did not begin to appear in gardening treatises until the fifteenth century.

Following the lead of the Conqueror's impressive White Tower in London, William's barons began to proclaim their power with a new kind of architecture, and Norse halls gave way to stronghold castles and to ostentatious manors with guttering wall lamps and enormous kitchen fires for roasting. At Penshurst Place the great hall soared 60 feet to a chestnut-timbered roof, vented so that smoke from the central fire could escape. In the shadow of these buildings, the mass of the population worked half-acre strips of land dotted around their villages:

freemen renting their land in return for tithes of grain and meat or *villeynes* who were forced to work part of the year for their lord. Most had their own small productive gardens of edible roots and herbs, and the Domesday record shows that almost every cottage kept swine in its own lean-to.

Helped by the nailed horseshoe, the new mouldboard plough and the development of crop rotation, more and more land fell under cultivation. In strip fields, peasants' crops were a mix of wheat, rye, tares, beans and wild flowers all growing to shoulder level: summer sanctuaries for children and the means of survival for their families.* But from the twelfth century, nobles began to convert common land to private ownership, enclosing it and imposing severe penalties for poaching. While withholding game from the poor, their own diets became marked by great quantities of venison, boar, wild birds, hares and the rabbits reintroduced to Britain by Norman lords and kept in warrens known as *coney heyes*. Until the mid-fourteenth-century Black Death halved the population and sparked the demise of the manorial system, the poor found themselves increasingly badly off.

Bread and ale, both packed with calories and nutrients, lay at the heart of all diets, and ale barm was so vital that it was sometimes known as *godisgoode* 'bicause it cometh of the grete grace of God'. But bread did more than appease hunger; it marked your station in life. The poor ate *maslin*: tough brown bread of roughly sieved wheat mixed with rye flour or even barley, millet, malt or beans, made at home or baked in the communal baker's oven. Wheat bread, known as *pandemaine* or, later, *manchet*, was the whitest and softest, but it was costly; everyone aspired to it, and the baker in William Langland's poem *The Vision of Piers Plowman* complained that even in times of dearth 'beggars refused the bread that had beans in it, demanding milk loaves and fine white wheaten bread.'

---

* Throughout the medieval period the Continent suffered from outbreaks of ergotism – poisoning from bread made of rye grasses infected with a fungus that caused nausea, seizures, even gangrene. LSD was ultimately synthesised as a by-product of research into the hallucino-genic symptoms of ergot, which was sometimes called 'St Anthony's Fire' or the 'Dancing Mania'. In Britain it seems to have occurred less often and without the force of the European outbreaks. The only recorded outbreak in England took place in Wattisham in Suffolk as late as 1762.

In her castles, Eleanor, Countess of Leicester, King John's daughter and wife of the infamous Simon de Montfort, had several grades of bread baked for different-ranking members of her household, using up to 300 pounds of grain a day for baking and brewing. Surviving household accounts from more modest manor houses are extremely rare, but we do have those of the widow Alice de Bryene, living on the Suffolk–Essex border in the early fifteenth century, which show that even her cooks baked more than two hundred white loaves twice a week, providing up to 2 pounds of bread a day for each member of her household.

Commercial bread prices had often been loosely regulated in attempts to minimise social unrest, but in 1266 Henry III's *Assisa panis*, or Assize of Bread, for the first time provided binding legislation tying the weight of the penny loaf to the price of grain. Penalties for flouting the law were severe: a baker found guilty of selling short weights could be drawn through the streets on a cart with his loaves tied round his neck, the target of abuse and filthy projectiles. Overcharging could be penalised by three days in prison and a hefty fine of 40d, and the third offence could lead to banishment from the city. So important was Henry's assize that it would exist in one form or another for the next five centuries.

In a society where water was viewed with suspicion, brewing was as essential as baking, and everyone drank quantities of ale: up to a gallon a day for adults, with weaker 'small' beer for children. Alice de Bryene brewed 112 gallons twice a week and served each of her guests around 3½ pints at dinner, while the household of Humphrey of Stafford, Duke of Buckingham, consumed more than 40,000 gallons a year. In London, tree branches or ale stakes were raised outside inns to alert the official *alcokers*, or aldermen, that a new brew was waiting to be checked by them, but adulteration and short measures were legion. In 1364 the alewife Alice de Caustone was charged with concealing an inch of pitch in the bottom of her quart pot with a sprig of camphorous rosemary, and a surviving wooden misericord in St Lawrence's Church in Ludlow depicts a demon with a cheating alewife flung over his shoulder, marching her off to the jaws of hell.

Aside from bread and ale, poor rural labourers like Piers Plowman had only a meagre store of cheap luxuries: pepper and peony seeds to flavour his ale, and garlic and fennel seeds for fish days. They ate pease pudding, baked apples, ripe cherries or the cooked shells of peas known as *peas-cods*, but summer was precarious. In a drought Piers lamented:

> . . . all I've got is a couple of fresh cheeses and a little curds and cream, an oat-cake, and two loaves of beans and bran . . . I haven't a scrap of bacon, and I haven't a cook to fry you steak and onions. But I have got some parsley and shallots and plenty of cabbages, and a cow and a calf . . . And with these few things we must live until Lammas [1 August] when I hope to reap a harvest in my fields.

Illustrations of smallholders, labourers and serfs like Piers cluster in the magnificently illuminated pages of the *Luttrell Psalter*, showing us a ploughman bothered by crows that threaten to steal his grain, a gooseherd scaring off a bird of prey, and women milking their sheep in pens. Elsewhere, a woman gleefully straddles a pig to wrestle it to the ground as her husband – preparing guts for narrow, flimsy sausages – watches with apparent unconcern.

A fourteenth-century woman stirs her cauldron with her baby at her breast while a toddler uses bellows to fan the fire.

Food was an obsession and hunger such an acute fear that contemporary poems are filled with fantasies of gorging on butter mountains, milk lakes and castles where 'All of pasties be the walls
. . . Wheat flour cakes be all the tiles . . . The rooftops are fat puddings' and the moats were filled with custard. Longing for escape from
the bleak subsistence of cabbages (or *worts*), dried peas and beans, the
poor dreamed of a life of idleness with macaroni falling from the sky
and roasted geese with garlic sauce calling out, 'Geese, all hot, all hot'.
But the contents of most rural families' pots included only boiled
cabbages, leeks, peas and beans, a handful of herbs, oatmeal and,
perhaps, a morsel of meat. Their daily reality included no kitchen
trickery, and their kitchens were unlikely to contain little more than
rudimentary brass and clay cooking pots, wooden pails and vats, and a
tripod for holding a pot above the coals. That of the poor country
widow in Geoffrey Chaucer's 'Nun's Priest's Tale' was melancholy:

> And there she ate full many a slender meal;
> There was no sauce piquante to spice her veal
> No dainty morsel ever passed her throat . . .
> Her board was mostly served with white and black
> Milk and brown bread . . .
> Broiled bacon or an egg or two were common.

Beyond the villages, monasticism flourished as the Norman kings encouraged the building of new abbeys and monasteries as extensions of their
power. As well as cultivating gardens, orchards* and art, the monks also
revived medical learning, turning to the ancient dietetic theories being

---

* Fountains Abbey had 2 orchards, of 8 and 12 acres. Glastonbury Abbey grew 3 acres of apple
and pear trees (Pearmanes and Custards were among the earliest apples, while most pears were
hard Wardens directly descended from Roman cultivars); Walter of Bibbesworth also mentioned
monks cultivating cornel cherries. Medlars, damsons, bullaces, mulberries and quinces were
common orchard trees. Other basic kitchen produce was grown in astonishing quantity: in 1211
the Bishop of Winchester spent more than 21s on shallot and onion seed, beans and a whole gallon
of colewort seed; and in 1333–4 Glastonbury Abbey produced more than 8,000 heads of garlic
and barrow-loads of onions and leeks.

reappraised by the remarkable Italian medical school in Salerno. Luminously illustrated translations of influential health handbooks, known as *Tacuina sanitatis*, began to circulate, filled with advice on moderation, abstention, exercise and hygiene; the balance of the humours became once more the defining factor in the way that fine food was prepared.

The *Tacuina* detailed the qualities and potential dangers of all foods and how they might be corrected in order to maintain a moderately 'moist' and 'warm' balanced state of health. Cabbage (considered warm in the first degree, dry in the second and bad for the intestines) could be neutralised with oil, marrowbone or egg yolks. Eggs were always strained, and the whites – disastrously cold and viscous – were often discarded. Cucumbers (cold and humid) were prepared with honey and oil, while leeks (warm in the third degree and dry in the second) were ideal for the old or temperamentally cold. Raw fruit was considered dangerously cold and was baked or balanced by cooking in wine and with spices. But with so much onion, cabbage and garlic in the kitchen, one pernicious physical complaint was unavoidable: *ventositye*, or wind.

Three of the most important elements of Norman cooking – the pulverisation of meat into pastes, the use of spices and sophisticated sauces – all sprang from the imperatives of humoural theory rather as they had with the Romans. We know from fragmentary records that different techniques also played their part, so that roasting had a warming and drying effect, while boiling, or *seething* (the origin of the expression about bubbling rage) counteracted 'dry' foods like beef. Cold fish were corrected by simmering in salt water or diluted wine or by frying, and the lamprey was considered so excessively dangerous that it was invariably drowned in red wine or salt before being roasted with warming herbs and spices. Humoural theories would remain at the centre of British food culture until challenged by the new sciences of the Enlightenment, creating a veritable minefield of ambivalent and even contradictory injunctions whereby milk was considered both nutritive and coldly dangerous, and cream, delicious though it was accepted to be, 'put men in jeopardy of their lives'.*

---

* Andrew Boorde, who loved strawberries – tiny, wild and sweet – and cream, recognised that they were a risky dish on account of both the raw fruit and the potentially dangerous malignancy of cream.

Sauces were again vital in tempering dishes, so that as we turn to mint sauce, medieval cooks paired acid with meaty richness, serving verjuice with capon and bacon. Bread-based sauces called 'camelyn' or 'gamelyne' could be spiced up with raisins, pine nuts, ginger, cloves or cinnamon and were served with most birds, including egret, crane, bittern and plover, but *chawdron* – a sauce of blood and livers – was the perfect companion for roast swan. A green sauce of sorrel or other sharp herbs with verjuice usually accompanied veal, and mustard made by grinding dried mustard seeds and mixing them with honey, wine or vinegar corrected the 'moistness' of pork, brawn and beef, warming the stomach and provoking appetite. A sauce *egredouce* (bittersweet) satisfied a particular craving in the medieval palate for mixing sweet and sour together, and even summer's heat could be alleviated with cool sauces of verjuice, vinegar or pomegranate. Medieval cooks used aromatics that have since fallen from favour: borage with its hairy leaves that taste of cucumber or the medicinal costmary, also used to repel moths. But the richest flavourings – all but absent from Britain since the departure of the Romans – returned overland from the Middle East with the Crusaders during the twelfth century. It was then that spices re-entered the British kitchen, inspiring new and vivacious culinary wizardry.

Spices were as unnecessary to survival as diamonds, the ne plus ultra of conspicuous consumption – costing the earth and yielding almost no nutritional value. By the time they arrived in Britain they had passed through so many traders' hands that few really knew where they came from. As a result, combined with their cost – a pound of pepper in the twelfth century was equivalent to two or three weeks' land labour – they achieved an almost mythical status, with some people convinced that they were harvested from the gardens of Paradise or found floating down the Nile. More than any other ingredient they quickened the medieval pulse, their heady scents wafting through élite medieval cookery to define its very character. And the range was striking: grains of paradise, *Aframomum melegueta*, from the cardamom or ginger family was the only medieval spice to come from Africa, while nutmeg and cloves came from the Moluccas and pepper from the forests of southern India. There was a variant known as *cubebs*, Celonese cinnamon and Chinese ginger with its relatives galangal and *zedoary*, as well as mace, gromwell and aniseed. The spicers, peppers and grocers (from *grossarii* because of their use of large weights) soon formed into powerful London guilds selling ready-ground mixes in small leather bags of various strengths known as *powdor fort, powdor douce* and *powdor blanche* – but if you could afford it and were wise you avoided adulteration by purchasing your spices whole.

In the past, historians sometimes assumed that spices were used liberally to mask the taste of partly rotten flesh. Certainly it was hard to keep unsalted meat fresh, but although surviving medieval recipes rarely include exact quantities there are good reasons to question such an assumption. Alice de Bryene's household account book reveals that in 1418, when prices had already dropped considerably, she purchased 3 pounds of pepper, 2 pounds of ginger, 2 pounds of cinnamon, a pound of cloves and another of mace, spending 56s at a time when a thatcher might earn 4 or 5d a day. These were large amounts, but when we consider that Alice provided for up to fifty householders and visitors each day, catering for almost twenty thousand people in 1418 alone, their use cannot have been heavy-handed.

Far from treating spices incautiously, cooks wiped out mortars with bread, which was then added to pottages, and kept the strained spices from jellies to reuse in sauces. It seems that what they were aiming for was a juxtaposition of the piquant with sweet fruits, nuts and sugars, the characteristic feature of many modern Moroccan recipes such as *pastilla* – a shredded-pigeon pie flavoured with mace, nutmeg, cloves, cinnamon, almonds and saffron, and powdered with icing sugar. If so much about the European Middle Ages seems bewilderingly remote, contemporary Moroccan food, robust and subtle by degrees, broadly unchanged for centuries, offers a hint of our own culinary past.

Intensely sweet dried fruits were therefore crucial, and exotic raisins of Corinth (currants), prunes, figs and dates were all traded by spice merchants besides the sacks full of almonds needed for thickening sauces and stews or for use as a creamy alternative to milk on fast days. By the thirteenth century, sugar was finding its way to Britain from Palestine and the Lebanon along new trade routes via Damascus and Venice and was beginning to replace honey; it too was considered a spice and was sold in hard cones wrapped in paper. Sugar was the ultimate culinary luxury: while Alice de Bryene used only a pound in a single year, during the same period royal household cooks used thousands of pounds of the glittering crystals.

Of all the medieval courts, the splendour and elegance of Richard II's in the late fourteenth century were legendary. The King spent his wealth on decoration, indulgence and sumptuous feasts rather than on foreign wars,* employing more than 300 kitchen staff to feed 10,000 courtiers and visitors a day and slaughtering dozens of oxen and 300 sheep daily. While his reign was marked by famines, plagues and hunger, it is from Richard's court that the earliest and most complete British culinary manuscript has survived: 196 instructions handwritten on fine calfskin by his own master cooks and physicians, known as *The Forme of Cury*.†

The recipes in *The Forme of Cury* and other manuscript fragments shed abundant light on a multitude of skilful 'made' dishes painstakingly constructed by professional cooks as foils to the great roasts and combining the savour of ancient Rome with the Saracen flavours encountered by the Crusaders, at times extravagant and fierce and at others restrained and subtle. The recipes often relied on several different techniques to construct a single dish, and many had probably been passed down from cook to cook for some generations. Now, as the culinary arts were flourishing across Europe, the very act of recording recipes was a self-conscious display of royal connoisseurship: just a decade before, the French King Charles V's master cook had compiled a similar collection known as *Le Viandier*.

Vague aides-memoires for the trained professional cook, reminding him to take just enough – *ynough* – of an ingredient, or to cook on a bright fire, these recipe collections tell us most of what we know about medieval courtly cuisine. Meats were often reduced to pastes, eaten on

---

* Handsome Richard was a great lover of fashion too, and is credited with the invention of the handkerchief, perhaps to save the fine velvet cloth of his sleeves. The greatest possible irony is that he was eventually forced to abdicate and starved to death.
† *Cury* from *curare*, 'to dress victuals', according to Pegge 1780.

the point of a knife or with the fingers: like *mortrews* made from a base of pork or chicken flesh pulverised in a mortar, then boiled and thickened with bread, spices and egg. Rissoles, or *raysols*, were made by forming balls of minced pig's liver, bread, cheese and spices and baking them with a crusting of egg yolk and saffron. Meat was regularly cut small into *gobbets*, and the cook's work was one of strenuous semi-violence as well as delicate modulation: along with *meddling* (mixing), he was told to hack, hew, stamp and smite, to *grynde*, cast into broths, *seethe*, *bray* and *do* on the fire.

One of the simplest recipes in *The Forme of Cury* was astoundingly modern for its time: proto-pastas boiled and layered with butter and cheese, known as *macrows* and not unlike modern macaroni cheese. The manuscript also gives us our earliest recipe for salad, using the smallest leaves of parsley, sage, borage, mint, fennel, cress, rosemary, rue and purslane mixed with minced garlic, small onions and leeks, and decorated with slivered and toasted nuts and glowing pomegranate seeds. The dangerous 'coldness' of the uncooked herbs was mitigated by a 'warming' dressing of oil and vinegar, a classic combination that would remain unchanged for centuries.

In a society still only marginally literate, people craved exuberant visual novelty and illusion and, like puzzle jugs that appeared to be filled with holes but did not leak, many of the dishes produced by medieval cooks were skilful, witty and strange. The *cockentrice* was a fantasy animal from the forepart of a capon and the rear of a piglet stitched together, stuffed and roasted. Peacocks were carefully skinned, their meat seasoned with cumin before being roasted, cooled and stitched back into their feathers, sent to the table apparently alive, their necks supported by wires, their tails spread and a phoenix fire bursting from their gilded beaks. Clearly a health risk, peacocks in their feathers were a triumph of style over substance, since everyone admitted that the flesh was stringy; but that was beside the point. They were centrepieces, designed to delight the eye as much as the palate and to emphasise social power through magnificent display; more than a hundred of them were presented at the installation feast for Archbishop Nevill of York in 1467.

The love of bright colour evident in medieval illuminated manuscripts, clothing and heraldry inevitably found its way to the table.

Transparent jellies were highly prized and took hours to make, with cooks laboriously boiling pigs' feet or knuckle of veal into a gluey gelatin that was scummed and strained repeatedly to remove each minuscule solid particle. Glowing medieval jellies were set in brightly coloured layers or encased whole cooked fish; sometimes they were gilded or carefully scented with spices ground so finely that they were indiscernible within the shivering mass.

Boiled blood was used to colour foods black, and a sandalwood-like bark known as *sanders* or mulberries or red alkanet were employed to turn them red or purple. Wheat starch, egg whites or crushed almonds were used for white; mint, spinach and parsley for green, and for blue the turnsole, or heliotrope, was mashed. Most desirable of all, egg yolks, dandelion petals or musty saffron were used to *endore* pie crusts and pottages. Saffron was a costly statement, with more than 50,000 hand-harvested crocus flowers needed for each pound of dried stamens. The fields around Saffron Walden in Essex must have been a mirage of smiling colour when in bloom, delighting thousands who could never hope to taste the kind of cooking in which they were used.

Flowers were in fact a particular feature of British courtly cooking, with violets used in meat stews and herb salads decorated with cowslip and broom petals, violets, primroses and gillyflowers. A sweet pottage called *rosee* mixed violet, primrose and rose petals with cows' or almond milk, flour and honey. *Spynete* or *espinee* called for hawthorn blossoms, boiled meat, ginger and sugar, and another concoction was based on the scented sweetness of spring elderflowers. Recipes like these demonstrate that whether savoury or sweet (or both), pottages were important elements of a meal even in wealthy households, the process of lengthy simmering in water, stock or even stale ale reducing the stringiest meat to tenderness.

Soupy pottages were known as *ronnyng*, while those thick enough to be sliced were called *stondyng* – a particular favourite was *blancmanger*, a thick mess of boiled rice and almond milk, lightly spiced, sweetened and mixed with the cooked flesh of capon or fish shredded patiently with a pin. There was also *mawmenee*, similar to blancmanger but more robustly flavoured with wine, sugar, fried dates, cloves, cinnamon and ginger. But it was frumenty, the ancient porridge of bruised wheat boiled in milk, that traditionally accompanied roast fresh mutton, venison or porpoise at feasts. Updated for medieval tastes, it was thickened with egg yolks, coloured with saffron and left to cool before being sliced like polenta.

The Romans had of course made a kind of pastry, but they had used oil rather than butter or lard so that it could not be 'raised' to a standing pie and was used mainly for sweet dishes drenched in honey, reminiscent of modern Middle Eastern patisserie. During the Middle Ages, pastry evolved into a rough, inedible casing – or *coffin* – filled with closely minced meats larded with marrowbone or oysters and flavoured with dried fruits, nuts and spices. Offal – livers, sweetbreads, lights and giblets – were all highly esteemed, and the original *umble* pies were not in the least bit humble, using a gallimaufry of entrails including testicles, tripe, hearts, palates (the tender roof of the mouth), gizzards, lambs' tails, cockscombs and fatty pigs' feet in a rich, spicy gravy. Valued as it was, offal was known as *garbage*, a word that would assume quite a different meaning as tastes changed.

The polite culinary style reflected in *The Forme of Cury* slowly made its way down from the court to the manor houses of country squires and to the merchants in towns where even more ordinary cooks had to know how to salvage burnt or over-salty foods, to be alert to the dangers of rotten meat, to prevent smoke from ruining their dishes, to set traps for the rats in their larders and to keep flies off the butter. Chaucer used several recipes from the *Forme* for his character Hodge, cook to the pilgrims in the *Canterbury Tales*, who makes boiled chickens with marrowbones, uses spices and prepares blancmanger and mortrews. But while Richard's court cooks had made scrupulous efforts to be clean – 'lay it on a clene bord; let the ovene be . . . clene swept . . . take a fayre frying panne' – Chaucer's cook had lower standards, showing a weakness for the bottle and having an open sore on his shin.

The Ellesmere Manuscript of Chaucer's great work illustrates Hodge as swarthy, brandishing a meat hook and riding in his long cook's apron. He might have used a sand timer or, more commonly, measured his cooking by the time it took to say a *Miserere*. He would have scoured his pans with sand or straw and carried with him bundles of birch twigs for beating eggs, feathers for glazing pastry, a mortar, a grater, a tripod, a cauldron and sieves of horsehair or cloth – all clattering and bumping on the flank of his horse as he accompanied his patrons towards Canterbury.

Chaucer's pilgrims left behind them in London the great snaking Thames, crowded with ships exporting wool and importing luxuries and supporting a population of around 25,000, most packed into subdivided tenements of wooden houses. Effluent and rubbish lined the alleys, rootled by foraging pigs. Wealthy residents had kitchens and cooks, but few of the urban poor had the means to prepare food and fire was a constant danger. So they were forced to turn to portable food easily bought. In the shadow of William's White Tower, the streets were filled with the sounds of peddlers shouting their wares: 'Hot pies! Hot! . . . Good piglets and geese, go dine!' At Cheapside hot peas-cods, fresh strawberries and cherries were sold; Candlewick Street specialised in sheep's feet, Eastcheap in beef ribs and meat pies, and at London Stone hawkers plied fresh oysters and mackerel.

London's main thoroughfares thronged with cattle and poultry driven to the city from Essex, Gloucestershire and as far as South Wales. Daily bread carts brought loaves baked outside the walls, the hawkers profiting by buying thirteen loaves for the price of twelve – the original baker's dozen. Streets took on the names of the trades plied along them – Bread Street, Fish Street, Pudding Lane, Pepper Alley and Ironmonger Lane – and markets developed like the ones at Gracechurch Street selling eggs, butter, cheese, herbs and fruit and at Leadenhall where grain lay in heaps. Butchers set up their stalls at the end of Stinking Lane, so called because until Richard II ruled that meat should be slaughtered beyond the grassy suburbs of Knights-bridge, the narrow streets were awash with animal guts and blood.* Across the city, the authorities struggled to remove putrid food and to control quality, sending butchers to the pillory for trading in rotten meat, setting prices and passing statutes that forbade the selling of 'venison pies' made of beef or the purchasing of leftovers from private houses to be commercially re-baked into pasties.

---

* By Chaucer's time, a sucking pig bought blind at market in a closed bag was already known as 'a pig in a poke' – or a shot in the dark, since its quality could not be inspected.

Hodge left behind him in London a scandalously filthy cookshop where fly-blown goose was reheated and disguised with a gritty parsley sauce, but others had good reputations. One flourishing establishment was described by William Fitzstephen in the late twelfth century as a place thronging with soldiers, travellers and the poor where, 'according to the season, dishes of meat, roast, fried and boiled, great and small fish, coarser meats for the poor, more delicate for the rich, of game, fowls and small birds' were sold. To such places those without ovens could take along their filling to be baked into pastry for a penny, or the town baker could cook their bread for a fee (and the risk of losing part of it to stealing fingers hidden under the counter).

The unchanging reality of medieval life was that control of food was linked to power. As abbots and aristocrats flaunted their wealth at table, food merchants rose to positions of authority in the towns: in 1347 and 1352 a fishmonger and then a grocer became Lord Mayor of London. But behind the vitality of the street cries and cookshops, beyond the gates of wealthy houses, lay the piercing hunger of the have-nots. Society was polarised between fine sauces and grey gruel, between feast and fast.

5

Feasts and Fasts

Sing a song of sixpence, a pocket full of rye
Four and twenty blackbirds baked in a pie
When the pie was opened, the birds began to sing
Wasn't that a dainty dish to set before a king?

As Erasmus later described them, the Middle Ages were a time addicted to splendid tables, and nowhere was the power of food more obvious than at the medieval feast, a public demonstration of privilege and power designed to emphasise the victory of courtly order, politeness and comfort over dearth and privation. Lavish hospitality was all about oiling the cogs of society, business and the politics of Church and State, and it satisfied social expectations of generosity. When Henry III attempted to control court expenditure it was thought shameful: 'an inexcusable act . . . bringing on him even the charge of avarice'. In failing to play the game, he did not grasp that as the father of his people he was expected, symbolically at least, to feed them.

Balancing the imperatives of a society that proclaimed its power partly through conspicuous consumption against those of a Church that urged restraint and a calendar peppered with fast days could be a tricky business, complicated by the fact that the Church also feasted publicly and without restraint. Thomas à Becket, though renowned for his personal abstention, kept grandly hospitable tables, and monastic indulgence had generally continued unabated: ecclesiastical gluttony was so overt that Chaucer's Monk developed a taste for swan and the Friar in the 'Summoner's Tale' revelled in rich capon's liver and roasted pig's head. The spiritual significance of their greed was not lost on a world in which you were defined, in part at least, by what you ate.

Banquets or feasts – even those enjoyed on fast days – meant marvels of culinary art elegantly served. In the medieval epic *Sir Gawain and the Green Knight*, the lord sits on a raised dais hung with silks and tapestries while his men take their places at trestles stretching away from the platform, sharing their dishes, or *messes*,* in pairs, served according to their degree. The hall is dim; firelight flecks the walls and ceilings. Pulling fur capes close, Gawain is served

> Delicacies and dainties . . .
> Fresh food in foison, such freight of full dishes
> That space was scarce at the social tables
> For the several soups set before them in silver

In verses designed to teach French to aristocratic children, Walter of Bibbesworth described the profusion of a court feast, the

> First course: the head of a boar, larded, with the snout well garlanded, and enough fattened venison for the whole household . . . a great variety of cranes, peacocks and swans, kids, pigs and hens . . . rabbits in gravy all covered with sugar . . . quite a different multitude of roasts . . . pheasants, woodcocks and partridges, fieldfares, larks and plovers, blackbirds, and song thrushes . . . and fried meat crisps and fritters with sugar mixed with rose water. And when the table was taken away, sweet spice powder with large dragees [sugar-coated spices], maces, cubebs and enough spicery and plenty of wafers.

The abundance of dishes was the embodiment of worldly success, even if the choicest ones were served only to the grandees, who might gracefully dispense titbits to their favourites. When Ralph de Borne was installed as Abbot of St Augustine's Canterbury in 1309, provisions for the 6,000 guests included 100 hogs, 30 oxen, 1,000 geese, 500 capons and hens, 24 swans, 600 rabbits and nearly 10,000 eggs. It all cost £287 8s with spices the largest single account: a hefty £28. A century and a half later, when Archbishop Nevill was installed at York,

---

* The old term *messe* for 'a dish' remains in the mess halls of the army and the expression to 'mess food about'.

his feast for some 2,500 guests took 62 cooks and more than a hundred servants to prepare; a thousand animals were slaughtered and 4,000 tarts were prepared. There are no records of the weeks of preparation, the cart-loads of fuel for the fires, the burning cheeks of the turnspits, the slaving for days in advance, the triumphs, the mistakes or the frayed tempers.

But we do know about some of the kitchens built to cope with the strain of feasting, like King John's at Clarendon in the early 1200s, which had space to roast up to three whole oxen, and those at Glaston-bury, Durham, Canterbury and Jervaulx abbeys. Durham's kitchen was separated from the main building to minimise the threat of fire and the nuisance of noise and cooking smells, and when Cardinal Wolsey began the building of Christchurch in Oxford in 1425, he started with a kitchen that rose more than 60 feet to a roof with open louvres: there were three vast roasting ranges with baking ovens set into their sides and a stone staircase leading up two floors to the great beamed hall.

As fireplaces began to be built into side walls, ornamental stone hoods developed from which pots could also be suspended. Kitchens expanded, their different offices arranged around a courtyard into separate larders, storerooms, cellars, butteries (for the wine and ale in butts), pantries (for bread) and sculleries (from *escuelier*, or 'keeper of dishes'). Passageways now linked the main hall to the kitchen and its departments, with serving or surveying places like those at Durham Castle, Knole, Eltham and Hampton Court where the steward would pass his eye over the food before it was presented. By the 1400s, carved wooden screens began to conceal the arches to the kitchen and buttery corridors, muffling draughts before they entered the rush-strewn hall.

There were new devices to help with the heaviest pots and cauldrons: ratchets to regulate their height, or vertical pivots with horizontal arms that acted like cranes to swing them over or away from the fire. Heavy metal stands were designed to hold a variety of spits at different heights, thick and heavy for whole animal carcasses, finer for small birds, and even smaller ones for artistic dishes like *pommes dorées* – spicy forcemeat balls rolled in parsley and saffron, or flour and egg yolk, and roasted golden to look like apples – or rolled stuffed slices of beef, or mutton known as *allowes*, a dish that would develop into the beef olives of the seventeenth century.

A thirteenth-century cook stirring an enormous cauldron. Note the ratchet device for raising and lowering the pot over the fire.

Stockpots bubbled away at the sides of the great fires, and waste was tipped into a chute that ran into an outside drain which had to be emptied regularly. Huge stone mortars and smaller wooden ones, ladles, sieves and graters swung from hooks; thick boards were set for chopping, and water stood ready in pails. On important occasions such as Nevill's enthronement at York in 1467, the master cook oversaw the main dishes but relied on a specialist sauce-maker, baker or confectioner and hired extra cooks and servants as well as labourers to chop and cart the wood, turn spits, churn butter or draw water. They and the scullions might have made their beds on the kitchen floor, but these rooms cooled fast and Norman laws ruled that all embers had to be covered at night with *couvre feus*, or curfews.

The three broad 'courses' of the medieval feast each contained an enormous variety of dishes. When the King feasted with Lord Spenser in 1397, contemporary records show that the first course alone consisted of venison and frumenty, capons, the head of a boar, roast swans, herons and pheasants, vast tarts and two *subtleties* (elaborate dishes meant to act as pauses in the meal). The second offered brawn, roast pig, rabbits, curlews, venison, peacocks and teal, a custard, fritters and a subtlety, and the third dates in syrup, roast cranes and gilded peacocks, roast plovers, quails and great birds, larks, small pieces of meat, apple fritters, cheese-and-quince dumplings and a final subtlety.

None of this would have been surprising, for lordly roast venison with frumenty traditionally opened feasts, with boar's head or brawn and a *peuerade*, or pepper sauce. Roast meat smacked of privilege, taken for granted by those who could afford the fuel needed, the dripping pans, basters and turnspits, and prepared crispy and sticky on the outside and juicy in the middle – quite literally done to a turn. An inexact science, the perfect roast came with experience, and early instructions all stress the importance of putting the spitted meat at the right distance from the fire, protecting its skin if the fire was too hot, interlarding dry flesh with fatty bacon, and watching for falling embers that might send up flares of ash. Often, entire carcasses were stuffed with a forcemeat of spices and fruits – combinations that survive today in applesauce and redcurrant jelly – and the joints were carefully secured to the spits to prevent them slipping as they turned, being basted regularly and finally *frothed* with flour or breadcrumbs mixed with fat or batter to make the hot skin sizzle and spit.

The King's second course was also typical in its inclusion of spiced pottages, *blaundeore*, or white puddings, and sliced pork and date 'cakes' known as *leche lumbard*, with smaller roasted birds like bustard,* curlew, woodcock, blackbirds, sparrows, linnets and quails. Carving manuals confirm that cranes were usually roasted with their necks wound round the spit and curved back until the beak touched the breast again, their wings cut off at the joint, or were boiled with their heads outside the pot so that with one pull of the neck, the stringy sinews could easily be removed. In addition, it would not have been unusual in the second course to see pigeons, rabbits and perhaps a great smooth wheel of custard tart cooked gently on the side of the fire.

---

* The heaviest flying birds in the world, with long, whiskery cheek feathers, bustards could grow to 25 pounds and were hunted with dogs. They became extinct in the UK in the early 1800s but attempts have recently been made to reintroduce them on Salisbury Plain.

Yet more small roast birds crowded the third course beside meat jellies, fruit dumplings, small fried pastries, *eyroun engele*, or eggs in jelly, and *doucettys* – cheesecakes made with soft curd cheese or with almond milk mingled with rosewater, sugar and spices. Apples and quinces were favourite tart fillings and were also served in *comfyt*, or sugar syrup, and creams and almond milks were scalded until they thickened. A separate dish of peas at King Richard II's table in 1397 was extremely unusual and must have been all but invisible in the mass of roasts, broths, spiced eggs and fat capons.

Designed especially for show and made well in advance of the meal, subtleties bought the kitchen staff time between courses: intricately coloured jellies or exotic sculptures made from sugar or almond paste. To make figures, sugar syrup was rapidly cooled by plunging a boiling pan into cold water so that it hissed and plumed with steam. Then the syrup was poured into oiled moulds and left to set before being delicately painted using fine feather brushes or assembled into three-dimensional objects. At their most fanciful, subtleties might be representations of saints or royalty, eagles or leopards, and some were truly theatrical: ships with the barons of the Cinque Ports on board, allegories or scenes from the hunt or the liturgy. Some were less impressive but sweetly edible, like *marchpane*, an early form of gingerbread made from honey, ginger, breadcrumbs and saffron baked into a great round biscuit and occasionally gilded (the original gilding of gingerbread). By the late Middle Ages, subtleties could be so large that they were paraded on carts or stretchers, theatrical punctuation marks in a complicated meal.

There was nothing random, however, about the multitude of dishes, nor were they served in capricious chaos. Almost all surviving records of great feasts show a similar procession of set dishes for, turning again to ancient dietetic learning, physicians believed that the stomach was like a cauldron with its contents all waiting to be digested; the order in which meats, custards and jellies were eaten was crucial to health. Most vital of all was a *voidée* to which only the most important guests were invited, a final course of spiced wine called *hippocras* and sugared seeds, nuts and spices called *comfits*. Fragile crispy wafers were made in large circular irons heated on the fire that stamped the brittle discs with figures of saints or coats of arms. *Crespes*, made by dropping batter through the fingers into hot oil, were served with honey or sparkled with finely rasped sugar, so headily enjoyable that they were also known as *nebula*, or clouds – the food of angels.

Stiff quince pastes, originally known as *charedequynce*, were the first marmalades – *marmelo* is Portuguese for 'quince' – and were accompanied by compotes of reduced fruit pulps mixed with wine and honey, salt and vinegar. Ginger was preserved in sugar and seasonal fruits cooked and tempered with a mix of mild spices to ease the stomach. Citrus fruits were so scarce that when Eleanor of Castile, wife of Edward I, was pining for the tastes of her homeland, she requisitioned the fifteen thick-skinned citrons and seven oranges that had arrived in Portsmouth on a Spanish ship entirely for herself. So exquisitely precious were they that they were either made into syrups, or *succades*, with quantities of expensive sugar or even left uneaten, pitted densely with cloves as supposed protection against the threat of infection or plague.

The spices and sugar of the voidée were considered medicinal and digestive – they sweetened the breath and warmed the constitution, pepping or gingering up the guests. With its expense and its resonances of Eucharistic wine and wafers, this final course cemented the bonds of power and loyalty in a semi-religious rite. But so extreme was some of this royal feasting that the knotty consideration of the sin of gluttony always lurked. As they had been in ancient Rome, sumptuary laws were passed in an attempt to restrain the gentry and merchants from emulating courtly fashions, but they were all but impossible to enforce. Leftovers, on the other hand, provided an ideal opportunity for easing consciences through charity since feeding the poor was one of the seven Acts of Mercy. Traditionally taken to the gates for distribution to waiting beggars, such alms were so important a part of lordly magnanimity that in the mid-1200s, Bishop Grosseteste advised the widowed Countess of Lincoln to ensure that hers 'be faithfully guarded and collected and not . . . wasted in suppers or dinners for the menservants, but freely wisely and moderately without dispute and strife distributed among the poor, sick and beggars'.

Fast days continued to balance the hedonism of the feast, and the forty days of Lent were particularly trying, dragging themselves out at the end of a winter during which fresh meat, eggs and butter were anyway in short supply. Fast meant fish and, though there was a thriving fishing industry, Lent was dreaded as a time when even 'the Dogges grow leane with the lacke of bones', uncomfortable even for those who had access to native freshwater fish and imported carp in rivers and monastic fishponds. Henry III ordered more than a hundred pieces of whale for Lent in 1246; beaver was also allowable, and barnacle goose, believed because of its fishy flesh to be born from excrescences on logs at sea, thereby achieved acceptance as flesh for fast days. Pike and bream were luxuries along with salmon – salted and expensive – from Scotland; plaice, skate, dab, sole, ray and a multitude of other sea fish and crustacea were all available to those living along the coast. But in the winter months and, particularly, in Lent the herring reigned.

Herring was so plentiful that the Abbey of St Edmond received a rent of 30,000 fish a year from the port of Beccles. It turned Lent into a trial to be endured, a monotonous round of herring cooked with onions or cabbage and served with mustard. Salted (white) or smoked (red) herring were stuffed into *cades*, or barrels, in their hundreds, soused or pickled in a salt-and-sugar brine so that their small bones turned to jelly, consumed in their thousands in all but the poorest households. Imported Norwegian *stockfish* was as inescapable – autumn-caught cod, salted and dried solid, made palatable only by lengthy soaking and repeated hard bashing with a stockfish hammer; its flesh stuck stubbornly to the fingers, and the skin was abhorrent. One schoolboy in the 1400s gave voice to the strain of it all when he wrote in his schoolbook, '. . . thou wyll not beleve how werey I am off fysshe, and how moch I desir that flesch wer cum in ageyn.'

For the well off with their master cooks and (irony of ironies) for the monastic rich, fast food meant a succession of ingeniously inventive dishes. Henry V's Queen was crowned on St Matthew's Day 1420 – a religious occasion at which the Archbishop of Canterbury sat on her right and Henry Cardinal of Winchester on her left – and of necessity the feast included whale in the first course and porpoise in the third. Fish were commonly poached in wine before being fried in oil, roasted on a spit, or chopped and mixed with raisins and fine spices; conger was encased in a delicate jelly with cinnamon and ginger, oysters poached in ale with pepper and saffron breadcrumbs, and lobster served with vinegar or green sauce. Fish rissoles were made of dried haddock or ling ground to a paste with boiled figs, shredded almonds and dates, all made into balls and fried in oil. Most complex of all, a single fish might be cooked in three ways – the tail fried, the head boiled and the middle roasted, each part differently coloured and the whole re-assembled and made to breathe fire by pushing a wad soaked in alcohol into its mouth and setting it alight.

For the rich, in other words, the very definition of fasting became elastic. When butter and milk were proscribed, the cook could fake them, grinding almonds in a mortar and adding stock, ale, wine or rosewater to make almond milk for use in custards, 'creams' and sauces. There were plenty of ruses: empty eggshells were carefully filled with a mush of crushed, blanched almonds mixed with sugar, a centre portion coloured with saffron to act as the yolk and the whole lot warmed gently until it set. If you could deceive the eye, you could fool the stomach too.

At last, as the seasons turned, fasting flowed back into feasting. Easter, Whitsun – when new ale was specially brewed and the villages danced – May Day, Harvest Home and Christmas were the days of all days, gastronomic highlights when drudgery was put aside in favour of fun and laughter. After the punishing forty days of Lent, Easter was the greatest release of all. Eggs were symbols of spring and rebirth, delivered up in their hundreds to feudal lords as tithes. Edward I distributed them like gilded gems to his favourites. Children took them to church to be blessed.

In the 1200s the Countess of Leicester bought more than a thousand eggs for an Easter feast for her tenants at Dover Castle and rewarded her labourers and tenants with succulent roast meats and spiced custards or *pain perdu* – bread dipped in egg, fried in butter and sprinkled with sugar, the forerunner of our eggy bread. In homes across Britain at Easter, real eggs were cracked into cooking pots or boiled and served in a green sauce to symbolise the banishment of thin fare, and the favourite *tansy*, or *erbolat*, appeared, an omelette coloured green with tart tansy juice or with spinach, fried golden in butter; if you were lucky, it might have a grating of nutmeg, a dash of cinnamon and a spoonful of cream or curds, but it was always a treat after the dietary rigours of abstention.

On Good Friday the fishmongers closed their stalls and butchers washed their aprons and chopping boards and sharpened their knives in readiness. As village congregations hurried from Easter services, fresh meat as much as the Resurrection must have been on their minds. Communal baking ovens were readied for pies; succulent veal, capon and pigeon were trussed for the pot; tender spring lambs and calves were led towards the kitchen; and the March rabbit ran dead into the dish. Spring greens were picked and pottage dressed with herbs as fragrant as the new grass. It was a time of rejoicing – 'a day of much delightfulnesse, the Sunnes dancing day and the earths Holy-day' – the start of the season of plenty.

At the other end of the year, in Advent, green (young) goose was ready for eating, and rich, fat brawn was prepared for Christmas's twelve days. Until the fifteenth century, wild boar were plentiful, and the head would be boiled in a great cauldron until the flesh was tender enough to be pierced by a fine straw, when it was carried into the hall whole. More modest homes were as likely to pickle the head in ale and serve the flesh chopped up with its unguent fat, with mustard or a dish of salt. Plum pudding was filling, sweet and steaming, a standing pottage of dried fruits and meat boiled in wine that banished cold and hunger and which, for the lucky few, was heavily spiced with sugar, mace and cinnamon. The sterility of winter lent it all glamour and savour.

And so the year turned. By 6 January, 'Christmas is ended, bid feasting adieu.' No more animals would be slaughtered, and larders would be carefully watched, eked out until the trees once again turned green.

6

Hospitality

Crabbe is a slutt to kerve
— JOHN RUSSELL

Medieval meals were organised not only by the imperatives of the religious calendar but also, increasingly, by complex ritual. Hospitality demanded that strangers should be welcomed into magnificent halls like William Rufus's Great Hall at Westminster, so large that two centuries after it was finished, in 1269, it became the site of the first true English Parliament. Inspired by the French cult of courtly love introduced by Henry II's Queen, Eleanor of Aquitaine, fine manners were considered the mark of a good and honest man, and as dining became more codified the various offices of the household multiplied, a steward overseeing the marshal of the hall, butlers, pantlers, ewerers, carvers and a veritable army of male servers. A glance at medieval manuscript illuminations shows that it could all become very crowded indeed.

At the top of the hall, furthest away from the draughts, the lord and his guests sat at their table on stools and under a canopy of state, the complex hierarchy of seating arranged by the marshal, wary of any potential for slight. John Russell explained some of the details in his *Boke of Nurture*, written about 1460, declaring that popes and emperors were socially equal, as were kings and cardinals; bishops, viscounts, barons, abbots and chief justices – and the Speaker of Parliament – could sit at the second or third rank, and all other social classes from knight to priors, deans to doctors should be spread out below them. Confusion could arise when a knight was married to a royal lady, a prince to a commoner, or when a Pope brought his parents, but the marshal could fall back on Russell's advice: the parents of a Pope should be prepared to sit far further down the table than their illustrious son, or even in a separate room.

In the 1240s Bishop Grosseteste advised the widowed Countess of Lincoln to ensure that her whole household ate together in hall and 'that your presence as lord or lady is made manifest to all'. But within a century some families sought the warmth and privacy of smaller rooms or parlours, often on the first floor up a narrow stone staircase, a habit noted by Piers Plowman in the 1370s:

Woe is in the hall in all times and seasons
Where neither lord nor lady likes to linger.
Now each rich man has a rule to eat in secret,
In a private parlour, for poor folk's comfort,
In a chamber with a chimney, perhaps, and leave the chief assembly
Which was made for men to have meat and meals in

Dining in hall did not lose its appeal, however, and wherever food was taken meals resonated with rules. Breakfast came after chapel at day-break, and some ate heartily: Lord and Lady Percy each sat down to 'a loif of Bred in trenchors, two manchets [white bread rolls], a quart of bere, a quart of wyne, half a chyne of mutton or ells a chyne of beif boiled' or, on fish days, salt fish, red herring, pickled herring or sprats. The main meal of the day, the dinner or *prandium*, was governed by the hours of daylight and usually enjoyed between eleven o'clock and midday. Supper, or *reresouper*, was generally a light meal often eaten in private and always by nightfall to minimise the use of expensive, rationed candles.

Though Chaucer's food-loving Franklin was so hospitable that the table in his hall was never taken down – it 'stood redy covered al the longe day' – more usually the narrow trestles, or *boards* (from which comes 'boarding school', 'board wages', 'bed and board'), were set up as dinner approached, the hall transformed into a bustling scene of activity as the sauces began to bubble in the kitchens. Napkins were folded, wine was brought from the cellars, and water and towels were prepared for the guests.

On to the tables went pristine cloths: for best, woven Syrian cloth or damask and for everyday use coarser materials like hemp. Costly and hard to launder, table linen was another outward mark of success and breeding; it was often included in a bride's trousseau, and instruction manuals devoted long pages to its preparation. John Russell suggested that the *cowche* should be thrown over the table, straightened with a rod and pleated at the edges before adding various further layers – the best *surnapes* on top, each overlapping to ensure that they fell to the ground at the ends and the front of the table. Sometimes separate bands of cloth that could be removed between courses would be folded just along the edge of the table. This process was performed with devotion and ceremony, and the lord's bread was wrapped carefully in 2½ yards of fine Rennes cloth.

Each place would be set with a napkin for the guest to throw over his or her left shoulder and a knife and spoon of wood, horn, silver or pewter, though most diners continued to carry their own knife and the christening spoon given to them at birth – the origin of the expression about the wealthy being born with silver spoons in their mouths – often with a little knob or saint's head at the end so that they were known as apostle spoons. Forks were used widely in the kitchen but, apart from a handful of royal forks made of crystal, precious stones or gold, they were conspicuously absent from the table. Bread rolls were set at each place – new bread for the lord, one-day-old bread for the guests and three-day-old bread for the household – so that one's social position continued to be defined by the age and quantity of bread as much as by its colour. Slices of four-day-old bread trimmed into orderly squares by the pantler and known as *trenchers*, from the French 'trencher', to slice, were stacked along the tables for everyone's use; from these come our use of the word *trencherman* to denote a hearty eater.

Meat was lifted from shared dishes using the point of a knife or the fingers, the trenchers were used less as plates than to suck up some of the thick gravies and protect the cloths. When sodden they were thrown to the dogs or discarded into a shared voiding plate or alms basket for the poor or, on occasion, poorly fed lower servants – one Italian in England noted that English lords were 'avaricious by nature', giving their household only 'the coarsest bread and beer and cold meat baked on Sunday for the week'. In the fifteenth century metal or wooden trenchers began to appear, often with indentations to hold a little salt; stale bread was then placed instead as a 'sop' on the plate or in the bottom of a bowl, with pottage or meat served over it. We still serve small game birds on toast in the same way and put bread into soups; 'soppy' still means to be a bit wet and useless.

Against the wall to one side of the table stood the buffet, rising in tiers like a dresser and designed as yet another stage for the ostentatious display of wealth. According to your social rank there were two, four or even five shelves filled with silver or gilt platters and precious table-wares, doubling as a place from which to serve wine. While the poor used wooden or leather cups, the rich now enjoyed fine pottery and drank from large carved wood or metal cups called *mazers* which often had curved bottoms. *Nefs* were a particularly British foible, elaborate galleons fashioned from precious metals, designed to hold the finest, whitest salt and set, symbolically, before the lord at the head of the table.

Once the hall had been made ready, it was time for the serving of food and the minding of manners. Before dining, guests and the household all ritually washed their hands with water scented with flowers or herbs, drying them on fine towels carried by the ewerer. Only the most powerful aristocrats and bishops then employed tasters to 'assay' their dishes in a highly formalised ritual relying not only on the courage and life of the taster but on substances like unicorn horn (in reality, elephant or narwhal tusk) to indicate the presence of poisons.

Jean Froissart, one of the first great chroniclers in the 1360s, noted that 'the gentry of England are particularly courteous', and a great flood of handwritten instruction manuals appeared from the fifteenth century, filled with advice on conduct and diet and anticipating the concept of mannered urbanity that would come to characterise the Renaissance. Aimed at children of the nobility, who, before schools were established, were sent to be educated by their neighbours and at *jentylls*, or rural gentlefolk, eager to ape the fashions of the court, these manuals were for those who appreciated that manners facilitated promotion. Erasmus also appreciated that expectations were not to be flouted if the goal was social success: in his work on civilising young boys he devoted his longest chapter to behaviour while eating.

Since manners marked you out, stylised conventions became so ingrained that to transgress was considered disgusting. Froissart judged the Irish by their rough courts where he found the people uncouth and slow-thinking with 'no respect for pleasant manners', and Chaucer's socially climbing Prioress fastidiously aped courtly manners, letting

> no morsel from hir lipes falle
> Ne wet hir fingers in hir sauce deepe . . .

The rules were designed to make sharing less of a trial as well as to protect the tablecloths. As Russell's *Boke of Nurture* advised, no guest should scratch as if he were looking for fleas, or strike his head to squash a nit; he must not pick his nose or allow it to run, nor should he put his hands down his trousers to scratch his *codware*. He must not laugh, gape or speak loudly; put his tongue into a dish or outside his mouth to clean his chin; or cough, hiccough or belch; nor must he pick his teeth (except with a newfangled toothpick) or breathe too heavily in case of bad breath. Farting was circumscribed. It was courteous to wipe your mouth before drinking from the shared cup and – even 600 years ago – considered rude to put your elbows on the table.

The courtly game of civility was thus minutely regulated by prescribed conduct mirroring the codified nature of society, all rather more uptight and restrained than the raucous dining scenes that some costume dramas would have us believe. On the contrary, most guides to manners stressed quiet behaviour at meals with little conversation or mirth; children, in particular, were taught to be seen and not heard, to look their parents full in the face before bowing to them, and to clear trenchers and serve wine, ale or beer before quietly bringing water and towels for washing.

One of the very first English printed books was a carving manual written by Wynken de Woorde, assistant to the first British printer, William Caxton, and it demonstrates in what regard the position of carver was held. Because he was expected to know the exact term for carving each kind of meat, Woorde listed them all, including 'tyere that egge', 'chune that samon', 'strynge that breme', 'side that haddocke', 'tuske that barbell', 'culpon that troute', and 'undertraunche that purpos', and he described the proper way to cut up, or *break*, each animal with finesse. Beef and mutton were always sliced neatly; partridges, doves and chickens were finely minced and the right wing of a capon always served to the hungriest guest; bitterns, egrets, curlews and herons were all *unlaced* before the lord and his guests.

This was the 'connynge of kervyung'. John Russell advised aspirant carvers to keep their knives clean and bright and to practise holding them tight in the palm of the hand, touching the meat only with two fingers and the thumb of the left hand. All meat was served to guests on the point of the carver's knife along with exactly the right sauce: mustard with beef and brawn, verjuice with boiled capon, garlic with roast goose and ginger for lamb. Sugar and salt were the correct condiments for curlew, lapwing, lark and venison; cinnamon was served with roast thrush; and there was a small handful of birds including woodcock and snipe that required 'no sauce but salt'. Russell explained that beaver must served with sliced frumenty and that the most succulent part of pike was its belly. 'Crabbe,' he wrote, 'is a slutt to kerve': by the time each claw had been broken, the meat seasoned with vinegar, verjuice and spices all mixed with the point of the carver's knife and returned to the clean shell, the crab had usually become so cold that it had to be sent back to the kitchen to be reheated.

Andrea Trevisano, the earliest Venetian ordinary ambassador to the English court, wrote in 1497 that the British were 'very sparing of wine when they drink it at their own expense . . . not considering it any great inconvenience for three or four persons to drink out of the same cup . . . and when they mean to drink a great deal, they go to the tavern, and this is done not only by the men, but by ladies of distinction'. In the hall, drink was served to guests by the butler only on request. Water, considered both bacteriologically and humourally unsafe, was rarely served, and five-day-old home-brewed ale was the norm, occasionally spiced and sweetened like cider. Costly wines were imported from Burgundy, Gascony, Anjou, Normandy and Germany, sweet wines known as malmsiy, *Vernage* and *Bustard* came from Spain and the southern Mediterranean, and Russell listed more, including 'Muscadelle, Rompney of Modon, Tyre, Ozney, Torrentyne, Greke, Jalelvesyn, Caprik'. All of these were made even more expensive by the two casks from each imported cargo that were forfeit to the King as *prisage*, or duty.

The butler also oversaw the production of spiced hippocras for the voidée – made by steeping ginger, cinnamon and sugar for nobles, cheaper spices and honey for the rest, in wine and leaving them to soften its harsh, acid rawness. The liquid was then strained through a hippocras sleeve, or cloth bag; the dregs were always returned to the kitchen to be used in sauces. Potent mead and its spicier cousin *metheglin* were also brewed, often stirred with the leaves of sweet briar or rosemary for flavour. So much were these pungent flavours an accepted part of life that even the village poor were accustomed to seasoning their ale with pennyroyal, mint, wormwood, sage or even horseradish, and for those rich enough to distil their own spirits *clarrey* could be made from sweetened wine fortified with *aqua ardaunt*.

Ambassador Trevisano was particularly struck by the British cult of hospitality, exclaiming, '. . . they think that no greater honour can be conferred or received than to invite others to eat with them, or to be invited themselves.' From great castle halls to timber-framed manor houses, meals were supplied not only to family members and retainers but to passing travellers, invited friends, religious visitors and estate workers. In 1412, 300 people sat down to dine at New Year's with Alice de Bryene at Acton Hall, and whatever the season there were rarely fewer than eight for breakfast, twenty for dinner and ten for supper. Her steward kept minute accounts of expenditure, and her cook typically balanced prodigality with simple dishes on days when the household ate without guests, using capon, coney, pig, goose, herring or stockfish and keeping waste to a minimum.

By the fifteenth century, wars, plagues and famine had begun to fracture medieval feudalism and its time-honoured notions of hospitality. As the population declined, so did manorial revenues; servant numbers were reduced and great halls were increasingly abandoned in favour of privy parlours. When the Wars of the Roses finally came to an end and the economy began to expand under the Tudor King Henry VII, new men were hired to do the lord's work for him and a professional class emerged. Profiting in the growing monetary economy, merchants and agents built themselves sturdy brick homes with smaller chambers and more fireplaces. Woollen gowns gave way to fine linens and silks, to velvets with rich embroidery and to square-toed shoes, and public eating began to decline.

Crossing the world's oceans, Vasco da Gama, Columbus and Magellan set out on their voyages of discovery, driven by the wealth that domination of the spice trades promised. Once the Portuguese discovered the sea route to India in 1498, their boats began to return to Europe with their holds bursting with aromatics – the price of spice tumbled.

A page from the Steward's account for Alice de Bryene's household in 1418–19, showing monies received from the sale of dairy produce, wool and empty barrels.

Pastry

When you come to think about it, medieval pie crust was an odd culinary invention. To make pastry strong enough to withstand a filling, hot water was used to turn the gluten in rye flour into an elastic grey putty that would stay upright on its own. The pastry, or *paste* as it was known, was raised up by hand either by using a wooden plug or by punching a fist into a ball of dough and pulling up the sides rather like a crude pot. Except that it was not crude – it was rather skilful and, above all, practical. Once the pies with their contents were cooked, the gravy could be drained out and clarified butter poured in through a pipe or funnel in the top. This sealed the meat from the air and kept it fresh in the larder for weeks or even months. It might then be reheated and, just before it was served, a fresh, hot gravy or a sweet, spiced and sometimes ale-spiked *caudle* of eggs could be added; at the table, the crust would be broken open and the contents spooned out as the steam rose. The tough, inedible pastry was either discarded or kept in the kitchen as a thickener for pottages.

Raised pies were important, highly decorated centrepieces at feasts as well as practical homely fare. They could be huge, pasty-like

The Battersea Cauldron, 800–700 BC. Pulled from the River Thames, this vast, elegant vessel was highly prized and used for grand feasting.

The Dunaverney Flesh Hook, circa tenth century BC – a four-foot wooden pole with cast bronze tubes and models of birds, probably used for hauling large pieces of meat from a cauldron or boiling trough.

Still life from the house of Julia Felix, Pompeii. Similarly luminous frescoes adorned the luxurious new villas that appeared in third-century Roman Britain.

The Mildenhall Treasure. This vast cache of Roman silverware was probably buried in AD 360 as the Roman Empire began to collapse. It includes sets of spoons with pointed ends called *cochleare*, used for eating shellfish and snails.

Bede was one of the first to disapprove of the gluttonous indulgence of the Church.

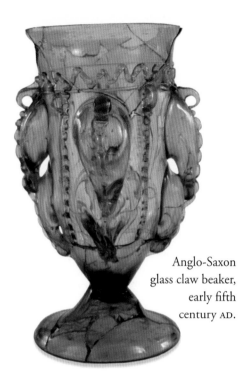

Anglo-Saxon glass claw beaker, early fifth century AD.

This page from one of the medieval health handbooks noted that leeks were warm in the third degree and dry in the second; they should be eaten in winter, by the old or those with cold temperaments.

Chaucer's swarthy cook, Hodge, from the Ellesmere Manuscript of *The Canterbury Tales*.

This sequence of miniatures from the *Luttrell Psalter* illustrates the physicality of preparing a fourteenth-century feast. Here, the meat has been roasted or boiled and is chopped with knives as long as the cook's arms before being sauced and served.

John of Gaunt feasting with the King of Portugal, 1386. Note the benches, the fine white cloth and trenchers, and the orderly presentation of food from a serving hatch to the left, while minstrels entertain the diners from a gallery on the right.

Fifteenth-century shops: a grocer selling sugar cones and a hippocras seller – part of the carnival of consumption played out on the medieval town street.

Baking bread in a medieval manorial household: once the ashes were raked out of the brick bread oven, large batches were inserted using a long-handled wooden spade or 'pele'.

The Cobham family in the 1570s. Attitudes towards eating raw fruit were beginning to change.

Still life with confections, Clara Peeters, circa 1615. A large, scalloped-edge marchpane decorated with coloured comfits dominates the banqueting table, surrounded by platters of knotted 'jumballs' and flowers made of sugar paste.

The Distinguished Visitor by Jan Brueghel
shows a valuable sugar cone offered as a gift.

Fragile Tudor glass, 1586, delicately
engraved and with the motto:
'In God is all my trust.'

Herring fishermen packing their fish in brine, 1619. Though fish was rapidly losing
favour, fast days were maintained by law to protect the British fishing industry, and 'cades'
or barrels of salted herring remained household staples.

The frontispiece from John Parkinson's *Paradisi in sole*, 1629, one of the great herbals of the age. The heaven-scented pineapple is at the very heart of Parkinson's Garden of Eden, though it had not yet been cultivated in Britain.

envelopes enclosing a great joint of venison – the largest of the ovens in the pastry house at Hampton Court was more than 12 feet wide – or smaller containers filled with a mixture of various meats, fruits and spices. Yet there are no real recipes for early pastry; perhaps, like bread, it was so widely understood and practised that the process was taken for granted. The only instruction in Richard II's *Forme of Cury* is that cooks should blow hard into their pastry casings before closing up the holes and putting their pies in the oven, in the hope that the lids would not cave in.

Pastry evolved throughout the Tudor period. With the addition of eggs and the use of cold fats like butter or suet, it became, for the first time, edible. Short-crust pastry was made using good-quality wheat flours, rich butter and cold water to create a dryish mixture that baked to a crumbling tenderness. One of the earliest Tudor cookbooks, *A Proper New Booke of Cookerye* (1545), included a recipe for 'short paest for tart', using fine flour, 'a curtesy of faire water and a disshe of swete butter and a little saffron and the yolkes of two egges and make it thik and tender as ye maie'. It needed delicate handling, but with this new method, pies began to attain even higher status.

Tudor standing pies were sometimes so finely wrought that they were edible works of art. When you start to look, you see them everywhere in still-life paintings of the Renaissance period, their laced patterns and panels, flutes and lozenges, heraldic emblems and devices mirroring the design of Tudor dress, plasterwork and gardens. Some-times, to signal their contents, rabbits' or hares' ears, or their entire heads, were left popping out of the top crust, and professional cooks kept stuffed birds or their wings as adornment so that a pie's appear-ance was really up to the cook's ingenuity, whimsy or sense of humour. For grand occasions it was not uncommon to perch an entire stuffed swan on the top of a garlanded pie – there is one waiting to be served in a painting of Archduke Leopold William's kitchen; a maid sits by it, exhausted or bemused, watching it like a hawk.

Standing fruit pies were sometimes replaced by flat tarts known as *florentines*, served in the final course and filled with thick fruit marmalades that could be imprinted with figures or laced with dec-orative strap-work – the bands of pastry folded, crossed or interwoven – and *struck*, or stuck, with sugared comfits. As was the fashion in still-life paintings of the day, the Flemish painter Clara Peeters arranged wafers and knotted biscuits around a central shallow marchpane* ornamented with rosemary sprigs in her *Still Life with Confectionery* (*c.* 1611). Her compatriot Frans Franken chose to paint a masterpiece of the art of pies, its exquisite top broken open ready for its contents – in this context probably spicy, sweet mincemeat – to be dug out with a silver spoon.

Although the Italian papal cook Bartolomeo Scappi included pastry recipes in his vast culinary guide of 1570, it was not until 1602, in a charming little book called *Delightes for Ladies*, that the courtier Sir Hugh Platt described for the first time in England how to make the several sorts of pastry in real detail. He explained that rich short paste was made with flour, egg yolks and cream rather than suet or butter, and that puff pastry required more work – the mix of eggs, butter, fine white flour and cold water had to be rolled out, dotted with butter, folded and rolled out again: '. . . drive out the piece with a rolling pin, and do with butter one piece by another, and then fold up your paste upon the butter and drive it out again, and do so five or six times together.' Platt's recipe would have made a rich but delicate crust with at least sixty-four frail layers of pastry designed to rise, expand and separate into light, crispy flakes. Ten minutes or so before it was ready, it was strewn with fine sugar and returned to the oven to bake, emerging crusty and steaming.

A decade or so after Platt's book, in 1615, Gervase Markham published his enormously popular collection of culinary and medical recipes called *The English Huswife*, aimed squarely at the well-off middling sort. Markham was the literate housewife's friend, always on the lookout for the detail that would make the difference, and here he gave even more specific descriptions of various pastry crusts than ever before, setting out the repertoire with care. First rye paste, kneaded with hot water and a little butter – tough and stiff enough to make a long-lasting, deep coffin. Next, for poultry, lamb, veal and peacock pies which might be served more than once over a few days but which

---

* During the Tudor period, marchpane evolved from its gingerbread-like medieval roots into something more like marzipan, with crushed almonds, sugar and rosewater as its main ingredients.

were not designed for extended keeping, a good white crust 'somewhat thick', made of wheat flour kneaded with hot water or mutton broth and 'a good store of butter'. Then the melting short paste, made from wheat flour dried in a warm oven, mixed very gently with butter, cold water and eggs, and rolled out as thinly as possible for enclosing delicate meats intended to be served hot: chicken, fallow deer or the fashionable new olives and sweet potatoes. Not all cookery writers were as reliable. In 1584, instructions given by the writer known only as A W must have driven uninitiated cooks to rub their temples in distraction: '. . . take fine flour and lay it on a boord and take a certaine of yolks of egges as your quantity of flour is, then take a certaine of butter and water and boile together . . . too many yolks will make it dry and not pleasant in eating and not too much butter or it will not raise . . .'

By the end of the sixteenth century, edible pastry was widely being made, and the British cook never looked back. Indeed the Tudors were so pleased by their pies that they sent them as gifts, especially at Christmas. In wealthy houses they were sculpted and flourished by trained cooks, while elsewhere housewives worked on the thick boards of their kitchen tables, first ensuring that the flour was sifted and put by the fire to dry – for keeping it entirely free from damp was always a problem – then fashioning pastry leaves and flowers, fluting the edges as they were fixed on the pie's top. Finally, strained egg yolk whisked with a bundle of slender sticks was washed with a broad feather over the decorated pie to form a glaze that would turn the crust a shiny corn-gold as it baked.

THE TUDORS

A garden arbour planted with sweet roses and set with a banqueting table, from Thomas Hill's *The Gardener's Labyrinth*, 1577.

7

Strange Vegetables, New Tastes

The situation of our region, lying near unto the north,
doth cause the heat of our stomachs to be of somewhat
greater force: therefore our bodies do crave a little more
ample nourishment than the inhabitants of the hotter
regions whose digestive force is not altogether so vehe-
ment

— HOLINSHED

Only seventeen on his accession, Henry VIII was the embodiment of modern monarchy: robust, glamorous and determined to spend the fortune that his father had left him in making Merrie England a little more like the glittering Burgundian court. Under his rule, lavish ceremony, rich taste, colourful dress, poetry and art would all flourish and be copied by a growing class of merchants and professional public servants – new men intent on establishing their own dynasties.

Henry was a passionate builder, amassing more houses than any other British monarch before or since, and, like the Conqueror, his grandiose mansions started an aristocratic building boom that would spiral through the century to culminate in vast Elizabethan prodigy houses like Longleat, Hardwick Hall, Montacute and Burghley.*

---

* Although York Place, renamed Whitehall, was the official royal residence, when the court despaired of its own stench it 'progressed' either to another royal palace or to one of these great new houses. Everything was packed on to carts, including beds, bedlinen, tables, stools, tapestries and entire kitchen contents, to rattle along the pitted roads in convoys which beggared belief. In the closing years of her reign, Elizabeth's courtiers tried so hard to outdo each other and gain her capricious favour that they regularly risked bankruptcy both in the houses they built to receive her and in the entertainments they provided during her stays.

Henry's Great Hall at Hampton Court, finished in 1535, was the last to be built in England: elsewhere, halls were being divided into two storeys with first-floor privy chambers whose windows looked out over gardens below and parkland beyond. In such rooms small tables were covered with heavy carpets – places to read, write, draw or eat; by the end of the century the bed would be removed, completing the transformation of the private chamber into a 'dining parlour'.

The King now dined in absolute and splendid isolation – quite different from the first-among-equals atmosphere of the medieval hall – witnessed only by invited guests, high-ranking courtiers and ambassadors. His daughter Elizabeth would retreat still further, dining almost entirely in private while the erstwhile public ritual of the hall took place in her absence. A German visitor, Paul Hentzner, watched it unfold at Greenwich; while the Queen was still at prayers, her table was laid

> with the utmost veneration . . . At last came an unmarried lady . . . bearing a tasting-knife . . . [who] approached the table and rubbed the plates with bread and salt with as much awe as if the Queen had been present . . . The yeomen of the guards entered . . . bringing in at each turn a course of twenty-four dishes, served in plate, most of it gilt; these dishes were received by a gentleman . . . and placed upon the table, while the lady taster gave to each of the guard a mouthful to eat of the particular dish he had brought, for fear of any poison . . . At the end of all this ceremonial, a number of unmarried ladies appeared, who, with particular solemnity, lifted the meat off the table, and conveyed it into the Queen's inner and more private chamber, where, after she had chosen for herself, the rest goes to the ladies of the Court.

Small privy kitchens connected to private quarters by a narrow stone staircase were sometimes designed for preparing food only for the monarch or the lord – though Elizabeth I, who famously hated kitchen smells, had her father's at Hampton Court removed. Conscious of the risk of fires like the one that began in the kitchens and gutted the royal lodgings at the Palace of Westminster in 1512, kitchens were increasingly built as separate complexes on the cooler, northerly aspects of houses. When Andrew Boorde – a jolly Carthusian monk who winningly believed that laughter was the best medicine for a truly healthy life – wrote his *Dyetary of Helthe* in 1542, he advised that 'the buttery and the pantry be at the lower end of the hall, the seller under the pantry . . . the kychen set somewhat a base from the buttry and pantry . . . the pastry howse and the larder howse annexed to the kychen'.

Henry and his court still had something of the Middle Ages about them, their tables shuddering under a profusion of meaty dishes, but the pattern of farming was changing as British wool began to make great fortunes, and more land was devoted to sheep pasture and less to crops, making traditional self-sufficiency almost impossible. Thus an important new role now developed under the steward: that of the *acater* – from 'acheter', to buy – who oversaw the purchasing of supplies from local markets and specialist merchants; unlike modern caterers, the acater was emphatically *not* the cook, but he *was* the man who got slapped if the cheese ran out.

Vast quantities of provisions were needed, for at Henry's Nonsuch, its white turrets rising from the fields to mark his love for Anne Boleyn, the kitchens were designed to feed more than a thousand courtiers a day. At Richmond Palace there were seventeen separate kitchens, and at Hampton Court designated rooms and out-buildings were devoted to spicery, buttery, pastry, confectionery, saucery and salting, slaughtering, scalding, baking and brewing, each with its own head clerk answerable to the clerk of the kitchen. Three enormous larders were provided just for meat, and a separate wet larder for fish rejoiced in its own piped water supply; there were six immense roasting ranges, an eighty-gallon copper pot for boiling stocks or meat, and three capacious cellars.

Among Cardinal Wolsey's Eltham Ordinances of 1526, designed to cut costs and raise standards at court, was a stipulation that part-naked kitchen scullions should be dressed and that no one should piss into cooking pots. But with kitchens heaving with the activity of hundreds of knife-wielding staff and master cooks barking their orders,* these

---

* Master cooks were valued professionals and well paid. Henry employed John Bricket and a French cook, Pero Doux, for the enormous sum of £23 16s 8d a year. Normally, these salaries were bolstered by 'perquisites', or perks – perhaps the dripping from roast meat, coney skins or strippings from prepared meat – which were all sold on at the kitchen door.

ordinances did little to mitigate the organised tumult: when Philip of
Spain visited Mary Tudor in 1554, one of his attendants described the
royal kitchens 'in full blast . . . they seem veritable hells such is the stir
and bustle in them'.

In the drama of such kitchens, coal – with its long-lasting, intense
heat – was being substituted for wood, necessitating iron fire baskets,
and discs of wet straw set on pikes before the fire protected the
turnspits from the fiercest heat as they basted and rotated the joints.
In specially built waist-high stoves and in chafing dishes, the gentler
heat of charcoal was used for simmering sauces, egg custards and other
subtle dishes. Copper pans, really efficient heat conductors, were used,
well tinned both on the inside and the outside to ensure that poisonous
verdigris did not form when acidic vinegar or lemon juice came into
contact with the copper – providing plenty of work for itinerant
tinkers who would call at the kitchen door offering to re-tin the pans.
Metal discs with long wooden handles called *salamanders* were heated
red-hot in the fire and held over dishes to brown their tops to a
satisfying crisp – the only effective way to grill the top of a dish until
the arrival of modern gas and electric ovens.

Mechanical innovation was in the air, and as weight and spring jacks
began to develop, Elizabeth's physician Dr John Caius, founder of the
Cambridge college of the same name, invented a turnspit operated by a
dog running in a wheel like a hamster, so performing a task, he wrote,
that 'no drudge or scullion can do . . . more cuningly'. At about the
same time, Bartolomeo Scappi filled the hundreds of pages of his guide
with careful technical illustrations of kitchen equipment, a beautiful
visual inventory of a well-equipped mid-Tudor kitchen. Scappi's
kitchen centred on a large table with drawers and cutting boards;
on pulleys, ratchets and levers for man-handling large equipment over
the fires, and on pans with long or short handles depending on how
close to the roaring heat they needed to be. His pages were crammed
with pictures of long-legged colanders, bellows, great boxes for bolted
flour, pestles and mortars, balances, little nut graters, large bread and
cheese raspers, and pasta or pastry cutters with crinkled edges. He
showed an army of knives, some with round and others with pointed
ends, these curved and those straight – and an array of equipment that
could be hung up when not in use. There were stools, cupboards with

The ideal Tudor kitchen as illustrated by Bartolomeo Scappi in 1570 included cranes, pulleys and poles for heaving great pots over the open fire, and various-sized roasting spits and large preparation tables.

bolts and odd little animal feet, lockable chests, pincers, presses, brooms and ladders; a sixteenth-century *batterie de cuisine* quite as wide-ranging as the equipment in any commercial kitchen today.

The cooking facilities and diet of the poor remained, as they had for generations, broadly unchanged, based on bread, boiled pottages, the produce from a couple of animals and a rough vegetable patch or, in towns, on the wares of street sellers and cookshops. But Henry's political expediency would bring about one of the most cataclysmic transformations in the diet of all classes, forever altering the British relationship with fish. His rift with Rome was hastened by the combination of a notoriously profligate Church and his urgent need to find both a new source of income and a way to divorce Aragon and wed Boleyn. In 1536 there were more than 800 religious institutions in Britain. Within five years there were none. The Dissolution of the Monasteries changed at a stroke the way the countryside looked and the rules according to which people ate. The monks, their masses and their fish-ponds disappeared. Roman Catholicism became treasonable.

By the time the London guilds of salt fish-mongers and stockfish-mongers merged to form the Worshipful Company of Fishmongers, fish days had already begun to lose their force. In 1541 Henry proclaimed that eggs, cheese and milk could all now be included in fast-day diets; total Lenten abstinence was abandoned, and the number of holy days was reduced by around three-quarters. Apart from the religiously tumultuous handful of years under the hard-line Protestant King Edward VI and, later, his Catholic half-sister Bloody Mary, a middle ground was reached: fast days were maintained by law in order to protect the fishing industry, and most people ate fish on Fridays and Saturdays. But attitudes to fish were shifting, and the status of butter and cream over olive oil and almond milk began to soar.

By the time Andrew Boorde wrote his *Dyetary* in 1542, he was already concerned that the lack of fasting would result in souls 'knockynge at paradyse gates to go in, wepynge and waylyng' at their rejection, but even he admitted to finding salt fish nauseating and river fish muddy. Lamprey were falling rapidly out of fashion, and fish was becoming political, 'popish' flesh that lost favour as fast as Anglicanism took root: in Shakespeare's *King Lear* (*c.* 1608), Kent vows to 'serve him truly that will put me in trust, to love him that is honest . . . to fear judgement . . . and to eat no fish'.

As British fish consumption began its long decline, novel ingredients from newly discovered lands including America were making their way into British kitchens, some to find immediate favour and others to languish for centuries before their true culinary potential was appreciated. Maize, known as Indian corn, came from the New World, the herbalist John Gerard writing that 'we have as yet no certaine proofe or experience concerning the virtues of this kinde of Corne, although the barbarous Indians which know no better are constrained to make a vertue of necessitie and think it a good food, whereas we may easily judge that it nourisheth but little . . . more convenient food for swine than men.' Chocolate and pineapples too would both wait a century or more for recognition. In about 1525 the turkey was introduced, rapidly displacing the stringy 'great birds' of the medieval table. Fabulously expensive, turkeys were sold at London markets for 6 shillings a piece,* but they were well enough established by the 1540s for the courtier Sir William Petre to cage them with pheasants in his orchard at Ingatestone Hall.

Slowly, these new foods began to alter the nation's tastes once again. Introduced from France, the dense sweet flesh of *pompions*, as pumpkins were known, was quickly accepted as a pie filler – a Tudor classic that later travelled with the Founding Fathers to survive in America as one of its national dishes. Sweet potatoes were commonly cooked in wine, while white potatoes, first noted by the Spanish conquistadors in the 1530s, only became regularly available from the mid-1580s. 'Virginia potatoes', as the white variety was known, were most often added to pies mixed with sugar and fruits but would not achieve a central place in the British diet for another two centuries. Gerard was among the first to illustrate and describe them, in 1579 – he roasted them in embers, or boiled and ate them 'with oyle, vinegar and pepper', but he

---

* Turkeys were so called because they arrived from Mexico via trade in the Levant. By the 1570s their price had dropped to 3s 4d for a cock and 1s 8d for a hen.

supposed that there might be fancier ways if you only had 'some cunning in cookerie'.

Red and green peppers, kidney beans, the French bean, red runners and a new variety of garden pea now jostled for culinary recognition along with the *tomata*, or love apple, which arrived from Mexico via Spain in the 1570s. Gerard wrote that in hot countries tomatoes were boiled with pepper, salt and oil or eaten with oil and vinegar as a 'sauce to their meate, euen as we in these cold Countries doe Mustard', but he and the rest of Tudor Britain considered them corrupting and devoid of nourishment. In the main, tomatoes were banished to the garden, cultivated as an ornamental and valued simply for their foliage and decorative fruit.

Greek olives and French capers were imported as appetite stimulants and, by the end of Elizabeth's reign, anchovies were arriving along with *botargo*, a Mediterranean relish made of grey mullet or tuna roes. The aubergine was broadly ignored – William Harrison, the Essex rector who collaborated with Holinshed on his 1577 *Chronicles* of everyday Elizabethan life, thought it 'very dangerous and hurtful'. Whereas that other important Elizabethan introduction, tobacco, found quicker acceptance: by the end of the century smoking had caught on – a seductive habit believed to air and perfume both the body and the breath.

Nothing could have been further from the medieval culinary tradition than all this fresh garden produce simmered in broth and served with butter, salt and pepper. Eclipsing spices in status, new plants arrived at an especially auspicious time, for nursery gardens were developing, stocks were being improved, and horticultural skills were making rapid strides, influenced by the advanced market-gardening expertise of Flemish Protestant refugees. As gardening became a gentlemanly pastime for the well-to-do, an entirely different attitude to vegetables emerged. Globe artichokes and asparagus became fashionable, served with a sauce of sack wine, butter and ginger or baked in pies with bone marrow and dates. Thomas Muffett, a contemporary of Shakespeare and Ben Jonson, observed that both vegetables, originally very scarce, had become common. He simmered artichokes and asparagus in butter and mutton broth until tender, and boiled artichoke leaves with sweet bone marrow, verjuice, pepper, sugar and gooseberries as a pie filling, or served them with a sauce of orange juice and sugar.

Like artichoke leaves and asparagus tips, the tender shoots of things were especially relished. Samphire was aptly paired with marsh mutton; cardoons (a kind of edible thistle) were trickily prepared by stripping and blanching their heads and stalks. Cucumber was eaten fresh or pickled, and the buds (or *knops*) of alexanders, purslane and broom were pickled like capers, tied into small linen bags and weighted down in a pot of brine until they went black, then boiled and stored in vinegar. Hop buds, astringent enough to make the lips smart, were scattered over salads and stews.

When Catherine of Aragon was a young Queen in England, salad plants were so rare that she had to send to Holland for the lettuce she loved. Within thirty years, a wide variety of salad greens were available, including chicory, endive, mallow, purslane, fennel, smallage and peppery rocket. Tudor gardening manuals were simply full of the range of vegetables that could be cultivated in the ever-expanding kitchen garden, all of them guarded fiercely from insects, slugs and the pigeons that sat in the trees waiting for the gardener to go home, all destined to be harvested, dew-fresh, for the cook. Small wonder that metal and earthenware colanders were becoming common.

The printed book both charted and stimulated these transitions in British taste. Though printed in English rather than Latin, the first such volumes were hand-sold and beyond the reach of the majority, but still they aimed at a growing aspirational and literate market. The earliest English printed cookbook, *A Noble Boke of Cookery ffor a Pryncis Household* (c. 1540), was old-fashioned and full of archaic Norman terms, but the *Proper Newe Booke of Cookerye* that followed hard on its heels suggested, perhaps for the first time, that cookery was not only a handy way to make an impression but something to *delight* in. By the 1580s and '90s, increasing numbers of little cookbooks were being printed, no longer aimed at professional cooks but at householders. Still vague by modern standards, their recipes were written with an increasing eye for detail, with some specific quantities –

spoonfuls, dishes or saucers – and occasional indications of timings, as clocks and watches were beginning to appear. In his *Good Huswifes Jewell* (1596), Thomas Dawson described how to boil a mallard with cabbage:

> Take some cabbage and pick and wash them clean and perboylle them in faire water, then put them into a collender and let the water runne from them cleane, then put them into a fair earthen pot and as much sweet broth as will cover the cabbage, and sweet butter, then taken your mallard and roste it half enough and save the dripping of him, then cut him in the side and put the mallard into the cabbage and put into it all your dripping then let it stew an hour and season it with salt and eat it upon soppes.

Such books demonstrate that the fresh flavours of green vegetables, herbs, butter and citrus were suffusing Elizabethan cookery. Perhaps it was Catherine's Aragonese background that led to the use of lip-smacking Seville orange juice in red-meat stews and pies and the novelty of pairing fish and poultry with lemons, for by 1534 Henry's household was using enough in its cooking to purchase an orange strainer. Oranges were an expensive taste: at the banquet to celebrate Anne Boleyn's coronation at the Company of Leather Sellers in 1533, there was only one citrus fruit. Tart barberries could be used instead, and the gooseberries that arrived in Britain in the 1530s provided similar acidity at a fraction of the cost. Yet as greater quantities were imported and prices somewhat reduced, the vibrant perfume of lemons, oranges and knobbly citrons began to waft through Elizabethan cooking, more fresh and subtle than vinegar or verjuice, ravishing bedfellows for meat and vegetables alike. Parboiled leg of mutton might be cut into strips and simmered with lemons, currants, verjuice and sugar; a capon could be cooked with oranges, currants, prunes, mace and white wine. The first five recipes in A W's collection of 1584 all relied on lemons or oranges, first slicing and parboiling the peel to dull its bitterness.

The taste for mixing savoury and sweet lingered alongside these new, bright flavours until after the Civil War, but mixtures of dried fruits with meat did began to feel old-fashioned, even to the Tudors.

Meat was still a sign of wealth: the German Paul Hentzner noted that the English ate far more than the French, and Andrew Boorde ranked it by status, with bacon 'good for carters and plowmen, the wiche be ever labouring in the earth and dung'. Venison still clung to its seigneurial significance – King Henry daringly wooed Anne Boleyn with gifts of it, writing that he sent 'some flesh, representing my name, which is hart's flesh, for Henry, prognosticating that hereafter you must enjoy some of mine'. Roasts too lost none of their aristocratic status, Cardinal Wolsey ordering that they should be 'neither raw neither over much . . . rosted'; Hentzner was not alone among visitors in acclaiming the British roast.

Some new approaches to meat were being explored. In his *Castel of Helth* (1539), dedicated to Thomas Cromwell, the physician Thomas Elyot noted a general turning away from 'old beife, mutton, geese, swannes, duckes . . . black puddynges' and from the heart, liver and kidneys of animals, which he thought were prone to making 'ylle iuyce', or bad 'juices', in the body. During Elizabeth's reign, as the court habit of dining in private was copied by merchants and families enjoying its warmer intimacy, smaller 'made' dishes like gently cooked stews and *fricassées* began to appear, thickened with eggs, cream and marrowbone rather than flour, breadcrumbs or crushed almonds, and flavoured with sweet herbs, wine and lemon. According to William Harrison, these dishes were the speciality of the 'musical headed Frenchmen' cooking for many of the nobility. Fuming at the excesses of his age, Robert Burton complained that simple, healthy ingredients were disguised in 'compound, artificial, made dishes.'

Burton had a point – this new style marked a turning point in the art of cooking and a bridge from medieval to modern cuisine. In dishes like these, slices of meat – known as *collops* – were stewed in broth, and wildfowl, hunted with newly available guns, was boiled and stuffed with herbs, vegetables and butter. The prolific culinary writer John Murrell gave a recipe for a terribly sophisticated leg of lamb cooked 'in the French fashion' – hollowing the meat out of the joint while leaving the skin intact, mincing the flesh into a perfumed farce 'with suet, bread, mint, orange peel, nutmeg, coriander seeds, barberries and pepper . . . worked with egg yolks and stuffed in again, baked in the [bread] oven with butter and serve strewed with yolks and parsley'.

As these smaller dishes took off, a new technique evolved and steaks that were too thin to be spit-roasted were now *carbonadoed*, or grilled over glowing coals.* According to Gervase Markham, small pieces of meat like the legs, wings or breasts of birds worked well if they were first scored deeply on both sides, salted and sprinkled with sweet butter before being put over the fire. He also suggested the use of a special iron plate 'with hooks and pricks on which you may hang the meate and let it close before the fire', toasting rather than barbecuing in order to avoid the acrid smoke caused by melting fat dripping on to the coals. As the fashion for carbonadoes took off, other cooks came up with alternatives: Hugh Platt fancifully suggested making little dripping pans from paper and starch, wetting them and placing the meat inside them on the gridiron so that the fats were contained – but this required vigilance to ensure that the boats themselves did not go up in flames.

Despite Boorde's opinion that pottage was 'not so much used in all Crystendom as it is used in Englande', this ancient dish was also growing up, often supplanted by lighter broths of chicken or capon thickened with lemon and egg yolk – in 1598 Queen Elizabeth rushed to her Chief Minister William Cecil's deathbed with just such a broth, ministering to him at his end with a motherliness lacking in her own long life. But away from the English court, change came more slowly. When the diarist and traveller Fynes Moryson dined in a Scottish knight's house in 1598, he was served great platters of pottage with pieces of sodden – or boiled – meat. There the servants still ate with their masters, and Moryson 'observed no art of cookery, or furniture, of household stuff, but rather neglect of both . . . much red Colewort and Cabbage but little fresh meate'. He found the Irish even cruder, scumming 'their seething pot with an handful of straw, and [straining] their milke . . . through a like handful of straw, none of the cleanest'; they boiled pig's intestines 'in a hollow tree, lapped in a raw Cowes hide . . . set over the fier', with 'whole lumps of filthy butter'. With no cloths or napkins gracing these Irish tables, Moryson thought there was a significant danger of the host devouring his very guests.

·   ·   ·

* The original term for grilling was *broiling* – the term that survives, like pumpkin pie, in most of the United States to this day.

In farms and manors, and in the abbeys like Beaulieu and nunneries like Ingatestone Hall, refashioned as new homes for wealthy courtiers, the old traditions of the hall and hospitality lingered and tastes evolved only slowly. William Petre's Ingatestone household accounts show that he regularly entertained forty strangers at his table during the winter months, despite having a separate dining parlour. Right into the 1550s, Petre purchased spices similar to those Alice de Bryene had bought a century and a half earlier – mace, cloves, saffron, currants, dates, ginger, cinnamon, pepper, caraway, almonds, enormous amounts of raisins and 3 pounds of rice – and for Lent there was still plenty of salt fish, cod, ling and herring. Petre valued his 40-shillings-a-year cook and gave elegant and expensive feasts, but his household was not unusual in continuing to rely on pigeons from the dovecote, carp from the fishpond, and roasts and raised pies, in its celebrations differing in degree rather than kind from his Plantagenet forebears.

Similarly, the culinary traditions of Christmas had not altered substantially from those of previous centuries. For most, it still meant brawn along with fresh beef, mutton, pork, goose, turkey, apples and cheese – and enormously hard work in the kitchen. Witty Nicholas Breton wrote that for the twelve-day festival

> capons and Hennes, beside Turkies, Geese and Duckes, besides Beefe and Mutton, must all die for the great feast, for in twelve days a multitude of people will not bee fed with a little. Now plumbs and spice, Sugar and Honey, square it among pies and broth . . . youth must dance and sing and the aged sit . . . and if the Cooke do not lacke wit, hee will sweetly licke his fingers.

Shred pies filled with meat, dried fruits, sugar and spices were still piled up beside good drink and a blazing fire. The Tudors welcomed the Lords of Misrule with open arms, revelling in magicians, fools and music and in a special new Twelfth Night cake, one of the earliest of all English spicy fruitcakes, into which a pea or bean was baked: whoever found it was crowned 'King or Queen of the Bean' for the evening, presiding over the fun and games.

What did conspicuously alter both in cities and in small country towns throughout the Tudor period were the amount and scale of inns and taverns, which swelled to meet the needs of burgeoning commercial activity. Some were so large that they could lodge and feed two or three hundred people as well as their horses; Fynes Moryson declared that 'the world affords not such Innes as England hath, either for good and cheape entertainment after the guests own pleasure, or for humble attendence on passengers.' Even in poor villages, he said, you could smell the variety of meats on offer at the tavern before you walked through the door, and you could choose between sharing a common table for 5 or 6p or dining in your own rented chamber on whatever you felt like ordering from the cook downstairs.

Inns also provided a really radical change of taste for the nation, as ale faced competition from the hops first imported from Flanders from 1525. Andrew Boorde was sceptical about adding hops to the mash to make beer, considering it an unnatural drink, but it caught on so fast that by the time Hentzner visited in 1598 beer had become 'the general drink . . . excellently well tasted, but strong and what soon fuddles'. The bitter antiseptic resins of the hops acted as preservatives so that now the brew could be kept for up to two years, strengthening as time passed. It could be made in commercial quantities and ordered by potency: March and October beer were the strongest, while weak 'small beer' was drunk for breakfast as well as by children. So pervasive was beer's influence that when hop crops failed, brewers resorted to broom or bay berries to achieve the same aromatic and bitter qualities.

Gentlemen and ladies generally preferred imported wines – around eighty different kinds according to Holinshed and often sweetened with sugar for the ladies. Like ale, though, beer was a vitally nutritious part of the ordinary diet, and it had a crucial advantage. Because the mash could be used more than once, it was often cheaper than ale and, as rampant inflation drove prices higher at the end of the century, that could mean the difference between survival and starvation.

Elizabeth's England with its population of more than four million was a country dotted with sheep-filled fields. It was a country of extremes –

of courtly intellect, artistry and lavish extravagance and of rising unemployment, inflation, poverty and homelessness. Yet outward show was the measure by which everything was judged: velvet skirts, fine *pantofles* and embroidered slippers were trailed through muddy streets, great ruffs of Holland or lawn were propped up with starch, and *supportasses* and bodies reeked of perfumes heavy with civet and musk – 'while at home perhaps they have not a piece of dried breads'. Visitors noted the fertile, fruitful ground, the temperate climate, crammed streets and poor roads; they wrote about bear-baiting, of the English love of hunting and of meat, of the occasional lack of sobriety and of affected manners, and, in the houses of the rich, they were struck by a particularly English foible – a growing veneration for sugar.

8

'Sugar Never Marred Sawce'

I will now proceed to the . . . setting forth of a banquet,
wherein you shall observe that March-panes have the first
place, the middle place and the last place, your preserved
fruits shall be dished up first, your pastes next, your wet
suckets after them, then your dried suckets, then yor
marmalades and godinakes then your comfets of all kinds

— GERVASE MARKHAM

Sugar's humoural qualities were unequivocal – perfectly balanced, dry and warm, it ran sparkling round the body, and it heated the stylish Tudor court; '. . . if sack and sugar be a fault,' wrote Shakespeare, 'God help the wicked.'

Once Spain began to cultivate sugar in the Canaries and Antilles in the mid-1400s, the quantity arriving in Britain surged. Shipped in cones weighing up to 30 pounds, it had to be broken into chunks with nippers and ground in a mortar before it could be used. It cost about a shilling a pound, or a labourer's daily wage – special enough to make an ideal present – but as merchant wealth grew, the taste for sugar inexorably trickled down to the gentry and yeomen farmers so that consumption expanded – the pound of sugar that lasted an entire year in Alice de Bryene's household in the early 1400s would hardly have been enough for one person in the sixteenth century.

Sugar's cachet came from its taste, conspicuous expense and lusty reputation, and it had one more crucial characteristic: like honey, it acted as a preservative. As pungent spices began to lose their allure and the Tudor palate woke up to the soft taste of butter, the tingle of citrus and a more pronounced use of nutmeg, the medieval voidée evolved into a final sweet course called, confusingly, the *banquet*: a profusion of sugary temptations that became one of the most characteristic markers of well-to-do Tudor England.

In the post-Armada world of 1602, Hugh Platt wrote that 'piercing bullets turn to sugar balls,' and with an entire course devoted to its pleasures, confectionery reached new heights of proficiency and artistry. Like gardening, it lent itself to symbolism, allusion and pattern, its knots and figures echoing the geometrical linen-fold panelling, brightly painted ceilings and slashed velvet sleeves of courtly house and dress. Henry VIII adored it, employing only one woman in the kitchen complex of his court – Mrs Cornwallis, who made the King's puddings – and under Elizabeth I tables glittered with sugar creations and courtiers outdid themselves to satiate their queen bee, whose teeth by her sixty-fifth year were black: 'a defect the English seem subject to, from their too great use of sugar', as Paul Hentzner recorded in 1598.

The production of 'sweetmeats' for the banquet course was not the preserve of the cook but the ladylike responsibility of the gentle-woman. Ladies of the middling and upper ranks transformed the produce of their kitchen gardens and fertile orchards into preserves, candies and 'banqueting stuffe', assisted by a swathe of confectionery books that showed them how. The first of these was translated from the Italian in the year Elizabeth came to the throne, but soon plenty of delightful English books were appearing, promising to unlock the secrets of sugarwork. Interest in the slim, pocketable guides was so intense that they were best-sellers – practical guides (Platt's even had an alphabetical index at the front) in a world where even the rich hoarded high-class preserves against crop failure and hunger but also selling a social fantasy. Their beguiling recipes released sugar from its medicinal stays, promising that culinary recreation might be as plea-surable as it was useful, enabling the housewife, partially at least, to emulate the strutting peacocks at court.

It may be that some of these books were only read for pleasure in the shade of a mulberry tree by ladies – and gentlemen – who had no intention of getting hot and sticky themselves, but there is no doubt that they were also actively used. Most were thumbed so repeatedly that their fine pages wilted and their spines eventually cracked, and the few that have survived are seldom pristine, often filled with recipes scrawled in Tudor hand inside the front covers or filled with ink-and-quill under-scorings and marginal pictures of hands with pointing fingers. The marks and frays are sixteenth-century reminders that, despite their lovely bindings, these volumes were pored over and interrogated by people who were eager to make Genoese pastes, musk sugars, liquorice paste, lemon marmalade, preserved roses, syrups, crystal jellies and candied fruits and flowers.

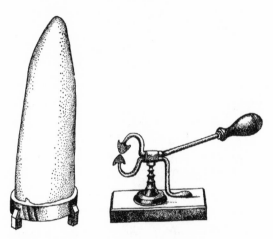

Sugar cones had to be snapped with sugar 'nippers' like these before being crushed and ground in a mortar.

The confectionery or stillroom was often situated in or near to the kitchen garden and orchard. William Lawson recognised that the two went hand in hand, placing the confectionery as an essential element in his plan for a perfect garden along with flower-beds, vegetable plots, beehives, an orchard and a mount. Tudor gardens were designed to thrill the senses, their gravel walks separating beds of roses, lavender, sage, chamomile and marigold that released their exhilarating perfumes as hands and skirts brushed against them. And the goodness of the garden – floral and vegetal – flowed into the confectionery with its charcoal stoves set at waist height, its small braziers and chafing dishes,* tin-lined shelves and cupboards for drying and storage.

---

* Chafing dishes had indentations in their lids into which embers could be piled to create gentle radiant heat from above as well as below. The earliest surviving confectionery in Britain, at Ham House in Richmond, dates from the last third of the seventeenth century.

The best sugar, wrote Platt, 'is hard, solid, light, exceeding white and sweet, glistering like snow' and might be scented with roses or violets or even with bruised musk* kept in a linen bag. In the mid-1500s there were only two sugar refineries in Britain, so it was more commonly cleaned and refined at home by breaking large lumps off the cone, grinding them roughly and boiling it up with bullock's blood, removing the scum that rose to the surface until the syrup was transparent, then straining it through a woollen cloth and leaving it to dry into crystals and liquid molasses.

Then the lady of the house might turn to the courtier John Partridge's recipe for her most important confection – a great disc of rich almond marchpane – grinding half a pound of blanched, skinned nuts in her pestle, using rosewater to stop them oiling, and adding a quarter of a pound of fine-grated white sugar over the gentle heat of a chafing dish or at the edge of a fire until the mixture thickened into a paste. Set on a piece of writing paper and banded by a hoop of rolled wafers, the paste was dried to a crisp and iced when cool with a solution of rosewater and sugar arduously rubbed through a gauze of lawn or silk. It might be scattered with upright coloured comfits or gilded, using coney tails to press fragile gold leaf through holes cut out of a paper pattern: when Elizabeth visited William Petre at Ingatestone in 1561, his hired confectioner demanded a quarter ounce of gold.

A similar paste was also used to make life-like painted fruits or figures, pressed into sugar-dusted moulds with the flat of the thumb and lifted out with the tip of a knife when dry. Fine moulding was encouraged by a new ingredient that arrived in the early 1500s: gum tragacanth – or *dragon* – derived from the sap of a Middle Eastern tree. A nugget about 'the bigness of a beane' was steeped in rosewater until it swelled and mellowed; then it was mixed with sugar, egg white and a drop of lemon juice to form a pliable paste that could be shaped, by hand or with pre-soaked wooden moulds, into the fanciest of shapes. Platt recommended tapping the moulds sharply on the edge of a table to release their contents. Sugar flowers were built up petal by petal,

---

* Musk, still used widely in modern perfumery, is the dried abdominal secretion of the Central Asian deer *Moschus moschiferus*. Confounding the nose as it hits the palate, it has a tinge of feral rankness about it, but its stridency is softened by sugar, rosewater and citrus peel in many of these late sixteenth-century recipes, where it replaced the most luxurious and exotic spices of the past.

drying as hard as translucent porcelain, coloured or painted according
to the confectioner's artistry.

Fruits were also preserved. In his *Paradisi in sole* (1629) John
Parkinson listed almost sixty varieties of apple, as many kinds of
cultivated pears, wardens (a hard variety of pear, ideal for cooking)
and plums, and thirty-five types of cherry, all waiting to be transformed by sugar. As exotic-fruit cultivation became the obsession of
men with deep pockets, delicate fruits like peaches and the apricot, or
apricock as it was known for generations – introduced in 1529 by one
of Henry VIII's gardeners – were grown on espaliers on south-facing
walls in gardens or in orangeries like those at Richmond and Nonsuch. Green melons were cultivated in pits heated with rotting
manure from the 1570s,* and figs, pomegranates and musk melons
were imported along with shiploads of oranges from Portugal –
sometimes known as *pottongayles* – whose bitter peel was repeatedly
soaked and boiled before being candied with a pound of sugar for
every four oranges.

With fruit increasingly revered and new varieties arriving regularly
from abroad, fruit-growing became popular, and Henry VIII's royal
gardener Richard Harris was among the first to establish a market
garden at Tenham Manor in Kent using grafts brought back from the
Low Countries and France to supply apples, pears, plums, damsons,
cherries and strawberries to the court. Some gardening handbooks
even suggested that a solution of water and honey poured into small
nicks in the bark of the trees would eventually find its way into the
fruit itself, and most of it was sliced and dried on pierced boards in a
warm oven to concentrate its natural sugars before being dusted with
grated sugar, or boiled in a sugar-and-water solution to make a wet
sucket or succade. Crystallised ginger was another Tudor favourite, as
racy as ever; Gerard judged it 'hot and moist in qualitie, prouoking
Venerie'.

Some people did begin to eat fresh, raw fruits at the ends of meals,
though Andrew Boorde was circumspect, writing in the 1540s that
peaches and medlars encouraged melancholy and that all raw fruit

---

* Melons were also baked with milk, butter and fennel seed or tempered with pepper or ginger
and wine, the forgotten origin of our own habit of serving raw melon with port and ginger.

provoked flatulence; he preferred the digestive comfort of sugar-baked apples with fennel, clove or aniseed comfits. Two generations later, even Gerard thought raw fruits prone to 'putrifie' in the stomach. But by 1599 Henry Buttes – also a believer in the benefits of tobacco – was suggesting that grapes, mulberries and cherries could all be eaten raw, recommending old cheese to balance the cold humours of melons and spiced wine with peaches. In the plague year of 1569, the sale of raw fruit in the street was banned – though Thomas Elyot's recommendation was probably still the safest: '. . . there is no better preservatyve,' he wrote, 'than to flee from the place corrupted.' Yet in the Cobham family portrait of the 1570s at Longleat, none of the children or adults anticipating a course of filiberts, hazelnuts and raw fruits looks in the slightest bit concerned at the prospect of polishing off the lot.

Nor did vegetables escape sugar's embrace: *eryngo* (sea holly), parsley and elecampane roots, green walnuts, lettuce or mallow stalks, borage, bugloss, alexanders, sweet potatoes and even carrot and parsnips were candied into soft, sticky-sweet suckets. The more you grew, the more you had to preserve, and it was hot work: Lady Gardiner's maid explained that her mistress had no energy left to write to Sir Ralph Verney, being 'almost melted with the double heat of the weather and . . . hotter employment because the fruit is suddenly ripe and she is so busy preserving'. Even flowers – especially cowslips, violets, primroses, borage and orange blossom – were candied, while the petals of gillyflowers and marigolds had to be pricked open one by one with a bone bodkin and laid out on papers in the sun or a warm room, a process that required infinite patience. Elinor Fettiplace, a cousin of Sir Walter Raleigh living in Oxfordshire, celebrated the start of summer on May Day by rolling sugar paste into twisted sticks coloured and scented with flowers, and she removed the bitter white cuticles of red rose petals, boiling them in water and using the juice to flavour and colour syrups.

Decorative comfits – or kissing comfits – required particular patience. The whitest, hardest sugar was beaten to a powder and dissolved until it streamed from the ladle like silky turpentine. Then fruit peels, fennel or caraway seeds, cinnamon sticks, ginger or cloves – all previously washed and dried – were rolled repeatedly into it and left to dry until they gleamed like tiny pearls. Without a thermometer, correctly judging the different 'degrees' of sugar boiling was a matter of experience. A few degrees or seconds too much and the solution coloured, caramelised or burned; too few and it would not set to the right consistency: 'see that you keep your sugar always in good temper in the basin, that it burne not into lumpes or gobbets . . . and let your fire always be without smoke or flame,' warned Platt. Even with such detailed instructions, the stillroom must have been a place not only of concentrated peace but of tempestuous frustration when things went wrong.

One more task remained to be achieved in these mini-laboratories of preservation. Since the Dissolution of the Monasteries, the distillation of 'wholesome and sweet waters' and herbal remedies had passed from the hands of monks to those of the Elizabethan housewife. With an alembic set over the coals, she became a scientist, extracting her own *vertues*, distilling damask rose-flower water for use in the kitchen, making spirits of wine, aquavit and alcoholic cordial waters as well as essences of spices, cosmetics, medicines and hand-waters for washing. Platt described a way to keep orange or lemon juice good for a year for use in sauces, distilling it until 'it is done boiling' and bottling the syrup with a barrier of salad oil at the top.

The balance to sugary preserves came from the dairy. Sage oil, cloves, mace and cinnamon were separately mashed into thick May butter; Andrew Boorde recommended mixing rosewater and violets into almond butter at Lent, when it 'rejoices the heart [and] comforts the brain'. As increased concentration on pasturing sheep for their profitable wool forced many smallholders to give up their grazing lands and their cows, milk and cream – for centuries a staple in the diet of the rural poor – rose in price. Holinshed observed that cream was 'never so dear as in my time,' and as it became exclusive it earned its place in the banquet, where its white purity and cool voluptuousness echoed the virginity of the bejewelled Queen. The poor paid their own particular price, for the more it became a luxury, the more their children's bones grew deformed with lack of calcium: rickets was known on the continent as the English Disease, not helped by the fact that humoural theory specifically prescribed that sufferers avoid milk.

But where expense was not an issue, 'white leach' was made by boiling new milk with Russian isinglass – an expensive, pure form of gelatin found in the swim bladders of sturgeon – sugar and sometimes rosewater, leaving it to cool and set firm until it could be cut into subtle, lubricious squares that might be gilded. Cream was thickened, or *clouted*, by heating it very gently and leaving it to stand and form a crust overnight, ready to be used in tarts and custards or kept safely for up to two weeks – clotted cream today is made in the same way. There were syllabubs, cream cheeses and cheesecakes, junkets set with rennet and moulded cream 'hedgehogs' stuck with slivered almonds. Bruised fruits and pulps were swirled into mounds of cool cream as fools, white pots of sweetened cream were sprinkled with comfits as our earliest form of trifle, and mildly titillating wobbly domes known as Spanish paps were made from cream, sugar and rosewater, warmed and left to set – rather like modern *panna cotta*. Blancmange shed its meat and was transformed into a milky rice dish, and for a centrepiece 'dish of snow' beaten cream, egg whites and sugar were mounded over a great sprig of rosemary stuck fast in an apple, the whole lot covered with a liberal dusting of more grated sugar.

Jellies were still made from bones but no longer contained shredded meats, being flavoured instead with fruit juices, claret or sack, rose-water, cinnamon, ginger and sugar, and isinglass now helped with the processes of stiffening and clarification. Published by an Italian master cook called Maestro Martino, a brand new refining technique was added to the cook's repertoire as lightly beaten egg white was added to the hot jelly mixture, trapping tiny impurities as it coagulated. Once Martino's secret was out, jellies began to gleam even brighter; some were gilded or 'made in the shape of castles and animals of various descriptions, as beautiful and admirable as can be imagined . . .', as after a royal joust at Greenwich Palace in 1517. Less royally, amber-coloured apple jellies were shaped in soaked wooden moulds or oiled bowls, the cooks holding their breath as they turned them out, praying that none would stick, focused on quivering success.

Wafers were puffed up with yeast in the Flemish fashion, and biscuits – from *bis cuit*, or 'twice cooked', because the dough was first boiled and then shaped and baked – appeared for the first time. French bisket was made from flour, egg white, ale barm, coriander and aniseed, baked in a roll for an hour and left for a day to cool before being thinly sliced and dusted with sugar – ideal for dipping into creams or compotes. Sarah Longe (*c.* 1610) made biscuits from pounded blanched almonds with rosewater, sugar, eggs and ambergris, baking them on papers in a cooling oven, and others beat their mixtures for two solid hours and used small tin moulds. Cinnamon-flavoured *jumballs* were made in the shapes of letters or knots, and rich batters were squirted into hot oil with a wooden syringe. There were fruit tarts and new spice cakes made with fine flour, a little damask water and sweet butter, three yolks, 'a good quantity of sugar and a few cloves and made as your cookes mouth shall serve him, and a little saffron and a little gods good [yeast] about a spoonful'. The dough was left to rise and then put on papers into a well-swept bread oven: 'do not burne them. If they be three or four days old they be the better.'

The allure of the banquet was often heightened by being served in the open air in summer, on a fashionable grassy mound planted with scented roses or in banqueting pavilions like the temporary structure designed in 1526 by Hans Holbein at Greenwich with silk carpets and a roof glittering with stars and zodiac signs. But throughout Elizabeth's reign, permanent banqueting houses developed as a particularly British architectural caprice. A two-storey domed structure was built at the Vyne in Hampshire; Longleat, Studley Royal and Theobalds each had one; at Lacock Abbey in Wiltshire in the 1550s you could climb across the roof leads to a small, octagonal tower designed by Robert Smythson that contained two intimate rooms, and at Cobham in Kent a tree house rose three storeys into the branches of a lime tree. Intimate and designed for flirtation – in *Measure for Measure* (1604) Angelo lustily attempts to trick Isabella into spending the night with him in a banqueting house – they enraged the puritanical and bad-tempered Phillip Stubbes, who believed that they were designed for women to 'plaie the filthie persons'.

Sweetmeats could be served on sets of *roundels* – wafer-thin syca-more or beech trenchers with entertaining verses, mottoes or songs painted on to their undersides for guests to recite or sing. Silver or gilt bowls were used, and English green glass and valuable imported Venetian glass were prized – vessels beautifully etched with mottoes and devices or rolled over water while being blown to produce a fine tissue of lines. Alternatively, Platt gave detailed instructions for making plates and glasses from sugar, pressing a paste on to saucers, letting them set and lifting them carefully. The edges could be brushed with egg white and gilded or delicately hand-painted. Such items were pretty and they were ephemeral: at the end of the banquet, according to Dawson, the guests broke 'the platters and dishes, glasses, cuppes and all other things, for this paste is very delicate'.

As she progressed about her lands, Elizabeth was offered the fantas-tically sweet foods she adored. In the summer of 1591 the Earl of Hertford constructed a temporary gallery on the hillside at Elvetham and organised more than a thousand sugar dishes to be served by the light of a hundred torches. With sugar models of castles, forts, lions, apes, eagles, unicorns, snakes, frogs, mermaids, whales and dolphins, fruits, preserves, suckets, jellies, pastes and comfits of all sorts, Hert-ford outdid the rest of Tudor England, delivering the apotheosis of all Elizabethan banquets.

9

The English Huswife

*She . . . must bee cleanly both in body and garments, she
must have a quick eye, a curious nose, a perfect taste and a
ready ear; she must not be butter fingered, sweet toothed
nor faint hearted*

— GERVASE MARKHAM

If the late Elizabethan court demanded lavish banquets, thrilling to the
luscious new music that swelled its halls, its Queen had not just the
heart and stomach of a King but, whether she liked it or not, the frail
body of a woman. Elizabeth was Gloriana, but she was also the mother
and mistress – the *huswife* – of her nation and, beyond the court, a new
focus on domesticity ruled.

As relative political stability bolstered the fortunes of prosperous
yeomen and gentlemen farmers in the counties, a multitude of chimneys transformed the roof-lines of villages and towns as each house
'made his fire against a reredos in the hall where he dined and dressed
his meat'. Furnishings and feather beds were making gentry homes
more comfortable than ever before; strewn rushes gave way to straw
matting and carpets; trestle tables became heavier, permanent and
embellished with carving, with stools or chairs lined up at their sides.
No longer was it unusual for a farmer to have 'a fair garnish of pewter
on his cupboard . . . a silver salt, a bowl for wine and a dozen of spoons
to furnish up the suit'; many homes owned full sets of knives and
pretty earthenware plates from Delft in Holland.

The old-fashioned ranks of stewards, marshals and expensive male
servants remained only in the most élite circles. Elsewhere, there was a
shift to cheaper female servants, and women found themselves managing the running of their households as never before. They were the

Merrie Wives of England, a growing band of literate women living in the shadow of the great Queen. Their houses had windows to the south and east, and larders filled with butter and milk, beer, wine and meat. They had spacious hen houses, corn lofts, apple closes, bakehouses, pantries and ovens for household bread, tarts and fine bakemeats.

The English huswife was ideally chaste, courageous, patient, diligent, witty and wise. Above all, she was tireless. Centuries before technology reduced the effort of making clothes, cleaning, laundering, fetching water, providing light and warmth as well as food, drink and home cures, the effort of providing for every eventuality was formidable. Young girls commonly learned the ropes from their grandmothers, mothers, aunts and sisters, but now they also looked to printed books. As society altered, many women had to learn the fundamental skill of making bread for themselves.

Gervase Markham's successful books on husbandry and huswifery were aimed foursquare at a growing slice of rural gentry and farmers, and, though they were published under Stuart rule in 1616, they conjure up a striking picture of the late Elizabethan housewife, illustrating the ancient and urgent need for her attentive and steady self-sufficiency, for abjuring 'the vanity of new and fantastick fashions' and for maintaining a wholesome, clean diet 'prepared at due hours and cookt with care and diligence'. In Markham's view, the housewife should provide for herself and her family without recourse to the market and without culinary pretension, serving good, plain English fare.

The foreign misconception of British gentlewomen was that they lived in a paradise of plenty doing very little. In fact, middle-class homes were veritable agricultural and domestic factories where relentless rounds of back-breaking brewing, baking, keeping back dough as sour leaven, distilling, butter-churning, cheese-pressing, sifting and scrubbing could not be forsaken. With her broad kitchen table, chopping boards, open fire with its range of pots and pans, hooks, spits and scummers, and small oven built into the chimney breast to one side, the huswife lived with an anxious eye on the next harvest. She stored up dried and salted meats, pickled artichokes, cucumbers and samphire for winter salads, and candied fruits, amassing her preserves for the freezing winters of the mini ice age that gripped Britain in the

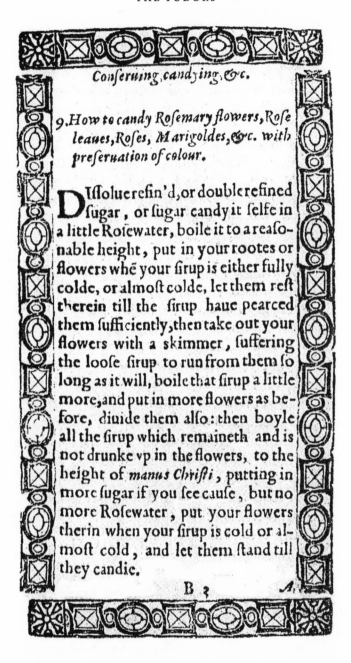

Conferuing, candying, &c.

9. *How to candy Rosemary flowers, Rose leaues, Roses, Marigoldes, &c. with preseruation of colour.*

Dissolue refin'd, or double refined sugar, or sugar candy it selfe in a little Rosewater, boile it to a reasonable height, put in your rootes or flowers whē your sirup is either fully colde, or almost colde, let them rest therein till the sirup haue pearced them sufficiently, then take out your flowers with a skimmer, suffering the loose sirup to run from them so long as it will, boile that sirup a little more, and put in more flowers as before, diuide them also: then boyle all the sirup which remaineth and is not drunke vp in the flowers, to the height of *manus Christi*, putting in more sugar if you see cause, but no more Rosewater, put your flowers therin when your sirup is cold or almost cold, and let them stand till they candie.

B 3

Gervase Markham's *English Huswife* of 1615 was something of a best-seller in a world waking up to the printed word and craving culinary instruction.

sixteenth and seventeenth centuries. She watched for beetles, rats and mice that nibbled at the paper or leather tops on her jars, encouraged her cats to hunt, and set falling-block traps or mounds of poison to keep vermin at bay. She made soap from ashes, lime and tallow, and candles from beeswax. There were the orchard, herb garden, kitchen garden and beehives to manage, the packing and carting of produce to the midweek or Saturday markets, as well as the ever-present pre-occupation with keeping food fresh.*

Markham believed that the huswife's principal skill was knowledge of the secrets of cookery, and the first step to this was to know her herbs and vegetables and to cultivate them successfully herself. As she tied on her bonnet, slipped her feet into her clogs and reached for her hoe, she might have turned to books by straightforward agricultural writers like Martin Tusser (1557) for advice on when and how to sow seeds, and when to prune and harvest. If she was lucky, she could pore over one of the exquisite, voluminous herbals like John Gerard's of 1597, filled with fine illustrations and compendious advice about every known plant. She could heed their advice to buy radish, turnip, cabbage, onion, parsnip and lettuce seeds in England and to send for the rest from abroad and might grow pompions (pumpkins), artichokes and melons as boundary plants to keep order in the kitchen plot. She collected herb seeds each year for sowing the next, and she might allow a handful of ducks on to the beds to pick off pests and slugs.

For those of us whose use of culinary herbs is restricted, say, to parsley, coriander, sage, thyme and basil, the cornucopia in use in the late sixteenth century is striking:

Thyme, Savourie, Hyssop, Pennyroyal . . . sage, Garden Clary, baulme, Mints, Costmary and Maudeline, tansie, Burnet, Monkes Rubarbe, Bloodwort, sorel (much used in sawses), langdebeef, arrach, blites, beetes, Alisanders, Smallage, Parsley, fennel, Dill, chervil, mallows,

---

* Hugh Platt worryingly recommended that tainted meat could be freshened up by cutting the flesh from the bone and burying it in the ground, wrapped in a coarse cloth, for twelve to twenty hours.

Succourie and Endive, spinach, lettice, purslane, tarragon, cresses, rocket, mustard, asparagus.*

Charmingly, Tusser urged his readers to gently stroke basil to bring out its flavour.

Some herbs were reserved for the pot and others kept for sauces, seasoning or decoration. Many found their way into the fashionable new *sallat*, no longer simply the preserve of courtiers, carefully composed for colour and shape. Primroses, violets, gillyflowers, bright blue borage, hyssop and bugloss, as well as the new nasturtium called 'Indian cress' all gave both taste and colour and were generally dressed with vinegar, olive oil, sugar and, sometimes, hard-boiled eggs. Pickled onions were bottled in sugar and vinegar, and roots like carrots were laboriously cut into fanciful shapes – knots, escutcheons, birds or beasts – to liven up these fresh summer dishes. Since it was the height of good middle-class taste to close a meal with lettuce or succulently salty samphire, Markham included pages of them – 'a world of sallats' – limited only by imagination. Some, like Robert Burton who remained convinced that 'all raw herbs and sallets breed melancholy blood,' but then Burton was so obsessed by melancholy that he wrote an entire book on it.

The combination of new horticultural skills and the opening up of the New World meant that the range of possibilities for the vegetable garden was ever-expanding. Cardoons stood sentinel in the beds beside cresses, colewort, summer savory, tansy, radishes, beets, *cowcumbers* and *skirrets*. William Harrison noted in his *Description of England* that even the poor were starting to grow melons, gourds, cucumbers, radishes, parsnips, carrots and turnips, yet these were also served as 'deintie dishes at the tables of delicate merchants, gentlemen and the nobilitie'. Roots and pulses were losing their social stigma, no longer considered food only for the very poorest and for animals, and were commonly boiled, buttered and eaten hot. In the 1590s Thomas Muffett favoured carrots above all other vegetables, boiling the tough roots for two to three hours and adding butter, prizing in particular

---

* Langdebeef was lamb's lettuce, bloodwort was dock, clary was a kind of sage, arrach was similar to spinach as a pot herb, and succourie was curly chicory.

their 'aromatical and spice like taste'.* Chopped spinach found its natural bedfellows in thick cream and eggs or was mixed with sugar and cinnamon as a filling for tarts.

When it came to meat, Markham's bible of domesticity also went into unprecedented detail on how to roast, advising the huswife to take her time over the chine of beef, to stir the fire to a quick sharpness for sucking pigs and small birds, to offset pink-fleshed meats with pale ones and never to keep her guests waiting. He explained how to fix the meat to its spit so that it neither shrank away from it nor slipped around it, and he described the different effects of basting with oil, butter, water or salt. Just as we do today, he advised his readers to poke birds between the wing and breast or to thrust a knife into the thickest part of the meat to see if the juices ran clear; then they were crisped with butter and breadcrumbs and sprinkled with salt. A good cook knew how to blister and skin a pig, to score its fat on the spit and to watch for the sign that it was ready – the moment when its eyes fell out and its body stopped whistling – then giving it a final but vital burst of heat to make its fat puff and crackle.

By the closing years of Elizabeth's reign, the fashionable 'made' dishes of the court had found their way down to the middling sort. 'Fricassees and quelquechoses,' Markham explained, 'are dishes of many compositions and ingredients, as flesh, fish, egges, hearbs and other thinges, all being prepared and made ready in a frying pan.' They could be simple combinations like eggs and collops – rashers of meat – fried together, but the point was that these dishes of mixed ingredients were considered 'things of great request and estimation in France, Spain and Italy and the most curious nations', and to be self-consciously Continental in your cooking had become quite the thing. *Quelquechoses*, for example, soon to be known as *kickshaws*, were fried dishes based on eggs and, usually, cream with the addition of almost anything that was to hand – boiled pigs' pettitoes (trotters), small birds, oysters, mussels, giblets, pigs' livers or blood puddings, lemons, oranges or other fruits, even pulses.

---

* Red, yellow and orange at that time, their pretty fronds were so pleasing to court ladies that, for a while, they wore them in their hair.

Another particularly exhausting new dish came from Spain, a casserole known as *olla podrida, olepotridge* or *hodge podge*, whose merit seemed to consist in throwing as many things as you could put your hands on into the largest pot available. Markham's recipe for hodge podge was one of the earliest, representing hours of patient culinary toil. A great pot was filled with water, bits of beef and roots were added, along with best mutton, pork, red venison and fallow dear, veal, goat, lamb, fat pig and pullet, and they were all brought to the boil and scummed continuously with a spoon or feather to keep the broth clear. Unchopped 'spinage, endive, succory, marigold leaves and flowers, lettuce, violet leaves, strawberry leaves, bugloss and scallions' went in, as well as a chopped chicken and partridge and 'quailes, railes, blackbirds and larks, sparrows and other small birds all being well and tenderly boiled'. It was all seasoned with sugar, cloves, mace and nutmeg, verjuice and salt, and then dished up 'on great chargers or long Spanish dishes made in the fashion of our English wooden trayes, with good store of sippets [small pieces of bread] in the bottome'. Still it was not over; Markham garnished the dish with 'prunes, raisins, currants and blanched almonds . . . with slices of oranges and lemons and . . . and [a] good store of sugar over all'.

It could clearly be a case of the whole feast in a single dish, and, though it sounds fairly nasty, hodge podge was rich, expensive, time-consuming and a fabulous way of showing off. In 1591, A W used fewer ingredients – a neck of mutton or a fat rump of beef, boiled and shredded into a broth thickened with onions, marigold flowers, parsley and breadcrumbs – but as far as Dr Thomas Tryon, a man wedded to plain gruels, was concerned, they were all a 'jumble' and he thought them unhealthy: 'what eye wouldn't loath, what stomach would not abhor such a gallimaufry? Yet this is done every day and counted gallent Entertainment.' Though its name came to mean something random and clumsy, the striking novelty of the hodge podge ensured its popularity, and it was exactly the kind of dish that paved the way for the table fork, another Continental habit poised to arrive in Britain.

For the huswife anxious to present her cooking in the latest style without the assistance of a phalanx of servants, Markham gave precise instructions on how she should serve a dinner for guests. She should

first marshal her sallets, delivering the grand sallet first . . . then greene
sallets then boyld sallets then some smaller compound sallets. Next . . .
all her fricassees, the simple first as collops, rashers and such like, then
compound fricassees . . . after them all her boyled meats in their degree,
as simple broths, stewd broth and the boylings of sundry fowls. Next
them all sorts of rost meates of which the greatest first, as chine of Beef
or surloine, the giget or legges of mutton, goose, swan, veale . . . then
baked meates, the hot first, as fallow deere in pasty, chicken or calves
foote pie and douset. Then cold bakd meates . . . then lastly the
carbonados both simple and compound.

Dishes were scattered about the table in broadly symmetrical patterns
and removed in even numbers to retain the artistry of the table.

And this was only the first course. Lighter meats came next, along
with quelquechoses 'thrust into everie place that is emptie and so
sprinkled over all the table'. Markham reminded the huswife not to
forget the fish (though it was hardly mentioned elsewhere) and not to
overreach herself with dishes beyond her status and budget, but to
limit profusion to her purse, taking particular note of seasonality and
erring on the side of sustenance rather than show. But when he was
into his stride, even reliable Markham found it hard to countenance a
plain feast of fewer than thirty-two dishes per course, becoming
unrealistically – if momentarily – carried away.

Clearly not all meals were filled with complex and rarefied dishes,
and, ordinarily, pigeon pies and sallets were more likely to appear
than fricassées. Harrison wrote that the middle class and yeomanry
usually lived on plain fare: stewed broth, boiled and stewed meats,
chickens and bacon, salted beef, pies, roasted lamb and capons,
conies, chickens and pigeons, baked venison and custard or apple
tarts, cooking three dishes when alone and six for company. A
typical dinner for a London bachelor in 1589 might have cost about
12d. Ben Jonson entertained a friend with a simple meal of chicken
with lemons and wine, a rabbit and a small game bird, with cheese
and fruit to finish.

Huswives made pies from sheep's or calves' intestines – known as mugget pies – for the workers to take to the fields, and large seed cakes to mark the end of the harvest. Cooking might have been the most important of their duties, but they still had to scour the dairy, bring in the laundry drying on the bushes in the yard, give the pigs their swill and prepare medicinal remedies like the mix of sugar, aquavit, betony and caraway for an old cough, or daisy root bruised with bay salt heated up in a cloth and applied to the cheek to dull the pain of toothache. Face creams were made of burned pigs' bones, broken, beaten, sieved and mixed with oil of white poppy; pimples were treated with salt and the juice of lemons; and for haemorrhoids 'a pint of ale and a good quantity of pepper and as much allome as a walnut' were boiled together with the juice of white violets and houseleek to make an embrocation 'as thicke as birdlime'. Ouch.

Prominent among the huswife's tasks were butter- and cheese-making, traditions that had changed little since Andrew Boorde's time, though most cheese was now made from cow's rather than sheep's milk: 'green' cheese was new and spongy, soft cheese was a little drier and more mature, while hard cheese like Cheddar was well pressed and left to age in great rounds. Fresh curds were still flavoured with any kind of green herb juices to produce *spermyse*. Cheese-making was another lesson in patience for, as Markham reminded his readers, they should be neither 'swete nor sowre, nor tarte nor salt, nor to fresshe . . . it must be of good savour . . . nor full of iyes, nor mytes, nor maggottes'. Cheeses were beginning their long journey up the social scale,* with Banbury, Stilton and Cheshire cheeses valued alongside those from Holland, Italy and France. The Scots valued theirs so highly that export was forbidden by law in 1573, and the English mocked the Welsh for their love of cheese, joking that when God wearied of the noise of the Welsh in heaven and asked St Peter to eject them, 'St Peter went outside of heven gayts and cryd . . . "Rosty'd

---

* Whopping amounts could be consumed. During 1552 the Petre household devoured the almost unbelievable quantity of 56 pounds of cheese a week. Sailors were also given rations of cheese, which kept better than butter on long sea journeys.

chese!", whych thynge the Welchmen erying ran out of heven a grete pace . . . And when St Peter sawe them all out he sodenly went into Heven and lokkyd the dore!'

Recipes for 'cookerye, physic and chirurgery' (or surgery) were collected side by side in the personal household books of educated British huswives. Begun with a view to setting up home upon marriage, surviving collections like those of the gentlewomen Elinor Fettiplace and Sarah Longe were cherished and passed down from one generation to the next, charting the growing experience of age, the advance of female literacy, and a confident, hands-on approach to cooking in which borrowed recipes were annotated with observations, additions and alterations – an extended cooking time here, a touch of lemon or wine there to pep up a sauce.

Huswives struggled to provide for all eventualities as competently as the Queen commanded her country, but by the end of Elizabeth's reign, seven successive wet winters and bad harvests had sent food prices rocketing; the cost of a chicken rose threefold during the century, and gnawing hunger had returned to the lives of the poor, leading to rioting and discontent. With no monasteries to act as safety nets for the truly distressed, homeless vagrants made the roads dangerous.

The Queen was ageing and heirless, and the country was concerned. In March 1603 she stopped eating. Perhaps because it charcterised the very breath of confident England, growing in the orchards of the nobility and the gardens of yeomen farmers alike, the apple was used by one witness as an image for the Queen's death; slender as her father had been corpulent, Elizabeth died 'easily, like a ripe apple from the tree'.

Blessed Puddings

Elizabeth probably did not live to see the greatest culinary discovery, first recorded in the early seventeenth century: the simple finding that a piece of sturdy cloth, dipped in water as hot as one's hands could bear, wrung out tightly and then well floured, could be tied up around a suety or batter mix – savoury or sweet – and boiled without the contents leaching out as they swelled.

The quintessentially British boiled pudding was born, spawning a repertoire of dishes that would lead the French visitor Henri Misson to exclaim in delight,

> . . . the pudding is a dish very difficult to be described, because of the several sorts there are of it: flour, milk, eggs, butter, sugar, suet, marrow, raisins etc are the most common ingredients . . . They make them fifty several ways: BLESSED BE HE THAT INVENTED PUDDING for it is a manna that hits the palates of all sorts of people . . . Ah what an excellent thing is an English pudding!

Finding English food broadly distasteful, Misson found in puddings a relief almost beyond words, and from the moment of its invention, it quickly became so much a part of British life that it would continue to develop over the next three hundred years.

Of course, mixtures of minced meats, blood, oats or other grains, fruits and spices had been stuffed through funnels into animal guts and boiled for generations. But the 'pudding cloth' revolutionised the process, leading to all kinds of new recipes for a multitude of savoury and sweet variations that could be made even when intestines were not easily to hand. Practical, quick and easy, the cloth produced a ripe cannonball of a pudding that threw off the aromas not only of its ingredients but of warm, wet cloth. In Scotland they were called 'bag puddings' or 'clootie dumplings', generally boiled as sausages had been for centuries, alongside the meat and vegetables in a large pot.

The earliest written record of a pudding boiled in a cloth comes from Cambridge in 1617 in a recipe for 'College Pudding' made of flour, breadcrumbs, suet, dried fruit, sugar and eggs – 'and throw your Pudding in, being tyed in a faire cloath'. Puddings might contain oats, barely or wheat flour, but what characterised them all was their solidity and their warming, nurturing qualities, rich in filling fats and starches. So effective were they in taking the edge off hunger that they were served in the first course, enormous round mounds of sustenance that arrived before the costlier meat was introduced. It was a practice that in Yorkshire led quickly to the expression 'them as has most pudding can have most meat' and that continued right into the nineteenth century: in Mrs Gaskell's novel *Cranford* (1853) Mr Holbrook served the 'pudding before meat' with no 'apology for his old-fashioned ways . . .'.

Like pies, puddings were often based on a rather old-fashioned medley of savoury and sweet ingredients, but unlike pies they were never spicy. In his 1617 collection, John Murrell gave a recipe for one made from meat with suet and breadcrumbs, dried fruit, sugar and eggs all boiled in a cloth. He, like most, continued to use guts, particularly for amber puddings* and for a sweet boiled-rice pudding, though

---

* Amber puddings, for example, were always made like sausages, from minced pork, almonds, breadcrumbs, ambergris, bruised musk and orange-flower water; they were a regular feature of traditional seventeenth-century dinners.

Gervase Markham conversely made his rice pudding in a bag from a rice mix of rice left to steep overnight in thick boiled cream, stirring in egg yolks, currants, dates, sugar, cloves, mace, salt and 'a great store' of shredded beef suet before tying the whole lot up to boil.

The fatty heart of most puddings came from cream, bone marrow and suet, which were often sweetened with dried fruits. Misson simply adored 'Christmas Pye', a pudding of neats' (ox) tongues, minced chicken, eggs, fruit and spices. By the end of the seventeenth century, this kind of pudding was firmly established as a classic, served with a syrupy liqueur sauce of sack, sugar and melted butter, a forerunner of modern brandy butter.

Filling, relatively simple to make, inexpensive and ideal country fare, puddings crossed the social divides. The eighteenth-century rural champion William Ellis wrote that they were perfect food for harvest workers – indeed, that 'Pudding is so natural to our Harvest men that without it they think they cannot make an agreeable Dinner.' Plum pudding, laden with fruits and meat, was prepared for the hardest-working periods of the farm year. At other times, farm workers would receive plain puddings made of flour, milk, eggs, raisins, chopped suet and salt, boiled in cloths for at least three hours to accompany good 'boiled beef . . . pork . . . bacon and roots and herbs' for their midday meal. The steak-and-kidney pudding as we know it – chopped meat in a thick gravy enveloped in a rich suet dough – was also on the point of evolution.

Quick puddings developed out of the old-fashioned flummery, a mixture of oatmeal with cream, a blade of mace, nutmeg, sugar, eggs, rosewater and cinnamon to make a sweeter, far more palatable dish than of old. In the Midlands, hasty pudding was made either from a crumbled penny loaf or from oatmeal steeped in milk or water, mixed with flour and boiled. Ellis suggested cooking such puddings in bacon water and serving them in slices with butter and a little sugar. In another recipe he transformed 'hasty pudding' from its humble origins into a richer confection of cream, rosewater, almonds, sugar, eggs, bone marrow and apples, acknowledging that you made your pudding to suit your purse.

Deliciously balanced between a custard and a boiled batter, 'shaking' or 'quaking pudding' was rich, sweet and wobbled like a jelly. In the

1670s, the cook Hannah Woolley served it with a sack sauce lifted with a little rosewater, orange, lemon or citron peel or sliced, blanched almonds – other cooks added white wine and candied or fresh lemon peel. No longer confined to fritters and pancakes, batter had found a new incarnation.

But as with all novelties, there were some who seemed unclear about the process of pudding-making, and their instructions were confounding. Take the Countess of Kent in 1653. Generally a stickler for detail, she suggested in her recipe for boiled pudding that the cook take 'a pint of cream of milk, boil it with a stick of cinnamon a little while, and take it off, and let it stand till it be cold, put in six Eggs, take out three whites, beat your Eggs a little before you put them into the milk'. On the other hand, Hannah Woolley's instructions were so comprehensive that she even advised her readers to find someone else to hold the four corners of the cloth while the mixture was being poured in; obvious, perhaps, but no other writer had taken the trouble to mention it. Others resorted to the use of a wooden bowl, wrapping the whole lot in a cloth for boiling.

Vegetables were perfect in puddings, infusing them with their scent and flavour as they dissolved to a mush. Pease pottage became pease pudding – the classic accompaniment to boiled pork. Bone marrow with a binding ballast of oatmeal and breadcrumbs was sweetened with grated carrots, or perfumed with ambergris, musk, rose- or orange-flower water, moistened with milk and boiled. Carrots were often mixed with sweet, sack-enriched custards and boiled, while potatoes were mashed into mixes of dried fruits, suet and flour. A Lancashire pudding using simply potato and butter was called potato pottage or *lobscouse*, marking the start of the potato's ascendancy in the diet of the poor.

In the early 1690s, Ann Blencowe, married to a Justice of the Peace in Brackley, Northamptonshire, filled her own household book with pages of handwritten recipes for puddings. As she scratched in the details of a recipe from Lady Clarke or Mrs Sydall with the cut end of a feather dipped in ink, cauliflower was beginning to be cultivated generally and gourds, pompions, cucumbers and French beans were also being tossed into puddings. Medieval tansies had metamorphosed from pancake to pudding, and within a generation that most British of all puddings, Yorkshire, would appear for the first time: a batter of milk, eggs, salt and flour poured into the hot fat of the dripping pan under roasting meat.

Wherever a recipe for a pudding existed, cooks emphasised the importance of using the most scrupulously clean cloth, paying particular attention to the removal of any soap with repeated rinses. They were advised to tie bread-based puddings loosely and batter-based ones tight, to ensure that the water was boiling before putting it to cook, and to move the pudding around in the pot to prevent it sticking to one side. No one described how to gingerly unpick the sodden knot as the pudding emerged from the boiler, however.

From the early decades of the seventeenth right through the eighteenth and nineteenth centuries, the British pudding bubbled away in its pot at the back of the fire or stove, swelling inside its floured muslin or baking to sultry glory in the oven. Once it had arrived, it was hard to think of a time when it had not existed. Along with the new tastes that swept in from France in the mid-1600s, it played its part in the final decline of pottages – took over from them, in fact, on tables long and short, fine and plain. Puddings were so very, very English that the most famous and influential French recipe book of the seventeenth century – La Varenne's *Cuisinier françois* (1653) – ignored them entirely. Yet, along with the roast, puddings seduced visitors from abroad – in the 1720s Caesar de Saussure agreed with Henri Misson, writing: '. . . this is a very good dish, and I have never yet met with a foreigner who did not appreciate it.'

THE STUARTS

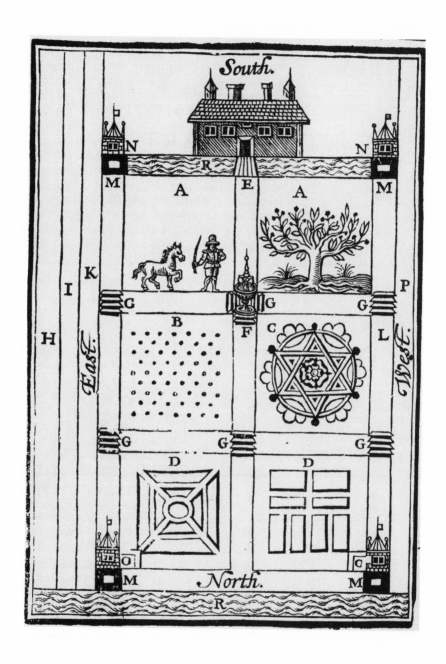

William Lawson's plan of the garden, 1618, showing the ideal situation of the orchard, patterned 'knots' of flowers, the kitchen garden (D), walks, a mount, beehives and south-facing still houses (N) close to the house and orchard.

10

Mad Master Cooks

A Master-Cook! Why he's the Man o'Men . . .
He is an Architect, an Ingineer
A Soldier, a Physician, a Philosopher
A general mathematician. Mad.

— BEN JONSON

Despite the enormous casualties of the bubonic plague in 1603 and 1604, the population of Britain continued to increase, stretching upwards to its mid-century peak of about six and a half million. The pressure on food, on land and on employment was intense, continuing to amplify the numbers of the poor for whom a monotonous diet and hunger remained facts of life.* Apparently insensible to all of this distress, in James I's palaces powerful and self-indulgent courtiers like George Villiers, 1st Duke of Buckingham flaunted their crimson stockings and high-heeled, beribboned shoes, exchanging the puffy Elizabethan ruffs for flatter, squarer lace neckware. The new King returned to the weekly ritual of eating in public and to excessive feasts involving literally thousands of dishes.

While extravagant, unbuttoned James, as the first King of both England and Scotland, was attempting to unify his island, the world continued to open itself up to unprecedented discovery and commerce. In honour of the new monarch, Shakespeare was working on his 'Scottish' play – *Macbeth* – the murderous spirit of which reflected the religious tensions that seethed under the surface of society. As James

---

* Despite this, by 1616 the Grocers' Company was reporting that 'the poor would not buy barley or rye, either alone or even if mixed with two thirds wheat', for they too wanted their bread to look as pale as possible.

made plans for an Authorised Bible, the Catholic Gunpowder Plotters were scheming to kill him and destroy Parliament.

But, unlike Elizabeth, James pursued a non-isolationist foreign policy; people were travelling again, and the East India Company raced to monopolise trade in the East. In the West, British colonies – Virginia from 1607 and the Bermudas from 1616 – began to lay the foundations of enormous fortunes. New sugar plantations in Barbados and the Leeward Islands flourished so rapidly that the quantity and quality of sugar reaching Britain surged: by 1640 John Parkinson would write that 'Sugar hath obtained . . . so continuall and daily use that it is not accountd Physicall'; there were now fifty sugar refineries in London alone, and during the seventeenth century consumption was set to quadruple.

Despite high prices, the diarist Fynes Moryson was entranced by Britain's domestic abundance, the famous mustard of Tewkesbury, Essex saffron, fat cattle and large cheeses in Suffolk, Worcestershire pears, Hull stockfish, the Isle of Wight's coneys, hares and pheasants, and the 'abricots, muske melons' and 'figges' of Jersey and Guernesy. He admired 'the great Oxen, the flesh whereof if so tender as no meate is more desired. The Cowes . . . with large udders yielding plenty of whitemeats'. The venison pasties, brawn – 'a proper meate to the Englishe, and not known to others' – and unmatched oysters; only the pigs of Westphalia trumped those of Britain by a fine margin. It was all superlative; 'no part of the world,' he wrote, yielded 'greater variety nor better of the kind', and much of it was flowing towards England's growing cities.

Live animals were driven to the cities in swelling numbers – cattle from Essex and Gloucestershire, sheep from Wales, even live poultry. By 1600, the network of about eight hundred regular markets across Britain was bulging with foods brought for the delectation of those who would pay the highest prices – and none more than the sixteen great markets of London. The city population had more than doubled in the eighty years to 1630, and 300,000 people crammed the streets. London was the 'Great Bee Hive of Christendome', full of playhouses, fencing and dancing schools, and fisherwomen crying out in the streets, so vast and overwhelming that the pamphleteer Donald Lupton was 'almost afraide to meddle with her'. Billingsgate sold grain from the Thames Valley and the Baltic, salt from France and some vegetables, but it began to specialise in fish, in stench and in foul language (giving rise to the expression 'to swear like a fishwife'). Leadenhall increasingly specialised in meat and live poultry, and in the 1620s the fruit market moved from St Paul's to a wide space laid out by Inigo Jones at Covent Garden on land owned by the Duke of Bedford – part of the newly fashionable West End.

Simultaneously, and as tulip mania raged in Holland, a home-grown passion for gardens flourished. Robert Cecil, the King's favourite courtier, set the standard for a kind of smart domestic gardening that matched the spectacle of court masques, building Hatfield on the top of a hill and surrounding it with seven ostentatious acres of gardens and madly extravagant waterworks. The Fruiterers' and the Gardeners' Companies were founded, and 'curious' gardeners like John Tradescant and the growing band of commercial seedsmen added fire to the gardening rage and grist to the mill of horticulture. Herbals and horticultural works like Parkinson's *Paradisi in sole* meanwhile proclaimed to the gentry that they too could anchor Eden in their very own gardens.

The frontispiece of Parkinson's great work put the exotic pineapple at the very centre of his paradise, a heaven-scented fruit whose time had still not quite arrived: with its crown of leaves, it would only begin to burst into the consciousness of the super-rich with the return of Charles II. In the meantime the Jerusalem artichoke – related not to the globe variety but to the sunflower – *girasole* in Italian – was discovered by a Frenchman in Cape Cod and by about 1615 had found its way via Holland to England, where it was washed and scraped, turning the cook's fingers brown, then boiled and buttered, mashed into tarts, thrown into simmering stews, pickled or preserved.

Mushrooms were cultivated and used in cooking in a manner almost unseen since the Romans. Truffles* too were being rediscovered. In 1620 John Tradescant the Elder introduced runner beans, native to high-altitude Central America and initially grown, like the tomato, as

---

* Visiting Lyon in 1644, John Evelyn tasted one for the first time, describing it as 'a certaine earth-nut, found out by an hogg, train'd up to it, and for which those Creatures are sold at a greate price: It is in truth an incomparable meate.'

an ornamental rather than a kitchen-garden variety. Tradescant also introduced a new species of apricot, while the East India Company brought the sweet China orange from the East to rival its bitter Spanish cousin. Walnut trees were planted for their wood, shape and nuts – which were pickled as an accompaniment to stewed meats, cold hams and salads – and rhubarb made the leap from the medicine shelf to the dinner table.

The scholar and purist John Evelyn translated Nicolas de Bonnefons' French treatise on gardening for gentlemen obsessed by their orchards, and practical gardening manuals gave advice for keeping toads out of the sage by planting it with rue and accelerating the growth of plants with heated beds. The British Library's copy of William Coles's *Art of Simpling* (1656) is among the most annotated of the Jacobean books in their collection, a horticultural bible for its original owner, studied hard for the secrets it revealed about his or her kitchen garden and its produce. Coles listed the range of edible plants available to 'Countrey people':

> the tops of Hops and turnips running up to seed, boyled and buttered, do eat like Asparagus: the buds of Broom being pickled are of an excellent relish: the roots of Tulip boyled and buttered make a rare dish. There be serverall wayes of dressing Mushromes to mak them edible: the leaves and stalkes of Alexanders being boyled, are eaten alone, or with fish to correct them . . . the root of Arum being raw, is exceeding biting . . . Ashweed, which some call Jump About boyled with Bacon when it is young, is a timely dish, and so is young Comfrey . . . With the buds of Elders, nettle tops, watercresses and Alexanders, good women use to make pottage, in the Spring time . . . And if you will have any more you must go to the Cooks, who can make many more dishes out of them. Yes, they can make good broath with the leg of a joyntstoole, if you allow them cost.

In 1617 Fynes Moryson recorded that the tables of the wealthy were so superabundant that there was no room for cups or glasses. Dinners were renowned for their length, and, he wrote, the 'Art of Cookery is much esteemed in England'. Caviar was introduced for the first time, almost certainly from Russia and still so suspiciously rare and odd that Nicholas Breton sent some as a gift only to have it returned with a note explaining that the servants already had enough black soap. In dark-timbered, tapestried houses still-life paintings glowed with citrons, lemons and oysters, with rimy grapes, bundled asparagus and lobsters propped against pewter tankards and rare glass which threw points of light black at the viewer.

The availability of all this fresh produce enlivened still further the fancy compound dishes, the carbonadoes, fricassées, *olios* (as the hodge podge was now more usually known) and *hashes* (from 'hacher', to slice) that aped the sophisticated fashions of Continental Europe. Turnspits had all but disappeared by the 1630s: jacks were becoming mechanised, propelled by gravity weights at the end of tightly wound springs, which unravelled over about half an hour. With cogs spinning, the Stuart roast was accompanied by a metronomical tick, but plain roasts, baked and boiled meats were being overtaken by time-con-suming compound dishes while highly paid professional cooks, often French or Italian, were sought by the nobility. In France, professional cooks had been raised to the rank of *chevalier* (for they were all men, still), and the finest of all wore the *cordon bleu*, a rosette of dark-blue ribbon.

Acutely aware of the drive to be modern and European in the kitchen, John Murrell included recipes from his travels in France, Italy and the Low Countries and promised to set out 'the newest fashion of cutting up any fowle' and to explore both 'exquisite English cookerie' and 'the new English and French fashion'. In fact, like most cooks his repertoire was a mix of the old – there is a recipe for a swan and for a bustard – and the very new – his 'Grand Sallat' and 'Potato Pye'. Murrell included no recipes for fricassées, but he stewed capon with oysters, pickled lemons and mint, and introduced his readers to veal olives – slices of veal rolled up around a forcemeat and simmered in gravy with eggs, developed from the roasted allowes of the medieval kitchen. Unlike his contemporary Gervase Markham, Murrell's kick-shaws were not stiff omelettes but pastes of finely minced veal or lamb's kidney mixed with mutton fat, sack and rosewater, pushed into moulded pastry cases and fried – or baked and iced with rosewater and sugar.

That very modern huswife Sarah Longe did make a fricassée (or 'ffrigasy', as she called it) from 'the flesh of six chickens cut to pieces, strong broth and swet herbs and mace . . . nine yolks and white wine and lemon', all bubbled together in a frying pan until the gutsy sauce thickened, serving the dish over toasted bread and garnishing it all with 'minced parsley'. This was the kind of food made for the table fork, small pieces of meat in a thick sauce where neither knife nor spoon were required. Each encouraged the adoption of the other in the self-conscious, urbanising south of England.

Apart from carving forks and tiny sucket forks, table forks had been so rare that Elizabeth owned only thirteen, made of silver; though the Italian merchant class had adopted them at table, in England they had been considered affected. Then, in 1611, Thomas Coryat returned from five months abroad to declare that he was the first Englishman to embrace the Italian habit, praising the politeness and cleanliness that came with proscribing the use of fingers at table. The acceptance of the fork appears to have been rapid, and by 1616 Ben Jonson was describing them in his new play *The Devil Is an Ass* as 'brought into custom here as they are in Italy, to the sparing of napkins'. Forks were soon being manufactured in Britain from iron, steel and silver, and John Manners, the 8th Earl of Rutland, was among the first to have a set made – squarish and with only two tines. Just one of them survived the rigours of the Civil War, the earliest known English silver fork, hallmarked 1632. It now sits humbly in a case in London's Victoria and Albert Museum.

Slowly but surely, eating with one's fingers went quite out of fashion, and as the country struggled towards a new identity, the kind of food cooked and eaten in well-off homes and at public dinners was more about taste and style than about the balance of the humours. Gone were the whales and porpoises of the medieval feast when the East India Company dined at their Merchant Taylors' Hall in January 1622. In their place were traditional dishes – boiled pheasants and partridges, whole roast kid, soused capon and eel, and a venison pasty – but there were also salads and roast mutton stuffed with oysters in the first course and oyster pie, *orringeadoe* pie, pickled oysters and *anchovees* in the second.

Those shallow pies show that new ingredients were invigorating the art of the tart. Often they retained just a whiff of the medieval in their sweet–savoury combinations: chopped spinach or carrots with dried fruits and rosewater; softened globe-artichoke bottoms layered with ginger, sugar, mace, bone marrow, dried fruits and 'a good store of butter', topped with pastry and served with a sack, orange-juice and sugar sauce; potatoes baked down to a desirable, sweet smoothness, oiled with bone marrow or butter (but rarely the heavy suet found in puddings). Potato pies were also made by layering them, peeled and chopped, with mace, cinnamon, sugar and a sweetly alcoholic sauce made thick with egg yolks and butter. Many had a separate, cut pastry lid whose gaps were filled with comfits or other sweetmeats.

It was also a time of flourishing domestic baking as the knot biscuits and jumballs of the Tudor banquet gradually developed into a whole repertoire of sweet sponge biscuits puffed up with egg whites rather than ale yeast: Naples biscuits like modern sponge fingers; Savoys, which resembled *langues de chat*; and macaroons, an almondy dough spooned into round drops and baked crisp on layers of paper to stop them browning. Almonds, hazelnuts and filberts were all widely used for biscuits, blanched and skinned before being pounded in a mortar with a little rosewater; apricot kernels were crushed into ratafia biscuits, whose closest modern equivalents are the Italian amaretti.

Great cakes, with their bucket-loads of ingredients averaging an alarming 20 pounds in weight, were beaten 'extreamely for an howre or more . . . for the longer you beat it the whiter it will be', according to Rebecca Price, brought up in London and married into the Hertford-shire squirarchy. Always on hand for guests, ideal for gifts and travelling, these leviathans generally included saffron, caraway seeds, orange- or rose-flower water, sack, earthy musk and quantities of dried fruits, and were glazed with a solution of grated sugar and rosewater spooned over the top a few minutes before they were ready to come out of the oven. There were tin, or sometimes wooden, cake hoops, and some were evidently made to expand and contract since Rebecca reminded herself to set hers 'at ye full bigness'. Such hoops ensured that, whatever the cakes tasted like, they at least held their shape – then, as now, looks were always half the battle.

These vast cakes were still raised with ale yeast.* Some called for scalded milk, others for thick cream and pound upon pound of butter – the Countess of Kent used 6 pounds in hers. Once the household bread was cooked and the oven was cooling, smaller cakes could be put in to bake, often flavoured with cinnamon and rosewater. Over the course of the seventeenth century, these small yeasted cakes began to develop specific regional variations – like the Shrewsbury cake, Eccles cake and Dewsbury or peppered fruitcakes from Westmorland; northern towns, above all, became renowned for their particular spicy or curranty breads, cakes and pastries.

In the year of his accession, as the plague raged yet again, the stuttering, obstinate new monarch Charles I, like his father before him, took a Catholic bride, Henrietta Maria, the sister of Louis XIII of France, ignoring the deepening religious fault-lines between Catholicism, Anglicanism and pious Puritanism. These were to be uneasy, unstable years during which few cookery books were printed as the country considered other issues. Only Lord Ruthven's recipe collection appeared, briefly, in 1639, with its mix of the old and new, its salad of lemons, its savoury *artichoak* pie and its shoulder of mutton with lemons.

Most people kept their heads down, perhaps dulling the sharp edge of their anxieties with a particularly seventeenth-century supper drink, the *posset*.† Growing out of the medieval practice of moistening pies with sweet egg gravies, or caudles, the posset was a spiced, sweet, warm confection made of ale, cider or wine – especially sack – thickened with eggs, cream or warmed milk which curdled as they were poured over the liquor. Rebecca Price wrote that it should be 'thine in the bottome, curd in ye middle and snow on ye top and if it be too cold before you eat it it will be tuff'. She poured hot cream and wine, sack or ale over

---

* The Elizabethan Martin Tusser was among the first to suggest in print that the whites of eggs be 'whipped to snow' to lighten the doughy mixture, though it would be generations before yeast was abandoned in favour of eggs as raising agents.
† In the United States, especially in the nineteenth century, the posset became known as eggnog.

whipped eggs from the greatest height possible to create both a curd and a whippy froth, letting it rest for a short while before the fire, sometimes grating Naples biscuits into it for body and flavour. Other cooks also added sugar, nutmeg and big sticks of cinnamon and ambergris or grains of musk for an even headier mixture.

Falling somewhere between a light meal and a drink, possets were served in special cups of earthenware, glazed Delft or even silver. The whey or warm alcoholic liquid could be sucked up through a spout that came from the base, leaving the custardy curds to be eaten with a spoon. Soon, it would be considered the height of elegance to carry a little silver nutmeg grater in your pocket – one quick rasp of the nut over your drink, your dish of cream or cup of chocolate transformed it into a rather addictive kind of aromatic heaven. But in the early 1640s, when the world was threatening to fall apart, when there was talk of war, revolution and regicide, silver was being packed away. Sack posset was one of very few comforts, bringing with it a somnolent, if temporary, respite.

THE COMMONWEALTH
AND PROTECTORATE

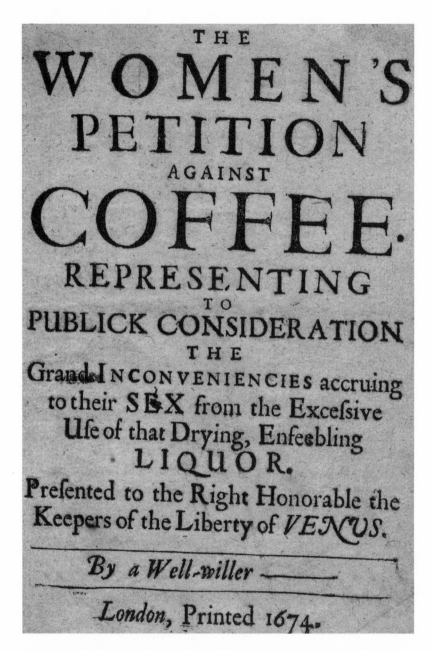

THE
WOMEN'S
PETITION
AGAINST
COFFEE.
REPRESENTING
TO
PUBLICK CONSIDERATION
THE
Grand INCONVENIENCIES accruing to their SEX from the Excelsive Ufe of that Drying, Enfeebling LIQUOR.

Prefented to the Right Honorable the Keepers of the Liberty of VENUS.

By a Well-willer ———

London, Printed 1674.

From the moment it arrived in London in the early 1650s, coffee was touted as a cure-all by coffee-house owners. A blizzard of tracts both for and against the Turkish brew only served to increase its popularity. This petition from 1674 is the earliest to have survived.

11

Unhappy Times

The unhappy and Cruel Disturbances of these Times
— ROBERT MAY

The 1640s must have felt like the longest decade in history to the people living through them, years of disruption, convulsing wars, the fracturing of communities and the final, violent reality of Charles I's execution. In the first months of the Civil War alone it is thought that more than 60,000 people were killed, a greater proportion of the population than in any other British war. Family members and villagers found themselves fighting on opposing sides, lands were forfeit, fields were burned, livestock was appropriated and slaughtered for marching armies, and silver and plate were hijacked for war chests. Harvests suffered; food was a trophy to be plundered or to be exhaustively foraged, and many – most – went hungry. It was a time for living by your wits, a time when wives and daughters across the country were left to fend for themselves and their families, trying to maintain their homes and their lands.

During the Commonwealth that followed, the colour was leached out of life. Puritans wore stark black with square white collars and linen caps or tall hats, Christmas and celebrations were banned, pleasure was repressed, and fish days and fasting were proscribed as Popish. Everything was pared down, economical, simpler. The world was altered; even the spoon underwent its first major design change for half a millennium: the Puritan spoon, as it was known, had a square end without any religious device and a flattened handle much as we know it today.

Noble robes were stored, and the surviving members of the upper classes retired to the country. William Russell, the 5th Earl and 1st

Duke of Bedford, went to Woburn, living on the provision of the estate and the produce of local markets. In fact, his household was remarkably unable to support itself: the estates provided venison, rabbits, pig and fish, but all other meat was purchased, along with artichokes (thruppence each in 1653), spinach, turnips, beans and peas, salads, herbs and summer fruits. Even so, bills were kept in check. In 1655, along with yards of cloth for cooking and cleaning, asparagus was bought only once (200 heads for 4s). After the Restoration the bills would more than double.

In the early 1630s, Donald Lupton had written about the departure of traditional hospitality, believing that 'pride, puritans, coaches and couetousnesse hath causd him to leaue our Land.' But if the growth of the towns, love of fashion and Puritanism had begun the process, the Civil War had sounded hospitality's death knell. Now the porter locked the gates at dinner time; high unemployment and rising prices continued to make the lot of the rural poor harsh, and in the towns the impoverished survived largely on bread, pickled fish and the very rare treat of a sheep's head or pig's trotter.

No one was really thinking about cooking, but only when Cromwell was dead, his son swept aside and the King safely returned to the throne was it was safe to mock the parsimony of the Puritans. Then, a satirical pamphlet, *The Court and Kitchen of Elizabeth Cromwell*, was published, accusing both her and her husband of unsurpassed meanness and of both absurd simplicity and arrogant extravagance. The anonymous author was perhaps Jos Cooper, chief cook to Charles I, and his attack was vicious, accusing 'Joan' (as Elizabeth was dubbed) of a niggardly refusal to make orange sauce for veal because the fruits cost a tiny groat apiece 'and for her part she never intended to give it'. In fact, the war with Spain had caused oranges and lemons again to become scarce and expensive, but to this writer Elizabeth was nothing but a 'baggage lady', lacking in both judgement and taste, frugal to the point of absurdity. He wrote that at Cromwell's 'private table very rarely or never were our French quelque-choses suffered' and suppers consisted only of the meanest slops.

The irony is of course that this slight book is today consulted less as an insight into the meanness of the Cromwells than as a rare reflection of the kinds of foods being cooked in homes during the Interregnum. It includes everyday meat dishes without a hint of sugar; plain sausages, gammons and legs of stewed mutton; a whole new emphasis on herbs like sage, thyme and savoury; a heavy-handed use of nutmeg and its earthy partner mace, and the inkling of a new preference for the assertive tastes of capers, anchovies and wine. Scotch collops (we are told that 'this was almost her constant dish') appear – slices of veal fried with oysters, capers, wine and eggs and served with sippets of bread, lemons and barberries – and there are beef olives, those thin slices of meat slashed, seasoned and stuffed with a mixture of sweet herbs, egg yolks, grapes or gooseberries.

Roast shoulder of mutton with oysters was becoming quite a time-consuming classic, now described in great detail by 'Joan', who parboiled the oysters before mixing them into a farce with minced herbs and hard-boiled eggs, grated bread and egg yolks: 'Your shoulder of mutton being spitted, lay it on the dresser and make holes with a sticking knife . . . put in your oysters with the herbs and ingredients after them – about 30 oysters will be enough – let it roast indifferent long.' She served the roast with a sauce of claret, onions, anchovies, nutmeg and sweet butter and garnished it with barberries and lemons. The relatively straightforward late Tudor fricassée was developing into an excessive and courtly preparation, utterly char-acteristic of the changing taste of the times with its multitude of ingredients and cloyingly rich gravy. 'Joan's' was far from frugal, a fried blend of six pigeons, six chicken *peepers* with their heads on, lamb stones (testicles) and sweetbreads, asparagus, boiled egg yolks, pista-chios, fried bone marrow, roast-mutton gravy, large fried oysters stewed in nutmeg, white wine and the yolks of ten eggs beaten with mace. As was becoming the vogue, the dish was garnished with a wild medley of fried sweetbreads, oysters and bone marrow, with pista-chios, sliced almonds and the juice of two or three oranges. The same oranges that Cromwell's wife was apparently too mean to buy.

When Cromwell was declared Lord Protector in 1653 and imposed military rule, relative stability began to return, hastening with it a flurry of very un-Puritan publications. The most important came two years after its first appearance in France: a translation of La Varenne's ground-breaking cookbook *Le Cuisinier françois*, a volume that caught up all that was newest in cooking, breathing a mantra of system, of stocks and sauce bases, of vegetables and of buttery, creamy textures. Britain was gasping for change: La Varenne's à-la-mode style delivered the strong flavours (or *haut goût*) of ragouts with cockscombs and sweetbreads alongside the cleaner flavours of broths with bundles of herbs and the gentle cooking of the *daube*. It was such a refined style that it would fall to aristocratic budgets and professional chefs to take up his clarion call only once the King was restored to his throne.

Other odd little English recipe books appeared, all rather old-fashioned, all overtly yearning for the return of the exiled court in France and nostalgic for a lost golden age, with few sparks of the new taste propounded by La Varenne. In fact, while proclaiming their royalist allegiances, their intent was to profit from those who had done well out of the war, a rising middle class who needed help to smooth over their rough edges with newly acquired recherché skills.

Attributed to the pen of the Countess of Kent, *A True Gentlewoman's Delight* (1653) was packed with mouth-watering recipes such as a rich loaf made of fresh curds and eggs, spiced with sugar and nutmeg. Hers was a new kind of painstaking instruction that had rarely been seen before; she suggested, for example, that to avoid turning her favourite custards into scrambled eggs, the whipped eggs should be warmed first with a little of the hot cream before they were added to the pan. Her recipe for mutton with oysters involved pulping the shellfish into a paste with butter, mace, cloves and egg yolk and using it as a stuffing, far more practical than trying to keep them intact while squeezing them into slits in the flesh. She boiled gammon with bay leaves and roasted a *giggit* of mutton with thyme and claret, garnishing it with sliced lemon and capers.

In 1654 Lord Ruthven issued a revised edition of his 1639 *Ladies' Cabinet Opened*, with a whole new section on cakes and baking, and with instructions for pickling oysters and vegetables. That same year, Jos Cooper, venturing less anonymously into print, filled his pages with recipes for mutton hashes, stewed oysters, artichokes and veal olives, as well as a terribly up-to-date recipe for roasted capon with white wine, bacon and pistachios. Then came a peculiarly pretentious collection purporting to be from the very mouth of the exiled Queen Henrietta

Maria, separated into medicinal, confectionery and general recipes, promising to divulge all the culinary secrets of a wealthy, bygone age; *The Queen's Closet Opened* was one of the most popular books of the period, recreating the savour of life under the late King. But neither the King nor his son – the future Charles II – were anywhere to be seen.

If people were talking about the return of the monarchy, they were doing it in discreet whispers, though now, in the heart of revolutionary Britain, political and intellectual conversation was about to be given its very own new theatre. The first coffee stall in Europe opened in London, quickly imitated in Oxford, Cambridge, Edinburgh and Glasgow – democratic establishments where anyone with a penny could purchase a tin or copper dish of the dark, bitter drink, peruse the parliamentary reports and take part in the debate of the day. In coffee houses across Britain an obsession with news and a new phenomenon – public opinion – were developing.

In 1627 Francis Bacon had noted that

> they have in Turkey a Drinke called Coffa, made of a Berry of the same Name, as Blacke as Soot, and of a Strong Sent, but not Aromaticall; Which they take, beaten into Powder, in water, as Hot as they can Drinke it. And they take it and sit in their Coffa-Houses which are like our taverns. The Drinke comfortheth the Braine and Heart and helpeth Digestion.

But it was not until the 1650s that the coffee bean began to be imported from Ethiopia via Constantinople along with that city's thriving coffee-house culture. The servant of a Turkish merchant, Pasqua Rosee's first British coffee stall in the vicinity of the bustling business of the Royal Exchange was so successful that within two years he had moved into a house across the rickety alley; his enterprise was swiftly copied.

Coffee houses appealed to a society in which ale houses and taverns were frowned on. They were social levellers, crucibles for the ideas of artists, scientists and writers, and convivial places for doing business. One would grow into Lloyds Underwriters and another into the Stock Exchange while others fostered seditious murmurings, so that by the late 1670s Charles II would try, and fail, to suppress them, fearing the dissent that brewed along with the strong coffee. They were masculine symbols of London's unique modernity, filled with babbling conversation, the smell of the roasting coffee bean, lawyers, rakes and, not uncommonly, prostitutes.

Hot drinks, apart from possets, were a whole new experience, and coffee's strong taste took some getting used to, described variously as a foreign fart, boiled soot, 'the Abominable, heathenish Liquor . . . base, black, thick, nasty, bitter, stinking, nauseous Puddle-water'. Samuel Pepys was not alone in finding it powerfully unpleasant. From the start, extravagant claims were made for its medicinal virtues: it was touted as the cure for gout, spleen, dropsy and sore eyes, for miscarriages and drowsiness, and as an ideal digestive. A blizzard of petitions and tracts both for and against coffee's various qualities flew through the cities – women said it made their men impotent and prone to gossip, men that it kept them awake and alert – all encouraged no doubt by coffee-house owners with a vested interest in maintaining the vibrant currency of their establishments.

Once the coffee-drinking habit had been formed, beans were bought privately and detailed instructions were circulated, describing how to roast them (too little and you risked missing the volatile oils, too much and they burned) and how to grind them, sieve the grounds and boil them in freshly boiled water. No one added milk or sugar, and no one bought very much at first: William Russell had been drinking coffee for some fifteen years by the time the beans started to appear in his household accounts. He began with small shilling's-worth packets, but by the mid-1680s his household was consuming around 3 pounds a year, at 3s a pound. The very earliest surviving English silver coffee pot, in the Victoria and Albert Museum, was made in London during the same decade.

Coffee was only one of a triumvirate of new hot drinks to find its way to Britain during Cromwell's rule. If it was the 'Egypte drinke' then chocolate or cacao was 'the Indian Drinke', with its own extravagant claims: 'it cleaneth the teeth, swetneth the Breath, provoketh Urine, Cures the Stone, Expells Poison', as one advocate wrote. But chocolate was far more complicated to make than coffee. In South America, the beans were roasted, crushed, mixed into a paste with water and dried into 'nibs' for export. Once in England, the nibs were scraped into sweetened milk and boiled rapidly, frothed with a 'Spanish instrument' called a *molenillo* or *molinet* – usually about a foot long, wooden and horizontally ridged, something like a modern honey spoon – and rolled vigorously between the hands until the cocoa particles, cocoa oil and milk had emulsified.

Chocolate was more expensive than the penny dish of coffee and quickly found its niche at the breakfast tables of the rich. Chocolate pots were made with removable finials in the lids and holes through which the Molinet could be inserted. With the addition of egg yolks or grated bread, it could become a breakfast in itself, or it could be fortified with Madeira wine, sack or (in the following century) brandy as an evening drink. More innocently, it was flavoured with its ideal partners, cinnamon, nutmeg, orange-flower water, hazelnuts or almonds, and by a new ingredient with a haunting scent: vanilla, an introduction that would be used only cautiously for several decades. Soft spices like these had now entirely replaced the smarting galingale, cubebs and zedoary of the Middle Ages, but a penchant for the fiery had not entirely disappeared: several of the earliest recipes for making chocolate to drink, many of them translated from the Spanish in pamphlets that circulated in the cities, included aniseed and crushed long red pepper or chilli. Another recipe was designed for that growing band of businessmen with little time on their hands. It suggested scraping the chocolate into warm water with a little sugar, pouring hot water over it, whisking peremptorily with the molinet and drinking the whole lot, fast, before a scum could form.

Given the amount we know about how we have lived, fought, invented and dreamed in Britain, it is striking to be reminded that, until the mid-seventeenth century, this sweet-toothed, confectionery-loving nation existed without even the knowledge of chocolate. Perhaps it is not surprising that, within a generation of its introduction, Georgian housewives were waking up to the delights of the cocoa bean, swooping down on this richly delicious new ingredient and including it in cakes, biscuits, creams and ices.

Tea, though, was the most rarefied of the new hot drinks to arrive in Cromwell's Britain. Made from the dried leaves of the Chinese

Camellia sinensis, it was first sold in England in 1658 at the Sultaness Head in the Royal Exchange to ladies who kept it locked in small decorative tea chests, the keys to which never left their persons.

Touted as a plague preventative, tea was a useless medical prophylactic and ruinously expensive at between 16 and 50s a pound. The first fragile teapots were correspondingly small, holding enough to fill just two tiny, Chinese, handle-less porcelain bowls set on saucers that curved high around them: there is a tiny beauty, a scant few inches high, at Ham House in Richmond and another luminous, almost transparent set at Penshurst Place. Choice was limited to just two varieties of leaf: the cheaper – Bohea – had small, dark leaves that could be topped up with water several times, while the delicate aroma of the finest Green leaves was lost if it was used more than once. All tea was so valuable that it was immediately taxed by Cromwell, a target for smugglers and profiteers who adulterated good leaves with sloe, liquorice, or re-dried spent leaves, repackaging them to sell as pristine.

The first English recipe for tea came from Sir Kenelm Digby, an oddball, charming mountebank cavalier, friend of Descartes and Thomas Hobbes, collector of books and aristocratic recipes. Digby criticised the English for letting 'the hot water remain too long soaking upon the Tea which makes it extract into itself the earthy parts of the herb. The water is to remain upon it no longer than whiles you can say the Miserere psalm very leisurely.' He also famously repeated a Chinese recipe – apparently recounted by

> a Jesuite that came from China, ann 1664: to Near a pint of the infusion take two yolks of new laid eggs and beat them very well with as much fine Sugar as is sufficient . . . Pour your Tea upon the Eggs and Sugar and stir them well together. So drink it hot. This is when you come home from attending business abroad and are very hungry . . . [it] strengtheneth exceedingly and preserves one a good while from necessity of eating.

The simple, restrained Doctor Thomas Tryon believed that tea was a triumph of style over substance, that it was esteemed not for its intrinsic benefits but 'Chiefly for novelty Sake and because 'tis Outlandish and dear and far-fetcht, and therefore admired by the multitude of ignorant People who always have the greatest esteem for those things they know not'. He preferred dandelion tea but, as he might have predicted, Charles II's wife, Catherine of Braganza, would take to tea with something like a passion, and silversmiths would soon begin to make not only kettles but curious little spoons for the after-dinner ritual of one-upmanship. After the Restoration, hostesses would begin to retire from the dinner table with their female guests, presiding over a spirit stove set up in the drawing room, measuring out small spoons of the expensive leaf and flaunting valuable tea wares that trumpeted their wealth and taste. These were the props for gossip and scandal or – as William Congreve would put it – 'genuine and authorised tea-table talk, such as mending of fashions, spoiling reputations, railing at absent friends, and so forth'.

The introduction of tea to Britain in 1658 ironically coincided with a failed harvest, a brutal winter and the death of Oliver Cromwell. As his inept son Richard, known as Tumbledown Dick, assumed the reins of power, grain prices spiralled and epidemics of fever swept through the land. The Republic began to unravel even faster than it had been established. Over breakfast chocolate, in coffee houses and over tiny cups of tea, whispers about the return of the exiled son of Charles I began to grow more urgent.

THE RESTORATION

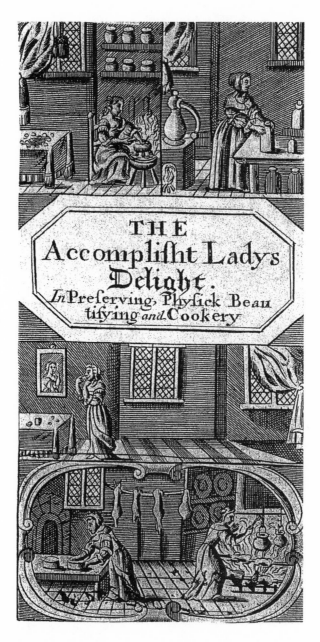

Title page from Hannah Woolley's *Accomplisht Ladys Delight*, 1686, showing (*clockwise from top left*) sugar work, distilling, fanning the embers for a roast and pie-making. Woolley was Britain's first professional female cookery writer in a society turned upside down by the Civil War.

12

A La Mode

Gluttons at Noon and abstinent at Night
— HENRI MISSON

Seven months after his father's death, Richard abdicated, the Protectorate was abolished, and the Commonwealth was re-established. Within another year General Monck marched his Scottish army down Whitehall, Members returned to Parliament, and celebration bonfires burned on street corners. On 3 February 1660, Samuel Pepys, then a young clerk to the Navy Board and still only twenty-seven, wrote in his diary that Monck's soldiers had entered the city. Everyone anticipated an official declaration of the restoration of the monarchy. On 23 May, Charles II landed in England from France, and on his thirtieth birthday at the end of the month, he entered London. Pepys's friend John Evelyn watched the 20,000 horse and foot soldiers brandishing their swords, the streets filled with 'many thousands of rumps, roasted publiquely . . . at the Bonfires . . . with ringing bells & universal jubilee'. For many, it was the signal for a return to the old order.

The royal chef Robert May was part of that world. In 1660, already seventy-two, he published his own significant and compendious cookbook, but as far as he was concerned, the old way of life was gone. Looking back to a time before the Civil War, he wrote of 'those Golden Days wherein were practised the Triumphs and Tragedies of Cookery; then was hospitality esteemed, neighbourhood preserved, the poor cherished and God honoured, then religion less talked on and more practised . . . then did men strive to be good rather than to seem so'. To May, the new order was one of 'seeming so', of outward observance and display rather than natural generosity. Yearning for the kitchen drama of old, he gave lengthy instructions for making 'a show piece for festival time', a subtlety more appropriate to the open, hospitable (if ostentatious) courts of Henry or Elizabeth, the last gasp of an old order:

> . . . make the likeness of a ship in paste board and cover it with paste, flags and streamers . . . guns . . . egg shells filed with rose water . . . In another charger have . . . a stag . . . with a broad arrow in the side of him and his body filled with claret wine . . . in another . . . a castle with battlements . . . gates and drawbridges . . . place it at a distance from the Ship to fire at each other, the stag being placed between them . . . at each end of the charger wherein is the stag place a pie made of course paste in one of which let there be live frogs and in the other live birds . . .

But if the magnanimity of the welcoming hall had disappeared, the return of the King meant for nobles at least that the years of belt-tightening and of physical, mental and cultural hunger were waning and purses were opening. Despite Britain's war debt, Charles's profligate court embraced all things Continental and gorgeous: loose coats slit at the sides with floating cuffs for the men; high, curling wigs for everyone; and exposed bosoms and face patches for women; Puritanism was exiled. At Woburn the Duke of Bedford's cook bought a greater variety of fruit and vegetables, fine Westphalia hams and confectionery from Monsieur de Villair in France. The cellars were restocked with sack and Malaga wines, Bordeaux, Rhenish and malmsey, and, in 1665, Bedford's first bottle of 'shampaigne'* – a delightful new wine that confirmed that life's sparkle had returned.

While noble families that had managed to survive with their wealth intact reminded themselves what it was like to live in comfort, new wealth flowed into the pockets of plantation owners, professional businessmen and commercial traders, creating an increasingly flashy bourgeoisie. No one wanted to think about the recent past. Being up to date, fashionable and à la mode were the pressing social priorities. Beside Henry Purcell's music and a newly thriving theatre, invention was sweeping through the cities and carrying its influence out into the

---

* Glass bottles were generally beginning to replace stone ones, and the invention of the cork was imminent.

counties, science and reason appealing to intelligent men (and sometimes, rarely, women) to unwrap the secrets of the physical world by
means of logical investigation, observation and analysis. In the country
too, innovation was transforming the quality and yields of crops, and
experiments with feeding herds on turnips and roots throughout the
winter meant more fresh butcher's meat was available during the
coldest months than ever before.

People began to let go of the tension and dudgeon of the previous
two decades and embraced the general feeling of renewal and
rebirth. The great inferno of 1666 that devoured 436 acres of
London's medieval heart, including Pudding Lane and Pie Corner
– watched by Pepys, who rushed to bury his papers, money, wine
and Parmesan cheese in the garden – swept away yet more of the
old. Soon a new, spacious city would rise from its ashes, with wide,
straight streets and terraced buildings with large sash windows and
wainscoted rooms. Above it all would rise St Paul's, dazzling in
white Portland stone.

At court and among the increasingly wealthy city merchant classes
and the rural gentry, food swung again into sharp focus. Pepys knew
how to dress his own fowl and revelled in the London markets, in the
prodigality of new, fresh goods, the cooked lobsters, a fine piece of
beef and his first taste of orange juice – though the risk of it left him
terribly anxious: 'I was doubtful whether it might not do me hurt'. The
wealthy were building south-facing brick-and-glass orangeries like the
one at Woburn where apricots and violet musk peaches were grown
alongside Roman nectarines and cherries, and melons were nurtured in
frames.

Pepys could not afford a hothouse, but he could pinch a small green
orange from Lord Brookes's garden and listen as Evelyn described his
first taste of pineapple at the King's table in 1668: '. . . in my opinion it
falls short of those ravishing varieties of deliciousnesse . . . it has yet a
gratefull acidity, but tasts more of the Quince and Melon.' Charles II's
gardener, John Rose, had presented his monarch with the first home-
grown pineapple seven years earlier, but it remained so rare that it
caught the public imagination with a force that made it the decorative
device of choice of a whole generation, appearing on pottery, garden
urns, gatepost finials and furniture; even new St Paul's was originally to

have sported a pineapple spire. Yet Henri Misson would write that, in general 'fruit is brought only to the Tables of the Great and of a small number even among them.' The banana had arrived in Britain for the first time from Bermuda – a great bunch hung up in a London shop window for crowds to gawk at – but would not be commonly eaten for a century and a half – even Victorian horticulturists were not entirely sure how it should be served.* Grapefruits – initially called *shaddocks* – and limes were also imported from the West Indies, but neither initially found favour. In 1665, the year of the plague, the public sale of fruit had again been banned as fear made even the most scientific minds revert to humoural doctrines: 7,000 Londoners died in the first week, and a sixth of the city were to perish before it had run its course.

Exotic fruits lent such extraordinary cachet to the lives of the rich, however, that in portraits ladies were painted holding not only tropical birds and flowers but plump grapes and felty peaches where a century before they would have been swathed in pearls. Food, cooking and dinners were all high on the agenda, and conversation buzzed about new ingredients, new flavours, new techniques and fresh ways of presentation.

Young gentlemen eager to make their mark in business were no longer interested in serving their apprenticeships in fine houses. Instead, less expensive female servants were taking over the servicing of households, compelled to use the new back stairs and service corridors being installed at fashionable houses like Blenheim Palace. At Calke Abbey in Derbyshire, a tunnel was built underneath the lawn to prevent staff from being seen from the windows. Following French fashions, the halls of new houses were filled with grandly sweeping staircases, and the great chamber and parlour descended again to the ground floor. Known as the salon or saloon, ideally it might be

---

* In the 1830s, the 6th Duke of Devonshire at Chatsworth was sent a banana with Lord Shrewsbury's compliments and a note: '. . . it may be eaten raw but I should think that it would be far more pleasant when cooked in a thin silver dish, like a pudding. I think (I speak in doubt) with butter' (Letter to the Duke in the Chatsworth Collection, 6th Duke's series, 2 December 1834).

A rome well wanscotted about . . . hung with pictures of all sorts, as History, Landskips, Fancyes etc. Long table in the middle, either square to draw out in leaves, or Long or round or oval . . . Side tables, or court cubberts for cups and glasses to drink in, Spoons, Sugar box, Viall and Cruces for Viniger, Oyle and Mustard pot . . . Turkey table cover, or carpet of cloth or Leather printed [and chairs of] turkey work, Russia or Calves leather.

Kenelm Digby's dining room had Turkey carpets on the floor and table, and Pepys, among the first to install a library with glazed shelves, was terribly pleased with his own draught-less room, complete with two-pronged forks and knives with modern, rounded ends. Dining parlours might be filled with several separate tables, perhaps the new gate-legged, drop-leaf varieties in oak or walnut, but the efforts involved in maintaining the cloths was still enormous. (Pepys's contemporary Mrs Ann Blencowe removed stains from her white linen cloths by soaking them in diluted sheep's dung, laying them on the grass and turning them several times before boiling them up with garden greens and strong lye.) Each place was set with a knife, fork and spoon, and we know that Samuel and Elizabeth Pepys copied the courtly fashion for fancifully pleated napkins, hiring a professional folder skilfully to transform starched damask into cockle shells, melons or even a pigeon in a basket.*

Old ceremonies and traditions of hand-washing and tasting for poisons had declined, the cruet set with its oil and vinegar had replaced the great salt of medieval tables, and the old-fashioned buffet had given way to sideboards with basins or cisterns for rinsing glasses and for keeping bottles of wine cool. French court fashions were profoundly influential, and the way that food was presented at table altered as a style known as *à la française* took hold, a vogue that required an enormous variety of dishes to be arranged like a Bach fugue in

---

* Despite such fashionable gentility, plumbing arrangements were still pretty basic, and pots were often kept in dining-room cupboards for the relief of (male) guests. On 21 April 1664, Pepys rushed home on hearing that his grand cousin, Lady Sandwich, was visiting. Flying into the dining room, he interrupted her 'doing something upon the pott', to their joint embarrassment.

kaleidoscopic, symmetrical, repetitive order, even raised up on mini platforms to create a landscape of dishes.

With presentation à la française, tureens of soup and fish were followed by *removes*, or *relevées* (because they literally necessitated the removal of the soup). The most important dishes were placed centrally, known as *entrées* or *surtouts* to denote their importance, and in every available space there were small, delicate dishes (later called *hors d'oeuvres*, for they sat outside the big, glamorous dishes) like small salads or pies, tiny bone-marrow *chewetts*, bone-marrow fritters, rissoles, stewed stuffed tongue, omelettes and plenty of other egg dishes. At important affairs, guests would bring their own servants to ensure that they managed to eat what most pleased their eye; without one, you were forced only to take from the plates nearest to you and to make the best of it. Asking for a dish to be passed plumbed the very depths of impoliteness.

It was all about grand formality, a theatre of shifting plates and pattern as dishes were continually removed and replaced. At its heart were complex French dishes, ragouts and thick gravies known as *cullises*, oysters, artichokes and asparagus, sturgeon and anchovies, lobsters, and crayfish and a fine roast – all sumptuous excess. At the coronation feast of James II, a two-course *ambigu** consisted of ninety-nine cold dishes and forty-six hot ones for the royal table's first course alone, with another thirty in the second. Six other tables in the hall were each laid with more than a hundred and twelve dishes, including monumental terrines of olio, beef *à la royale*, ragoued rabbits, tarts and spectacular pyramids of fruit and sweetmeats, all placed in elaborate symmetry. In 1710, the erstwhile royal cook Patrick Lamb added fold-out paper diagrams to his recipe collection to show the ideal *placement* of over fifty large, middling and small dishes at the table.

The Baroque aesthetic of the court cooks meant that all the almost wantonly lavish conglomerations of olio and ragout were copiously garnished with cockscombs, palates, tongues, oysters, truffles, sweet-breads and other rich titbits, piled up into pyramidical forms that

---

* A conflation of all the courses into a vast buffet: ambiguous by sheer dint of variety.

mirrored the tall, ringletted wigs of the courtiers and the topiary of the formal court gardens. In 1671 Madame de Sévigné described to her friend Madame de Grignan a dinner at which the pyramids of fruit were piled so high that the doorways were hardly tall enough for them and where the view across the table was so obscured that to communicate with anyone opposite you had to write them a note. No one described the tortuous difficulties of serving yourself from such a stately construction.

Piles of fruit were now served during the last course, increasingly known by its French name, *dessert*, though jellies were still very much a magical part of it all. 'Crystal Jellies' were the finest, made in the time-honoured way and flavoured and perfumed with rose-water, sugar, ginger, nutmeg, oil of mace, lemon juice or grains of musk. Isinglass was joined by the extraordinary gelling qualities of a new ingredient: *hartshorn*, shavings from the antlers of deer that were also used in the production of ammonia for smelling salts. In addition to clarifying with the whites of eggs, recipes now suggested that the tops and bottoms of jellies should be cut off and discarded, the middle part melted and set again in order to ensure an un-alloyed, jewel-like clarity. Soon tables were adorned with expensive little jelly glasses that gleamed on the white cloths or were arranged to rise up on tiered salvers, glittering above the arrangement of dishes below.

At tables like these, the complexity and elaboration of English pies and 'fifty angled custards' reached their zenith. Robert May produced differently coloured shallow tarts in asymmetrical tin cases that could be slotted together to form a mosaic effect, using bright yellow and red fillings from preserved fruits like quince, apricot, green plum, cherries and redcurrants and concocting a 'black tart stuffe' from 12 pounds of prunes and 16 pounds of raisins boiled to a pulp with sugar and ginger. For all of them, he used a robust hot-water, fat-free pastry, first baking it blind to make sure that it stayed crisp, with balls of crumpled-up paper pushed into the corners as supports; they were so fragile that May used a special funnel to pour the fillings into the pastry while it was still in the oven. Remarkably delicate fretted or canted puff-pastry lids were baked separately and slipped on just before serving.

Robert May's designs for tarts from *The Accomplisht Cook*, 1660.

May was the first British cook to include illustrations in his book (1660), woodcuts of spectacular pastry work that would set the standard for the next hundred years, the most complicated of which was a celebratory 'Bride Pye', shaped with several concentric circles of paste, each containing a different mixture of both sweet and savoury fillings. William Rabisha, another professional private chef, also gave instructions for producing swathes of geometric tarts whose shapes interconnected and whose coloured contents – custards, jellies or leaches – formed an intricate geometrical parterre.

Indeed, so pervasive was the influence of this French style of dining that on 12 May 1661, on the advice of his periwig maker, Pepys – a man accustomed to roasts, pasties, boiled meats, a plate of anchovies and a boiled lobster – took his wife Elizabeth to dine at a 'French House': 'In a moment' they had 'the table covered . . . and all in the French manner, and a mess of pottage first and then a couple of pigeons a l'esteuve, and then a piece of boeuf a-la-mode exceeding well seasoned and to our great liking.' It cost Pepys 6s. For presentation of food at home, householders could now fashionably choose between cool blue-and-white Delftware or the fresh 'white plates' being manufactured in Lambeth and Bristol; further down the social scale, they might choose little *cheney* dishes that allowed them to arrange side dishes neatly around the central set pieces of a dinner.

By the end of the seventeenth century, recipe books were being filled with illustrations of how to lay a table in the à la française style and 'bills of fare', or menus, that balanced cooking techniques, ingredients, colours and textures. These books not only fulfilled a desire for an unprecedented level of detail but also responded to the needs of a growing number of town-dwellers so removed from the sources of their food that they could not plan a dinner without knowing what was likely to be available at the market.

Breakfasts, however, remained rather old-fashioned in Restoration Britain: broth and pudding or mutton, chicken, cold pie or goose if you were Pepys. Kenelm Digby preferred oatmeal porridges, but he was also the first to suggest that 'two poached eggs with a few fine dry fried collops of pure bacon are not bad for breakfast.' Dinner, still the main meal of the day, was just beginning to shift back an hour to between midday and one o'clock, and it was the habit to sup between six and seven – or much later if it followed a visit to the revitalised theatre – on cold meats, pies or cheesecakes, a dish of asparagus or neats' tongues, a lobster bought ready-cooked or, very commonly, oysters bought by the barrel. Even so, Henri Misson clearly went to bed on more than one occasion with the pangs of hunger rumbling in his stomach, characterising the British as 'Gluttons at Noon and abstinent at night'.

The Pepyses were not unusual in installing their own small bread oven in the recess of the kitchen fireplace, eliminating the anxiety of sending their ready-made pastries through the crowded streets to the neighbourhood baker. The iron grate was also developing, with a solid iron fire-back that reflected heat forwards and with sliding iron 'cheeks', or panels, that could be pushed in or pulled outwards to alter the width of the fire according to the job at hand. Elaborate mechanical spits were hung from andirons one above the other in front of the fire, each turned by jacks operated by weights, gears or springs, all with intricate parts that had to be kept scrupulously clean and well oiled.

Kenelm Digby's will shows that, in his smart Covent Garden townhouse in the early 1660s, he enjoyed an impressively well-equipped kitchen with a buttery for washing glasses, a linen press, white earthenware fruit dishes with scalloped edges, small syllabub glasses, a butter churn and even a feather bed – presumably for the maid, but perhaps he fell into it himself after a hard day mixing his beloved spiced wines. Wooden trays, rolling pins, salting tubs and flour barrels were stored in the larder, and in the wash-house there was a great copper furnace and eight tubs for both brewing and laundry.

The kitchen was stuffed with forty pewter dishes of various sizes, a dripping pan, kettle, boiler, fire fork and tongs, tin colanders, frying pans, numerous brass skillets and scummers, brass-tinned saucepans and stewing pans. Digby had four spits, a hundred different weights, iron pestles and mortars, wooden pastry plugs and two wooden *peles* (bread spades) for removing loaves from the oven. Tin goods were made by the local smith or bought from a roving tinker – all inexpensive, efficient and particularly perfect for cooking pastry to a crisp. Cauldrons now had lids to prevent soot from falling into them, and earthenware pipkins came in various sizes for boiling and stewing. Reams of brown baking paper were bought from mills by the quire, and yards of cotton canvas, wool, lawn and even silk cloths were kept for straining soups and sauces and for boiling puddings. Digby's kitchen might have boasted one of the new silver basting spoons with a rolled hollow handle to prevent hands from burning;* it certainly contained hair sieves and jelly bags, baskets and basins, gally pots for storage, mustard pots, soap and ashes for cleaning, and mousetraps for the larder.

The heavy kitchen table was commonly built up on blocks to prevent its wooden legs from rotting when the floor was wet. At Ham House, the Duchess of Lauderdale had two modern kitchen dressers made, each occupying the full length of their wall, with shelves over and drawers underneath. New charcoal stoves for gently simmering ragouts, soups and sauces were built against the wall, close to a window through which their noxious carbon-monoxide fumes could escape. Few homes, however, would have luxuriated in the French physicist Denys Papin's 'digester': a tightly closed vessel with a safety valve that could reduce bones to the softness of marrow like a modern pressure cooker. In April 1682, John Evelyn attended a Royal Society dinner at which Papin's invention reduced the hardest beef and mutton

---

* These were beautiful things but not hard-wearing: due to their design and the softness of the metal, once dented they often split.

bones to the consistency of cheese using a mere 8 ounces of coals. It produced, wrote Evelyn, an incredible 'quantite of gravie, and for close, a gellie made of the bones of Beife, the . . . most delicious that I had ever seene or tasted, so as I sent my wife a glasse of it to the reproach of all that the lady's ever made of the best Harts horne'. Papin also developed one of the earliest prototypes for a steam engine, but neither invention would be taken seriously for a century.

Which is odd, because meat remained at the heart of the British diet, and Papin's 'digester' would certainly have lightened the load. Foreigners continued to be astonished by the extravagant amounts of meat consumed at British tables. In the 1690s, Henri Misson noted, 'I always heard that they were great flesh-eaters, and I found it true.' In his native France it would have been a scandal for a gentleman to be seen in a cookshop, but 'here a gentleman of 1500 livres a Year enters a Cook's shop without fear of being at all despised for it and there dines for a shilling to his Heart's Content'. There were 'generally four Spits, one over another [with] five or six pieces of Butcher's Meat, Beef, Mutton, Veal, Pork and Lamb, you have what quantity you please cut off, fat, lean, much or little done, with this a little salt or Mustard upon the Side of a Plate, a Bottle of Beer and a Roll and there is your whole Feast.'

Despite his passion for puddings, Misson longed for the cooking of his native France. Although he encountered noblemen who employed professional cooks and who ate 'after the French' manner, the middling sort enjoyed a plainer kind of fare: '. . . ten or twelve sorts of common meats which infallibly take their turn at their tables and two Dishes are their Dinners: a pudding, for instance, and a Piece of roast beef . . . with five or 6 heaps of Cabbage, Carrots, Turnips or some other Herbs or Roots, well peppered and salted and swimming in butter.' Misson was describing two recognisably different cooking traditions developing in tandem that would form the centre of culinary debate throughout the eighteenth century.

13

Chefs and Sweethearts

*Sweethearts, So Strong, so great, so vehement is my Desire
for your Benefit and Advantage, your Prosperity, and
Preferment in this world . . . to make you capable of
serving the Greatest person of Quality, or a gentleman or
Gentlewoman in City, Town or Country*

— HANNAH WOOLLEY

There had not been so much interest in French cooking in Britain –
a fashion driven by Charles II's passion for all things French and by
the return from the Continent of exiled nobles with their foreign
tastes – since the arrival of the Normans. French cooking, court
cooking, was self-consciously *haute*, using endless rarefied ingredients in dishes that required formidable resources and skill to
execute. French chefs (or at least chefs trained in France) were
paid exorbitant wages and treated like princes. Pepys thought his
cousin the Earl of Sandwich had become a 'perfect courtier [with
his] French cook'.

Set against this was the domestic cookery of the middling sort
propounded by a new breed of female cooks that featured the kind
of dishes which for the first time are broadly recognisable as the basis
of our national tradition – jowls of salmon, chines of beef, boiled
crayfish and legs of mutton. This was solid, plain 'English' cooking,
reliant on roasted and boiled meats and beautifully done puddings, pies
and cakes, food for those who derided the wasteful excesses of the
fancy French, or who could not afford them.

Court recipes were about abundance, refinement and the presentation
of snazzy dishes markedly different from anything that had gone

before. Behind it all lay the influence of La Varenne, the French master cook, who stressed herbs and pepper over any other spice and who was the first to give real meaning to the notion of the celebrity chef. La Varenne's recipes reflected a palate that had shifted from sweet to savoury, towards anchovies rather then raisins. He introduced the use of cooked flour rather than breadcrumbs to thicken sauces, calling it *fleur frite*, stirring flour with fat and letting it cook gently before adding stock, onion or mushroom for flavour and leaving it to thicken; then it was strained, bottled and kept aside for constant use.

La Varenne insisted on the constant presence of a pot of clear, fine broth made from copious amounts of expensive butcher's meat as the basis for thin soups and for poaching. Intensely reduced, this broth also formed the thick cullises, used to drench pyramids of labour-intensive and highly flavoured meat dishes. It was partly this cullis, requiring hours of work and endless ingredients to make, that gave the French style its reputation as overblown and expensive. Cullisses were not the juicy by-products of cooking meat but intricate and expensive undertakings all of their own. Yet La Varenne also popularised simple stews with wine, herbs and a gentle scattering of lemon or orange peel, served with parsley and flowers; by the 1680s, his simple 'Boeuf à la mode' – the meat thickly larded, stewed in broth, wine and herbs and spices – had become a culinary classic.

Throughout the closing decades of the seventeenth century, a slew of cookbooks by professional chefs like Robert May took advantage of the profitable vogue to publish, aiming at other chefs serving in noble households and at their rich employers stretching out in fashionably new libraries to flick through such collections in search of a stunning new dish. Some of the books were translations from the French and some were home-grown, but all included complex dishes based on refined foundation stocks and recipes that were both inspirational and aspirational.

May was perhaps envious of the French master cooks who had 'bewicht some of the gallants of our nation with epigram dishes' when he wrote that 'a la Mode is not so worthy of being taken notice of'. Another court cook, Giles Rose, also criticised the expense, perhaps anticipating Middle England's antipathy towards the indulgent expense of the French style. Yet they both packed haute-cuisine recipes into their own garrulous books, and May could not hide his reliance on an unlimited budget, declaring that 'to be confined and limited to the narrowness of a Purse is to want the Materials from which the Artist must gain his knowledge'.

May's *Accomplisht Cook* was one of the most clearly written collections of the century, containing more than a thousand original recipes organised for the first time into logically themed sections that echoed the systematic order of La Varenne. May devoted about a tenth of the book to soups, or *bisks*, all based on broths with small amounts of meat or fish. One of the most popular was 'Soop a la reine', in which a French roll stuffed with chicken farce and garnished with sweet-breads floated in a clear broth – a dish particularly difficult to eat with a spoon. But May still served soups over toasted bread in the bottom of the dish, unwilling to embrace a newer style that used vermicelli or even the new sago, or that floated broken pieces of French bread in the broth just seconds before serving.

May's was in some ways an old-fashioned collection with savoury dishes laden with sugar and dried fruits. Nonetheless it nodded firmly at the new French style with recipes for snails, copious amounts of butter,* a tentative use of cream in sauces and its deliciously novel combinations like slashed pork carbonadoed with fennel seeds. He was fanatical too about the orderly rigour that characterised service à la française, carving the sippets for boiled meat into dainty shapes, notching the edges of sliced lemons and being careful about exact presentation: 'three pieces of Mutton and one in the middle, and between the mutton three Chickens, and up in the middle the Par-tridge.' He decorated the rims of dishes with vegetables diced into perfect squares, made fritters in the shapes of fish, animals or coats of arms to garnish boiled meats, and used soft-stewed oysters to pile over

---

* Butter was not cheap, costing twice as much as meat per pound, and its lavish use was an extravagance. To denote various qualities, the pats were often printed with the maker's mark; Cambridge butter was sold by the yard, and Epping butter was considered the best. Butter was so widely used in late seventeenth-century cookery that you might have thought there would be none spare to export. Not so. Indeed it was one of Britain's most successful exports, and in the year 1662–3 more than 21,000 firkins of butter with a value of more than £18,000 were exported from London.

meats so meltingly boiled that the flesh fell away from its bone at the lightest touch.

Court cooking meant bravura ragouts of fried, chopped meats garnished with rich sauces of mushrooms and capers, cockscombs and truffles, mace, cloves and nutmeg. Fricassées contained a profusion of intensely flavoured ingredients: pigeons and peepers (scalded and trussed), lamb stones and sweetbreads (blanched, parboiled, sliced, fried and floured), asparagus, hard-boiled eggs and bone marrow cooked together in good sweet butter; as if that wasn't enough, they were garnished with pistachios, sliced almonds and a final squeeze of orange. One French chef even suggested that 'Tortoises may be put into a fricassee of chickens . . . having cut off their heads, feet and tails, let them boil in a pot with pepper, salt, onions, cloves, thyme and Bay leaves.'

The tortoise was the idea of François Massialot, whose books were translated into English in the 1690s, ten years after they appeared in France; he also suggested using tortoises for a new dish known as the *pupton*, or *poupeton*, a rich mixture of stewed meats encased in a crust of forcemeat, covered close with rashers of bacon 'as long as your hand and as thin as a shilling'. Pigeon was a more usual choice in Britain, the bird first trussed, singed and blanched, fried in butter or larded and stewed in gravy, and then mixed with sweetbreads, morels, mushrooms, blanched chestnuts and a roux of butter, onion and gravy. The whole creation was baked, loosened from the sides of its pan with the tip of a knife and turned out on to a presentation dish: 'if it is well baked it will stand up right like a brown loaf. Squeeze over it an orange, lay round it fried parsley, the sauce in the middle. So serve it for first course.'

Along with the cullis, new sauces were the heralds of the French style, such as Sauce Robert, an emulsion of mustard, vinegar, pepper and onion – described by John Evelyn as the 'Passe par tout in France for Turkey, goose, pig, ducks, pettitoes etc'. Chefs kept separate bouillons for sauces, and Massialot softened the sharp wine-and-anchovy sauces of the past with butter and herbs like parsley, thyme, chervil and tarragon and, most particularly, with cream. In refined sauces, chives, or *chibbols*, replaced strong brown onions, while garlic, mint, sorrel and rosemary achieved an entirely new prominence.

Above all, court cooking stressed the importance of careful mixing and seasoning, and while timings were still a proper question of trial and error, quantities did become far more precise. Robert May's recipe for 'Olio Marrow Pie', for instance, paid close attention to the needs of his readers, listing 'butter, three pound, flower one quart, lamb-Stones three pair, Sweet Breads, six, Marrow bones eight, large mace, Cock Stones twenty, interlarded Bacon one pound, knots of Eggs twelve, Artichocks twelve, Sparagus one hundred, Cock's Combs twenty, Pistaches one pound, Nutmeg, Mace . . .' Ironically, it was just this kind of detail that allowed even amateur cooks to attempt to follow his upmarket receipts.

Despite being so impressed by his dinner at the 'French House', Pepys preferred plain meats, yet he also wanted to feel himself to be up to date. On one occasion he refused an old-fashioned sweet sauce with his mutton, sulking over a dish of marrow bones instead; conversely, he was full of self-congratulation after sharing a chicken for a simple dinner at home with his wife: 'it pleased me much to see my condition come to allow ourselves a dish like that.' Compared to the penny prices of a century earlier, chickens were luxuries, sold at market for as much as 1s 4d; eating chicken was a sure sign that you had risen well in the world.

Details of food fill Pepys's diary. His wife often rose at five in the morning to prepare a dinner, buying a chine of beef and fowl at the market and hiring a female cook to help her with plates of oysters, a hash of rabbit and lamb, roast beef, fowl and a tart, which might all cost £5. Within a few years of the Restoration, tricksier fare was finding its way on to their menus, 'a ffrigasy of rabbets and chicken' joining the boiled leg of mutton, roast pigeons, lamprey pie and dish of anchovies.* Beef was served on special occasions, and the Pepyses were far

---

* A dish of anchovies had become an accepted way to finish a meal, and other savoury foods like eggs or toasts spread with melted cheese, chopped kidneys or mushrooms were becoming very popular, lingering in our very British habit of serving cheese and biscuits at the close of dinner. By the 1660s, anchovies, like oysters, had found the place we now reserve for crisps and nuts – being offered to visitors as salty whets; they were imported in their shiploads, mainly from Italy.

more likely to buy cheaper cuts of pork or rabbit when dining alone, despite the fact that Robert May included more than 112 recipes for beef. Calf's head boiled with a piece of bacon had become a standard dinner-party dish – the brains peeled from their clinging membrane and mashed with pungent sage, vinegar and butter into a standard sauce. Ann Blencowe's recipe was typical:

> Let your Calve's head be half boyled and cut it in small peses toung and all. Put it into a stupan; put to it prettie deel of salt and anchove pepper, cloves and a Onion, a bundell of sweethearbes, and as much sider of white Wine and water as will cover it. Stu this till ye licker be half wasted, then put in 7 yolks of egges beaten with a spoonful of Viniger; put it in and stir it on ye fire till it is thick and sarve it up with ye brans fried and forsed Meat Balls and slised Lemon.

Cod's head and fleshy shoulders was another dish fit for entertaining, generally boiled and coated in an anchovy, oyster and butter sauce, but, along with expensive sturgeon and salmon, it was the exception to a growing rule. For though well-ships with large water tanks were now able to transport live fish over great distances, fast days were rarely observed. Consequently, apart from cheap lobsters, anchovies, smelt and oysters – and despite a thriving French tradition of fish cookery – fish had begun to come a very poor second to meat unless it was costly enough to be presented as a 'remove'.

While French cooks concocted side dishes like asparagus with a thick *jus*, mushroom ragout or a dish of peas in cream, most domestic cooks boiled new vegetables like broccoli in the same way as spinach, carrots, cabbage, lettuce, turnips, radishes and cucumbers, serving them with a simple butter sauce. Another newcomer, cauliflower, was generally poached in milk and served with cream, though court chefs like May also added mace, sack and butter to the recipe.

Domestic cookery was dominated by one woman – Hannah Woolley, the first Englishwoman to set out to make her fortune by instructing the middle classes on all aspects of household management. From her first book in the early 1670s, Woolley addressed both those women who were rising up the social scale and had to learn it all from scratch and those who were tumbling down it, conscious of the great numbers of 'gentlewomen forced to serve, whose parents and Friends have been impoverished by the late Calamities'. Woolley had emerged from the Civil War liberated, a servant able publicly to express her own opinions, and she believed in the education of women, scornful of 'the great negligence of parents [who let] the fertile ground of their daughters lie fallow, yet send the barren noodles of their sons to the university'.

Woolley's books addressed servants for the first time, not only advising them on how to cook good, plain English dishes but explaining how to make preserves and how to take over the jobs of distilling and candying from their mistresses. Orphaned at fourteen, living by her wits, Woolley, whose experience was domestic, whose recipes were cheaper and whose advice was more homespun and certainly less daunting than that of professional French chefs, was the cloth from which the Victorian Isabella Beeton would be cut.

For all the heightened emotion of French chefs with their dramatic concern for reputation,* domestic cooks like Woolley focused on practicality and economy. The preparation of meat and soup – rather than medieval pottages – was a litmus test for the two styles, for, as Henri Misson recorded, the tables of the English 'who do not keep French cooks are covered only with large dishes of meat. They are strangers to bisks . . .' Woolley did in fact include a recipe for a complicated *bisk* in her *Gentlewoman's Companion* but only in order to scorn it:

> Gentlewomen, I must crave your pardon, since I know I have tired your patience in the descriptions of a Dish which though it be frequently used in noblemen's houses and with all this cost and trouble put together by some rare whimsical French cook, yet I cannot approve of it, but must call it a Miscellaneous hodg-podg of studied vanity: and I have here inserted it not for your imitation, but admiration.

---

* Famously the Sun King's chef, François Vatel, began to panic at Chantilly in 1671 when the meat ran out at the twenty-fifth table; the next day, believing that the fish was not going to be delivered on time to prepare properly, the hissy fool fell on his sword. Almost as soon as he died, the fish began to arrive.

Woolley had learned her craft not in Paris nor in a noble household – though she boasted that she had once cooked for the King – but from her mother and sisters, practising it in the homes of the gentry. Yet even she could not escape the spell of the intense flavours of the French style, for there was not a cook in the land who did not want her cooking touched with the razzmatazz of the Continent, however much she might rail against its excesses. Rebecca Price was a case in point, fashionably up to date with a taste for cream sauces to flatter rabbit, veal and poultry, and her use of the milder flavours of oysters, bacon, mushrooms and red wine mixed with butter to make sauces. Price used a burnt-butter sauce with flour for thickening gravies and copied into her household book one of the earliest recipes for hollandaise: an emulsion of eggs, water, white-wine vinegar and shallots. She enjoyed the punchy flavours of the 'frikesy' (as she called it), mixing veal, sausage, eggs, butter and bacon with wine or putting chickens with cockscombs, veal sweetbreads, mushrooms, truffles and oysters.

Price's contemporary Ann Blencowe also liked to show off a little with her fashionably smooth pea soup or her Greek recipe for vine leaves, or *delma*, and she made 'dobes' and 'beef-a-la-mode' as well as soups with garnishes – all imitations of French court cookery. John Evelyn – an advocate of home-cultivated, slender-stemmed asparagus plunged quickly into boiling water – was almost unique among his male contemporaries in keeping a handwritten recipe book. Like his female contemporaries', it combined old-fashioned recipes with others that were terribly up to date, comfortably and unselfconsciously putting the French and English styles side by side, demonstrating that cooks picked and chose according to their budget, taste or purpose.

Where Woolley succeeded was in her recognition that people wanted to offer upmarket, modern dishes on a constrained budget. Weaving the fashionable tastes of anchovies, capers, cream and wine into her recipes, she set about simplifying. For a general 'fricasie' she advised that veal, chicken, rabbits or anything else that was lying around would do quite well. She had a long list of ingredients, but not one of them was terribly expensive. Indeed, because she was addressing, in particular, women in service and those in towns where food was expensive and self-sufficiency impossible, Woolley laid down the law of frugality, stressing the importance of collecting up leftovers for re-use. In her hands, fricassées and ragouts were good ways of using up bits of raw meat or leftovers, and faking it was often a necessity rather than a duplicity: venison had become so rare and costly that a sirloin of beef or a loin of mutton left to sit in sugar before being rolled into a paste the thickness of a thumb often took its place.

'To make a ffrigasy of rabbit or chickin', from Elizabeth Fowler's recipe manuscript, circa 1684.

Although she set out to simplify, the disordered arrangement of Woolley's books, in which pickled cucumbers appeared next to orange pudding, was a far cry from the model of clarity presented by May, and a handful of her recipes would have floored a cook of average competence. Her olio, for example, included a myriad of ingredients all cooked separately and laboriously. But perhaps it was all relative: the piled-up profusion of the royal chef Patrick Lamb's olio recipe covered six long pages; La Varenne would certainly have loathed them both. Woolley did on occasion also quite ignore the perfect simplicity of a La Varenne recipe: his lamb pie was cooked only with a few herbs and a good stock, while hers was an old-fashioned circus of contrasting flavours – grated Naples biscuits competing with cloves, mace, nutmeg and cinnamon, rosewater, orange peel and citron with a caudle of egg, sugar and butter.

Yet in the main, Hannah Woolley was a fine, solid cook, confidently chopping boiled tongues into pies, roasting pigs with puddings in their bellies, frying garden beans (another novelty) with parsley and butter, and larding calf's tongue with lemon peel and bacon, braising it in a pipkin with claret and caraway seeds. She was not above roasting woodcock 'The French Way' with strips of bacon over the breast and served on toast, and she made a classic shoulder of mutton with oysters. She offered carefully detailed monthly bills of fare: for April, ideal dishes included goslings, a turkey, a side of jointed lamb, turtle doves, sucking rabbits, pickled beef, a buttered apple pie, an almond custard or a syllabub – the dessert of the age.

Frothy, fruity versions of the posset without its custardy eggs, syllabubs had been all the rage since Charles II was reputed to have sent his milkmaid into the fields with a dish of warmed spiced wine or fruit syrup into which she was to milk the cow. What everyone agreed was that the milk must be poured from a great height, whisked violently or squirted through a syringe known as a 'wooden cow'. Kenelm Digby left the cream, sack, white wine and sugar to stand overnight, 'quicken[ing] the taste' with rosemary or bruised lemon peel, and Ann Blencowe spooned just the froth into glasses, though in all likelihood even this separated again into whey and curds. Pepys often stopped to enjoy one on his way through the park to work, though in general syllabubs were offered as female party drinks, arranged in glasses in a pyramid stack on a silver salver.

Whipped cream cut with sharp fruit purées were also part of a very English tradition. Rebecca Price had six separate recipes for her favourite lemon cream and was among the first to experiment with chocolate – grating it into sweetened, heated cream, milling it constantly, adding eggs and sugar, and then pouring the chocolate custard from a height to make it froth, leaving it to cool and set until the following day. Then there was the bizarrely difficult but highly fashionable 'cabbage cream' – whipped cream layered until it looked like the vegetable – as well as gorgeous confection of clotted cream with bruised raspberries, sugar and rosewater. One of Woolley's recipes was halfway to being a modern trifle, the sweet cream flavoured with mace, set with rennet and strewn with French comfits.

Woolley was not alone in her approach, but she was unique in her desire to offer the most comprehensive advice. Sympathising with the greasy, smutty work of the under-cook maids, she advised them to rise up the scale by dint of keeping themselves 'from being Nasty', carefully stirring the pot, minding the oven, scumming the broth and, above all, never grumbling. She also guided the cook through the difficulties of the market, pointing out the black legs and short spurs, the bright eyes and moist feet of fresh poultry, the clear eyes and sweet smell of a good fish. She described how to look for the fresh blue vein on the neck of the forequarter of a lamb and for the open grain and oily smoothness of fresh, tender beef; there were also instructions on how to wash plate, answer letters, mind your manners, keep accounts and save for retirement.

For young ladies inching their way up the social ladder, Woolley explained how to behave at table, to keep the body straight and the elbows in, to use a fork and spoon to take out the contents of a pie and the point of a knife for offering a slice of cake. Copying courtly notions of balance and height, she suggested that a large wooden tray should be made for serving dessert with recesses to stop the small plates from sliding around. She also chided her readers to learn the skill of carving neatly, for this uncomfortably tricky public ritual was no longer the preserve of a male servant, and 'I have seen the good gentlewoman of the house sweat more in cutting up of a fowl than the cook did in rosting it, and when she had soundly beliquor'd her joints, hath suckt her knuckles and set to work with them again in the dish.'* And, lest they end up with husbands who failed to come home for dinner – Pepys grazed his way through the day at taverns and 'ordinaries' despite his wife's cooking – Woolley enjoined her readers to lure them back to the family nest: '. . . let whatever you provide be so neatly and cleanly drest that his fare, though ordinary, may engage his appetite, and disingage his fancy from taverns, which many are compell'd to make use of by reason of the continual and daily dissatisfaction they find at home.'

Unlike his friend Pepys, the courtly, horticultural John Evelyn was so enamoured of the salads now playing a fashionable role at the table that he published the first book devoted just to them. The recipes in his *Acetaria* (1699) were a world away from May's showy mounds of shredded capon, boiled meats, minced herbs, onion, capers, olives, samphire, broom buds and pickles; as well as being a purist, Evelyn was slender, as intellectuals were supposed to be, and favoured simple mixtures of leaves and herbs, picking out the tiniest leaves, potatoes or roots and mixing them so that each fell 'into their places like the notes in music'. Loathing garlic ('. . . we absolutely forbid it entrance into our salleting by reason of its intolerable rankness . . . sure tis not for ladies palats'), his ideal dressing was simple oil, vinegar and salt with, on occasion, a shaving of horseradish or a spoon of mustard, and his perfect salad bowl was made of porcelain or Delftware – pure, cool and untainted by the astringency of the very best vinegar.

However, whether or not you had a French chef, part of the garden and orchard produce still had to be transformed into food for the unproductive months, and manuscript household books of the period are crammed with instructions – after years of war, extreme hunger and hardship, the mania for hoarding and preserving was unabated.

---

* Twenty-odd years later, the printer J. Moxon produced a pack of playing cards to accompany his book *The Genteel Housekeeper's Pastime* and give precise and detailed instructions on carving. This was one of the very first step-by-step guides ever produced.

Rebecca Price was among the first to make an orange marmalade soft enough to be spooned out of its jar; another professional chef, William Rabisha, included plenty of recipes for pickling vegetables in his book; and Ann Blencowe had a recipe for 'Pickile Lila' – one of the earliest piccalillis, coloured with turmeric. Blencowe also used a new method to preserve meat into a 'collar' by soaking beef in brine for two days before rolling it with spices and herbs, tying it up tight, cooking it in ale, pressing it and baking it again so it would keep for up to three months tied into a clean cloth hung in the larder.

Potting offered a new way to store meat: a smooth paste of chopped, seasoned and cooked meat pressed hard into a pot and covered with clarified butter or thick suet to seal out the air. Kenelm Digby threw lamprey alive into scalding water (for as long as it took to say an Ave Maria), scraped off the skin and mud and gutted them, baking them in a hot oven to concentrate their flavour with onions and butter before potting them: he said they would keep for a year 'if the buttr stays hard.'

But at the heart of Restoration cooking, common to court and domestic cooks alike, was the knowledge that the kinds of foods you chose and the way you presented them at table proclaimed your social status. Woolley wanted her readers to know how to serve a bowl of raspberries (between two spoons) and how to set out a table 'with Vine leaves and Flowrs between the Dishes and the Plates', and she wanted them, on occasion, to shine. The final recipe of her *Queen Like Closet* (1670) covered three whole pages. She warned that it was not simple to make, but it was a perfectly bourgeois kind of culinary statement: a thick plum cake studded with biscuits and decorated with fruit, candied quinces, dried apricots, pears and pippins all in the likenesses of snails and worms, the whole confection held together with gum and sugar.

Ice

British taste had moved right away from the Arab influences brought back by the returning Crusader knights in the Middle Ages. But a thrilling innovation that sprang from the spiced and sweetened fruit syrups and cordials of Turkey and the Near East was about to take fine Georgian dining by storm.

Ice cream – or cream ice as it was called for the first hundred or so years of its existence – not only looked divine but presented an extraordinary, utterly unique taste experience: the shock of the frozen mass hitting the teeth and the explosion of flavour and perfume as it melted in the mouth. It made eyes fly open with surprise. So exquisitely rare at the time that it might have been part of the Crown Jewels, a single sweetened cream ice was served to Charles II at the Garter Feast of 1671 at St George's Hall – its first written record in Britain. Unfortunately there is no description of Charles's face as he took his first taste and, unlike the pineapple, no evidence that any courtier was invited to share the divine confection. It was the ultimate in snob appeal, its exclusive sparkle beyond culinary compare.

Since the start of the seventeenth century, Neapolitans, like their Roman ancestors, had been using the eternal snows of Mt Etna to cool their drinks. Now they were influenced by *sorbetti*, the sherbets of Turkey: fruit syrups that were chilled but (and this is important) never frozen. It became quite the thing in Naples to mound pyramids of snow on to the dessert table and to serve wines chilled in an ice bucket. The French followed suit, and, between them, the two nations continued to experiment with the process of freezing syrups and creams into moulded centrepieces.

The difficulty in Britain lay in finding ice at the height of summer. James I had snow pits dug for storing ice cut from lakes and rivers in winter. Two brick-lined pits were constructed at Greenwich in 1620 and another at Hampton Court five years later, but there is no real record of how the ice was used: Francis Bacon was experimenting with the use of ice as a preservative but had reached no absolute conclusions when he caught a chill on Highgate Hill while collecting snow with which to preserve a chicken and died. Forty years later, ice's qualities were more certain, and, in the year of his coronation, James's grandson, Charles II, began to construct ice-houses in Upper St James's Park. The Duchess of Lauderdale was one of the first to copy him, at Ham House, and by the time Celia Fiennes toured the country on horseback in 1702, she was able to note several ice-houses without surprise. Ice pits were dug from Painshill to Scotney Castle, and at Chatsworth in the Derbyshire peaks a 1693 ice pond had its own controlled water-feed and outlet and a gamekeeper installed to keep birds and animals away from the water.

Getting ice was relatively easy if you had your own lake and the staff to hack and cart it in winter – according to Giles's *Instructions for Servants* (1682), it was the responsibility of the steward to oversee its winter collection – but preserving it was expensive for these designer ice pits were works of art. John Evelyn gave instructions: 'first digge a pitte on the side of some shady hill . . . line the pit with reeds . . . bulrushes or sedge being the best.' He created a false bottom with a metal grille through which the meltwater could escape and layered clean ice with straw to a 12-foot height, thatching the whole to make it airtight 'and so conserve the snow for many yeares'.

The next step on the culinary path was salt – particularly cheaper salt nitre or saltpetre, introduced almost certainly from India in the Tudor period and already widely used in the salting of hams. Put the two together around a separate container of water or cream and the effect was swift even if the science was perplexing: as the salt melted the ice in the outer bucket, it sucked the heat from anything it touched, reducing its temperature and causing the contents of the inner bowl to freeze.

The discovery of this puzzling process is lost to history, but the first British book to explain it and to offer a recipe for the extravagant novelty was the 1702 translation of Massialot's *Court and Country Cook*. Massialot – a professional chef – used boiled, filtered water or creams and sweetened and flavoured them with fruit compotes, herbs or flower waters, including chervil, burnet, jonquil and tuberose, immersing the bowl in a bucket of ice and salt until its contents froze into a rather crude lump, serving the ices in pyramids on china dishes beside fruit, creams and jellies. What Massialot appears to have latched on to at this very early stage was that the kind of aromatics and scents so adored by the court at Versailles added to the surprise of it all – at low temperatures, scent is barely discernible, it blossoms only as the icy mass liquefies in the mouth. Cherries, apricots, peaches, lemons and oranges – even chocolate – all found their way into his ices. Ever the perfectionist, he reminded cooks to strain fruits like raspberries, finding the pips terribly 'troublesome to the teeth'.

In 1718 – some fifty years after it was first served to Charles II – Mary Eales, self-styled confectioner to Queen Anne, published the very first home-grown recipe for ice cream. It was confident, practical and detailed, if slightly roundabout:

> Take Tin Ice-Pots, fill 'em with any Sort of Cream you like, either plain or sweeten'd, or Fruit in it; shut your Pots very close; to fix Pots you must allow eighteen to twenty Pound of Ice, breaking the Ice very small; there will be some great Pieces, which lay at the Bottom and Top: You must have a Pail and lay some Straw at the Bottom; then lay in your Ice and put in amongst it a Pound of Bay Salt; set in your Pots of Cream, and lay Ice and salt between every Pot, that they may not touch; but the

Ice must lye round 'em on every Side; lay a good deal of Ice on the Top; cover the Pail with Straw, set it in a Cellar where no Sun or Light comes, it will be froze in four Hours, but it may stand longer; then take it out just as you use it; hold it in your Hand and it will slip out. When you would freeze any sort of Fruit, either Cherries, Rasberries, Currants, or Strawberries, fill your Tin-Pots with the Fruit, but as hollow as you can, put to 'em Lemmonade, made with Spring Water and Lemon Juice sweeten'd; put enough in the Pots to make the Fruit hang together, and put 'em in Ice as you do Cream.

Eales was among the first cooks to develop jams, or *giams* – cherry, apricot or raspberry mixtures which were not designed to set into firm pastes for slicing but which remained runny, stored in jars with paper lids. These were especially handy for flavouring ices. As the secret of making ices spread, *sorbetières* – cylindrical pots with lids, designed to be plunged into wooden freezing-pails filled with crushed ice and salt – developed. Tiny pewter or tin moulds about 1 to 3 inches high and in the shapes of fruits, flowers or animals were also produced, but these early ices were neither churned nor beaten during freezing, resulting in a rather solid mass that must have been hard to eject from the moulds; many novices must have found that merely holding them in your hand was as likely to give you a bad frost burn as loosen the contents from their little prisons. As with moulded jellies, cooks had to perfect the art of extraction using any means at their disposal, and many chose to dip the moulds swiftly into warm water.

In the 1730s the Duke of Chesterfield's renowned cook Vincent La Chapelle developed the technique of making ices by stirring the mixture from time to time as it set, breaking up the crystals and creating a much creamier effect. He also experimented with egg-custard foundations as smooth as butter and described how to make imitations of citrons, plums, strawberries or peaches, pouring the mixtures into moulds with a funnel and painting them when they were done. La Chapelle also made his ices in the shape of cheese wedges, known as 'cheeses' though they were more usually sweet than savoury.

By the second half of the eighteenth century, the gentry and merchant classes were beginning to enjoy these tantalising frozen creams. They were sold by confectioners or, if ice could be got, made at home, served in flourishing peaks in small glasses or painted cups. As she prepared the fifth edition of her *Art of Cookery* in 1755, Hannah Glasse added an up-to-the-minute recipe for a raspberry-and-cream ice, though she gave only peremptory instructions for the process – probably aware that few of her readers would have the wherewithal even to begin to attempt it but pointing them in the direction of the pewterers for the requisite bowls. Within ten years, however, she announced that 'ice cream is a thing to be used in all desserts as it is to be had both winter and summer and what in London is always to be had at the Confectioners.' By the 1760s cream ices had become ice creams and syllabubs had been pushed into second place.

The confectioner Borella's *Court and Country Confectioner* (1770) was the first British book to explore the creation of sugar syrups in specific detail, guiding his readers through the 'degrees' or tempera-tures of sugar required for different functions. Borella filled his sorbetière only half full, regularly opening it and scraping the sides with a paddle or long spoon to detach 'all the flaks which stick to the sides in order to make it congeal equally all over in the pot. Then you must work them well as much as you are able, for they are so much the more mellow as they are well worked, and their delicacy depends entirely upon that'. His ice pails had a bung at the bottom for the removal of meltwater so that fresh ice and salt could be added, and he kept the salt content light so that the mix would chill gently, delivering a soft, highly prized texture.

Water-, cream- and custard-based ices were now flavoured with a wide variety of gorgeous and imaginative flavours including pounded coriander, cinnamon and even tea. Brown bread, pistachio, coffee, chocolate and Seville or China orange were all popular, as were scented flower waters like elderflower, rose or jasmine; punch, burnt filberts, pineapple, pear and barberries were all great favourites.

Rather than fill his moulds with unfrozen creams and syrups as La Chapelle had done, Borella whipped the frozen mixtures again, break-ing up any lumps before spooning them into hinged moulds which he then wrapped in paper, sealed with wax or lard, and set to freeze again. When they were done, he slipped them out and painted them with fruit and vegetable pigments, storing them until dessert in ice caves – lead-lined boxes filled with ice that were kept in a cool, dark corridor or basement. As they were sent to the table, a frosty rime would develop, turning their surfaces dreamily, softly opaque – miniature mouthfuls of whimsical delight.

Nearly two decades after Borella's celebrated publication, Frederic Nutt, an apprentice working at the famous London confectioners Domenico Negri, published his own enormously expensive publication, *The Complete Confectioner* (1789), priced at 10s 6d: It included more than fifty simple, elegant recipes for scintillating ices flavoured with aromatics like bergamot and the fulsome, salty kick of Parmesan cheese, and his mixtures were coloured before adding them to moulds which came in several parts, so that he could create yellow pineapples with green leaf crowns sitting in pretty woven baskets of pink ice. There were even moulds in the shape of fish.

Nutt accompanied his ices with lovingly made wafers flavoured with coffee or flower waters and rolled round a narrow stick to set in thin tubes. Or he scented a mixture of whipped egg white and sugar with sophisticated bergamot, burnt orange or peppermint, leaving the semi-transparent meringue discs to curl gently over the warmth of a stove, the perfect crisp companions to the spectacle and melting entertainment of the ices.

WILLIAM AND MARY, ANNE, AND THE HANOVERIANS

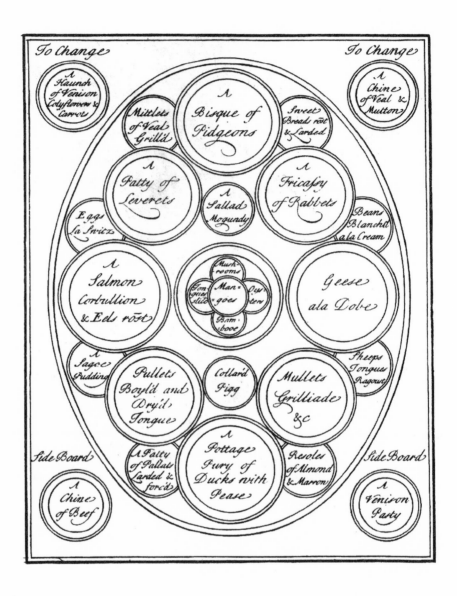

Table plans like this one from Charles Carter's *Complete City and Country Cook*, 1732 became more common in cookbooks throughout the first half of the eighteenth century, as readers sought assistance in planning seasonal menus and presenting them in the balanced order of service à la française. Note the removes for the soups, roast beef and venison pastry now placed on the sideboard.

14

Human Nature

*We shall represent Human Nature at first to the keen
appetite of our reader, in that more plain and simple
manner in which it is found in the country, and shall
hereafter hash and ragout it with all the high French and
Italian seasoning of affectation and vice which courts and
cities afford*

— HENRY FIELDING

When Charles II's brother, the autocratic Catholic James II, retreated
to the Continent in 1688, ice-making was still in its infancy and politics
were to the fore as his daughter Mary and her husband, William, sailed
from Holland at Parliament's invitation to plug the royal gap. Within a
year, the Act of Religious Toleration was passed and then the Bill of
Rights, establishing 'free' elections and annual parliaments; monarchy
was becoming constitutional, bounded by an increasingly powerful
parliamentary system. Nineteen years later, Queen Anne's Act of
Union finally brought the Scots and English under one government.
Britain had become a stable, tolerant country enjoying high wages and
low prices, and its population had rarely been so well off.

The 'long century', as the period stretching from the 1690s to the
1820s is often called, was a period of singular energy and exuberance,
riddled with paradoxes. It wove together commodities and trade, wit,
reason, tolerance and manners but also slavery, taxes, political corrup-
tion, crime and constant wars. It was characterised by enormous
wealth and urgent poverty; by vogues for both artificial formality
and wild, informal nature; by expansive imperialism and entrenched
domesticity; by aristocratic élitism on the one hand and the breaking
down of social boundaries on the other – for in pleasure gardens like

Vauxhall and Ranelagh and in health spas like Bath, the quality rubbed shoulders with tradesmen and servants, a proximity of classes that startled tourists. Under Mary, William, Anne and then the Hanoverian Georges, the centre of political and social influence continued to shift away from the court towards the great country houses of the landed aristocracy – the Whigs – fanning out to the expanding ranks of the middling sort. Under Queen Anne, the Prime Minister Robert Walpole promoted the kind of self-interest and greed that could only result in a moneyed population intent on leisure and consumption and a 'Beggar's Opera' underworld peopled with thieves, highwaymen and the gallows. While the urban poor grew wraithlike, ruining themselves on cheap gin, improving roads and the Penny Post encouraged what Oliver Goldsmith called 'polite society' to take up socialising as a national sport. At the fashionable new spas and in town there were balls, routs and assemblies for crowds of guests; *ridottos*, or concert parties; musical and card parties; informal suppers and socially competitive dinners for smaller groups of guests where witty conversation was the dernier cri. Well-to-do waistlines expanded, buttocks swelled, and constitutions began to suffer, a surfeit memorably satirised by Hogarth's engravings.

It was a century of appetite, and the demand for possessions was increasingly satisfied by an infinite array of decorative goods: elegant, light furniture, wallpapers, damask curtains and mirrors that filled the candlelit rooms. Pretty china charmed the ladies: in the very first year of her reign Anne commanded that 'all pickles, salades, jellyes with other cold meats and intermesses brought up to our table be served on fair china plates', and the upper classes collected 'tee' cups and 'jacolite' (chocolate) dishes from Holland and crockery sets stamped with crests or monograms from the German factory at Meissen. In 1735 Lady Elizabeth Finch wrote to the Countess of Burlington that her sister 'is become china Mad, frequents all the shops in town in order to get either old or Dresden China', and in the 1740s the Chelsea Factory began to produce its own English bone china. Painted china sets, the like and extent of which had never been seen before, flourished on polished mahogany dining tables whose prized surfaces were protected by a wad of leather beneath the linen cloths.

As society played the envy game, tables began to shine with more than polish. Elegant sets of silver cutlery strengthened with 'rats' tails' or spines down the centre of their backs were laid with the three-tined fork to the left and the broad-ended knife and spoon to the right, face-down so as not to catch on lacy sleeves. Silver was flaunted: candelabra and *épergnes* with connecting branches to hold jellies and sweetmeats held sway down the centre of the table, replacing the great salts of the medieval hall. Silver salt and pepper pots, sugar shakers, gravy jugs with hot-water compartments and coasters for holding decanters added to the gleam of it all, and delicate silver teaspoons, sugar tongs or nips and tea strainers were arranged on special tables whose edges were lipped to prevent the china from slipping off. Thomas Bolsover's development of a new kind of plate at his factory in Sheffield would in the 1770s lead to the mass production of cutlery for the aspirational gentry classes.

With Ravenscroft's invention of lead crystal, chandeliers appeared called 'lustres', and sets of heavy, clear drinking glasses returned to the table from the cool marble sideboards, always held by the base and always rinsed in a cistern by a footman before they were refilled. When glass was taxed in 1745, the glasses' weight was reduced by cutting deep jags and slices into their surfaces so that they sparks of light ricocheted off them, or they were blown thin and fragile with exquisite etching. The rage for these luxuries was so pervasive that by mid-century Hannah Glasse was giving instructions for mending broken china with a glue made of egg white and ground oyster shells or glass with alabaster. And by 1777 even the bachelor country parson James Woodforde would find himself sending his servant to Norwich to buy him a complete 'Table service of the cream coloured Ware'.

Unlike any other city in the world, London's streets were filled with shops like Betty's fruit shop in St James, Fortnum & Mason, Wedg-wood's showroom and Hamleys, the greatest 'joy emporium' on earth. By the end of the century they would be joined by Swan & Edgar, Hatchards and the business that would become Debenhams, all offering the trappings of riches to anyone with a full purse. The hanging wooden signboards of these up-to-the-minute establishments creaked in the breeze, obscuring the sun from the rutted pavements below.

The leisured classes were inclined to breakfast as late as ten in the morning and in the parlour rather than the dining room, ale and sides of meat giving way to tea (now taken with a little milk), chocolate, and bread enriched with sugar, eggs and milk. Some breads were served in wedges – called 'wigs' – but there were also regional spiced breads like Bath buns with caraway comfits and Sally Lunns brushed with butter; the Swedish botanist Per Kalm* drooled over 'slices of wheat bread which they had first toasted at the fire and when it was very hot had butter spread on it'.

Dinner for the smart set was delayed to as late as three in the afternoon and service à la française, still consisting of three main courses each with their many dishes, was increasingly governed by new conventions of balanced order and pattern. As guests entered the dining room they found their food waiting for them. Soup traditionally came first or, better, a pair of soups contrasting in colour and texture, placed at each end of the table in ornate matching tureens and served with small decorative toasts in place of old-fashioned sops. 'White' and 'brown' soups were traditional companions: the 'brown' a thickish veal or mutton broth with the torn flesh of a roasted duck, some onion and chopped herbs, and the 'white' a clear stock with some finely shredded pullet's flesh, made velvety with cream and mace, thickened with bone marrow or egg yolk. Pea soup was a favourite, the biggest of the shelled peas boiled and sieved to a pulp and the smallest stirred in with spinach and mint to lift both the flavour and the colour, with a little green spring onion fried gently in butter as a garnish. Clear broths commonly included vermicelli, macaroni and rice, making careful timing a necessity lest these turned into a distasteful mush while waiting for the guests to arrive at the table. In Scotland, medieval tastes survived in cock-a-leekie, with its mixture of meat and prunes in a barley broth, while further south soups with chestnuts or crawfish were also catching on.

In 1715 Lord Orkney served his dinner guests a pea soup followed by 'removes': a boiled ham and chickens, spinach stacks, pigeon pie and stewed beef. The second course included dishes of roast turkey, fricassée of cockscombs and sweetbreads, pickled sole and roast partridge; and dessert rounded it all off, consisting of old favourites

---

* Linnaeus' pupil, after whom he named the American shrub kalmia.

like thickened cream, apples, pears, confections, peeled walnuts and chestnuts. The fricaseés may well have been, like the soups, a balance between 'brown', based on dark meats, and 'white', which used poultry with a cream, white-wine and egg-yolk sauce. The vibrant colours of the medieval table had almost entirely disappeared, and no fine eyebrow was raised when meat and fish were served together. In fact there were quantities of oysters and lobsters, anchovies were almost inescapable, and salted fish was still bought in barrels in preference to the dubiously 'fresh' fish transported to towns from the coast in hulking, stinking water carts.*

The precise position of each dish in relation to the others at table was more crucial than ever, and tablecloths were ironed with a sharp centre fold that functioned as a guide for the footmen. Damask napkins had grown enormous – the origin of the phrase 'to make ends meet', for the richer you were, the more cloth there was to tie round your neck. Small fringed or lace cloths called 'd'Oyleys' developed to protect the table surface during the dessert, when the cloths were generally removed.

With the eagle-eye of a Tartar, Grisell Baillie – daughter of an earl and wife of a future Lord of the Admiralty – obsessively scrutinised the exact composition and placement of each dish wherever she dined, memorising and recording it all in her diary when she returned home. From a dinner at Lord Mountjoy's in 1722, Baillie was able to recall the giddying variety of both French and English dishes with astonishing precision. A tureen of beef was at the head, with matched pairs of similar foods balanced each side of the table including puddings, stewed beef collops and a small mutton. Smaller dishes – known as *reliefs* – of smelt, ragoued breast of veal and young ducks were arranged with due symmetry, and apple tarts, sweetmeats and vegetables like asparagus in cream filled the gaps. The dessert, on the other hand, was arranged specifically with an eye for height. Preserved fruits, jellies and ratafia or lemon creams were each served on footed gilt salvers, on raised glass plates or on épergnes holding small glasses. It

---

* Daniel Defoe, in his *Tour thro' the Whole Island of Great Britain* . . . in the 1720s, wrote that the carts arrived in London stinking 'yet the people are so eager of them that they buy them, and give dear for them too'; Smollett's Matthew Bramble railed that fish came 'sixty, seventy, fourscore, and a hundred miles by land carriage; a circumstance sufficient . . . to turn a Dutchman's stomach'.

The service of a dessert from Massialot's *New Instructions for Confectioners*,
1702, shows ices, patisserie and fruits arranged in symmetry and,
particularly, in fashionable pyramid forms.

was just the kind of arrangement admired by Joseph Addison, editor of
the influential magazine the *Tatler*: 'Pyramids of candy'd sweetmeats
that hung like icicles, with fruits scattered up and down and in an
artificial kind of frost and creams like heaps of snow with sugar-lump
hailstones'.*

As Britain found itself continually pitted militarily against France –
during the War of the Spanish Succession (1701–13), then during the
War of Austrian Succession (1740s) and, later, the Seven Years War –
patriotism extended to the kitchen. Criticism of French cuisine became
as much a political as a culinary statement, fanned by insecurity and a
smidgeon of sour grapes, for professional French chefs were still paid

---

* For anyone born before the 1970s, resonances of this kind of table setting are still often found on
the Christmas Day table with its dishes of vegetables intermixed with small plates of chocolates,
candied fruits and nuts, and its central arrangement of fruits, candles, crackers or flowers.

perhaps £60 a year, while plain English domestic cooks got £10 at the most. Despite the war of words, however, French chefs *were* still courted, and Continental influence still settled ineluctably among the pots and pans of British kitchens even as a robust repertoire of plainer dishes suited to Bulldog Britain continued to develop in parallel.

At the level of haute cuisine professional cooks like La Chapelle, Pierre Clouet and, later, Clouet's pupil William Verral began to move away from the pyramids of heaped meats, the dense ragouts and the thick, strong gravies of the Restoration court in favour of dishes with fewer ingredients, simple garnishes and thinner broths and sauces which they called 'essences' or 'quintessences'. Like Handel's music and the landscape gardening of 'Capability' Brown which swept away severe parterre gardens in favour of blurred boundaries, theirs was a style that reacted against strict rules of symmetry. The *bon ton* also adopted a studied informality so that ladies' chemises began to show at bosom and sleeve, and aprons were even worn over silk dresses – the ultimate irony since these were the very ladies who preferred to sit at cards while their housekeepers ran the show.*

The new generation of French chefs created recipes that leaned towards a single dominant flavour rather than the wild mixture of the haut goût, but the effort and the cash required to create the impression of simplicity could be enormous. While Brown's labourers moved hills with spade, cart and bucket to create artificial landscapes, chefs like La Chapelle continued to make cullises which took two pages to describe, using entire legs of veal, loins of ham and even champagne, simmering and scumming them for hours and straining them through silk to produce a smooth, rich sauce with a prodigious concentration of flavour.†

The books written by these professional chefs were successful, but they offered rather a vicarious thrill, conjuring up an illusion that was

---

* Among the well-to-do, gambling was something an obsession and fortunes were staked at the card tables. In the 1760s, John Montagu, 4th Earl of Sandwich, invented a snack of thin bread and butter with a filling of finely cut beef, veal or ham in order to continue to eat without leaving the gaming table, a fact that remains debatable but is generally accepted.

† Can it be a coincidence that this first super-refined, self-consciously *nouvelle cuisine* sprang from an acquisitive, self-interested, consuming generation in the same way that the flash, cash-rich Thatcherite generation embraced its own version more than two centuries later?

rarely practised. In the back of the British Library's copy of La Chappelle's *Modern Cook* is a handwritten recipe for something far simpler than its author's offerings: *ramakins*, or baked cheese, made from a paste of half a pound of mild cheese, an ounce of butter and an egg yolk, spread thickly on toast and browned with a red-hot salamander. Dishes like this were commonly served for supper, and there was nothing particularly French about them – indeed they would soon develop into the much-loved rabbits (sometimes known as rarebits today) as the great English cheese industries around Cheddar, Stilton and Cheshire expanded.*

Hedging his bets like Robert May before him, the royal chef Patrick Lamb proclaimed the virtues of unfussy 'English' cooking while compiling plenty of recipes for tricksy French dishes. Others began to voice their disapproval in more strident terms, criticising 'disguised foods' that took precedence over the substantial sirloin often set apart on a side table, 'banished in so ignominious manner, to make way for French kickshaws'. A pamphleteer in the late 1720s wrote of his horror on seeing a dozen marvellously fat roast partridges whipped off the spit by a rascally cook simply to be mashed into a thick cullis. The antipathy to French sophistication would grow: fifty years later, Sarah Hurst, a young tailor's daughter in Horsham, would write that she would rather starve than eat any more over-rich, French-style food.

The divide between town and country was widening, and much of the hostility towards the French style emanated from the rural gentry, who could not or did not want to compete in the teeming, materialist waters of London. The swaggering capital with its swelling merchant classes was a jungle of opportunities where the new 'West End' with its fine terraces distanced itself from the poverty of the fire-ruined medieval city. Beyond the city, farmland was changing under Jethro Tull's newfangled seed drill. There, squealed one pamphleteer, 'Honest' folk sat down to dine at noon, a world away from townsfolk easily seduced

---

* Daniel Defoe encountered all of these on his great tour – Cheddar, he noted, was around 6 to 8d a pound, while Cheshire was rarely more than tuppence ha'penny for the same quantity. Cheese consumption rocketed in the eighteenth century, but not all foreign tourists appreciated it. In 1782, Carl Moritz was given roasted Cheshire at an inn: '. . . in England, it seems, [it] is reckoned a good eating, but not unfortunately for me, I could not touch a bit of it.'

by expense and hard names, and from 'sumptuous Side Boards, Sycophants and little Sincerity'.

In the country, the provision of the larder was still a priority. There, practical middle-ranking housewives and housekeepers were less busy with cullises than with potting and pickling. Sides of meat, particularly pork and beef, were still submerged in a brine tub or rubbed with a mix of dry salt, saltpetre and just the right amount of rough brown sugar to counteract its toughening and pink-dying effects. William Ellis, the writer who gave puddings to his harvesters, stressed the importance of taking salt pork from the barrel with a fork rather than by hand, to save it from tainting. At Bilney Hall in Norfolk, Elizabeth Freke scribbled numerous recipes for pickling and salting in a notebook given to her by her daughter, tying sides of beef into great collars for preserving, drying gammons, and pickling her home-slaughtered pork in barrels of brine salty enough for an egg to float in it until the meat turned what she called a lovely red colour 'without being rusty'.*

Freke had her eye fixed on the future – she potted venison, stored fruit sweetmeats, cordials, cheeses and biscuits for the winter, and kept a coffin in the dining room ready for her own death, filling it in the meantime with blankets. Typical of her era, she had a mania for pickling. Fish, walnuts, mushrooms, samphire, small cucumbers and oysters were all scalded, spiced and stored in jars of vinegar sealed with paper or leather, and even peaches, nectarines, apricots and apples were pickled. Ann Blencowe also pickled walnuts, mushrooms and lemons as a relish for salads and salted meat for several days before boiling and immersing it in a solution of vinegar, sharp wine and spices.

There was nothing new about delighting in fresh seasonal produce, but in the face of urban sharp practice, rampant food adulteration and the inexorably attenuating connection between towns and their food sources, the purity and plainness of country fare began increasingly to be eulogised. Matthew Bramble in Tobias Smollett's novel *Humphrey Clinker* (1771) relished his home-reared chickens, the game on his moors, and the trout and salmon in his streams, all eaten 'in four hours

---

* A process that would have horrified the satirist and poet Alexander Pope, one of the few British vegetarians to write in the *Guardian* of 1713 of his disgust at 'kitchens covered with blood and filled with the cries of creatures expiring in torture'.

after they are taken'. But he fumed at London bread – nothing but 'a deleterious paste, mixed up with chalk, alum, and bone-ashes' – and at the city population who knowingly exchanged wholesomeness for whiteness. He criticised London veal, bled until it was so tasteless 'that a man might dine as comfortably on a white fricasee of kid-skin gloves', and he excoriated the milk from overcrowded, filthy town dairies, peddled in open pails by dirty girls, 'the produce of faded cabbage-leaves and sour draff . . . frothed with bruised snails', or thickened with cheap flour into a bad likeness of cream. Adulteration was also potentially murderous: pickles and sweets were coloured green with toxic lead, and vinegar was faked with poisonous sulphuric or vitriolic acid.

Addressing themselves not to the urban élite but to the yeoman farm households of the counties, two men in particular vigorously promoted the advantages of simple rural self-sufficiency. Richard Bradley was the first Professor of Botany at Cambridge University, a horticulturist growing exotic wall-fruits, figs and unusual kidney beans in his gardens at Vauxhall, and the first journalist to write monthly gardening bulletins which made a point of seasonality in pamphlets called *General Treatises of Husbandry and Gardening*. He also wrote a recipe book aimed, he said, at farming families earning around £300 who aspired to the lives of gentlemen with incomes of £800. Bradley's *Country Housewife and Ladies Director* (published from 1727) included recipes for traditional collars of meat, cheeses, pies, potting and preserving, as well as less usual ones for smoked-fish sausages poached in white wine and herbs and eaten cold. He was a passionate believer in the little world of the garden and the farm as the core of society at a time when continuing enclosure was making the rural lower classes increasingly destitute, and his writing was infused with an enthusiasm for all growing plants, from the seed to the stomach.

One imagines him returning from the orchard or kitchen garden, his boots wet, his arms lush with greenery, his earthy hands filled with herbs, his mind coursing over their culinary possibilities. Paring down recipes to suit constrained budgets and limiting dinner to two courses with five simple dishes in each, Bradley's answer to coping without servants was to cut a hole in the centre of his table and fix a rotating plate in its place that would spin the dishes round to each guest;* the great advantage of this arrangement, he wrote, was that once the hostess had served the soup 'everyone is at Liberty to help themselves by turning the upper Table about'.

Along with his recipes for seasonal foods, home-slaughtered goose, jams and chutneys of plums and bullaces, Bradley was also – contrarily – the first to describe the successful cultivation of the pineapple and to publish a recipe for it. Stewing slices with sugar and sweet wine, he baked it in a pastry and served it, appropriately, with cream. The pineapple was still so rare and expensive that it inspired devotion, turning up as a decorative device on table and chair legs, gateposts, mirrors and ceramics. In London pineapples were hired out as centrepieces for dinner parties, passed between houses for weeks on end, and it may be for this reason that Bradley also concocted a recipe for pineapple marmalade, using up the over-ripe fruit by boiling it to a pulp with sugar, white wine and pippins.

A generation after Bradley, William Ellis's *Country Housewife's Family Companion* (1750) also targeted the rural smallholder, giving advice on fattening swans and geese and stressing the savings that keeping a pig could make. He considered it 'very ill Housewifery to buy Bacon or pickled Pork at shops (as is done by thousands) where there is a Conveniencey to prevent it, by feeding Swine at home . . . for if Servants cant live upon a Piece of Bacon or pickled Pork and a Pudding, or Apple Dumplins for Dinners and Supers, let them fast, I say'. But Ellis was also generous with his own farm workers: they breakfasted at four in the morning on bread, cheese, apple pie and small beer, and took milk or porridge, more bread and cheese and an apple pasty or cold minced meat at light; '. . . dinner is at one o'clock in the field with broad beans and bacon or pork one day and beef with carrots or turnips or cabbage or cucumbers or potatoes another day . . . 4 o'clock in the afternoon is what we call Cheesing time.'

Like Gervase Markham a century and a half before, Ellis gave

---

* Normally free-standing, these spinning devices were also known as dumb waiters and, in the twentieth century, lazy Susans.

fastidious instructions on essential kitchen tasks like bread-making, brewing and distilling, practices still not generally described in print. He explained how to preserve the yeast from beer barm, drying and then rolling it into thin logs with salt so that it would keep for a month, making it 'work' again by mixing it with warm water. It could also, he wrote, be submerged in water in a pitcher or close-covered stone bottle, the water changed regularly and the pot watched like a baby during frosts to keep it from harm. Alternatively, he kept back a piece of leaven about as big as a fist from the previous batch, pouring salt into a small hole in its centre and leaving it to dry in a box until it crumbled. He also described how to clean pigs' guts and how to hold open their necks with a whalebone in order to push the stuffing in with a clean napkin 'lest, forcing it with your hands, you break the Gut'.

Filling his pages with careful economies, Ellis encouraged his readers to keep the rendered fat from roasts for frying, for greasing cartwheels and for softening leather harnesses. He reminded them that meat for smoking should first be wrapped well in brown paper to protect it from the acrid fumes of the coal, and he faked Westphalia hams with bay-salt herbed with hyssop, winter savory, thyme and pennyroyal, smoking the meat with juniper wood. He made mock oysters from sheep's trotter meat, and he ignored the notion of fancy French food entirely, borrowing only the process of slow-cooked stews that transformed cheap cuts of meat into manna: braising ox cheeks and bones together for five hours with wine or ale, onions, herbs and lemon peel and adding, right at the end, a very English sauce of flour and butter.

Ellis and Bradley's cooking was reliant on what was home-produced, gathered from the back garden, smallholding and hedgerow, and it sidestepped class distinctions, for a carrot tasted as good pulled from the mud of a smallholding as it did from a kitchen garden on an important estate. Plain cooking, they both demonstrated, could be altered according to one's income: the less well off could make their pancakes with flour, milk and eggs or with water, frying them in lard and eating them without sugar; the rich could use butter and cream, adding sugar, sack, rosewater and nutmeg, while the gentry might add round slices of apples fried in butter. Like puddings, onions, celery, leeks, winter savory, carrots, beans and potatoes all made meat go further, and everyone ate them in a quantity directly proportionate to the state of their finances. Indeed, it appeared to the tourist Caesar de Saussure, visiting England in 1729, that the very wealthy ate no vegetables at all unless they were served with meat.

15

Good Gravy and Hooped Petticoats

*It being grown as unfashionable for a Book now to appear
in publick without a Preface, as for a Lady to appear at a
Ball without a Hoop-Petticoat, I shall conform to Custom
for Fashion sake*

— ELIZA SMITH

Throughout the eighteenth century, households that could not afford
French cooks or cooking came to form a growing audience for books
by women that contained unpretentious recipes cut to suit a less costly
cloth, for pickling and collaring rather than ragouts. Where Hannah
Woolley had led, plenty of female cooks with their eye on the
profitable middle market followed, with books like Mary Kettilby's
collection of recipes (1714) and Eliza Smith's *Compleat Housewife*
(1734) containing dishes ranging from shoulder of mutton with oysters
to marinaded leg of lamb with shallots, boiled fowl, cabbage puddings,
sponge biscuits and lemon cheesecake. These writers aimed at the rural
and urban gentry who had a taste for entertaining but whose budgets
were not elastic.

Such books confirmed the arrival of a golden age of domestic,
middle-class cookery. Here were vast cakes rich with the earthy
flavour of mace and saffron or flavoured with almonds, caraway seeds,
honey, orange or lemon and baked for up to four hours. Rice soups,
lamb pies, sides of bacon, roast meats, buttered vegetables and fruit
tarts were joined by general instructions for the maid or mistress at
market: how to taste butter from the middle, judge cheese by its
smooth coat and test the freshness of eggs by holding them up to the
light. From Leeds, Elizabeth Moxon's *English Housewifery* (1749) was
one of the first cookbooks to be published outside London; it too was

filled with straightforward recipes for puddings, roast lobster, beans and bacon, stewed breast of veal, green goose, young rabbits and stewed apples. This was the kind of food served, less elegantly, in eel-pie houses, in 'shilling ordinaries' offering traditional plates of beef shin, tripe, cow-heel, sausages or boiled beef and greens, and in town *alamode* shops that signalled their presence with signs promising 'hot every night'.

By the 1740s about 40 per cent of all women could read and England was the most literate nation in Europe, driving the establishment of new newspapers and providing a market for the ground-breaking novels of Defoe, Fielding, Richardson and Smollett. On his travels through Britain, the German Carl-Philip Moritz recorded that he had even come across a Derbyshire saddler quoting Homer and Virgil, for though books were still not cheap, many were pirated and sold second-hand, or printed in part-works like Fielding's *Joseph Andrews* (1742). Beside novels and newspapers, a veritable mania for cookbooks gripped the British public, and hundreds of new works appeared during the century. But two women – Hannah Glasse and, later, Elizabeth Raffald – would dominate the Georgian market for books which instructed in the 'plain English style'. Both wrote with an easy confidence, and both brought out new editions of their best-selling works with such regularity that they could lay claim to being the first culinary 'brands'.*

Hannah Glasse understood as well as anyone the need to lay out her wares, and the preface to her *Art of Cookery Made Plain and Easy*, first published in 1747, made typical claims for straightforwardness. She was also the ideological child of her namesake Hannah Woolley and claimed that her intention was 'to instruct the lower Sort', ordinary girls who would not understand 'the high polite stile'. Glasse promised straightforward language – bits of bacon, in other words, rather than *lardoons* – and she characterised French cooks as confidence tricksters who used six pounds of butter to fry twelve eggs: 'But if gentlemen will have French Cooks, they must pay for French tricks . . . so much is the

---

* Glasse was the originator of the phrase 'first case [skin] your hare', a phrase which not only became mangled in the retelling but that also came to be ascribed to that far more modern Queen of the Kitchen, Isabella Beeton.

blind folly of this age that they would rather be impos'd on by a French Booby than give encouragement to a good English Cook!'

Widowed and with a clutch of children to support, Glasse wrote from expediency and, like most of her contemporaries, stole recipes shamelessly from other books. What she clearly appreciated was that she must appeal to the rising crowd – more Mrs than Lady – of ordinary, if financially comfortable, townswomen, the kind who shopped for crockery in Mrs Ashburn's shop where Glasse's book was first sold. At 5s, *The Art of Cookery Made Plain and Easy* was an investment for women who wanted to slough off the burden of teaching their staff how to cook; Glasse promised that it would assist them in the culinary rat race, improving 'the Servants and [saving] the Ladies a great deal of Trouble'. It quite quickly appeared in a 3s version, more affordable but still three weeks' wages for a hired female cook.*

Believing that her readers had enough practical common sense to know how to lay a table, Glasse decided against including the kind of engravings that were appearing in books by professional male chefs. Instead, she discussed how to substitute sprats and salt for anchovies and explained the startling innovation dating from the late 1720s of using eggs rather than yeast to make cakes rise – beating the whites hard – and firmly reminded her readers that there must now be no dawdling between the bowl and the oven. Her 'rich cakes' were so large that they took some four hours in a 'quick oven'. Glasse made her own vermicelli from an egg-and-flour base and offered a handful of substitutes for French cullises and essences, though, as her critics were quick to point out, even these were by no means cheap, requiring half a pound of bacon, a pound of veal in slices, sixpence worth of beef, a pigeon, morels and truffles, carrots, onions, sweet herbs and spices – and 'you may also add an old cock beat to pieces'. Nor could Glasse entirely help herself from bowing to the age-old social pressure for a certain amount of culinary grandeur, including recipes for hostesses who wanted to present alamode dishes with recherché ingredients like truffles, cockscombs and morels – even though these were the kinds of dishes that, higher up the social scale, were already becoming rather

---

* A shilling was still a week's wages for a woman cook.

The frontispiece from Hannah Glasse's bestselling *Art of Cookery Made Plain and Easy*, this edition circa 1775, which aimed to appeal to mistress and servant alike. Here the mistress has copied out a recipe for the cook to produce.

passé. Her 'Beef a la Daub' browned a buttock, or rump, in butter and stewed it for four hours with stock, pepper, cloves, mace and herbs, garnishing it with an outlandish mix of sweetbreads, truffles and morels, palates, artichoke hearts, mushrooms and fried forcemeat 'fingers'.

What set Glasse apart were her careful judgement and her complicit, galvanising style. There was a randomness about the order of her recipes, but she timed them to the very minute, giving specific weights and measures and scrupulous directions for all the basic culinary principles like roasting and boiling. Nothing escaped her attention as she described how meat should never be dropped into boiling water but brought slowly to a simmer from cold. She explained how to make fires bright and cautioned the cook not to fuss over them but to leave them alone lest the raked ashes settled over the meat or fell back into the dripping pan. Roast beef, she wrote, should be cooked for about ten minutes to the pound until it had a caramel crust and a pink centre; pork needed longer; turkey breasts were papered to stop them scorching; and steaks for grilling were cut to a maximum thickness of half an inch, absolutely not to be turned until they were properly done on one side.

Glasse was clear, concise and comprehensive with the common sense and practicality that made the Yorkshire pudding possible. Taking her cue from French chefs, she expanded the repertoire of egg dishes, buttering (or scrambling) them with quantities of butter and thick cream, mixing them with tripe or celery, serving them with scalded lettuce garnished with orange or frying them in deep oil. Sometimes she did get it wrong: her recipe for omelettes, or *amulets*, stirred eggs into warming cream and would have resulted in custardy failure.

Her book was suffused with a very 'British' kind of cooking. Her roast ham or gammon – with its fat removed, soaked in and basted with sweet canary wine and finally crisped with a bread, parsley and butter crust – is not unlike many modern recipes, and her jugged hare, boiled for three hours in an earthenware pot with nothing but its own juices, bacon, mace, onion and herbs, would not be out of place on the menu of a proper country restaurant today. She left out no standard favourite: scotch collops bashed with a rolling pin, dipped in yolks and fried brown with a gravy of fine mushrooms, wine, egg and cream;

stewed ox palates simmered softly; hashes – or slices – of meats with capers, gherkins and shallots; beef olives made of thin rump steaks rolled around veal forcemeat, egged, breaded and roasted or fried brown in French butter.

Glasse also included plenty of recipes for traditional English pastry work, like her Christmas pie made from a pigeon, a fowl, a goose and a turkey all packed into a strong crust designed to withstand being boxed and sent off as a gift. Savoury pies were the only foods to hold on tight to the medieval medley of meats, dried fruits and even sugar,* but she also included fruit pies which used fine puff pastes and updated the savoury pastry kickshaws of the previous century into small fruit creations that she baked or fried. Although she suggested using a teacup for cutting the pastry, ornate tin cutters were also appearing, some in the shape of holly and oak leaves, for garnishing such creations.

Glasse adored using nutmeg, mace and cloves, and for her sauces she reached for anchovies, horseradish, lemon, shallots, oysters and lots of cream. Meat was commonly rolled or stuffed: ox tongues were blanched, skinned, stuck with cloves and rolled up, and udders were filled with a forcemeat of veal and roasted, served with a sweet sauce in a separate cup. Most impressive of all, and reserved for company, was calf's head. Glasse offered recipes both for a standard 'hash' and for a 'surprise'. In both cases she carefully cleaned and boiled the head in water until its flesh was tender. For the hash, half the meat was sliced, mixed with spices and eggs, and kept warm by the fire ('and take care no Ashes fall into it') while the other went into a creamy sauce; both were served in an ornate pile garnished with the calf's eyes, little brain cakes, forcemeat balls and fried oysters. For the 'surprise', the head was painstakingly boned and stuffed with a ragout of sweetbreads, truffles, artichokes, asparagus, gravy, eggs, cream, wine, breadcrumbs and suet, baked and served with forcemeat balls and mushrooms. But Glasse's most stinging critic, her contemporary Anne Cook, rightly remarked

---

* In more remote areas of Britain, baking on stones or under inverted pots continued. At the end of the eighteenth century, Eliza Melrose described the Cornish and Irish making their pies under pottery cloches surrounded by hot cinders, letting them bake for up to six hours while they worked in the fields.

that the stuffing was not stiff enough and that the head would collapse, the filling streaming out of the nose, eyes and ears.

The heads and fleshy shoulders of cod or salmon were still favourites for 'company', simmered in barely bubbling water or a court bouillon of wine, stock and herbs and presented whole, served with a new table implement, the fish *trowel*. Although interest in fish had declined since the Reformation and most fishponds had been infilled or turned into ornamental waters, Glasse (like her French professional contemporaries) included plenty of recipes for them: carp was baked, tench fried, lobsters boiled and split or roasted (for far too long, by our standards), and all of them were sauced with mixtures of shrimp, oyster, anchovy and lobster and garnished with oysters, cockles, butter, wine or lemon. Small fish like smelt or roach were floured and fried brown in butter* and assiduously drained on a rack by the fire before being garnished with ever-present slices of lemon.

Glasse served horseradish with roast salmon or cut the fish into steaks and grilled it, saucing it with a mixture of butter and wine; she may have 'crimped' large fish as was then the cruel practice, slashing them diagonally with a sharp knife while they were still alive to make their flesh contract to a palatable firmness. Like most of her contemporaries, she also included instructions for a Dutch dish known as *water sokey* or *souchey*, boiling small freshwater fish like perch, gudgeon or even eels with parsley root and serving them in their broth with a separate dish of butter.

This 'dish of butter' or 'melted butter', a sloppy emulsion of butter and flour often with stock or cream, had become a standard accompaniment to fish, meat and vegetables, replacing the raw green sauces of the past, and it now dominated middle-class cooking. It was the base from which mornay, parsley, anchovy and all the other very British 'white' sauces sprang, commonly flavoured with shellfish or shellfish roe and with fennel, lemon or herbs, and it was the focus of persistent discussion and discontent. Glasse put it right at the beginning of her book, warning: '. . . you must be very careful; let your Saucepan be well tinn'd, take a Spoonful of cold water, a little Dust of Flour, and

---

* Later cooks would point out that it was better to fry fish in hog's lard or beef suet, as butter was apt to burn and often left fried fish soft rather than crispy.

your butter cut to Pieces: be sure to keep shaking your pan one way for fear it should oil; when it is all melted, let it boil, and it will be smooth and fine.'

Plain it certainly was, but not so easy; melted butter is one of those fundamental processes better demonstrated than described, which perhaps accounts for its apparently regular failure. Foreigners on the whole loathed its blandness, its proneness to oil and to lump, grateful at least when it was served in a separate cup.* They were by no means alone. In the mid-1750s a modest Sussex village shop-keeper called Thomas Turner was furious that the roast pig and good turnips prepared by his uncle's cook were ruined 'by almost swimming in butter and also a butter pond pudding and that justly called for there was almost butter enough in it to have drowned the pig'. Despite widespread grumbling, melted butter reigned at the Georgian middle-class table. Martha Bradley, almost the only published female cook in eighteenth-century England to espouse the French way of doing things, made clear her preference for vegetable-based sauces, especially lettuce, onion, celery and sorrel, but despite her clear and seductive manner, she went broadly unnoticed.

Directions in mid-Georgian recipe collections confirm that vegetables were coming of age, taking their place on the table as distinct, albeit subordinate side dishes. Peas partnered duck and pork; boiled beef was rarely without its carrots or calf's head its cabbage. Peas and lettuce were stewed together, cucumber sauce went with lamb, tongue and turnips with mutton, and cabbage with bacon. The Finnish traveller Per Kalm discovered a passion for sea kale – 'one of the best flavoured green vegetables which anyone can wish for' – eaten young and tender with butter. He also admired the samphire from the banks of the Thames at Gravesend – washed in vinegar, boiled, pickled and served

---

* So ubiquitous was melted butter on English tables that early the following century Napoleon's Foreign Minister Talleyrand famously complained that the British had plenty of religions but only one sauce, while the French were the other way around.

with steak – and the thriftiness of the women who harvested the
delicate leaves from turnips grown as animal fodder, serving them like
spinach with roast meats. Few published cooks omitted recipes for
celery fried with cream, eggs or herbs, for mushrooms stewed with
cream, or for boiling and buttering vegetables almost unknown today,
like alexanders, cardoons and scorzonera.* Fennel and celeriac had
both been brought to Britain by Dutch horticulturists around the time
of the Restoration, but the dearth of recipes for either clearly suggests
that neither had yet found favour.

As a result of all this fuss over green stuff, once again its cultivation increased dramatically. Richard Bradley estimated that market-
gardening around the edges of London – in Kensington and Chelsea in
particular – had grown eleven-fold between 1688 and the 1720s yet,
despite all the novel varieties, cooks concentrated on an ever-narrow-
ing selection. On big estates, as hothouse technology flourished, out-
of-season vegetables were considered the very last word in elegance,
sent down to London where they were purchased for small fortunes:
peas that were usually 6d could cost 7 guineas out of season for the
same weight, and kidney beans forced in hotbeds could command 2s a
dozen. Sacrificing taste at the altar of ostentation, out-of-season
vegetables were among the stars of the table.

At the other end of the scale, the potato was beginning its ascent.
Richard Bradley advocated its cultivation as a food crop for the poor,
while his contemporary the botanist and commercial nurseryman
Stephen Switzer wrote that while potatoes had once been considered
good only for 'the vulgar . . . Irishmen and clowns', they had now
become 'luxuriously polite'. The reality was that potatoes were popular with both the northern poor and the southern middle classes,
especially – as Per Kalm recorded – 'with the roast meat. They are
cooked as we cook turnips and either put on the same dish as the meat
or on a special one. A cup of melted butter stands beside it to pour on
to them.' William Ellis boiled potatoes with bacon or salt beef and

---

* Alexanders were an old-fashioned, bitterish, celery-like root that was about to be replaced by
celery; cardoons are artichoke-like thistles; scorzonera is black salsify. The word *vegetable* had
previously referred to any member of the plant kingdom but was first used in print by the
agriculturalist Arthur Young in 1767 to refer to the cultivation of specifically edible plants.

slipped off the skins, or put them in the dripping pan under the roast beef. He also boiled and sliced them to accompany herring or baked them raw in a pie with meat or with dried fruits. Hannah Glasse was among the first to do the seemingly obvious thing and fry potatoes in butter until brown, but she rather ruined the effect by sprinkling them with sugar. She also mashed them with cream, sugar and dried fruits and cooked them in boiled puddings or sweet pies. By mid-century mashed potato would find its ultimate refinement, spooned into scallop shells kept for the purpose and grilled with a salamander to become 'scalloped potatoes' – a dish that would enjoy a renaissance two centuries later during the 1970s freezer and prepared-foods boom.

Vegetable preparation was laborious: before they could be peeled, chopped and pared, the clinging mud had to be scraped off, and cookbooks emphasised the need for repeated washing in the deep kitchen sink* to remove bugs, caterpillars and dust. The worst were Jerusalem artichokes, arriving in deepest winter when one's hands cracked in the freezing water (mutton fat was used by cooks and maids as a salve) while the chill from flagged floors seeped into weary feet.

In general the cook was advised that vegetables were done when they sank to the bottom of the boiling pan. To pep up their colour, some added copper salts to the water or used a copper pan with vinegar for boiling, a habit that might have worked, but that also risked poisoning the diners with highly toxic verdigris. Georgian writers continuously warned their readers to carefully wash and dry their copper pans and ensure that they were kept well tinned to avoid the green killer, and there were similar warnings about storing pickles in pottery with lead glazes. John Farley's *London Art of Cookery* (1784) included a whole appendix on culinary poisons, and others recommended the use of silver pans for sauces, but these were, unsurprisingly, the preserve of the terribly rich.†

---

* Made of slate or stone, perhaps, but lined with wood or lead for preference, to minimise the breakage of china and glass.
† In Jonathan Swift's satirical *Directions for Servants* he reminded the slovenly cook to keep her pans clean, bright and well-tinned, asserting that 'if your butter when it is melted tastes of brass, it is your master's fault, who will not allow you a silver saucepan, besides . . . new tinning is very chargeable.'

Hannah Glasse believed that 'most people spoil garden Things by over boiling them; All things that are Green should have a little Crispness for if they are over boil'd they neighte have any wetness or beauty.' She always boiled green vegetables in their own pan in well-salted water, though she simmered cauliflowers in milk and water and cooked spinach only with the clinging drops of the water it was washed in. She gave little carrots about half an hour and 'Old sandwich Carrots . . . two hours'; potatoes were boiled and skinned as they cooled, and globe artichokes were boiled fast for an hour and a half, turned upside down so that any trapped dirt would fall out. Asparagus, cheap and plentiful, were cut evenly, their stalks scraped white, tied in little bundles, boiled until just tender and served on toast, as was broccoli – accompanied by melted butter or a vinaigrette and a garnish of nasturtium buds in place of capers.

Salads were eaten at the end of dinner, and Per Kalm described how only the succulent hearts of lettuce were mixed with salt, vinegar and oil, surprised that 'I never saw sugar used here with salad.' Cucumbers were sliced in succulent combination with lettuce, mint, sage and watercress, and a new supper dish grew out of the 'grand sallets' of the seventeenth century, the *salmagundi*, a large mounded salad layering minced cold meats with anchovies and pickles.* Glasse sometimes piled each ingredient into little interconnecting bowls raised higher than the other dishes in the centre of the table, and in the late 1750s John Thacker, the cook at Durham Cathedral and master of a cookery school in the town, made a showy salmagundi with layered white meats, minced eggs, capers, apple, lean ham or neat's tongue, pressing them down into a funnel which was then inverted and given a 'good thump on the dresser'. Once out, and assuming it retained its pointed shape, the dish was decorated with sliced lemon, small onions and anchovies.

As savoury toasts began to join the salad at the end of meals, Glasse was again among the first to give recipes for toasted-cheese rabbits, her 'Scotch rabbit' prepared as we would today, the toast for 'Welsh'

---

* Surviving still in Canada as Solomon Gundy.

rabbit rubbed with mustard, and 'English' rabbits made by dipping the bread into red wine before toasting and lathering it with melted cheese.

Two particular culinary developments were reflected in Glasse's pages, the first especially appropriate to the sea-faring age in which she lived. 'Portable Soup', also known as *glue*, was usually made from veal – sometimes beef – stock, reduced into a jelly that could be dried and stored. It was practical and, like the modern stock cube, would keep for years, easily reconstituted into a broth with the addition of hot water: ideal for both ships' captains and for cooks. Like the vilified French cullis, *glue* required quantities of meat – Ann Blencowe used a whole leg of veal to make a piece no bigger than her hand, and Glasse's recipe called for 50 pounds of beef to 9 gallons of water. It also took hours to prepare, but at a time where fresh stock could sour in the space of a hot summer's afternoon, it could be a saviour. Glasse left hers to dry on a fresh flannel and stored it in tin boxes, within two decades Mrs Raffald would spike hers with the pugnacious bite of cayenne pepper, the taste of Empire.

The second culinary evolution was curry. Glasse had been the first in England to publish a recipe for 'Currey the India way' in the earliest edition of her book (1747). Adding browned and pulverised coriander seeds to a simple stew of pieces of fowl or rabbit with onions, salt and butter, she observed that the sauce must be reduced until it was 'pretty thick'. She added other dishes savouring of the East: the *pillau* – or *pellow* – based on slow-cooked rice that 'must be very thick and dry and not boiled to a Mummy', and 'Mutton the Turkish way', a stew of mutton with rice, turnips and ginger. Curry was the taste of the arrogant nabobs returning from positions with the East India Company, and as it grew more popular, Glasse updated her work, including in the fifth edition (1755) a recipe for 'India Pickle' that used a gallon of vinegar, a pound of garlic, long pepper, mustard seed, ginger and turmeric.

From calf's head to curry, Hannah Glasse's *Art of Cookery Made Plain and Easy* steered a careful middle ground between hostesses aping the grand manner or curious for novelties and squires or their wives whose main interest was in a plain mutton chop. As the regularly updated editions of her great work showed, mid-Georgian Britain was a society once again throwing open its arms to the exotica of an unfolding world.

16

Brave Stomachs

*'Once,' said the Mock Turtle at last, with a deep sigh, 'I
was a real Turtle'*

— LEWIS CARROLL

Into Britain's widening arms flew one particular colonial import that
would become one of the most unforgettable elements of Georgian
dining. From the moment someone discovered that the West Indian
green sea turtle, a gentle beast weighing between 60 and 100 pounds,
could survive transportation to England in the water tanks of ships, a
turtle dinner became a byword for success, the venison of the middle
classes. The first recipe came in 1727 from Richard Bradley via 'a
Barbadoes Lady'. It involved laying the flesh in salt water for two
hours, sticking it with cloves, and roasting it with a baste of wine and
lemon juice, crisping the outside with flour and breadcrumbs and
serving it with lemon peel and a little sugar, the gelatinous green fat
rendered into a sauce. Bradley also used turtle meat in a pie with cloves,
herbs, lemons, olive oil, white wine and its much-prized, unguent fat.

The fact that no turtle recipe was included in Glasse's book until
its fifth edition in 1755 is a good indication of the dish's progress to
popularity. In fact, Bradley's roast turtle sounds more delicious than
the classic treatment that followed in which the flesh was made into a
pretty insipid soup lifted only by copious amounts of Madeira,
lemon pickle, cayenne pepper and anchovies, served in a great ornate
tureen or in its own *callepash*, or upper shell. One shell still hangs on
the wall over the original roasting ranges in the kitchens at Wolsey's
Christchurch in Oxford, a forgotten relic of Georgian and Victorian
ostentation.

A turtle dinner was not an easy production, typically taking at least eight hours to prepare, so that the recipes that used up every part of the reptile often covered several pages, typically observing the importance of killing 'your Turtle the Night before you want it, or very Early next morning, that you may have all your Dishes going on at a Time'. What no one ever fully detailed was how you managed to hoist it up, secure it firmly and then cut off its extended head while the large turtle protested strenuously, without an army of brawny helpers.

Some cooks suggested starting two days in advance since, to complement the soup itself, six or seven other dishes were made from various parts of the turtle, designed to fill the spaces at the top, bottom and corners of the table. The flesh was sliced into collops, the guts stewed, the heart ragoued, the lights fricasséed, and the gravy alone 'for a Turtle a hundred weight [could] take two Legs of veal and two Shanks of beef'. It all took a cook 'equal to the task', one with the patience to clean out both shells, scrape the intestines and whiten them with lemon juice, make the broths and farces, guard against the dishes becoming slimy and poach the turtle eggs as garnishes. There can have been few domestic cooks who embarked upon the process with anything like equanimity.

With turtle dinners so much of the moment, it did not take long for recipes to begin to appear for faking, or 'mocking', them with a calf's head. It was still labour-intensive and far from cheap: the head had to be scalded, split and boned, a strong gravy made with cayenne (according to one cook, 'as much as will lie on a shilling'), and the whole lot served with sweetbreads, palates, the shredded tails and claws of lobsters, oysters, morels and truffles, plenty of Madeira, Lisbon and port wine, and lashings of butter to simulate the fat. Some even said that turtle soup was 'incomparably improved by leaving out the turtle and substituting a good calf's head'. By the turn of the century, the great French epicure Grimod de la Reynière was astounded that this 'supposed soup' had caught the interest even of the French, who 'adore novelties, and are always kind enough to envy those dishes which their neighbours prize at a far higher value than their worth. Such is the case with mock turtle soup, which has had Parisian tongues wagging for several years'.*

---

* A little over a century later the culinary world had changed to such a degree that the great Escoffier would suggest that turtle soup should be bought in tins.

In 1766, the newly built London Tavern in Bishopsgate Street constructed great tanks for keeping live turtles, and others followed suit, including the King's Head Tavern and the Shakespeare in Covent Garden. Already famous for its 40-pound turbots, the Shakespeare served around 6 pounds of live turtle per head at the shattering price of 3s 6d a pound – in total more than the poorest families might survive on for two weeks, or about half a craftsman's weekly wage.

In an age of sociability, Samuel Johnson declared taverns like the London, the King's Head and the Shakespeare to be the very arbiters of happiness. Parties and entertainments spilled out into public places, into the clubs that were developing out of the original coffee shops, and into inns and taverns, all vying with each other to produce the best foods and wines.* John Farley, stealing most of his recipes from other writers, made the food at the London Tavern famous and produced one of the first restaurant cookbooks, tempting diners to replicate his cooking in their own homes. As Edinburgh began to buzz with a modern and commercial spirit, the cellars of some of the houses were turned into public oyster bars where both men and women of standing occupied large tables covered with oysters, and pots of porter, brandy and rum punch. Edward Topham assured his correspondents that, despite appearances, these were not places of intrigue; the ladies, he wrote, were witty and lively, but they called for their coaches after dancing reels.

By the end of the 1760s Elizabeth Raffald was addressing a new generation of domestic cooks. Her *Experienced English Housekeeper – for the Use and Ease of Ladies, Housekeepers and Cooks etc* was so popular that it would remain in print for almost fifty years. Like Glasse, Raffald recognised that her book might be bought by

---

* Walpole spent more than £1,000 a year on food and wine at the most fashionable of Whig clubs, the Kit-Cat Club, founded in the 1720s. He spent more on chocolate there than he paid his housekeeper or cook in a single year. This fashion for eating out soon spread to France, from where, in the following century, the 'restaurant' would be re-introduced to Britain. Separate though many declared them to be, the French and British culinary traditions remained, in part at least, symbiotic.

housewives but was as likely to be used by housekeepers For while at the turn of the century Lady Mary Wortley Montagu and her friend Grisell Baillie had each taken carving and cookery lessons, 'polite' ladies were now fleeing as fast as they could from the kitchen to the parlour. As housekeepers took over the running of well-to-do houses, cooking began to be seen less as an honourable accomplishment than as a chore, beginning its descent down the social hierarchy.

An educated interest in food had clearly been a mark of taste in the early years of the century, but as the decades progressed the expression of appetite was considered, ironically, rather disgusting, so that in Fanny Burney's 1788 novel *Evangelina*, Lord Merton and his dissolute friends

> displayed so much knowledge of sauces and made dishes, and of the various methods of dressing the same things, that . . . it would be very difficult to determine, whether they were most to be distinguished as gluttons, or epicures. I should have been quite sick of their remarks, had I not been entertained by seeing that Lord Orville . . . not only read my sentiments, but, by his countenance, communicated to me his own.

Yet Raffald's success did in some measure confirm the feminisation of cooking after centuries of domination by professional males. She was well ordered, lucid and dependable, explaining how to make the kind of dishes that Middle England craved: shredded calves' feet, hot chicken pies and carrot puddings, poached eggs on toast, macaroni with Parmesan, and lettuce stewed in gravy and mint. She could, occasionally, be just a bit bizarre – her 'surprised' rabbit was indeed surprising, stuffed with a pudding, and 'when they are roasted, draw out the jaw bones and stick them in the Eyes to appear like horns.' But she was generally supremely practical, urging her readers to work slowly, to follow her recipes closely, and to keep their provisions and vegetables free from mould by careful storage.

Like Glasse, Raffald promised to be 'Instructor to the young and ignorant as it has been my chiefest Care to write in as plain a Style as possible'; there were French names, she warned, but it did not mean that the dishes themselves were expensive. Her book was not cheap at 6s – she too had a bevy of daughters to support – but it was an investment, filled with instructions for making preserves and wine vinegars or bottling sauces, giving the kind of clear and precise directions that many of her contemporaries failed to provide. She began the different sections of her book with general comments and advice, reminding her readers to get everything ready before they began, to cream the butter, beat the eggs, dry the fruits and seeds, and prepare the oven before starting on a cake. She was, characteristically, among the first writers to explain to her readers that wine should always be added to a dish while there was still some cooking to be done, to 'take off the rawness, for nothing can give a made Dish a more disagreeable Taste than raw Wine or fresh Anchovy'.

Typical of her generation, Raffald liked her vegetables crisp, was liberal with cayenne and with scraped horseradish, and did not count herself among the small band of brave cooks introducing garlic – unlike Sir John Whiteford's cook, who wrote, '. . . many people (more particularly in the country) have an aversion to the taste or smell of garlick. I nevertheless presume to say, that its effects are very good when used with moderation . . . Taste must direct'. Like Glasse and emphatically unlike La Chapelle's new purism, Mrs Raffald filled her dishes with forcemeat balls, pickled vegetables, mushrooms and artichoke bottoms; like the rest of Middle England, she stood for hours over her brown sauces, assiduously skimming every last droplet of fat from the surface. She did have a lovely turn of phrase, reserving the water from a raised-pie paste until the last minute so as not to 'make the Crust sad' – and she was an astute businesswoman, following the lead of glittering London shops to open her own establishment in Manchester selling high-class ready-prepared foods to those who could not be bothered to make them at home: New-castle salmon, Yorkshire ham, tongue, potted meats, cold suppers, confectionery and 'portable soups'. She seemed quite indefatigable, also setting up an agency for the supply of domestic servants and publishing the first street-and-trade directory for the city of Man-chester.

Recipes for using up leftovers were appearing for the first time in print, and, among directions for making for boiled neck of veal with onions, plum puddings, swine's cheek and pea soup, a growing preoccupation with frugality leapt from Raffald's pages. Few households still had the staff to finish off the remains of the family food; the shopkeeper Thomas Turner regularly recorded that his 'family at home dined on the remains of yesterday's dinner', even while he entertained his customers on neats' tongues and turnips. The last of the roast or boiled meat could be made into beef olives with a plain stuffing of bread, onion and suet; hashes were simple ways of reheating sliced leftovers; and toad-in-the-hole delightfully developed as a way of using up slices of cold meat in a blanket of puffed-up Yorkshire-pudding batter. Indian curries were also good for leftovers, generally using turmeric, ginger, stock, cream and, occasionally, a little lemon juice. As the taste for them spread inexorably, ready-mixed curry powders – from the 1780s – trounced the gentler flavours of mace and nutmeg so highly prized in the early decades of the century.

Raffald's recipes conclusively demonstrate that meat had not stirred from the core of well-to-do life. Winter-feeding and selective breeding had continued to improve livestock so that by the close of the century animals had doubled in size since the Middle Ages. And there was plenty of it. Butchers' meat was around thruppence a pound at mid-century – half the price of butter – and the 80,000 cattle that were driven to market in London in 1750 was set to increase to nearer a hundred thousand by 1800. Unsurprisingly, there were tourists who wrote that they did not 'believe that any Englishman who is his own master has ever eaten a dinner without meat'.

Despite the warnings of Dr William Buchan, whose *Domestic Medicine* (1769) had become something of a national medical bible, meat was such an addictive mainstay of the eighteenth-century middle-class diet that thousands began to suffer from bulging veins and mottled noses, from gout, kidney stones, dyspepsia, diabetes and degenerative diseases caused by eating too much animal protein and fat. Thomas Turner resolved to give it up for the sake of his health: 'to leave off during life . . . eating any sort of meat unless sometimes a bit of boiled lamb, mutton or veal, or chick, or any such harmless diet'. But even with so many caveats his resolution soon faltered. For him and for many, beef was the *ne plus ultra*. With Henry Fielding's 'Roast Beef of Old England' ringing in their ears, the Sublime Society of

Beefsteaks* tucked into enormous steaks, and Parson Woodford's final diary entry, some months before he died in 1803, was, appropriately, 'Roast Beef'. Foreign visitors still swooned at the British roast cooked rare in the middle while France continued to cook its roasts to the core.

In the 1760s, more than 80 per cent of the population still lived in the countryside, where squires, parsons and their families preferred the comfort of 'plain' food. At Houghton, Horace Walpole threw twice-yearly dinners at which the guests sat, according to Lord Harvey, 'up to the chin in beef, venison, geese, turkeys etc, and generally over the chin in claret, strong beer and punch'. But the medieval resonances surrounding food had shifted; meaty profusion was less about over-arching power than about the more provincial preoccupations of stability and guiltless comfort. Stoutness now demonstrated not only prosperity but rock-solid strength and unwavering resolve.

This was life in the spirit of 'Farmer' George III, a small, dutiful man with a taste for home, family and economy and for morality over intellect, a King reputed to like toasting muffins at the fire while Queen Charlotte fried sprats. When foreigners noted that the aristocracy and gentry in the country all lived like little kings, it was as much a comment on the bourgeois monarch as a record of rural prosperity. And when Samuel Pegge rediscovered and published the *Forme of Cury* in the 1780s, the hostile reaction to this gallimaufry of 'disguised', French-inspired dishes said as much about the late eighteenth-century preference for culinary plainness as about the medieval manuscript.

The dinner enjoyed by the Cornish clergyman John Penrose on his visit to Bath twenty years earlier had therefore been ideal:

First course – pair of large soals, one fried with Parsley, the other boiled, the Dish garnished with Horse radish. At the lower end, roast rump of beef. On one side crab-sauce and melted Butter, the othere side Cucumbers, A Sallet in the middle.

---

* Formed in a room at the top of the Covent Garden Theatre in 1735 to protest against French cooking. The members, called 'steaks', assembled weekly to devour grilled steaks weighing between 3 and 5 pounds with baked potatoes and beetroot. Members included George IV when he was Prince of Wales, his portly brothers the dukes of Clarence and of Sussex, William Hogarth, Colley Cibber and David Garrick.

Second course – at Higher end 6 pigeons roasted lower end a large dishe of Asparagus; one side a goose-berry Tart, the other side an hundred large Prawns Afterwards – Cheese sound and rotten . . . like Stilton . . . Pats of butter, Radishes . . . a dish of sweetmeats viz 2 preserved Pine apples in a high Glass, which stood in a salver of preserved peaches, preserved in Brandy . . .

Dr Johnson, by his own admission a man who minded his belly very studiously, found to his delight on his tour of the Hebrides that Scotland might be isolated and impoverished, its poor living on potatoes, but its wildfowl, moor game and fish were bountiful and delicious. Unlike Fynes Moryson almost two centuries before, Johnson's contemporary Edward Topham also enjoyed delectable Scottish dishes of salted cod (*cabbiclow*) boiled with parsley and horseradish and of friar's chicken – pieces of fowl boiled with parsley, cinnamon and eggs in a strong beef soup. But just as Johnson had found the fish-fed geese to be quite rank,* Topham also described a dinner of Scottish food that left him 'almost famished with hunger and tantalised to death of Scottish haggis . . . cocky leaky . . . sheep's head . . . and Solan Goose', or gannet. The haggis made his stomach lurch: '. . . my Politeness got the better of my delicacy, and I was prevailed on to taste it; but I could go no farther.'

Further south, in the village of Weston Longeville in Norfolk, the life of Parson James Woodforde marched to the steady pulse of marriages and burials, social visits, fishing, cribbage and hiring-fairs, all recorded in his inimitable diary. Woodforde detailed the day his niece was overcome by charcoal fumes when making jam, as well as his irritation at his maids for breaking china bowls and at the fire in the kitchen chimney. He also recorded the detail of most of his meals, which were usually a single course of several dishes. In common with

---

* In a 500-year-old tradition, men still scale the 300-foot cliffs of Sula Sgeir north-west of Lewis to collect thousands of baby gannets – *guga* – from precarious ledges, salting and barrelling them on the spot. Before cooking, they are scrubbed to remove the grease and salt and boiled in clean water, constantly skimming off the grease. They are then roasted. While coastal communities survived on these gannets for generations, they have a limited gastronomic appeal: apart from the people of Ness, most now find them greasily revolting with a taste something like fishy beef. The smell of boiling guga is said to be repugnant.

many of his class, anything too sophisticated made him uncomfortable so that dining with a neighbour he found 'most of the things spoiled by being so frenchified in dressing'. For his own guests he was more likely to serve 'a large Cod, a Chine of Mutton, some Soup, a Chicken Pye, Puddings and Roots etc. 2nd course Pidgeons and Asparagus. A Fillet of Veal with Mushrooms and high Sauce with it, rosted Sweetbreads, hot Lobster, Apricot tart and in the Middle a Pyramid of Syllabubs and Jellies . . . Dessert of Fruit after Dinner and Madeira, White Port and red to drink as Wine'. When his niece Nancy overate, he dosed her with a pint of brandy and warm water, water gruel and a rhubarb-and-ginger cordial, and when he gorged on currant tarts and cream, he was reduced to 'purging and vomiting almost the whole day'.

In Woodforde's culinary circle, brawn had been transformed into the dish we know today, a preparation of meat from the head and feet of a young pig, moulded with its own jelly, and the alamode beef that had been such a novel delicacy only half a century before was now a relatively simple stew with carrots and spices, served cold with mushroom pickle; haricot mutton – a stew made of diced neck of mutton, floured, browned and braised with gravy, turnips and carrots – was a favourite. But although tripe, kidneys and other innards were still widely used, they were descending the social scale, now known as offal because they literally fell off during butchering.

By the second half of the eighteenth century, thick gravies and cullises were giving way to *catsups*, or *catchups*: home-prepared sauces used as instant flavours for melted butter, or to enliven a stew or made dish. Hannah Glasse had given an early recipe for a sauce of anchovies, shallots, stale beer, mushrooms and spices all boiled together and reduced. Walnut catsup was now popular, and mushroom catsup was made from large mushrooms left to lie in salt overnight, then stewed and strained through a coarse cloth, the liquid simmered with ginger, pepper, mace and cloves until it had reduced to a thick syrup.

Home-made catsups were becoming culinary mainstays for the domestic cook. Elizabeth Raffald used lemon pickle and gravy browning as the foundation for many of her recipes, finding them so essential to her work that she opened her book with directions on how to make them, promising that they were far cheaper 'than Cullis, which is extravagant'. It still took twenty-four lemons to make her renowned pickle, rubbing them with a lump of ragged salt, steeping them in white-wine vinegar with cloves, mace, nutmeg, garlic and mustard seed, and leaving the whole lot by the side of the fire for five days. Once it had stood in the cool larder for three months, the pickle could be sieved and bottled,* perfect for melted butter or fish sauces so long as it was added *before* the cream to prevent it curdling.

Raffald's 'browning' was made with caramelised sugar, butter, red wine, shallots and spices, and her green-walnut catchup used anchovies, horseradish and fiery cayenne. Both it and her lemon pickle were sold at her Manchester shop, predating the commercially bottled condiments produced by Peter Harvey† and his sister Elizabeth Lazenby at the end of the century. They caught on so fast that by the 1780s home-made catsups in bottles were being slipped into cruet frames at the dining table, adorned with silver neck labels.‡ They were useful, but catsups did also mark the beginning of a decline in culinary skills in Britain and the relinquishing of centuries of pride in the slow refinement of a perfect sauce. Early in the following century the Irish novelist Lady Morgan would mourn the loss, complaining that 'fines herbes are no longer known in the English garden, gravies made with water, entrées dressed with cream and hard eggs, soups (great occasions) flavoured with catsups and cayenne'.

---

* Corks were now appearing for stopping bottles; the British were the first to use them for wine, allowing it to age properly.
† Harvey's Anchovy Sauce was produced from the end of the century; it was made from anchovies, walnut pickle, soy and shallot, cayenne, three heads of garlic, a gallon of vinegar and cochineal for colouring.
‡ Imported from China and Malaya, salty soy sauce was popular, though few had any idea how it was made. The professional cook Martha Bradley believed it was made from a purplish mushroom with a wrinkled surface.

Drunkenness

Silence, scientific minds and courage, wrote Caesar de Saussure in 1725, characterised the British, along with a contempt for foreigners and an arrogant self-regard. In London, the greatest commercial city in the world, he saw wealth and plenty wherever he looked. Manners and taste were refined, political freedoms relished, furniture fine and delicate, and fabrics sumptuous. There was vibrancy in the thriving theatres, the opera, the pantomimes, the taverns and the tea gardens, and in the midst of it all was a kind of full-blooded, roaring life characterised by hearty eating, swearing, gambling and prodigious drunkenness. 'The English,' he wrote, 'are Almighty Swearers.'[*]

Throughout the eighteenth century it is true to say that there was an unprecedented amount of drinking, but with water still mostly contaminated and therefore out of the question and ale no longer a household staple, the majority turned to wine and spirits to quench their thirst. From the 1690s on, it was the fashion to drink endless toasts at dinner, necessitating quantities of wine and an appreciation of

---

[*] De Saussure 1725.

confounding etiquette. Toasts quite befuddled Henri Misson until he realised that anyone could jump up and propose one to another guest at any moment: the subject of the toast had to remain very still even if mid-gulp and had then to make a great bow without dipping his 'Peruke in the Sauce'. Misson found it all, as we might, faintly ridiculous.

Wine was brought to the dinner table only at the close of the meal, the ladies taking a glass or two and withdrawing to their tea, gossip and games while the gentlemen lingered. To many foreigners this was another surprising custom, and though La Rochefoucauld enjoyed the relative freedom of these moments in the mid-1880s, he was appalled by the risqué conversation and the chamber pots commonly stored in the sideboards.* Toasting gradually went out of style; within four years of La Rochefoucauld's visit, a bright little etiquette book was warning that they were already considered vulgar and silly.

At the start of the eighteenth century there had been 207 inns, 447 taverns, 5,857 ale houses and 8,659 brandy shops in London, and more than eleven million gallons of spirits were drunk a year – or about 7 gallons for each adult. Although it was rarely brewed at home, beer did still come in various strengths. Thick black porter cost about thrupp-ence a pot, and there were clear ales that could cost as much as 18d a bottle, some of them 'as transparent as fine old wines'. De Saussure reckoned that 'more grain is consumed in England for making beer than for making bread', much of it clarified with isinglass or adult-erated with dangerous copperas (ferrous sulphate) to make its head froth 'like a cauliflower'.

Wine was imported from France, Portugal, Spain, the Rhine, the Canaries and Madeira – there was even sweet Tokay from Hungary – though the supply was constantly interrupted by wars, and French wines attracted particularly heavy taxes. This encouraged the middle classes to develop a taste for port while the rich stuck to champagne and French Hennessy or Martell brandies. Yet none of these were quite sufficient for a society that craved novelty.

---

* He noted, '. . . the sideboard too is furnished with a number of chamber pots and it is common practice to relieve oneself . . . one has no kind of concealment and the practice strikes me as most indecent.'

The most popular new drink was punch. Introduced by East India merchants and served in ornate silver or decorated china bowls, punch had five main ingredients (hence its name – *panch* means 'five' in Hindi): brandy, wine, lemons (even better, rare limes from the West Indies), sugar and spice. Sometimes rum, or *rumbullion*, made from the fermented residues of the sugar-refining process – molasses – was also added. Unsurprisingly, the mixture was incredibly potent. Like Scandinavian *glögg* (claret, aquavit, orange peel, sugar and sometimes raisins), British punch was also taken hot in winter with an aromatic scraping of nutmeg. Widely drunk though it was, for some reason lost to history punch became associated with the thrusting Whig party, while sack and claret remained the favoured tipple of the Tory old guard.

However, the spirituous scourge of the age came not from home-grown liquors but from Dutch genever, or gin. Made of corn spirits and flavoured with the juniper that gave it its name, gin was also brewed in grimy back alleys, but even the imports were cheap and potent enough to ruin the poor. From the 1690s and particularly through the 1730s and '40s, gin became a craze, sold for a penny a dram or on spirit-soaked rags, beggaring its victims, driving them to crime and prostitution, and contributing to a surge in infant mortality.

Between 1700 and 1735, imports of gin rose from half a million gallons to five million, a figure not including the quantities that were smuggled or faked, so that Henry Fielding wrote of it as 'the principal sustenance (if it may be so called) of more than 100 thousand people'. Slums collapsed in an orgy of lethal drinking, foundling hospitals were established simply to deal with the plight of babies and children orphaned or abandoned by their intoxicated, syphilitic parents, and when the government tried to impose a tax on spirits, there were riots. Gin continued to be sold under the name of 'Parliamentary Brandy'; only when the price of grain rose in the 1750s, taking the price of gin with it, were the poor forced to turn elsewhere for comfort and oblivion.

At balls and assemblies, chilled waters were flavoured with raspberry, apricot, currant, bergamot, orange flower, peach or pear; *orgeat* was made of pounded almonds; and potent lemonades were fortified with brandy or white wine and sugar. Arrack came from the Indies, distilled from rice or coconuts, and ratafia – a brandy flavoured with peach or apricot kernels – complemented the same taste in biscuits and baking. Few ladies or their housekeepers now practised the art of distillation, though Elizabeth Raffald did give recipes for lemon and orange wines (in reality, cordials mixed with brandy and sugar) and for home-made wines made from fruit, cowslip, elder and even walnuts. Jacob Schweppe's artificial mineral waters, developed in the 1740s, would not arrive in Britain from Germany until the closing decades of the century, so the well-off did penance at the thriving spas, gagging on their sulphurous waters. As far as De Saussure could see, it was 'not the lower populace alone that is addicted to drunkenness. 'Debauch,' he wrote, '[ran] riot with an unblushing countenance.' In Thomas Turner's Sussex shop, his customers spent so much on 'spirituous liquors' that they often had 'little money to spare to buy what is really necessary'.

It seems that just about everyone spoke plainly, played hard and drank alcohol – heavily. An Edinburgh student, Sylas Neville, recorded that he had 'Dined at the Fox and Goose, Musselburgh . . . Lucky I did not go yesterday, as a company of only 8 or 10 . . . drank 27 bottles of claret and 12 bottles of port, besides Punch, and were all beastly drunk'. La Rochefoucauld believed the damp climate was to blame, while Frederick Eden noted mildly in his report on the state of the poor at the close of the century that 'temperance does not appear to be an English virtue'.

17

Taste

Everyone talks of Taste, or the taste, or the good Taste,
but few affix any idea to the term

— EDWARD TOPHAM

Taste, no longer just about the palate, had become a social concept in a modern society overflowing with material goods and opportunities for financial gain. It was the very fact that taste was uncertain, varying as fast as it was established, that kept the middle classes and their servants busy. In a theatre of envy that propelled society onwards and upwards, no sooner had you fixed on the 'proper' way of doing things 'than you are obliged to despise what you have been labouring at'.

Nowhere were the fluctuating concepts of taste more obvious than in the 'dining room', a new and – for many – vulgar expression that just made it into Dr Johnson's 1755 dictionary. The dinner hour was also becoming a social signpost, pushed back until six o'clock in town while in the country, as the novelist Fanny Burney wrote in the 1760s, '. . . we breakfast always at 10 . . . we dine precisely at 2, drink tea about 6 and sup exactly at 9.' In the 1780s Parson Woodforde, in common with Jane Austen's family at Steventon, habitually dined at three o'clock, but only ten years later the Austens were dining at five. With habits in such flux, it was easy to be caught out: the novelist Maria Edgeworth assumed that her friends the Hopes maintained town hours even in the country; she was wrong and kept them all waiting.*

---

* So fast were fashions moving that between the first (1740) and later editions of his novel *Pamela*, Samuel Richardson changed his text to accept that Mr B's habit of dining at two o'clock and supping at eight had become 'old-fashioned'.

Horace Walpole, arch critic of the folly of modern manners, jeered at the affectation of Londoners who went out of their way to be late, arriving at tea gardens like Ranelagh two hours after they closed and supping at three in the morning. Others mocked the fact that town suppers were becoming so late that they were in danger of getting confused with breakfast, and some began to plug the widening gap between breakfast and dinner with 'lunch' – another new word for Johnson's dictionary, defined as 'as much food as one's hand can hold'.

The fashion for afternoon tea with cakes may also have developed in response to the lateness of dinner, for although the Duchess of Bedford would claim in the middle of the next century that she had been responsible for starting the fashion, it seems clear that it had begun well before her time. When Thomas Twining opened his first tea shop for ladies in London in 1717, various different leaves were being shipped directly from Canton by the East India Company – among them Congo, Souchon and Pekoe – and consumption had already more than quadrupled since the start of the century. The Georgians were, in truth, tea-obsessed and by mid-century they were flaunting fine crockery now sporting handles and flattened saucers. As tea clippers raced back and forth across the oceans to fulfil demand, annual consumption rose from around quarter of a million pounds in 1725 to twenty million pounds by the end of the century.

Encouraged by popular tea gardens and falling prices, the tea habit spread to the middle classes and on down the social scale until the promise of two cups a day was even included in servants' wage agreements. Dr Johnson was so addicted that he admitted his kettle rarely had time to cool. The philanthropist and hospital founder Jonas Hanway (coincidentally said to have been the first man habitually to carry an umbrella) attacked the addiction, declaring that 'your very chambermaids have lost their bloom', but when Pitt's government reduced domestic duty from 100 per cent to 12.5 per cent in 1784, consumption surged.*

---

* Parliament's stubborn insistence on its right to tax its colonies – including thruppence a pound on tea – so enraged the Americans that when a tea surplus was exported duty-free in 1773 it was destroyed at the infamous Boston Tea Party, signalling that the struggle for independence had begun in earnest.

Of all European countries only Russia took to tea with the same avidity as the British. Coffee, on the other hand, did not fare so well, and eighteenth-century tourists excoriated Britain's apparent inability to make it palatable. In 1782 Carl-Philip Moritz wrote, 'I would advise anybody who wants to drink coffee in England to mention before hand how many cupfuls should be made from half an ounce, otherwise he will get an atrocious mess of brown water set before him such as I have not yet been able to avoid in spite of all my admonitions.' Such criticism would continue for centuries; somehow coffee was never destined to be one of Britain's culinary successes.

As dinners shifted further into the evening, the etiquette of the dining room was also in constant modulation. At the start of the century, hostesses were kept so busy helping their guests that they hardly had time to eat themselves, but by mid-century studied informality had become fashionable: servants were dismissed for small groups who wished to dine flirtatiously at *soupers intimes*, and at bigger dinners the host and hostess were more inclined to leave their guests to help themselves. In the 1750s, the cookery writer Alice Smith accepted that 'our grandmothers made too much racke with their guests' but saw that 'we are in danger of making too little'. Counselling a middle course, she thought it better that 'the truly polite lady take some notice of these things, though not too much, and let her praise a dish that is good, though her own'.

Then, during the 1770s, the code of manners once again became so rigidly prescribed that La Rochefoucauld was tempted to think that stiff evening dress and hierarchical progression into dinner 'was done for a joke'. He wearied of four- or five-hour-long dinners punctuated continually by the host or hostess asking 'whether you like the food, and [pressing] you to eat more'. Amid all this formality, men and women began to be seated next to each other rather than at separate ends of the table, and once again the assistance of etiquette manuals was required. John Trusler, the first to record the new style of 'promis-cuous seating' in 1788, also gave discreet advice about what to do if you needed to pee during dinner: '. . . steal away silently and return without announcing where you have been.'

Reflecting the changes in manners, the design and decoration of the dining room also evolved, particularly under the influence of architects like Robert Adam whose mannered Rococo rooms were 'fitted up in elegance and splendour'. Damasks and tapestries that 'retain[ed] the smell of the victuals' were removed in favour of stuccoed walls, large pier mirrors between the windows, and gilded or painted sideboards and ceilings – the kind of rooms we can still see at houses like Osterley Park outside London and Saltram in Devon. Often, the several small tables of old were replaced with one big, permanent table made up of several leaves that could seat upwards of a dozen guests: Walpole was one of the first to install one – extending to 16 feet – at his mansion in Norfolk. Opinion was divided of course: parsimonious Mrs Norris in Jane Austen's *Mansfield Park* (1814) considered these great tables absurd, 'filling up the room so dreadfully!!' But they were particularly useful for a style of table decoration and arrangement that would breathe a whole new lease of life into dessert.

As with ladies' extravagant, flower-filled hairstyles, from the 1760s table decoration went horticultural and mimicked the grottoes, temples and follies of the modish landscape park. Known as table plateaus, swirling patterns of coloured sand or sugar were arranged as centre-pieces, often on long, mirrored panels. Hannah Glasse described one in her 1760 book devoted to confectionery: a mirrored panel that came in five parts, joined by 'gravel walks, hedges and a variety of things, as little Chinese temples for the middle or any other pretty ornament, which . . . are to be bought at the confectioners and will serve year after year'.

The effect was amplified by pyramids of fruit (real or made of sugar with real stalks and stones) and figures made of sugar or porcelain – 'puerile puppet shows', according to Walpole, who grumbled that 'jellies, biscuits, sugar plums and cream have long since given way to harlequins, gondoliers, Turks, Chinese and shepherdesses of Saxon China'. The vogue was so influential that within a generation it had arrived in the counties: dining with the Bishop of Norwich in 1783, Woodforde found the table dressed as 'the most beautiful Artificial garden . . . one of the prettiest things I ever saw, about a yard long and

about eighteen inches wide, in the middle was a high round temple . . .'
Within a decade, he was spending sixpence on two figures in 'Plaister
of Paris, one of the King of Prussia and another of the present Duke of
York, both on horseback and coloured', for his own table.

All this decorative fanfare was designed to show off the new highlight of the meal – the dessert, a glorious array of sweet foods presented
in glasses and porcelain baskets, or on gorgeous plates and silver
salvers. Fuelled partly by an increase in tea drinking and partly by this
show-stopping final course, consumption of sugar rose from 8 pounds
a head in 1720 to 13 pounds by the end of the century, and the price fell
to around sixpence a pound – firmly and finally consigning raisins to
the culinary back seat.

The favourites at dessert were lemon creams, orange custards and
brandied fruits. Savoy or French biscuits were scattered along the table
with others made with almond and ratafia, lemon, orange and even
pepper, all designed to provide a crunchy contrast to fruits, compotes,
creams and ices. Celery seeds, cardamoms and chips of orris root had
joined the list of ingredients used for comfits – increasingly known as
nonpareils – and Elizabeth Raffald explained how to spin sugar into
decorative webs, boiling it to the cracking point and drawing it out on
the point of a knife so that threads formed over an upturned bowl,
warning her readers not to stand for too long in front of the fire for fear
of fainting.

Cream was the Georgians' darling, and new metal whisks made its
transformation into desserts easier for the cook. Some were subtly
flavoured by rubbing citrus peel with a knob of rough sugar before
crumbling it into a dish or by tying a piece of peel to the whisk itself.
Chocolate also nudged its way into creams, along with seductively
scented essences like vanilla, bergamot, burnt almonds and coffee.
Junkets were produced by curdling milk, flavouring it with flower
waters, sweetening it, setting it with rennet and decorating the dish
with comfits. Everything was in place for the final development of the
trifle – or *whim wham* – a supposedly inconsequential mixture of
biscuit, jelly and cream concealing a powerfully alcoholic punch that
would become one of the great classics of the British table.

As early as 1747 Hannah Glasse had developed the idea of a trifle
with a recipe for 'Floating Island', layering sack-flavoured, thickened

cream with slices of French roll and currant jelly, finishing it off with a froth of whipped cream decorated with sweetmeats: 'very pretty in the middle of the table with candles round it, and you may make it in as many different colours as you fancy'. By the 1760s Elizabeth Raffald's recipe was substituting Naples biscuits for bread and adorning the top with a rural idyll of sheep and swans fashioned from sugar, which, she warned, must be put on at the very last minute 'or they will sink into it'. The trifle had arrived.

With so much emphasis on creams, *darying* became a hobby for the likes of Queen Charlotte and the duchesses of Bedford, Rutland and Norfolk, who all had enchanting dairies built – rather like Marie-Antoinette's model farm at Rambouillet – a flush of romantic pastoralism in the face of advancing industrialisation. As dukes fantasised about ditching their duchesses and wedding soft-skinned servants, the pretty, plump, mob-capped dairymaid became one of the archetypal Georgian symbols of seductive purity. At Ham House the Duchess of Lauderdale's north-facing dairy had tiled walls and marble work slabs supported on ceramic cows' legs, a room where maids could beat milk to butter in a plunge churn and warm cream until it coagulated into curds. At Uppark, Humphrey Repton designed a dairy room as much for outdoor entertaining as for productive labour, and in response to the dairying craze Wedgwood began to produce patterned tiles and dairy wares including large cream and syllabub bowls and perforated curd moulds that turned the dairy into a fashionable lady's delight.

The syllabubs of the Restoration contained, by mid-century, a greater proportion of cream so that the mixture no longer separated into curds and whey and became 'everlasting'. Tudor 'hedgehogs' developed into a creamy marzipan paste set into the shape of a hedgehog and stuck with blanched slivers of almonds; Hannah Glasse liked to lump jelly around them, using currants for the eyes and making an alternative to the more usual custard sauce with sorrel juice, hot red wine and sugar. Norman fritters and pain perdus survived, and a new, whisper-thin pancake called the 'Quire of paper' was invented – made as big and as thin as possible and served with sugar, butter and nutmeg. Meringues, introduced by Massialot at the start of the century, were now established, sometimes sandwiched together (or 'twinned') with a little fruit compote.

With her finger firmly on the competitive culinary pulse, Elizabeth Raffald devoted more than a third of her *Experienced English House-keeper* (1769) to confectionery – including one of the earliest recipes for 'burnt cream', or crème brûlée as we know it today – and she was the undisputed queen of the jelly, flavouring them with lemon, orange or Madeira and colouring them with cochineal, syrup of violet blue or the old-fashioned fallbacks of saffron and spinach. Raffald's jellies were painstakingly built up in elaborate layers to produce domed mounds which magnified their amusing contents – fish made from flummery or hens' nests from thinly sliced, syrup-poached lemon rind, each layer set firm before the next was added, each new syrup cool enough so as not to melt the one below it. They might have been stiff compared to modern jellies, but they still wobbled and quivered delightfully, sometimes prettily supported by flowers with long, slender stems pushed in at the corners.

Moulded foods like Thacker's conical salmagundi were becoming de rigueur, and workshops like the Staffordshire potteries produced bizarrely shaped moulds for boiled puddings, including pretty fluted rounds with practical central pipes that not only took the heat to the centre of the dish but left a hole that made the steaming dome easier to cut without the whole structure collapsing. Staffordshire also produced glazed creamware jelly moulds with relief designs of wheat sheafs, corncobs, fruits and animals, while Wedgwood designed copper and tin moulds in the shapes of fish, shells, cards, birds and flowers – a quick rinse with cold water before filling them usually ensured that the jellies would slide out with relative ease. Like multi-part ice-cream moulds, pyramid or obelisk moulds allow-ed a core of decorated jelly to be set in one colour while an outer layer of clear jelly magnified the interior – Woodforde noted one at a dinner in 1782, 'a pretty pyramid of jelly in the centre, a landscape appearing thro' the jelly'. Leaving Raffald to her complicated models of the moon and stars, of eggs and bacon, Solomon's temple or cribbage cards, less ambitious cooks simply poached strawberries very gently and set them in glasses surrounded by clear jelly, working patiently, for leaving pips in the jelly bag or squeezing it – a dreadful temptation for a busy cook – reduced the sparkle of the finished result.

Confectionery was, however, no longer the job of the lady of the house as it had been two centuries before. Raffald sold her decorative sugar webs at her Manchester shop, and in London specialist confectionery could be bought from professionals – famously the Italian Borella in the 1770s, John Nutt in the 1780s and, later, Jarrin and Gunter, each of whom also published their own specialist books. Negri's shop, at the sign of the Pot and Pineapple in Berkeley Square in London,* was famous for its 'Cedrati and Bergamot Chips, Naples . . . Syrup of Capilaire, orgeate and Marsh mallow . . . All sorts of Ice, Fruits and Creams in the best Italian manner'. It also sold *diavolini*, or little icing-sugar drops scented with violet, barberry, peppermint, chocolate and neroli made from the blossom of bitter orange. For those who could not stretch to the luxury of shop-bought produce but who could afford a book of recipes, a long struggle with the complexities of sugar science ensued.

Most ladies delegated to their cooks and housekeepers since, as early as the 1740s, magazines had begun to caution them against too much involvement in household matters lest they forfeit their reputations as women of taste. Despite plenty of cookbooks promising to shoulder the burden of training kitchen staff and notwithstanding the existence of a handful of cookery schools like Elizabeth Raffald's in Manchester, a basic culinary skills gap was developing, compounded by the difficulty of finding and keeping good staff.

This was not an entirely new phenomenon. Eight cooks had come and gone at Grisell Baillie's house in 1715; one had stayed for less than twenty-four hours. 'Plagued to death' by his staff, Jonathan Swift wrote his satirical *Directions to Servants*, advising them that 'when you have done a fault' always be 'pert and insolent and behave yourself as if you were the injured person'. He told the cook to use the tablecloth to

---

* The dangerous, heavy, creaking wooden signs that had signalled commercial establishments for centuries were now on the verge being replaced by street numbering.

clean the pots, leave the spits greasy, buy cheap meat and account it as expensive, and 'if a lump of soot falls into the soup and you cannot conveniently get it out, scum it well and it will give the soup a high French taste'. Daniel Defoe found the 'pride, insolence and exorbitant wages' of his servants alarming, along with their lax morals and penchant for fine clothes. As maids paraded in their mistresses' cast-offs or copied their figured silks, chintzes and muslins with cheap calicoes imported from India, foreigners wondered at how alike mistress and servant appeared to be; Carl-Philip Moritz certainly thought 'there is, through all ranks here, not near so grate a distinction between high and low as there is in Germany'.

When the government imposed a tax on male servants in 1777 to help fund the war with America,* only the most aristocratic could afford their liveried footmen, and the demand for female servants grew ever more pressing. With so many jobs on offer, it was a seller's market: if a cook or a maid did not take to her employer, she could simply move on or, worse for her mistress, just stop making an effort. In the sort of houses that could afford to install a network of bells attached to hidden wires with which to summon their staff to work, separate servants' quarters were appearing for girls as young as twelve, but elsewhere the majority of female staff were housed in the attics or basement kitchens of their employers. Glasse's *Servant's Directory or Housekeeper's Companion* (1760) taught enthusiastic novices how to organise weights, collect bills from traders, melt candle stumps and triumph over a stream of unremitting chores.

Day after day, the kitchen staff were faced with clarifying stocks and soups and rendering dripping by melting, scumming and letting it set and then scraping the top and bottom clean and hanging it up on a thread in the larder. They drew meat and singed, trimmed and trussed it, they scaled fish and prepared vegetables, and at the end of it all they scoured the tables and dressers and sieved the cinders to collect reusable lumps of coal. Copper was cleaned with vinegar, with old lemon skins dipped in salt and silver-sand or – more safely – with boiling water and a little bran or lye made from wood ash; pewter was

---

* Directed at the richest of the rich, this was not just any tax but a whopping guinea for each male member of staff. It was not abolished until 1937.

burnished with whiting;* and the ironwork of the stove had to be blackened. After a dinner party, the washing of the dishes and glasses with soda and softsoap might stretch well beyond midnight, working in the half-light of inferior tallow candles while the guests rattled away in their carriages. Kitchen labour was hard and physical, and for many maids-of-all-work barely past childhood it was a tedious, relentless purgatory.

There were, however, some kitchen advances which made their life a little easier. When William Verral, pupil of the Duke of Newcastle's famous chef Pierre Clouet, arrived at a house in Sussex to prepare dinner, he found only one frying pan 'as black as my hat and a handle long enough to obstruct half the passage of the kitchen'. Frying was rarely acceptable for dinner-party food, and Verral might have expected great sets of copper pots with which to execute his boiled and braised dishes. In this disastrous Sussex kitchen there were none, nor any tiffany silk or cotton lawn for sieving: just one battered sieve which had recently been used for sanding the floor.

Verral was appalled, for elsewhere kitchens were being brought rapidly up to date by technological improvements. Block-and-tackle cranes – or lug-poles – swung pots over the fire, and sophisticated devices attached to a gallows beam within the chimney made it easier to regulate the pot's height. Soon there would be smoke jacks which used the chimney draught to spin a fan and rotate the spit. Movable wooden screens, sometimes lined in tin – called hasteners, Dutch ovens or roasters – were set before the fire to reflect heat back on to the roast while protecting it from draughts. Some even had a sliding door to allow the cook to baste the roast from behind the screen, or shelves fixed on to their backs that could be used to warm dishes or bake small custards. At Uppark, the food was raced from a separate kitchen wing to the dining room along an underground passage on charcoal-heated wooden trolleys in an effort to keep it vaguely hot for the guests.

But the most vital change of all was happening in the fireplace itself. From about the middle of the century cast-iron plates were attached to the front of the grate on each side, with metal supports for pans at the front and the whole grate was sometimes built into a masonry support.

---

* Ground chalk.

Then, from about 1770, cast-iron side boilers and baking ovens began to appear. How proud the owners of Shugborough Park Farm House near Stafford must have been, and how alarmed and nervous their cook, when faced with a range patented by Thomas Robinson in place of the traditional open fire.

Soon, boilers like the one at Bretton Hall in Yorkshire were being installed at the backs of ranges to supply ready hot water and steam for cooking. Then Joseph Langmead patented a design from which all future closed ranges would develop, using flues to spread a more even though still rather inefficient heat to the side ovens. At the same time the American Count Rumford, a prolific inventor and one of the founders of the Royal Institution, also developed plans for a closed oven heated by flues and blow-pipes and another that covered the fire with an iron plate, creating a hob and reducing the amount of heat charging up the chimney.

These developments would change the course of cooking more radically than any other culinary invention. On 27 February 1802 an Exeter man, George Bodley, would patent the first practical closed range in which the fire heated the oven and hotplate before expelling hot air and smoke into the chimney. With such devices, products of the Machine Age, ash and charcoal dust no longer blew around the kitchen, and the era of the open fire was drawing to a close.

THE LONG REGENCY

Carême's 'Cochon de lait en galantine', with his signature 'architectural' styling and 'hatelets', or decorative skewers, used as garnishes. The base of this dish of sucking pig is ornamented with coloured paste medallions, everlasting flowers and cut pieces of tongue, fowl breast, egg whites and truffles; it is piped with Montpellier butter and studded with 'croûtons' of aspic jelly.

18

Mad for Innovation

Tell me what you eat, and I will tell you who you are

— JEAN-ANTHELME BRILLAT-SAVARIN

During the last decade of the eighteenth century, George III appeared increasingly deranged, America declared itself independent, and in France the guillotine shook the structure of European society to its core. Public executions at Tyburn in London had been abolished, and Dr Johnson fumed that the age was 'running mad after innovation'. The world was again in flux: soaps, candles and starches were less often made at home than bought from the shops; within twenty years, gaslights would appear on London's Pall Mall and in theatres along Drury Lane. Among the intellectual and social élite, ladies put aside their stays and hoops for body-hugging, high-waisted muslins and fine cottons, and men started to wear top hats, swapping their breeches for tight trousers. Bawdiness was out of style, litheness was chic for the first time, and to look fragile was an outward sign of a forceful intellect and a romantic sensibility.

Britain was the richest nation on earth. Although two-thirds of the population still lived and worked on the land, everyone appeared to be caught up in a collective race for riches, propelled by business, production and timetables, and there were plenty of losers. Decades of war and a series of poor harvests had wrecked the economy, sending prices and unemployment spiralling while wages fell. By 1790, the population had exploded from five to almost eight million, and a new wave of enclosure had partitioned around three million acres of land, wrenching yet more villagers from their roots and destroying their ability to remain self-sufficient. In the growing towns, slums housed the thousands of human drones sucked in by the rapacious appetite of the factories: in 1795 John Aitken of Manchester wrote that the poor were 'crowded in offensive, dark, damp and incommodious habitations, a too fertile source of disease!' As the boom decades passed, the rift between the haves and the have-nots widened, breeding a whole new kind of social and political instability and resentments that would seethe for the next half-century.

The poor in Britain were now subsisting not on the diet that had remained broadly unchanged for centuries, of ale, grain, vegetables and a modicum of fatty meat, but on a vastly less nutritious mix of often-adulterated white bread, cheese, tea and sugar. Even these devoured up to two-thirds of their weekly budget so that they struggled to pay for rent, clothing and fuel. The voices of physicians and political reformers alike were raised in concern – William Buchan was one of the first in a long line stretching well into the twenty-first century to advise that the poor should be encouraged to return to a healthier, cheaper diet of grains and pottage. But if his advice reached them at all, they, in the main, turned a deaf ear – and for very good reason. Fuel for even the most basic home-cooking was often too expensive, equipment and skills were sparse, and the price of grain was sky-high. Parliament introduced Standard Bread – a mix of barley, potatoes and rye – but it was so unpalatable that it was often simply ignored. Even the middling sort were running out of flour: when Parson Woodforde dined with a neighbour in 1796, he wrote that there was 'no kind of pastry, no wheat flour made use of . . . the bread all brown wheat meal with one part in four of barley flour'. Families like the Lamonts in Edinburgh bought ornate stoneware casseroles designed by the Dalton factory to imitate fluted pastry coffins so that 'pies' could still be served, albeit without the pastry.

For the poor, tea brought immediate if unsustaining comfort – not the Hyson of the well-to-do but cheap leaves often adulterated with poisonous black lead. As early as 1784, La Rochefoucauld noticed that the 'humblest peasant' brewed tea a couple of times a day – but it, and the sugar that went with it, ate into their incomes. The radical politician and journalist William Cobbett, also known as Peter Porcupine, was not alone in inveighing against 'this vile concoction, the corrosive, gnawing and poisonous powers of tea', often substituted for solid food but containing nothing nutritious; that it, 'besides being good for

'The Coffehous Mob', 1674, is the earliest known image of a British coffee house; smoking and debate lay at the heart of these establishments' allure.

The frontispiece from the translation of La Varenne's *Cuisinier François* of 1653, showing a chef at work in his kitchen.

Charles II Being Presented with a Pineapple by the Royal Gardener John Rose, Hendrik Dankerts, 1675. John Evelyn was disappointed by his first taste of pineapple in 1668, considering it inferior to the 'ravishing . . . deliciousnesse' of other hothouse fruits.

Illustration detail from Francis Sandford's *History of the Coronation of James II*, 1687. James's feast was prepared by the royal cook Patrick Lamb and served *à la française*, with an extravagant plethora of highly decorated dishes presented in rigorous symmetry. Drinks were served to each diner on request, from a sideboard shown here behind the guests.

The dairy at Ham House was one of the earliest of its kind, with cool marble worktops supported by legs in the shape of cows' legs. Potteries such as Wedgwood supplied a growing market for cream-coloured or patterned dairy wares.

Eighteenth-century glassware. The 1745 tax on glass led to the production of lighter glasses which were beautifully designed and cut or engraved.

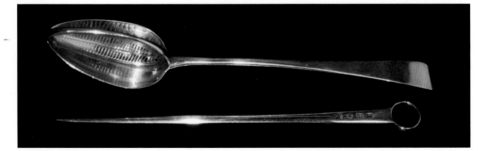

During the eighteenth century silver gravy-straining spoons (this from 1795) were made in several different designs, some with a slotted bridge which was occasionally removable for cleaning. Silver meat-skewers came in different lengths for large roasts, game and poultry, and were used for holding together boned, stuffed cuts of meat as they cooked.

Grace before a Meal, by Joseph van Aken, circa 1725, was painted at a time of relative plenty. Aken depicts an unadorned country meal served on pewter plates and in salt-glazed bowls; the dripping pan is hung behind a spit over the chimney.

Gin Lane, William Hogarth, 1751. Between 1700 and 1735 legitimate imports of gin rose from half a million gallons per year to five million, and slums collapsed in an orgy of lethal drinking.

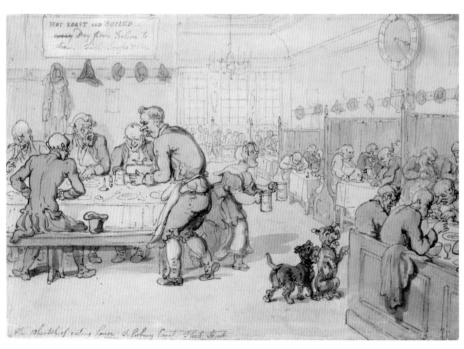

City chop house, Thomas Rowlandson, 1790s. These bustling establishments served the Englishman's ideal diet of roasted or boiled meat washed down with plenty of ale or claret.

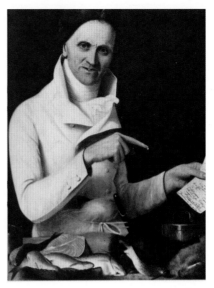

The Burthens of Plenty by Matthew Darly, 1777. While the broad-waisted and well-off gorged on turtle, rabbit and beef, the poor found themselves increasingly subsisting on bread, tea and beer.

The cook at Drumlanrig, Dumfriesshire, circa 1817. Smart and keen-eyed, the Drumlanrig cook was surely either French or French-trained – his fine portrait indicates that he was highly valued, and highly paid.

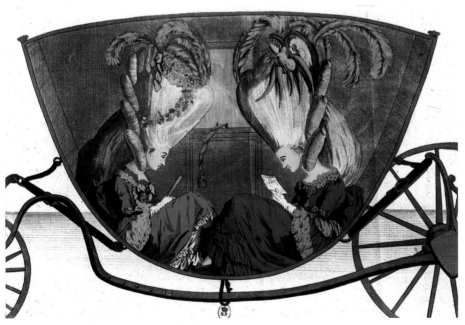

From the 1760s, hairstyles and table decoration went horticultural.

Plumb Pudding in Danger, James Gillray, 1805. William Pitt and Napoleon divide up the world – represented here by a great steaming pudding – between themselves. This etching appeared just before the victories of the British at Trafalgar and the French at Austerlitz.

The Royal Pavilion kitchens, Brighton. In 1816, Carême worked around a great steam-heated, central serving table, while enormous ranges were used for roasts and copper hoods projected from charcoal stoves. The copper *batterie de cuisine* was arranged on a great dresser and the room was flooded with light from high windows and gas lanterns.

nothing, has badness in it, because it is well known to produce want of sleep in many cases, and in all cases, to shake and weaken the nerves'.

While the comfortably complacent gorged on turtle and pudding, proud of their new decanters and dinner sets, the landed gentry set man-traps in the woods against poachers and fed their hogs and horses on pea, bean and barley mash which might have fed the hungry. Poor Relief was predicated on the availability of cheap corn and on the assumption that a labourer's family could survive on a day rate of 1s 4d if the price of corn was no more than 1s 1d a half peck,* but the price was already over 2s. Frederick Eden's 1797 'Report on the State of the Poor' – the first of its kind – painted a shocking picture of the plight of impoverished southerners 'habituated to the unvarying meal of dry bread and cheese', the once-a-week bit of meat returning from the local bakers as a shrivelled lump, cheap bacon creating a thirst relieved only by porter. Northerners were marginally better off, holding on to the old traditions of pottage, frumenty, and pease and hasty puddings, and already reliant on vitamin-rich potatoes.

Eden's well-intended suggestion that the southern poor could turn salt-fish to appetising account with an egg-and-butter sauce showed that he, like Buchan, was simply missing the point. Indian corn – maize – and rice were both imported cheaply in an effort to relieve suffering, but no one thought to explain to the poor – who had never seen them before – how they should be cooked. Ominously, given the famine that waited to devour Ireland's population in the following century, Buchan observed that the Irish were the only ones happily to substitute potatoes for bread and urged fine ladies to economise, using their legs in place of carriages. The urban poor, dislocated from the land, had lost the skills and the appetite to cook, and few had the equipment to do so even if they did have the will or the ingredients. Ancient traditions of economical and nutritious gruels and pottages were now broadly overlooked in the rotting slum-houses of sprawling new cities so that *The Times* barked out moralising advice with its 'Rules for the Rich', urging them to give up gravy soups and second courses, to make broths and rice puddings for the poor, and to teach 'them to make such things' themselves.

---

* About 4 pounds in weight.

As feeding soup to the indigent grew into a fashionable, philan-
thropic pastime for ladies with little better to do than visit their
neighbours or cut intricate patterns out of paper, charity soups became
a veritable passion. Now recipes for cheap dishes became de rigueur in
cookbooks, weak concoctions improbably made with sago, brown
sugar, lemon peel, raisin wine and gin, or a gallon of barley broth made
for a groat (about fourpence) using Scotch beef, mutton dripping, fat
bacon, oatmeal and seasonings like celery, cress seed and cayenne.

Inhabitants of workhouses and prisons were fed less on broth and
rice pudding than on a grim diet so lacking in goodness that it was close
to the starvation limit. In the crowded prison hulks at Woolwich, men
were given small quantities of meat, often green with rot, and biscuits
made of unwholesome grit. At Christ's Hospital School, the essayist
Charles Lamb remembered Thursday's fatty, grey, boiled beef 'poisoned by detestable marigolds floating in the pail' in cheap imitation of
saffron.

If one of the culinary realities of the long Regency and brief reign of
George IV was frugality, elsewhere the aristocracy were hell-bent on
spending to 'improve' their mansions and gardens. In the north, James
Craig's classical New Town was transforming Edinburgh into a city of
palaces, 'the Athens of the North', its royal street names proclaiming
loyalty to London as it prepared to flex its industrialising muscle. In
London's Regent's Park, in Bath and in Brighton, John Nash's grandiose, stuccoed terraces and elegant crescents were rising.

The Prince Regent, a profligate dandy variously nicknamed Prinny
and Georgy-Porgy, was sinking his funds into the lavish decoration
of Carlton House in London (now the site of the National Gallery)
and Nash's transformation of the Royal Pavilion at Brighton into a
whimsical Indian palace. The very opposite of his parsimonious
father, the 'Prince of Whales', as Charles Lamb dubbed him, was
a gourmet and a glutton who would suffer from an early age from
gout and die weighing more than 22 stone. The Carlton House
kitchens were the largest in London, and Nash's new kitchen at the
Royal Pavilion, remodelled between 1815 and 1823, was not only

enormous at 1,600 square feet but among the most technologically advanced of its day.

A world away from the northern city slums, here slender, cast-iron columns surmounted by painted copper palm leaves rose to the ceiling; the space was flooded with light from high, broad sash windows and hanging oil lanterns. The open fire was capable of roasting various-sized joints on several spits simultaneously; extensive charcoal stoves were fitted with copper hoods; an army of pots and pans lined the shelves, and several semi-circular preparation tables flanked a central 'butler's table' famously heated by steam. A local newspaper gushed that 'in the furnishing of the new kitchen . . . every modern improvement to facilitate the process of the culinary art has been introduced in all its perfection'. Steam was indeed new – Sir Walter Scott would be among the first to introduce it to heat his mansion at Abbotsford in 1823 – and it was indispensable if the Regent was to lure Antonin Carême, the greatest chef in Europe, to his coastal palace.

In post-Revolutionary France, in reaction to the perceived greed of the nouveau riche, a cult of epicurism had emerged characterised by the publication in 1803 of the *Almanach des gourmandes* by Grimod de la Reynière and, later, Jean-Anthelme Brillat-Savarin's *Physiologie du goût*, a book that treated dining as an art and famously proclaimed, '. . . tell me what you eat, and I will tell you who you are.' With so much attention being paid to fine dining but with few aristocrats left to serve, French chefs turned to Britain, importing the artistry and science of haute cuisine with its male-dominated kitchen world of professional efficiency and discipline.

Even more than their forebears at the Restoration, many of these displaced French chefs became celebrities. The Earl of Sefton paid Louis-Eustache Ude 300 guineas a year before Ude moved on to the United Service Club and the even smarter Crockfords Club in St James's, and Carême's name was shorthand throughout Europe for signal culinary excellence and elegance.* Carême cooked for the Russian tsars, for the great French diplomat Talleyrand and for the

---

* When Carême's books were translated posthumously into English and published in 1836, they were dedicated to Viscount Canterbury, Speaker of the Commons, demonstrating once again the liaison between haute cuisine and political power.

socially ambitious de Rothschilds in Paris. In 1802, after dining with
the de Rothschilds on a dinner cooked by Carême, Lady Morgan
wrote of the demonstrable innovation of his work: its

> character was that it was in season, that it was up to its time, that it was
> in the spirit of the age, that there was no . . . high-spiced sauces, no
> dark-brown gravies, no flavour of cayenne and allspice, no tincture of
> catsup and walnut pickle . . . Every meat presented in its own natural
> aroma; every vegetable its own shade of verdure.

With his stress on seasonality, freshness and gentle flavours, Carême
and his contemporaries used steam as almost never before, relying on
the water bath, or bain-marie, for exquisite sauces and delicately
poached meats. They cooked *en papillote* – wrapped in paper – to
preserve the moisture of fish or chicken, and the carbon-monoxide
fumes from the charcoal stoves ruined their lungs as they refused to
open the windows for the sake of culinary perfection. Carême *was*
lured to Brighton, where he praised the quality of British ingredients,
but the British climate and palate-dulling gluttony of his patron sent
him scurrying back to the Continent in little more than a year. Yet
his system with its new methods and utensils would dominate
'classic' French cuisine in Britain until the rise of Escoffier a century
later.

Like the fine wrought-iron balconies fronting Regency houses,
these detailed, fancy dishes trumpeted elevated taste and wealth.
Taking their lead from Grimod de la Reynière and Brillat-Savarin,
the terms 'gastronomy' and 'alimentary science' and the high-
falutin' language of the epicurean dandy tickled the lips of the
fashionable and urbane, marking their superiority over the vulgar
new wealth of the industrialists. To talk about food, to write about
it, to indulge in it at its finest, became a mark of a gastronome: the
duty of a good sauce, as Launcelot Sturgeon rather ludicrously
wrote in *Essays Moral Philosophical and Stomachical* (1822), was to
'titillate the capillaceous extremities of the maxillary glands and thus
to flatter and excite the appetite'. In such a climate, Lamb could pen
his elegant if moderately ironic tribute to the roast pig, memorably
describing the 'coy, brittle resistance, of its crackling, the tender

blooming of fat . . . the cream and quintessence of the child-pig', a dish so vulnerable that, like a young child, it should not be left untended for one instant.

Sauces were once again crucial,* and the eighteenth-century cullis developed into three basic 'foundation' sauces from which hundreds of more complex ones could be produced: *velouté*, made with a white stock, *béchamel* and piquant, brown *éspagnole*. Simple egg mayonnaises came into focus: Carême carefully described the delicate process of emulsification needed to make one, adding alternate drops of tarragon vinegar and oil to beaten egg yolks in a bowl set over ice, and serving it with a little aspic jelly made from veal knuckle. *Sauce maître d'hôtel* was also quickly established – a bright combination of olive oil, butter, parsley and lemon that went particularly well with veal. Smart dinner services began to include more sauce boats and tureens, and, on the tables of the aristocracy at least, melted butter was banished.

Stocks and broths, the cornerstones of the professional kitchen, were once again made with no thought of economy, using astonishing quantities of meat to make a liquid for moistening roasts, poaching white meats, and preparing *consommés* and sauces. Ude wrote that 'for a small dinner with four entrées . . . twenty pounds of beef would be required to be used for broth only, independent of the roast', and court bouillons were prepared separately, for poaching fish, from fish, butter, carrots, onions, parsley, wine and, less frequently, garlic. Ude also made a *vin de champagne* sauce and articulated a general abhorrence of the smallest bit of grease being left in the stock, an insufferable vulgarity that indicated only 'bad cookery and a cook without method'.

Novelty was so feted that chefs were driven to create endlessly imaginative dishes from costly ingredients, naming them sycophantically after important and influential patrons – à la Richelieu, Régence, Financière, Dauphinoise and the like. Once the large tureens of soup had been removed, it was these entrées, or made dishes, that booted the roast from centre stage, proclaiming the reputation and skill of the

---

* Grimod de la Reynière commented that a dinner without sauce was as bare as a house that had just passed through the hands of the bailiffs.

cook and the discrimination of his employer.* The language of service à la française expanded as important *assiettes volants* (or flying dishes) were brought in with fanfare by the head footman or the chef himself in advance of the great centre plate, or *dormant* (because it was not removed). In the second course, set-piece roasts were surrounded by *flancs*, or larger side dishes, all still arranged in studious symmetry.

French names, French terms: in the upper-class kitchen there was a whole new language as well as an array of brand-new cooking techniques and forms. Fluffy soufflés were invented in the late eighteenth century by increasingly egg-obsessed French chefs working with the more regular heat that could be coaxed from the new enclosed ovens. They began to appear in British recipe books from about 1813, often flavoured with rabbit, white meat or fish; getting them to the table before they collapsed back on to themselves presented quite a challenge, and it was not uncommon for the footman to walk backwards to the dining room to protect a soufflé from draughts. Forcemeat balls became *quenelles* – melting meat pastes mixed with cream, shaped into ovals and poached in clear broths – or, alternatively, forcemeat sausages called 'boudins'. In place of little pies like old-fashioned chewetts, croquettes appeared – bite-sized shapes of pounded meat or vegetable, breadcrumbed and deep-fried; other amuse-gueules included stuffed puff-paste balls fried in hot lard or, in 'the Russian manner', little pancakes filled with minced fowl or game, dipped in egg and crumbs and fried.

With the shapes of foods high on the agenda, meat and vegetables were primped, tamed and moulded into eye-catching forms: timbales, *turbanes, salmis* and *macedoines*, painstakingly layered or pressed, studded with chopped truffles, embellished with broken aspic or glazed with clever sauces. Carême pioneered the 'artistic' use of silver skewers, or *hatelets*,† and decorated his creations with different-coloured wax medallions, or *pâtes d'office*, with piped Montpellier butter, sliced egg whites and truffles; fish or fowl were presented in moulded rings with heaps of aspic jelly and cut truffle garnishes.

---

* Entrée remains the term for the main course in America and Australia, just as in America 'to broil' has kept its original meaning while British cooks 'grill'.
† Precursors of the club-sandwich cocktail stick.

Small birds were again much in demand: quail, woodcock and snipe were roasted or served *au gratin* – a new term for a baked dish with a deliberately crispy top, sometimes with the addition of cheese – or were baked with bacon or with a rabbit farce, or served on toasts on to which their intestines oozed, dark and bitter. Plovers and pigeons were simmered in orange juice, went into compotes and ragouts, or were poached in the bain-marie, their flesh then pounded and moulded into richly seasoned salmis, or game stews. Larks were stuffed with quenelles and served on fried toasts, and ortolans – songbirds no larger than a plum, supposedly asphyxiated in brandy or vinegar – were roasted and eaten whole. Lord Alvanley's chefs prepared fricassées from the tiny, tender breast morsels – or *noix* – of vast numbers of snipe, woodcock and pheasants, discarding the rest of the meat.

French chefs used cayenne sparingly, relying instead on thyme, burnet, chervil and parsley. Garlic, hardly tolerated a generation earlier, was now acceptable in small quantities. Mixed garnishes of cockscombs, sweetbreads, kidneys and brains were derided as inharmonious fandangoes, and Carême banned the 'ridiculous' combination of fish and meat, inventing 'Pike à la Régence', garnished specifically and only with all kinds of other fish. In between all these culinary works of art, as something of a relief from their elaboration, small saucers of simple hors d'oeuvres replaced the 'pretty little side-dishes' of the previous century: anchovy salads, lemon or orange salads, radishes and figs. Cucumbers were stuffed, celery stewed in broth, chicory braised in a jus, and haricot beans prepared *lyonnaise* (with butter and onions), *françoise* (with butter and lemon) or *provençale* (with garlic, butter and lemon). Full of aphorisms, Grimod de la Reynière contended that a grand dinner without hors d'oeuvres was as improbable as a pretty woman without rouge.

In the French lexicon soups proliferated: 'English soups' of turtle, hare, pearl barley, veal and partridge with soft quenelles floating in them, a clear broth called 'potage de santé' thickened with puréed white meat, or others using finely sliced – julienned – vegetables sautéed in butter in place of rice or pasta ribbons. In the inventive atmosphere of the haute-cuisine kitchen, egg dishes were, according to Ude, 'indispensable in cookery'. He served omelettes ('the middle part must be kept mellow') or poached eggs in water with vinegar; he fried them in boiling oil, served them with maître-d'hôtel butter, stuffed them (*en surprise*) or baked them *en cocotte* in small pots in the ashes of the fire with a little tarragon or concentrated gravy.

Chiming neatly with Prinny's passion for pageantry and visual amusement, this refined modern cooking found its apotheosis in extravagant dinners like that given by the Regent for 2,000 guests in honour of the exiled Louis XVIII in 1811. On this occasion a stream of water ran the 200-foot length of the table, with a fountain and fish-filled lake. Ridiculed in the popular press, these occasions were often graced by rigidly ornate *pièces montées* designed to make the guests gasp: the final flourish of emblematic, architectural confectionery in Britain. Carême had begun his career as a pastry chef, was passionate about architecture and was renowned for his painstaking Georgian equivalents of the Renaissance subtlety: harps, lyres, Gothic towers, rustic rotundas, Indian pavilions or Athenian ruins made out of wire, cardboard, gum paste, pastry and sugar. Impossibly difficult to create, these creations were feted and copied by professional confectioners; few dinner parties of any substance were without their boastful artistic confection.

With or without its pièces montées, Regency Britain had not lost its sweet tooth, and the dessert course lost none of its appeal, though the elegant new French desserts were characterised less by billowing clouds of whipped cream than by small meringues poached in milk, sailing on a sea of *crème anglaise*. They were infused with perfumed essences and the subtle, bruised tastes of ingredients like chestnuts, vanilla, frangipane and neroli. Regency fancy was tempted as much by capillaire syrup (flavoured with dried maidenhair fern), chartreuse and brandies as by the taste of nougat, pistachio, maraschino, mint, aniseed and even – for the first time – caramel made from gently browned sugar and cream.

Beside tiny cups of steamed custard, delicately flavoured meringues and gently spiced fruits, desserts in the high style were layered into bombes or moulded into extraordinary shapes, titivated with ribbon and foliage decoration, iced friezes and glacé fruits. From the con-fectioner's separate kitchen* came little almond cakes known as

---

* Carême was unusual in combining the skills of both confectioner and chef.

pithiviers, rum babas, madeleines and the successful new charlottes, moulded with a lining of sponge fingers or buttered bread, filled with stacked apple or apricot slices, and inverted. 'Nesselrode Pudding', supposedly created by Carême, epitomised the character of the culinary era in which it was born. It was a complex mixture of chestnut purée whipped into an egg-and-cream custard, spiked with maraschino, perfumed with candied citron and vanilla, and either steamed or, in Carême's case, frozen into the shape of a pineapple and garnished with stoned or sugared fruits.*

There were flaky millefeuilles, delicate vol-au-vents and a whole new kind of sweet pastry, choux or pâte royale, made with a paste of boiling water, sugar, butter, flour and eggs, baked into little puffed-up balls to be filled with praline, almonds, fruits or creams or served with crème patissière, as delicate and as apparently slight as the sprigged-muslin dresses won by the ladies. Carême even attempted to modernise the English *pouding*, using a bowl rather than a cloth to produce a perfect dome enriched with chestnuts, rum and macaroons. Hard as he tried, one suspects that the heavy English pudding of tradition was not entirely successful in its high French incarnation, though 'Pouding de cabinet' was swiftly embraced, made from sliced brioche and dried fruits soaked in brandy, sugar, vanilla, candied peel and a cream custard, all steamed in a mould.

Since the foundation of the Royal Society of Horticulture in 1803, soft and exotic fruits had begun to pour from aristocratic greenhouses – pineapples, grapes, apricots and peaches, lemons and oranges, figs, currants and melons among them. The passion for ices was so insistent that in September 1804 Cassandra Austen wrote from Weymouth to her sister Jane, bitterly vexed by the lack of ice in the town. Smart confectioners like Guglielmino Jarrin coloured ices with burnt sugar, indigo and saffron or new commercial colourings like cochineal, carmine, vermillion, Prussian blue or Spanish green – adding real stems and leaves or the leafy fronds of maidenhair fern. Jarrin was the first to write about the *bombe* mould – shaped like a shell from the

---

* He was also credited with the invention of the Bavarian cream, or *bavarois*, a rich custard and whipped cream (*fouetté*, for those in the know), set or moulded with isinglass and variously flavoured with nuts, star anise, chocolate or fruit purées. A *bavaroise*, on the other hand, was a later, caudle-like drink of hot, milky tea with egg yolks and kirsch.

Napoleonic War – in which a frozen mixture enveloped a core of an entirely different colour and flavour. Jarrin's *Italian Confectioner* (1820) was also the first book in England to include engravings of kitchen utensils, illustrating how to make sugar-paste petals by hand and how to undo the special screw at the bottom of the new ice moulds so that you could blow into them, loosening the ice from the sides for successful de-moulding.

Regency ices were sugar's final glittering fanfare, for as it became cheaper, the cachet that had surrounded it for half a millennium began to fall away. Books like Jarrin's were really directed at the trained chef, with their technical definitions of sugar syrups as the thread, pearl, blow, feather, ball, crack and caramel. As for gilding, wrote the confectioner Gunter, '. . . always employ a journeyman gilder'.

In an irony and contradiction typical of its period, a famous tract recommending the pursuit of an epicure's life – *The School of Good Living* (1822) – was published in the same year as William Cobbett's *Cottage Economy* championing rural values. Between the extremes of the inordinately overfed and the distressingly underfed, of excessive refinement and the call for charity, economy and rural self-sufficiency, the strong domestic culinary traditions of the eighteenth century were still fighting their own corner, but the march of progress was against them.

Carême's style of cooking was refined and innovative, but its influence began to hobble the vibrant domestic culinary tradition characterised by Glasse, Raffald and their contemporaries. Part of the point of Carême's haute cuisine was that its elaborate preparation and impressive presentation were exclusive. No 'plain' cook should have tried to imitate it, but the published works of the self-styled culinary masters served only to encourage emulation, and the style *was* soon mangled by the untrained and aspirational.

A La Russe

Since the arrival of Norman courtly ceremony in Britain, dinners had been presented as two or three courses, each one rich in a variety of dishes. With service à la française, guests entered the dining room to see the table painstakingly patterned with dishes, each course conceived and presented with structure and symmetry in mind so that shapes, colours and flavours all matched or complemented one another. Much of the food went cold before they could get their hands on it.

Gradually, a radically new style of presentation at table emerged. Known as *à la russe* in imitation of the tsarist court, it – confusingly – began in France, possibly in honour of Alexander I's liberation of Paris from Napoleon in 1814. It was characterised by two novel features: food was now served straight on to plates from a sideboard and handed to guests, and the courses therefore progressed much as they might today, with soup, fish, meat, vegetables and dessert now entirely separate. By 1821 the 'plain cook' Maria Rundell was observing that while some people still preferred the old practice, others allowed the roast to be carved by the host or hostess while smaller dishes were

served directly to the guests by servants. She was not entirely convinced that it was a good idea, disliking the awkwardness of it all and
concerned that smart clothes were often spoiled by clumsy staff.

Alternatively, smaller fricassées or curries could be arranged on the
table for the guests to help themselves, while larger dishes and roasts
would be carved separately and carried to them. Both were a sort of
'demi russe', a hybrid style that was for many the first step on the way
to change. The anonymous 'Lady' author of *Domestic Economy* (1827)
suggested that if the hostess was to carve, she should make her chair a
little higher so as to give herself the advantage of command over her
table; others left their cooks to carve the joint in the kitchen, skewering
it back together, or asked them to run lines of cloves across the joint to
ensure that it was carved neatly enough for its remains to be put aside
for serving cold at another meal. Increasingly, hosts and hostesses gave
up any qualms about having the troublesome carving done in the
kitchen, recognising that this was 'now the general practise of France,
Germany and Russia'. Indeed in 1827 the cook Meg Dods claimed that
'in this fastidious age, the sanguinary spectacle of an entire, four-footed
animal at table is anything but acceptable.'

The upshot of the new style was that guests got their food faster and
hotter and with less need for them to help one another. Chairs could be
set further apart, and arms need never touch at all. The uninitiated
could be shocked or confused on being shown into a dining room in
which the table was empty of food. When Tennyson's friend Arthur
Hallam gave an à la russe dinner party in 1849, 'his guests went down
to dinner and found nothing on the table, not even soup. Harry began
to redden in embarrassment, Julia and I to giggle.' By the mid-nineteenth century Charles Dickens and his wife Catherine were among the
liberal-minded group that approved of the vogue, enjoying the quicker
pace of the meal and the fast flow of conversation that it encouraged.
Others mourned the social distance it created, missing the opportunity
for flirtation and intimacy; it was all a long way from shared messes
and the benches of the Great Hall.

Jane Carlyle was shrewish about the style when she dined with the
Dickenses in 1849, deriding the overabundant piles of fruit that filled
up the spaces at the table, for without tureens, platters and bowls
crowding every available surface, service à la russe allowed more room

for candelabra and elaborate centrepiece épergnes, and for several wine glasses to be set for each guest. The Regency épicure Dr Kitchiner found the latest fashion for grand candelabra that threw light at the ceiling rather than on to the plates both pompous and impractical, recommending only 'half as many candles as there are guests . . . the flames . . . about eighteen inches above the table'. Flowers were used as ornaments in their own right, and the author of the popular *Domestic Economy* steered unwary hostesses in the right direction, pointing out that delicate nosegays were appropriate, while 'great Covent Garden bouquets are an abomination'.

Jane Carlyle was equally snippy about the Dickenses' use of artificial flowers as decoration, and by the 1860s books were appearing that taught flower-arranging for the table: Henry James poked fun at the pretentious ladies who 'did' flowers for the smart, fast people 'whose names were in the papers'. For those without plate or crystal, well-presented cold meats – a glazed ham, a salad or a fish in jelly – could serve as centrepieces, and hostesses wary of blank spaces could arrange small dishes of fruit or biscuits around the table or provide newfangled finger bowls – to the horror of those who were either disgusted by or unsure of how to use them.

Of the generation of French chefs to follow Carême, only the royal cook Francatelli gave instructions in 1846 for middle-class housewives wanting to dine in the fashionable new manner. 'Tabitha Tickletooth' – in reality the culinary-minded actor Charles Selby – was also open to change, recommending in 1860 that 'her' readers should consider serving 'one dish at a time, and only one – one soup, then one fish, and so on', without any absurd and pretentious French titbits like vol-au-vents or boudins to ruin the appetite and make the rest of the food go cold. Those without access to a delightful set of Sèvres china or a gardener to set the table with an abundance of flowers and hothouse fruits, Selby wrote, would have to make do with a plaster cast of Napoleon or the figure of a church with coloured windows, bought for a few pence. He sounded so sure, but even he recognised that many were still not ready for change, comforting them with the thought that 'to see our dinner in its integrity in all its parts is an English comfort we still cling to'.

Selby's contemporary Isabella Beeton cautioned her readers vehemently against the new fad. They might aspire to ranks of footmen, but

Beeton clearly understood that the majority of them were unlikely to
have more than a general maidservant who would struggle, and fail, to
juggle everything by herself. An à la russe dinner required a quantity of
china, glass, knives and forks which, along with the pressure to make
each course a culinary triumph, simply put it beyond the management
of the suburban villa family. It was 'scarcely suitable for small establishments', wrote Beeton – which all seemed clear enough. But even the
perceptive Isabella felt the pull of novelty and could not help herself
from including illustrations for setting the table in the new style,
demonstrating how to trail flowers and ferns about the edges, pile fruit
and flowers down the centre, and place an army of shaded candlesticks
among the prodigal decoration.

The later Victorian dining table bristled with handwritten menus
which showed guests what to expect so that they could pace themselves
accordingly, and with parvenu implements, all part of that very
Victorian desire to define class visually. Broad-ended knives – so
useful for eating peas – gave way to narrower versions; new fruit
and cheese knives were developed along with cutlery for fish (sup-
planting the old-fashioned use of two forks) and soup spoons; cruet
stands came in every imaginable design; and electroplate stood in for
silver for the less well off. The heavy sideboard groaned with ornament
as it had in the medieval hall, and the cloth was set at the last possible
minute to preserve its shiny whiteness from the sooty air, creases no
longer needed. Everything, as a pretentious little manual of 1859
declared, presented 'an opportunity for the display of taste'.

Mrs Beeton knew that dreams were potent and that anxious young
suburban housewives aspired even to what they could not currently
afford. Consequently, she also allowed herself to construct sample
menus for dinners in the new style, offering five courses in a garbled
mix of French and English and an over-profusion of dishes more in
keeping with the French style of serving:

Ox tail soup ~ Soup à la jardinière

Turbot and Lobster sauce ~ Crimped cod and oyster sauce,
Stewed eels ~ Soles à la Normandie
Pike and cream sauce ~ Fried filleted soles

Filets de boeuf à la Jardinière ~ Croquettes of game aux champignons
Chicken cutlets ~ Mutton cutlets and tomata sauce
Lobster rissoles ~ Oyster patties
Partridges aux fines herbs ~ Larded sweetbreads
Roast beef ~ Poulets aux cressons
Haunch of mutton ~ Roast turkey
Boiled turkey and celery sauce ~ A ham

Grouse ~ Pheasants ~ Hare
Salad artichokes ~ Stewed celery
Italian cream ~ Charlotte aux pommes ~ Compote of pears
Croutes madráes aux fruits ~ Pastry ~ Punch jelly
Iced puddings

Dessert and ices

By contrast, some fifteen years later the Countess Onslow had the measure of the style when she planned her menu for sixteen guests, putting quality and substance above quantity:

Potages:
Julienne ~ Purée de petits pois

Poissons:
Saumon ~ Sauce tartare ~ Blanchaille

Entrées:
Cotelettes de riz de veau à la Tina ~ Cotelettes d'agneau aux petits pois ~
Foie gras en aspic

Rotis:
Selle de mouton ~ Chapons jambon d'York ~ Leverets ~ Cailles

Entremets:
Crèpes froides ~ Gelée aux fraises ~ Boudin glacé aux abricots ~
Paile de parmesan ~ Glaces

Finger glasses on doyleys

At the same time as the Countess Onslow's dinner, a pompous retired army officer, Colonel Kenney-Herbert – known as Wyvern – demonstrated that it was not only the aristocracy who felt at home with the à la russe style; advising anxious returnees from India on how to manage without armies of native servants, he believed that dinner should take no more than an hour: 'soup, fish, two well-contrasted entrées, served separately, one joint only, game and a dressed vegetable, one entremets sucré, an iced pudding, cheese with hors d'oeuvres and dessert'. Similarly, his contemporary Mrs Pendler-Cudlip brushed aside her husband's concerns that their dessert service was not good enough to stay on the table throughout the meal, relying instead on her silver, glass and flowers (which were expensive) to set the right tone. Serving gravy soup, salmon with shrimp sauce, fillets of sole, lobster patties, saddle of mutton with roast game, Nesselrode pudding, creams and ices, she, in common with most of her contemporaries, relied on food that was easily portioned.

Amid the flurry of advice and instruction, there was nothing swift about the change in table presentation, and service à la française lingered for decades after its first tentative introduction. It would take until the turn of the twentieth century for service à la russe – our modern style of service – to find its way resolutely under the skin of the middle classes, establishing itself once and for all at dinner tables the length and breadth of the British Isles.

19

Painting the Lamb,
Roasting the Mutton

*. . . with a mistress within who is stuck up in a place she
calls a parlour with, if she have children, the 'young ladies
and gentlemen' about her . . . Good God! . . . they flee
from the dirty work . . . What a misery is all this!*

— WILLIAM COBBETT

Widespread acceptance of the à la française style was still almost a
century away when, in 1796, John Lamont purchased the brand-new
No. 7 Charlotte Square, in Edinburgh's New Town. From the elegant
hallway, eighteen stone steps descended to the draughty kitchen
corridor with storerooms for coal, wine, silver, chamber pots and
Wedgwood crockery. Here was the tradesmen's entrance and an
impressive flagstoned kitchen dominated by a semi-enclosed range
with side cranes and spits and a separate bread oven. For stewing,
braising and sauce-making and for drop-scones and pancakes there
were two charcoal stoves, each set under a window.

With the fin-de-siècle vogue for prettily coloured walls, the kitchen
was painted blue;* From the ceiling hung cured hams, strings of onions
and dried herbs; baskets were piled with coal, and barrels of anchovies
were stacked against the walls. Salt, spice boxes and flour-
dredgers were set over the fire to keep their contents dry, beside a

---

* Less – as one modern paint company would have it – because flies were repelled by the colour
than because both ultramarine and Prussian blue were relatively non-toxic compared to other
colours laden with arsenic, lead and chromium. I am grateful to Dr Peter Morris, Head of
Research at the Science Museum, London, for this insight.

tinderbox,* and there was a small side pantry for storing pickles, jams and preserves. The house's only water pump would not be fitted for twenty-odd years, but there was a stone sink to cope with the laborious food preparation and washing up: a kitchen maid would have had to stand on a box to reach into its depths.

In this kitchen, damping the cinders at the back of the fire to keep them under control, building up the sides to project 4 inches beyond the length of her roast, replacing candles that burned too fast in the heat, the Lamonts' cook is more likely to have been mopping the sweat from her brow in the half-gloom than living up to the prettily cool example often engraved in the frontispiece of contemporary cookbooks. As she juggled the roast with the sauces, casting her eye over the bubbling vegetables, she was blessed with a kitchen simply stuffed with pots, pans and equipment, an impressive copper batterie de cuisine arranged on the vast side dresser beside tin and copper jelly moulds, sugar-nippers, graters, hammers, horn spoons, biscuit presses, spice boxes and clockwork jacks.

Much of the available floor space was taken up by a substantial wooden table arranged with chopping boards, knives and a three-sided wooden tray for rolling pastry. To one side was a tin-lined plate-warmer and to the other a 3-foot-high wooden pestle and mortar for grinding wheat, essential now that flour was so scarce and adulteration so widespread. The cook would have used yards of worsted woven in the new mills, known as tammy cloth and sold, according to the Regency cook Dr Kitchiner, 'at the oil shops . . . made on purpose for straining sauces'. Once the cloth had been filled with a thick liquid or purée, tammying was a job for two – the cook and a maid each twisting their end in opposite directions over a large bowl until their wrists cried out for mercy.

In an increasingly time-obsessed world, the vast black-lacquer kitchen clock urged the cook to punctuality, as grandfather clocks in the hall and dining room struck the quarter hours. In the formal

---

* The earliest matches, made of wax paper and phosphorus sealed into a glass tube, burst into flame on contact with air. In 1810, wooden chips began to be dipped in potash and sugar; then came acid matches, which had to be dipped in vitriol (a highly corrosive acid made from sulphur dioxide) to spark. All three versions were unstable at best and explosive at worst. In 1826 the first friction match, or Lucifer, was finally developed.

The frontispiece of E. Hammond's *Modern Domestic Cookery*, 1826, shows
a dresser stuffed with platters and dish covers, an open grate with its gear-driven
clockwork spits, a dripping pan and baster, and a capacious wooden screen
that also warms dishes.

dining room on the ground floor, a large sideboard was set into a recess, mirrors and portraits hung on the walls, and the dining chairs were covered in fashionable red leather. A 'dumb waiter' – a piece of wooden furniture with a central shaft and two, sometimes revolving, trays set one above the other – stood at each end of the table to carry dishes when servants were not required, and in front of the fireplace stood a tin box for keeping food or plates warm, prettily painted with Chinese figures.

In such a household, Meg Dods's *Cook and Housewife's Manual* (1826), rather than books by cooks like Carême, was welcome. Dods was the fictitious, sharp-tongued landlady in Sir Walter Scott's best-selling tale *St Ronan's Well*, cooking for an epicurean group of gentlemen styling themselves as the Cleikum Club; the manual's real author, Christian Isobel Johnstone, was both genial and accomplished. Writing with a broad Scots accent, she combined plain domestic cookery with pride in perfection: 'boils done to a popple, the roast to a turn, the stews to the knick of time'. Her recipes were aimed at middle-class families who aspired to the best seasonal foods cooked with precision and thoughtfulness. Assuming diligence on the part of her readers, Dods described how to wind a strip of pastry round the edge of a pie dish before adding its top, reminded her readers that eggs had always to be strained and was rationally exact in her quantities.

Far from the foppery of society London, Dods's accomplished cooking allied her firmly with the epicurean spirit of the times, while epitomising the middle-class obsessions with reining in waste, using up leftovers and eschewing superfluous finery, preferring to leave out an ingredient rather than substitute it 'with the desire of being genteel'. She explained the general rule about boiling meat for twenty minutes to the pound, how to keep the skin of a boiled ham to cover it when cold, and how to fix meat to the spit and gauge the weather's effect on the roast. Under her supervision, sausages were fried slowly to prevent them bursting, and bacon and eggs were delicately done, the eggs simply 'slipped' into the hot fat. She explained how to keep separate gridirons for meat and for fish and to make soups in earthenware containers like the French, and she counted it foolishness to hanker after the 'meagre, hard' meat of venison, preferring to leave the deer alive and to cook well-hung mutton with its far superior taste.

Dods was among the last few generations to home-salt, collar, pickle and smoke her meats for keeping, and her successful book continued in many editions well into the 1880s. However, two other cookery writers of the period found the kind of commercial success that Glasse and Raffald had achieved in the previous century: Maria Rundell and Dr Kitchiner. Rundell's *Domestic Happiness* – first published in 1809 and later called *Domestic Cookery* – was compiled when she was already sixty, ostensibly for the use of her own daughters but in reality aimed at the growing band of anxious housewives who had not been taught how to run a home. Starting with the basics, Rundell gave advice on everything from paying ready money to keeping minute accounts and using up leftovers, and she was firm in guiding her readers to weight-check all their provisions the very moment they got home from shopping.

Rundell despaired at the dearth of kitchen skills among educated but socially pretentious young women and argued that domesticity should not be an excuse for a contraction of the mind: 'When a girl, whose family moves in the higher ranks of life, returns to reside at her father's house after completing her education,' she wrote, 'her introduction into the gay world . . . persuade[s] her at once that she was born to be the ornament of fashionable circles rather than to stoop (as she would conceive it) to undertake the arrangement of a family.' She was not alone. In 1805, Abraham Edlin published the first full treatise on bread-making since Gervase Markham two centuries earlier, attempting to educate householders who had given up baking. Mary Wollstonecraft wrote scathingly of the reduction of women to dolls in a growing cult of home life and motherhood; Jane Austen gently satirised mothers who cultivated imbecility in their daughters – mothers who studiously kept their girls out of the kitchen, but who remained simperingly impressed by flashy French cooking.

William Cobbett fumed at mistresses who 'flee from the dirty work', taught to be divine rather than sensual, to paint a lamb but not to roast a mutton. Rundell was determined to lift such women out of their ignorance. She gave precise instructions for making pastry, preserves

and bottled sauces, explained how to boil, roast and fry, how to curry
cod in flakes, to mock turtle, and to boil rice slowly on a moderate fire
until the grains were loose and dense, pinching them between finger
and thumb to see if they were ready. Her smart new 'spunge' cakes
beat egg whites into a great froth before adding the yolks, sugar and
flour. So successful was her plain-speaking book that it sold more than
half a million copies in her lifetime, making her publisher John Murray
the fortune that allowed him to continue to print the work of authors
like the infamous Lord Byron.

In parallel, with his eye-patch, his collection of fifty-one telescopes
and his odd air, combining dilettante and connoisseur, the self-styled
'Cook's Oracle' Dr Kitchiner relied upon a 'Committee of Taste',
including Sir Joseph Banks, Sir John Soane and a medley of actors,
musicians and journalists, to pass judgement on the recipes he included
in his 1817 collection *Apicius Redivivus*. Matching Rundell's direct
approach with that of the gourmand and scientist, Kitchiner promised
to unfold a system of cooking that combined method and carefulness
with elegance – that much-desired Regency commodity – offering a
standard repertoire glossed with humorous eccentricity. His curlicued
language and recipes with raffish names – 'Wow Wow Sauce' and a
beer punch he called 'Tewahdiddle' – slipped the whiff of smart
London society into his pages even as he admonished his readers
against pretentiousness in cooking.

Kitchiner's readers could flatter themselves that they too were
epicures while following recipes that set a new standard in precision
of measure and weight and that included final 'observations' that aimed
to clarify essential details or offer alternatives. Despite initial appearances, Kitchiner's rule was also to keep things simple, to pay and treat
the cook well rather than leaving her to rely on extras from the sale of
unwanted bones, dripping or candle stubs,* to deal directly and only
with the best shops, and to be prepared to pay a little more in ready
money for quality produce – hints that no Tudor housewife would
have needed and that few, now, could do without.

Like Dods and Rundell, Kitchiner paid attention to the basics, giving
careful instructions for bashing steaks of meat to tenderise them and

---

* The rights, or 'perquisites', of the cook to make money on the side.

for broiling or grilling them upright at the fire, catching the fat before it hit the coals. Fish was poached at the gentlest simmer, and, for the sake of economy rather than deception, he showed how to mock pheasant with cheaper fowl hung longer than usual, and how to make gravy with water, beer, herbs, onions, cloves, flour and catsup. In common with Charles Lamb and many of his generation, roast sucking pig stuffed with sage, onion, breadcrumbs and eggs was a dish beyond compare (an 'ortolan with four feet', as Dods called it), the ears and tail crisped separately in buttered papers. For a man who made a virtue of dining, perhaps it was not surprising that Kitchiner's first recipe – emphatically *unlike* his female contemporaries – was for 'peristaltic persuaders' designed to combat the effects of constipation.

Instead of fiddling with meat baked in paper – tricky stuff even for a trained French chef – or struggling with difficult made dishes, the middle-class cooking of Rundell, Kitchiner and Dods was focused on recipes for jugged veal, hashed calf's head and Scotch collops, ox tongue in a thick brown gravy, potted rabbit, apple dumplings or mashed turnip. With a little care and attention, stuffed haddock, barley broth, scrag of mutton with a caper or parsley-butter sauce, scalloped oysters or fish pie were all well within the capability of any moderately well-equipped cook. Instead of hors d'oeuvres, simpler savouries were served at the end of dinner – 'baked or pickled fish, done high, Dutch pickled herrings, sardinias [sic] which eat like Anchovy but are larger . . . caviare and sippets of toast . . . radishes, French pie and cold butter', if you heeded Mrs Rundell.

Fish, on the other hand, was expensive food for dinner parties where the cod's head and Dutch turbot ruled, each served at their best one day old. Already a great affair in the previous century, cod's head had a kind of bulky magnificence, almost always presented with a crisp egg-and-breadcrumb coating, garnishes of pickled samphire or fried parsley, and a cucumber sauce or melted butter jazzed up with fish stock, oysters, lemon juice and chopped lobster flesh. Sole, John Dory, mullet and skate were all widely available, if not cheap, and traditions were hard to shake even if most cooks were unaware of their origins. Lamprey was rarely served without a sauce containing wine, and it remained a tricky fish to kill: while medieval cooks had bloodily skinned it alive, Kitchiner suggested fixing it while still thrashing to a thick board with a sharp knife through the base of the skull, pulling off the skin the moment it died.

The whitebait that swarmed in wide rivers like the Thames was inexpensive, though its preparation was laborious, with tails being fixed into mouths before being floured and fried in a heavy pan. Oysters were still abundant, costing only about 2s a hundred, and were parboiled and used generously in sauces to accompany fish, enriched with cream and lifted with essence of anchovies. Lobster was also used for sauces or was pounded with butter, eggs, breadcrumbs and mace, and potted to eat with toast. Cobbett, however, noted that the old fish-ponds in country houses were still being filled in – a continuing symbol of the population's growing divorce from the land – and few now ate freshwater fish aside from salmon. Fish came a clear second to butcher's meat, and though few people still observed Lent, the confectioner Gunter sounded positively medieval when he wrote in 1830 that by April fish and vegetables 'soon tire the stomach and in this month fish is fairly hissed from the theatre of good living'.*

From Edinburgh's New Town to Jane Austen's Chawton, cooking with which Parson Woodforde would have been comfortable, if not quite so much of it, was served according to the seasons; as Jane Austen wrote, '. . . good apple pies are a considerable part of our domestic happiness.' When the Austen girls went walking, inspired like so many of their contemporaries to a new appreciation of natural scenery by the Romantic poets,† their friend Martha Lloyd made them pigeon or rabbit pie and packed cold lamb, hard-boiled eggs, dishes of butter and bowls of strawberries; printed recipes for sandwiches also began to appear from the 1820s, filled with ham, tongue and mustard, roast beef or potted shrimp, cut small and 'served upon a napkin'.

---

* Gunter would continue to dominate ice-cream sales in London, owning great orchards and market gardens around Earls Court. He and his daughter Edith are immortalised in Gunter and Edith Groves in London, which stand on the land he once owned.
† The word 'picnic' was taken from the French *pique-nique*. In 1802 the Picnic Club was formed, its members sharing the cost of meals sent from a local tavern, but the word soon developed its modern meaning of sharing food out of doors.

Breakfasts, especially in Scotland, were becoming hearty affairs – fish, ham, cold meats, sausages, pies, eggs and a variety of breads and rolls with honey and marmalades – all taken at leisure in a designated breakfast room while perusing daily breakfast papers with names like *Dry Toast*. But dinner remained the culinary highlight of the day; Dods believed that soup was the foundation of the meal, and the mantra was scum, scum, scum, the cook throwing cold water into the pot to set the fats and make particles rise to the surface from where they could be lifted out. From Carême to Kitchiner the cry went out for cooks to simmer meat and vegetables very gently to coax out their flavour and to serve soups at the very last minute to prevent them from forming a skin at the table. Gentler seasonings and caramelised onions took the place of the bitter browning of burnt sugar and the over-powering taste of cayenne – fit, wrote Kitchiner, 'only for an iron throat and adamantine bowels'. Heading most dinner-party menus were the 'brown' soups of hare, giblet, beef and oleaginous ox rump and the 'white' soup of almonds and sieved chicken, but nudging in next to the elegant lobster and the smooth carrot or celery purées, a new soup – mulligatawny – had captured the public taste, the exception to the rule when it came to liberal use of cayenne.

'Mullga-tawny', or pepper-water soup, was a favourite among those returning from India and the East, made of meat in a clear stock flavoured with pounded coriander seeds, cinnamon-like cassia, some black and cayenne pepper, turmeric, browned onions and garlic, with a little lemon juice and cream swirled in just before it was served. Everyone had a recipe for mulligatawny, and most served it with a ballast of boiled rice. In fact, the confident taste of curry continued to colonise British kitchens: devilled biscuits were served as *provocatives*, or appetite stimulants, and the original owner of the British Library's 1821 edition of Rundell's work filled its blank opening pages with several recipes for curry powders, Bengal chutney and even a recipe for a condiment with tamarinds, red chillies, sugar and spices that, like the Romans' liquamen, had to be left in the sun for two days.

Even Middle England agreed that sauces should each have a decided character and be sent to the table hot and in a separate dish. Kitchiner thought that nothing bettered natural meat juices, but melted butter was still found on most solid British tables, alongside little mounds of grated horseradish and cream, pickled red cucumber, home-made mustard and sauces based on browned onion or shallot and oyster. Meg Dods home-flavoured vinegars with chilli, shallots, garlic, celery, cucumbers, anchovies and even curry powder, and used them to create different sauces from a base of melted butter. She recommended mushroom and celery sauces for boiled fowl and used many of the herbs favoured by professional chefs – especially tarragon, chervil, burnet and basil – and she even gave a recipe for garlic sauce, bruising two cloves with butter and oil, sieving the mixture to a smooth emulsion. 'Poor Man's' or 'Miser's' Sauce with its mix of parsley, onions, oil and vinegar, copied the grander 'Sauce maître d'hôtel', and even soy was faked with water, treacle or sugar and salt, reduced to a syrup the thickness of oil.

Walnut and mushroom catsups were still relied on, but, to the disgust of William Cobbett, 'to buy the thing, ready made, is the taste of the day. Capitalising on the popularity of Harvey's and Lazenby's sauces, Kitchiner ran advertisements for his own commercially pre-pared, bottled ZEST – an invention of 'piquant and savoury quintessence of ragout . . . to awaken the palate with delight, refresh appetite and instantly excite the good humour of (every man's master) the stomach'. For those who preferred to do it at home, his 'Wow Wow Sauce' was made by simmering parsley and pickled cucumbers in beef broth and table beer, and his 'Sauce Superlative' could be rustled up from port wine, mushroom catsup and vinegar.

With so much interest in concentrated, sharp flavours, the tomato – or tomata as it was still known – shyly entered the kitchen from the garden, where it had waited patiently for more than two centuries. Jane Austen adored them, writing to ask her sister Cassandra whether she had any spare. The first two printed recipes for tomato sauce came from Maria Rundell, who baked them in an earthenware jar once the bread had finished baking and the oven was cooling. Once they were cooked, she slipped off their skins and mixed the pulp with capsicum vinegar, ginger and pounded garlic or, alternatively, with white wine, vinegar and cayenne. Corked and stored, the sauce may have been used at table or added to gravies, but Kitchiner also embraced the taste, presenting his own 'tomata or love-apple sauce', stewing the ripe flesh with beef gravy, pressing it through a tammy and boiling it thick with lemon juice. Others remained suspicious, mocking tomato sauce with sharp apples instead.

The anonymous author of *Domestic Economy* (1827) cooked ripe tomato flesh to a bold mush with butter, garlic, thyme and chillies, but she was one of the bravest and most liberal of cooks, more ready to experiment with foreign flavours and textures than the majority of her broadly conservative contemporaries. Whereas most domestic cooks knew only a few 'foreign' recipes, keeping them quite separate from the rest of their cooking, she wrote inspiringly of the Continental love of calf's liver and encouraged her readers to dredge it in flour, fry it and serve it with an exemplary sauce of wine, ale, garlic, spices and herbs. Among now-standard recipes for mulligatawny and curry, she daringly fricasséed frogs with garlic, simmered snails with truffles and introduced the sweet pillaus, yogurts and cold soups of Persia, *cubbubs* (kebabs), couscous and African honey-pastes. Against directions for more prosaic ox cheek, ox heart and salted udder jostled recipes for pigeons with apricots, mutton with dates and mince in vine leaves – dishes so startlingly far ahead of their time that among Regency cookbooks they are entirely unique.

If a few adventurous housewives ever cooked such dishes for their husbands or guests, we can only guess with what amusement, joy or even disgust they were received, jolting the diners from their traditional expectations. For this was a society in which even coffee was still made terribly weak, over-boiled or unnecessarily brightened by isinglass, and where the majority were more at home with cauliflower poached in milk until tender to the tip of a knife. Yet attitudes to vegetables were on the move again. During the eighteenth century, the priority was to serve them crisp, but Regency cooks boiled them until they were soft, believing them otherwise 'tremendously indigestible, and much more troublesome to the stomach than underdone meats'. No one advocated boiling them to a pulp, but the change in taste did mark the start of the over-boiled, tasteless vegetables that would characterise the worst of English cooking from the heyday of Victoria until long after the First World War.

Potatoes too were becoming something of an obsession. Freshly dug and scrubbed, boiled whole and rubbed from their skins, mealy potatoes were drained and left by the side of the fire to burst and powder, were browned on a gridiron or crisped in beef dripping under the roast. Kitchener mashed them with butter, milk and even onions, spooning them into scallop shells, scattering breadcrumbs over them and browning them with a salamander much as Raffald had done; he also made them into balls which he floured and fried like dumplings, or rubbed them through a sieve to make a light 'snow'. Potato starch, known as *mucilage*, was treated as a thickener for soups and stews, though from the 1820s its use would be overtaken by arrowroot, imported from the East Indies.

Cold potatoes could also be reheated with leftover meat for supper or the 'lunch' dishes that were rapidly establishing themselves among the non-working classes. In towns there were no longer pigs and chickens to fuss around the kitchen door for peelings and scraps, prices continued to rise, and most cooks lived in a flurry of worry about waste as 'economy' became, of necessity, a concept equal to happiness. Accomplished cooks skilfully used small quantities of cheaper cuts of meat in French-inspired stews, and the repertoire of leftover meat expanded from beef olives and hashes with a thick sauce to 'bubble and squeak', which fried chopped meat and cabbage together. Mutton or fish from the day before were curried with stock, onions, a little cream and – preferably – a home-made curry mix of turmeric, ginger and cayenne; soups were strained and reheated, and jellies were melted and remoulded. Kitchener moulded meat scraps into an aspic seal for supper, but he also adored the bizarrely fashionable 'toast and water' that would soon be served to invalids: browned toast infused in boiling water, cooled and strained.

Economy was not the only pressing concern for harassed housewives and servants. There were pastes to be made for chapped hands and potpourris to sweeten rooms; chimney pieces had to be blackened, creaking doors rectified and rooms with their accumulation of decorative furniture to be dusted daily; and there were the children to consider, treated previously as miniature adults. Eighteenth-century Rousseau-esque philosophies were changing the status of children to that of idealised, vulnerable animals, and, beginning with William Buchan's medical dictionary in the 1790s, a whole repertoire of new dishes developed for the nursery and for the sickroom based on rice, sweetened sago or *salop*, arrowroot jellies, *panadas*,* chicken broths and boiled meats with mashed potatoes. The author of *Domestic Economy* even warned mothers to ensure that the nurse did not eat most of the food herself.

The anxious question of the dinner menu fluttered amid the tradesmen's calls, the deliveries that did not arrive or came with too little of this, too much of that and below-quality meat. Everyone was cautioned to deal only with respectable tradesmen, and every cookbook and manual had its tips for detecting adulteration, practically turning the cook into a chemist. From 1820, when Frederick Accum's *Treatise on Adulterations of Food and Culinary Poisons* created such a furore that he had to leave the country, housekeepers found themselves ever more vigilant regarding vinegar made of vitriol, pickles greened with copperas, bread bulked and whitened with chalk, bones or plaster of Paris, and 'cream' made from milk thickened with potato starch.

In response to such fraudulent and widespread practices, prepacked and branded goods marketed with the promise of quality flourished, and in 1806 the details of a new method of preservation that – unlike smoke, sugar, vinegar or salt – did not change the taste of meat, fruit or vegetables were published by a Frenchman called Nicolas Appert. Appert bottled his materials, corked them carefully, boiled them in a water bath, sealed the bottles with pitch and stored them in a cool, dark place – and it worked. New-laid eggs could now be boiled with bits of bread to stop them cracking. The technique worked for gravy, soups, fruits and reduced cream; even meat could be thus preserved, and new-gathered asparagus, beans and petits pois – 'prepared with the utmost rapidity so that there should be as it were but one step from the garden-bed to the water bath' – were declared delicious.

---

* Bread soaked in water with sugar and wine or rum and butter.

Food adulteration reached a peak during the nineteenth century and did
much to encourage the growth of tinned and bottled branded goods.

Driven by the needs of soldiers fighting in the Napoleonic Wars,
Appert could see the potential benefits of his discovery to the military
and to hospitals, but with chemistry still in its infancy and bacteriology
unknown, he had no notion of how important his discovery would
prove to be.* By the time his work was translated into English in 1811,
technology was speeding ahead and his method was already being
adapted to tinned metal containers by British businessmen. Brian
Donkin's first canning factory opened in 1812 – the year in which
Charles Dickens was born – producing goods in heavy metal containers which had to be opened with a hammer and chisel.† Hitherto,

---

* In America, the process of sterilisation that resulted from Pasteur's experiments was first
known as 'appertising'.
† Ice was also finally beginning to be used as a preservative. In 1785, Alexander Dalrymple of the
East India Company described the ancient Chinese practice of packing fresh fish in ice and the
penny dropped. His friend George Dempster passed the information on to his Scottish fish
merchant; the Scottish fishing industry was transformed, and fresh salmon was despatched
countrywide, safely and without the need for salt or pickle.

cooks had had to cut off rusty or sour pieces from their home-cured bacon, or wipe the slightly off joint with vinegar before cooking it; in hot weather many found themselves having to change their plans – like Mrs Grant in *Mansfield Park*, frustrated 'that the turkey, which I particularly wished not to be dressed till Sunday . . . will not keep beyond to-morrow'. With Donkin's method, even meat could be preserved indefinitely.

In 1815 the medieval Assize of Bread was abolished, only a year before the arrival of steam shipping. In the 1820s the ancient European pig was crossed with imported Chinese breeds, and the long-snouted, slope-backed animal gave way to a shorter, rounder, meatier variety. The Indian tea plant was grown commercially, slashing the cost of imports, and the hated British salt tax was abolished after almost four centuries of resentment. Industrialisation and the growth of towns continued to displace cooks and diners even further from the sources of their food. By 1830, along with omnibuses in London, there were Thomas Telford's roads and the established rumblings of George Stephenson's *Rocket*. As cooks tried to get to grips with the new iron monsters in their kitchens, everything around them was speeding up.

THE VICTORIANS

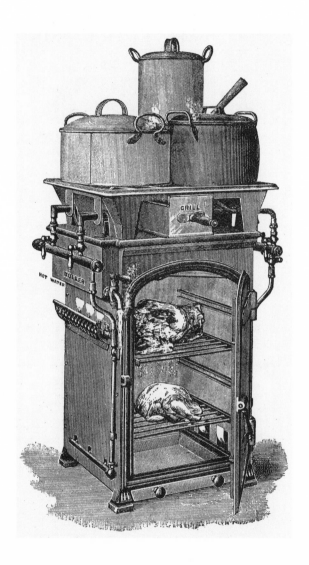

Technology bored its way into all aspects of Victorian life. By the 1890s, free-standing
gas ovens competed with cast-iron enclosed ovens or 'kitcheners' and the warmth
began to go out of the domestic kitchen.

20

The Great Laboratory

From kitchen ranges to the implements used in cookery is but a step. With these, every kitchen should be well supplied, otherwise the cook must not be expected to 'perform her office' in a satisfactory manner

— ISABELLA BEETON

In the Victorian society of seemingly limitless ambition, time was money and speed was progress, the drumbeat to which everyone marched. Railway schedules, business meetings, clocks on town halls and watches on chains, bells and gongs that warned that dinner was imminent all proclaimed that every minute mattered in the race for improvement. A vast semi-circular clock welcomed the six million visitors to the Crystal Palace where the Great Exhibition proclaimed Britain to be the workshop of the world, and Big Ben's tower dominated the new Houses of Parliament. Kitchen and dining-room clocks were synchronised – though there were no doubt plenty of unpunctual cooks who nudged the hands back with their broom handles as the dinner hour approached.

A population that had doubled to eighteen million between 1801 and 1851 would double again by the end of the century, and in bourgeois Britain advancement appeared to be there for the taking; the industrial economy thirsted for bankers, clerks and managers, and the cult of diligent work replaced the cult of taste. What had been a nation of shopkeepers was becoming a nation of shoppers in which the middle classes scoured vast emporia and department stores for the accoutrements of refinement that poured out of the manufactories. As everyone struggled for preferment, the cut of your dress, the type and extent of your furnishings, and the food you put on your table all proclaimed who you were – or who you wanted to be.

As the diminutive, plump, eighteen-year-old Victoria was crowned and Prinny's extravagant Pavilion in Brighton was given to the town Corporation, the nation began to slip off the expansive mantle of Georgian permissiveness in favour of buttoned-up earnestness, suffocating ceremony and a developing obsession with economy and waste. Within ten years of Victoria's accession, 5,000 miles of railway track were streaking across the land, transforming the possibilities of mass travel and transportation. Respectability was the fashion and muscular prosperity – echoed in the very landscape, in Isambard Kingdom Brunel's bridges and tunnels, in lamp posts and pillar boxes – the goal.

In the Derbyshire peaks, Joseph Paxton, the gardener who would design the Crystal Palace nearly twenty years later, was putting the finishing touches to the Great Stove glasshouse at Chatsworth, the biggest glass structure in the world at that time, an icon of horticultural as well as engineering progress. From it and a thousand smaller imitations in gardens large and moderate poured fruits and vegetables of extraordinary quality, and on the edges of towns and cities market gardens expanded still further to supply the great city markets. Strawberries and peaches were bigger than ever; rhubarb was becoming popular and pineapples cheaper. At Covent Garden in London, in Liverpool's new covered market and in towns across Britain, railways were delivering sacks of apples and potatoes, bundles of broccoli, mountains of cabbages and turnips, 'the roads stained green with the leaves trodden underfoot'. London's docks were crammed to breaking point; from Billingsgate and at Smithfield came a 'low murmuring hum . . . like the sound of the sea at a distance', the sound of restless, bustling food provision, a din that confounded the senses.

Crosse & Blackwell were soon selling nearly forty different pickles and sauces; Mr Bird invented instant custard powder for his delicate wife who could not take eggs but who loved the sweet, creamy sauce that had taken Regency tables by storm. Colman's mustard removed from cooks the eye-watering process of grinding seeds, curry powders were sold widely, and a returning Governor of Bengal pressed not a cook but a local chemist, Lea & Perrins, to invent Worcestershire, or 'Indian', sauce, so successful that its sales rose from 636 bottles in 1842 to 30,000 a decade later. New industrial methods created 'Dutched' or powdered chocolate, removing part of the butter fat to make it easier to dissolve, and Cadbury's factory at Bournville and Fry's followed soon after. Arrowroot thickened everything it touched and centrifugal machines began to produce the low-cost, high-quality granular sugar that would consign to history the paraphernalia for breaking down and grinding great sugar cones.

Technology bored its way into the kitchen too, turning it into the laboratory of the household. Isabella Beeton would rule in 1861 that kitchens had to have 'easiness of access, without passing through the house . . . [and] be sufficiently remote from the principal apartments . . . that the members, visitors, or guests . . . may not perceive the odour incident to cooking, or hear the noise of culinary operations'. At Mentmore in Buckinghamshire, the extravagant pile built for Meyer de Rothschild in the 1850s, an underground railway delivered food from the separate kitchen block to the dining room; at Chatsworth a separate brewhouse delivered beer via an underground pipe. Elsewhere, as at Petworth, circuitous passages – to the despair of the cook – distanced the dining room from the clamour and confusion of the kitchen, its offices and its legions of back-stairs staff.

From basement kitchens in terraced London to cramped suburban quarters, behind the green baize door and in the separate wings of country mansions, new gadgets were quickly adopted. Hinged moulds which produced raised pies emblazoned with decoration, baking sheets, soup ladles, vegetable cutters, fluted patty pans, boiled pudding moulds,* cutlet choppers, tongue-presses, freezing pots, and labour-saving fruit pressers, peelers and stoners all filled the inventories of the Victorian kitchen. Tea kettles, sausage machines, scales, brushes to replace feathers, fish and egg slices, fish-kettles, cheese toasters, and bright pans with close-fitting lids, flat bottoms and shorter handles to suit the new ranges all crowded the shelves. Reviewing cooking appliances for Charles Dickens's weekly journal, *Household Words*, George Dodds mocked that 'a coffee pot is not a coffee pot now; it is a mechanical psuatico-hydrostatic piece of apparatus.'

---

* The pudding cloth was becoming obsolete, and by the end of the century there would be metal pudding-boilers with clip-on lids.

The only note of discreet caution was directed at families in India whose native cooks, it was felt, were unlikely to use modern gadgets properly, or at all. In general, Victorians could be so proud of their up-to-the-minute kitchens that they photographed them using the new technology of Edward Fox Talbot. However, in an age of stinking sewers, ravaging cholera and the belief that smell transmitted disease, they could also be obsessed with odours, fitting the scullery sink with a bell-trap to catch refuse, pouring vegetable water away in the remotest corner of the garden (if you had one) and regularly flushing the drains. There was an arsenal against vermin – rat poison, beetle wafers or traps and fly papers at 2s 5d a dozen – and since cleanliness was still next to godliness, Calais sand or crushed soda was kept for scouring wooden surfaces and mounds of soap for swabbing stone floors. Rabbit skins, feathers and bones were collected for the rag-and-bone man (though slatternly servants put them in the dust heap and poured greens water down the sink), and old lemon rinds were salvaged for the tricky business of cleaning intricate moulds.

Plenty of cooks still toiled over open-grate ranges, though cast-iron ranges sporting mightily stolid names like the Eagle and the Conqueror were slowly taking over. Known generically as combinations or kitchiners,* these enclosed ovens with water boilers and hot plates came in every shape, size and pattern, but they were expensive, sulky and 'apt to be out of order', and it paid to understand and explain their working in detail to the cook. Taking a coveted first-class medal at the Great Exhibition, the 'Leamington Kitchiner' had an enclosed oven with movable shelves, an open fire for roasting, gridirons for chops and steaks, and a large boiler with brass tap and steam pipe. It cost £5 15s – or about a year's salary for a scullery maid. A larger, family-sized version was a dizzying £23 10s, or more than the housekeeper in a really grand house might earn in twelve months – none of which put off the owners of the fine house at Saltram in Devon from installing one, still in its place in the heart of the old kitchen.

These ranges often smelled strongly and were chancy at the best of times – especially for baking, which did not take kindly to the uneven

---

* Nothing to do with the Cook's Oracle, Dr Kitchiner.

heat many of them produced. They were tyrants eating into precious time; the filthy dampers and flues had to be regularly swept, the cinders sieved, the insides scoured, and the outsides burnished and black-leaded. When the wind changed, they smoked as badly as open fires, and temperature control was still inexact, so that the cook still tested the heat with flour or paper – if it burned, it was too hot; when it went dark brown it was suitable for pastry; light brown was for pies, dark yellow for cakes, and light yellow for puddings, biscuits and small pastries. The point at which any of these merged could still only be gauged by experience.

At the new Reform Club in Pall Mall, the excitable, extravagant and celebrated chef Alexis Soyer luxuriated in state-of-the-art basement kitchens meticulously ordered and equipped with the very latest steam technology, gas ovens and a plethora of his own cunning culinary innovations. So famous that more than 15,000 people were said to have visited them in 1846, Soyer's perfect kitchens inspired him to publish designs for kitchens of all sizes, paring down the eighty stew-pans of the Reform to four in a cottage kitchen, along with six black saucepans, a flat-bottomed egg bowl, wire baskets and a spoon drainer for deep frying, one hair sieve and, improbably, two bain-maries. An omelette pan, scissors, knife, pastry cutters, meat hooks, four wooden spoons, two meat saws, rolling pin, pudding cloths and towels completed his idea of the cottage cook's most basic needs.

Soyer also licensed his sauces and relishes to Messrs Crosse & Blackwell, and designed one of the very earliest domestic gas cookers, the unpronounceable Phidomageireion,* but it would be another fifty or so years before power stations supplied gas widely enough for most people to benefit from its instant heat. The Phidomageireion's great novelty was that it needed no chimney and could stand in the very centre of the kitchen, but cooking with gas remained controversial: the smell was off-putting, while poor ventilation and the cooker's tall, narrow shape meant that food was more often steamed than baked, and items placed at the top frequently remained raw.

In the misplaced hope that such domestic order would have an effect on his dubious morality, the indolent Eugene Wrayburn in Dickens's

---

* 'Thrifty kitchen' in Greek.

novel *Our Mutual Friend* (1864) fitted out a small room as a kitchen, complete with 'miniature flour-barrel, rolling-pin, spice-box, shelf of brown jars, chopping-board, coffee-mill, dresser elegantly furnished with crockery, saucepans and pans, roasting-jack, a charming kettle, an armory of dish-covers'. But not everyone benefited from a well-stocked culinary haven; in tenements, cooking facilities remained limited to a precariously balanced kettle or small pan on the grate, and terraced basements could run with damp. Many families in towns and villages alike still used the communal bake-oven, boiled over an open grate or used a poor man's spit: a skein of twisted worsted, weighted with a key, from which the meat dangled and rotated in front of the fire. Like many throughout Scotland, Ireland and Wales, the poor crofter widow Sheila MacFaddyen, in her simple cottage on the Western Isle of Ulva, relied on nothing but a small open fire until the early decades of the twentieth century, even as her close neighbours at Duart Castle on Mull installed the latest cast-iron range.

Cooks in middling households were advised to rise at six to scour and light the stove, to roll out dough for breakfast at eight, and to spend the morning making pastries, jellies, creams and fancy dishes which could be put aside in a cool room before the attenuated process of preparing dinner began. The evening meal was the core of the housewife's day whether she was giving instructions to the cook or setting out to plan, provision and prepare it all herself.

Dinner was also the perfect way to keep pace with one's neighbours and business acquaintances, but, badly managed, it could easily blow the domestic budget – and, as everyone knew, in overspending lay the road to ruin. Just as Dickens's Mr Micawber memorably – if vainly – repeated, 'annual income twenty pounds, annual expenditure nineteen, nineteen six, result happiness', everyone urged the cautious keeping of accounts. Books, papers and journals promised to navigate the difficulties of running a household as insistently as had the manners handbooks of the fifteenth century. Revolutionised by new steam presses, cheaper paper and mass distribution by the rail network, monthly journals like the *Magazine of Domestic Economy* – one of the first such to appear, in 1835 – ranged over advice on how to manage servants and nurture indoor plants, reviewed the latest publications, and gave the odd recipe for parsnip wine and boiled fowl.

Then came a cook who made thousands sit up and take notice. Published in 1845, Eliza Acton's 650-page *Modern Cookery in All Its Branches for Private Families* was an instant success, concentrating on plain foods for modest households: well-dressed vegetables, unadulterated home-made bread, fine-flavoured preserves, well-steamed rice, baked whiting, mackerel and John Dory, Irish stews and saddle of lamb. Acton liked to keep it simple and slow; she transformed the written recipe not only with her exact quantities and detailed instructions on things like boning and trussing but, also for the very first time, with closing summaries of all the ingredients needed and the time that each one would take to complete.*

'Eat to live', rather than to impress, was Acton's motto, and with her poet's eye for the written word and her wry humour about things going wrong, she filled her pages with an amused, frank intelligence quite the opposite of the de-haut-en-bas delivery of her French contemporaries. With advice to put skewers under roasting meat to stop it sticking, that dredging roasting meat too late meant that it went to the table tasting of raw flour, and that all sweet dishes benefited from a pinch of salt, Acton inspired her readers to thoughtful and imaginative cookery, complementing her fine recipes with simple woodcut engravings. She was the kind of practical cook who, in an emergency, would make a dessert soufflé flavoured with citron, coffee or chocolate in a 'plain round cake mould, with a strip of writing paper 6 inches high placed inside the rim', holding a hot salamander over it to maintain its shape as it was carried to the table – or a heated-up kitchen shovel if nothing else was to hand. She rarely used expensive tinned foods, preferring roast and boiled meats, pies and tarts, boiled suet and batter puddings, jellies and cakes, taking pleasure in the adept preparation of fine pastries with butter rather than suet, handling the paste as little as possible, taking it smartly to the oven and patiently leaving it alone to cook.

---

* Listing ingredients at the foot of a recipe, when you think about it, makes sense, since it assumes that the recipe itself has been read thoroughly first. It was Isabella Beeton who copied Acton's innovation but moved the list to the beginning, giving us, finally, the form of the modern recipe.

Cooks in Acton's mould firmly believed that there was no excuse for purchasing rather than making bread, letting the yeast ferment slowly by the fire and using the increasingly old-fashioned brick bread oven. They slow-cooked French stews and braises, soaked vegetables in brine to kill insects, were careful to break eggs – still small and often stale – separately, straining and whisking them for omelettes, and they rolled hard-boiled eggs carefully over a wooden table to remove their shells. Thoughtful cooks like her used spring onions – *eschalots* – in place of astringent brown ones and crushed cayenne with the back of a spoon, mixing it in warm liquid to prevent it forming lumps. Curry powders were home-made and used sparingly, the very opposite of Mrs Sedley's abominable sauce in Thackeray's *Vanity Fair* that tormented Becky to gasp for 'Water, for Heaven's sake, water!'

There was a palpable satisfaction in Acton's cooking that mirrored the best kitchens in the land. She recommended making soups – including coconut, chestnut, Jerusalem artichoke and one using old mutton with apple and ginger – the day before to ensure that not a drop of fat tainted their surfaces, and she added only the freshest vermicelli, sago and tapioca, cooked just to the point of tenderness. She also turned away from melted butter to its French equivalent – rich, unguent mayonnaise made by working drops of oil carefully into whisked egg yolks to form a smooth custard, coloured green with parsley juice or flavoured with a pea-sized piece of bruised garlic or a drop of tarragon vinegar. Salad creams were fashioned from a spicier, denser mix of hard-boiled egg yolks, cream, oil and vinegar with just a dash of chilli vinegar.

An ideal blend of writerly enthusiasm and practical confidence, Acton's remarkable cookery book was such a perfect resource for any hostess contemplating 'the dinner problem' that it stayed in print for seventy years. Four years after its first publication and under the pseudonym of Lady Maria Clutterbuck, Charles Dickens's wife Catherine also sprang to the rescue of hostesses struggling with the worry of constructing a straightforward but impressive menu for their guests. As the world flocked to the shimmering bird cage that was the Crystal Palace, she published *What Shall We Have for Dinner?*, a collection of menus for all occasions, with a few recipes attached for good measure.

Catherine Dickens's menus reflected solidly upper-middle-class life in London, where dinners were created around a traditional backbone with more expensive cuts of meat than would be used for a family meal. Typical for a small-scale affair might be:

Fried Soles. Shrimp Sauce.

Roast Fillet of Beef, stuffed. Turnip Tops.

Mashed and brown Potatoes.

Spanish Pudding.

Toasted Cheese.

Grander dinners retained the same tone:

Green pea Soup.

Broiled Salmon. Turbot. Lobster Sauce. Cucumbers.

Mushroom Patties. Lamb's Fry. Lobster Curry. Rissols.

Roast Saddle of Mutton. Mayonnaise of Chicken.

Broccoli. New Potatoes. Roast Duck. Peas.

Pudding. Clear Jelly. Italian Cream. Macaroni.

Cheese. Brunswick Sausage.

It all still felt rather eighteenth-century: salmon was served to good company, codling came with oyster sauce and lobster with shrimp sauce, and there were plates of Yarmouth bloaters (lightly salted smoked herrings, less dry than kippers)* and splendid mounds of fried whiting; the vegetables were soft-boiled.† Notably, Catherine Dickens rarely served poultry, though it was on the verge of changing

---

* The kipper was 'invented' in the 1840s by John Wodger – split, salted and smoked for long-term preservation.
† Unless you belonged to the Vegetarian Society (formed in 1847 from an offshoot of the Swedenborgians), whose members prided themselves on eating vegetables cut into pretty shapes, savoury omelettes, mushroom pies, moulded rice and the like. They were widely regarded as insane, even suicidal.

status as the incubators of the following decade increased production and reduced prices. In the meantime game, legally offered for sale only from 1831, retained its cachet.

Catherine Dickens loved a good brown gravy made from meat juices and a bit of walnut catsup or Harvey's sauce, or from the meat scraps and leftover gravy from the day before. Indeed, so sacred was gravy to nineteenth-century dinners that the Empire might have been founded on it, or, as Mrs Todgers says in another of Charles Dickens's novels, 'there is no such passion in human nature as the passion for gravy among commercial gentlemen'. What had been called 'essence of meat' was all of a sudden confounded by the advancing science of chemistry as the notion of ozmazome briefly appeared, described by Carême as the 'most savoury part of the meat', by Soyer as its 'very essence' and by plenty of others, including Mrs Beeton, as the soluble part of the meat that gave its perfume and savour to stocks. Whether ozmazome was in fact the caramelised meat juices found in the roasting pan or a hazy notion of the most nutritious part of the meat (red meat had more of it than white, fish had none), the befuddling concept was soon exploited by Justus von Leibig, a German chemist, who developed his own 'Meat Extract', a concentrated powder achieving a cult-like status. It would later be renamed Oxo, the first in a long line of artificial gravy powders.

Catherine Dickens's dinners generally closed with tingling water-cress and savoury toasts – melted cheese or soft fish roe made into a paste with butter (usually cod's but never slippery herring roe or the grey, waxy roe of the mullet). Her cheese soufflé was an unfussy addition of six eggs to 4 ounces of grated cheese and a quarter of a pound of melted butter: 'mix well, whip the whites of the six eggs, stir gently into the other ingredients, fill small paper cases . . . bake about a quarter of an hour in a moderate oven, and serve very hot.' Like most cookbooks, Catherine Dickens's was partly aspirational, but her menus were enviably thoughtful, and her husband was bristlingly proud of his dining room, rich with brocade curtains, fashionable flock wallpaper, Turkey carpets, a heavy mahogany table and hot, smelly, hissing gas jets – which is just as well, for the stroke that floored him during dinner in 1870 ensured that it was the last room he ever properly enjoyed.

Amid the whirling criticisms of domestic waste, French chefs like the flamboyant Soyer at the Reform Club or Charles Francatelli – Queen Victoria's cook until he hit a maid and was dismissed – continued to cook in the haute-cuisine style of their Regency forebears. Famous for his 'Mutton Cutlets Reform', in which the meat was coated with a ham-and-breadcrumb crust (still on the club's menu after a century and a half), Soyer was renowned for showy marathon banquets like the one given in honour of the Egyptian army commander Ibrahim Pasha at the Reform in 1846. Carving turkey legs into the shape of ducklings, garnishing veal consommés with blanched cockscombs, saucing hare with redcurrants, and roasting barons of beef, haunches of mutton and saddles of lamb, Soyer's tables were crowded with fine vol-au-vents, curried lobster and waves of piped mashed potato; there was a cake in the shape of a warship with a cargo of iced peach mousse and a 2½-foot-high meringue cake studded with sheets of crisped sugar, fluffed with pineapple cream and crowned with the likeness of the Egyptian Governor Mehmet Ali drawn on a satin cartoon.

A dandy to the core, Soyer's first book, *The Gastronomic Regenerator* (1846), was published just a year after Acton's and was its absolute antithesis, filled with artful, shiny foods, ornamental pastry *croustades*, and advice for steaming scraped carrots and sticking them into mashed potato in the shape of a crown. It should have surprised no one that Soyer was so fascinated by the bill of fare for the extravagant feast of Archbishop Nevill of York in 1467 or that he reprinted it in the back of his own book.*

This was French food beyond the abilities of the untrained cook. But Soyer also turned his hand successfully to recipe collections not only for the poor but for the middle classes, and a slight section on economical or 'plain' dishes even found its way into his *Regenerator*, containing recipes for roasts, julienne or vegetable soup, Scotch

---

* Soyer was also a philanthropist, justly celebrated for his efforts to relieve the suffering of the poor in London's East End and of the Irish during the Famine with quantities of cheap soup. Passionate about the possibilities of mass catering for the wealthy or the indigent, he also travelled to Scutari during the Crimean War, revolutionising hospital and military catering.

cock-a-leeky, oxtail or mutton broths, mock turtle, mulligatawny, green-pea soup and Palestine (artichoke) soup. Here he included the white-bellied turbot à la crème which everyone who could afford it loved, salmon boiled with a sauce matelotte of anchovies, oysters and Harvey's sauce, plain boiled cod and sole meunière. There were recipes too for fruit jellies and bread puddings, and it was just as well for, as Thackeray put it in the magazine *Punch*, '. . . everybody has the same dinner in London, and the same soup, saddle of mutton, boiled fowls and tongue, entrees, champagne and so forth.'

Soyer liked to boast that, with all the pretty girls in his kitchen, there were 'no plain cooks here' – but the phrase was now riddled with double meaning. Depending on your point of view, 'plain' was used either as a compliment for well-made, traditional dishes or as an insult for un-trained, uninterested and clumsy cooks. As the nineteenth century got into its swing, there was plenty of comment about the worsening state of English cookery. *Blackwoods Magazine* thought '. . . the aim of foreign cookery is to make it tender, of English to make it hard,' and Dickens's *Household Words* stated in 1851 that 'the real art of stewing is almost unknown in Great Britain . . . Everything that is not roasted or fried is boiled at "a gallop" till the quality of tenderness is consolidated to the consistency of caoutchouc [rubber]'. Eliza Acton had already called for the establishment of cookery schools for domestic servants, believing that they 'would be of far greater benefit to them than is the half-knowledge of comparative un-useful matters so frequently bestowed on them by charitable educationists'.

As the cry went up to make cookery a branch of female education, Harriet Martineau, a woman who had no sense of taste or smell, called in the pages of *Household Words* for a new 'School for Wives'. As daughters found themselves at increasing distances from their mothers and as female education continued to ignore the need for domestic skills, the situation was – Martineau wrote – in danger of becoming a case of the blind leading the blind.* Eighteenth-century criticism of

---

* In 1874, John Charles Buckmaster wrote that 'mistresses ought to be what they once were, the superiors and teachers of their servants', denouncing culinary ignorance as a national misfortune. He established a 'National Training School', but it had space for only ten students. Formal instruction in 'domestic economy' was introduced in 1876 in the new Education Code, but no financial provision was made for it, and where it was practised, women were more likely to be taught nonsense organic chemistry or unsuitably elaborate dishes.

flighty maids and insolent footmen developed into unceasing complaint about the depravity of servants, the proud, ill-tempered minxes
who broke crockery, built the kitchen fire up to the very flames of hell,
bullied the children and pilfered or squabbled over the accounts.
Pampered, spoiled mistresses and their wilful, sluttish 'Mrs' cooks
were endlessly satirised, each so derisive of the other that the mistress
feigned a headache while the cook took to drink and sentimental
penny-romances, 'her toes cocked upon the fender . . . our cat . . . in
the frying pan, and the house flannel and the scrubbing brush in the
fish kettle'.

Where neither good cook nor firm mistress existed, poorly hashed
mutton and the 'cold shoulder' – both the terror of normally jovial
husbands – could drive men to dine at an array of male-only alternatives away from wife, home and hearth. Upmarket members' clubs
clustered around Pall Mall, many made famous by chefs like Soyer at
the Reform who sent forth the best food on the shoulders of an army of
footmen for a handful of shillings. In any neighbourhood with a large
enough working clientele, cavernous taverns and dining houses sprang
up offering enormous joints and stews like the one that transported Mr
Codlin in Dickens's *Old Curiosity Shop*: ' "It's a stew of tripe," said
the landlord smacking his lips, "and cow-heel," smacking them again,
"and bacon," smacking them once more, "and steak," smacking them
for the fourth time, "and peas, cauliflowers, new potatoes, and
sparrow-grass, all working up together in one delicious gravy." '
New West End hotels like the Clarendon, Bedford and Clunns and
restaurants like Simpsons in the Strand with its great joints of meat
catered to the wealthy; the Albion in Little Russell Street or the
Provence in Leicester Square attracted middle-class play-goers; and
taverns on the Thames like the Trafalgar at Greenwich specialised in
whitebait dinners. For the rest, the pie-and-mash shops of London's
East End, alamode shops, cheap chop houses and 'ordinaries' with
sawdust and spit on the floors and greasy cloths on the tables served
boiled meat and vegetables. In 1851 the first restaurant guide for
London was published to assist the masses streaming to the Great
Exhibition, but it noted that there was almost nowhere for ladies, who
were limited for the time being to the elaborate ritual of 'visiting'
instead.

Poverty's Larder

At the heart of Britain's Empire, beyond the dinner parties and the smart clubs, lay the underbelly of its glutted cities. In 1815 only a fifth of the population lived in towns, but as people flocked to find work the statistics were reversed. Green spaces were diminishing, and the filth of life and industry flowed into inadequate sewers and polluted the waterways, housing the grim spectre of cholera. Poverty and grind were the fuel of material progress, labour was plentiful, and wages were low; the urban underclasses fended for themselves as best they could.

The Poor Law Amendment Act of 1834 provided a system designed to keep the poor just on the right side of starvation without diverting capital from the wage pool, and the twin faces of the nation with its hellish city slums and its comfortably off bourgeoisie were captured in Benjamin Disraeli's novel *Sybil* (1845) and widely debated by social reformers. William Cobbett wrote of the misery of villagers, and a twenty-four-year-old Friedrich Engels witnessed the wretched fate of the factory workers in Manchester in the 1840s, painting a vivid picture of a 'submerged tenth' whose diet was dominated by tea and who hoped at best for an onion or 'a small bit of bacon cut up with the potatos; lower still, even this disappears'. These hollow-eyed ghosts were starving, literally unable to bring home the bacon. While a handful of enlightened factory owners like Samuel Oldknow at Mellor Mill fed their workers on porridge, bacon, meat pies and puddings, others compounded labourers' adversity by paying a portion of their wages through the 'truck' system – giving credit which could only be redeemed at the owners' high-price, low-quality shops – a practice that drove workers into debt.

Leaving their factories late and exhausted, the best food in the markets already purchased, the poorest bought wilted vegetables, old cheese, rancid bacon, tough meat taken from diseased cattle, decaying potatoes and miserably adulterated goods. Reeling from the problems caused by rapid urbanisation, adulteration of goods was reaching a fraudulent and dangerous peak,* and they bore the brunt of it. But in an atomised society nobody much bothered about the undernourished, deceived and poisoned who, Engels believed, were lurching towards a revolution like those already ravaging the Continent. Indeed, despite the Reform Act of 1832, with its extension of the vote to propertied working people, the nation only drew back from the brink of potential revolution with the repeal of the Corn Laws, which had maintained an artificially high the price of corn, and the failure of Chartism in the last years of the 1840s. If it had not been for the lessons learned from its earlier civil war, Britain too might have tumbled into political turmoil during the worst of the 'Hungry Forties'.

In 1854, Elizabeth Cleghorn Stevenson, better known as Mrs Gaskell, shocked the readers of her novel *North and South* with unflinching descriptions of the appalling food of the factory workers, their greasy cinders of meat, the 'miserable black frizzle of a dinner'. In another of her novels – *Mary Barton* (1848) – workers bought opium

---

* The *Lancet* investigations in the early 1850s horrified the medical journal's readers when it found each of forty-nine bread samples to be adulterated. Coffee was commonly bulked with chicory or mangle-worzel and acorn, milk was watered, and tea had up to half its weight made up of iron filings. As William Wills wrote in *Household Words* in 1852, 'Whatever the British consumer may feel inclination to devour, let him devour it at his peril.' Against such 'death in the pot' fraudulence, the Food Adulteration Acts of 1872 and, particularly, 1875 at last outlawed the practices of short weights, bulking out and adding poisons to fake superior goods.

'to still the hungry little ones, and make them forget their uneasiness in heavy troubled sleep'. But of all the nineteenth-century novelists, it was Mrs Gaskell's contemporary Charles Dickens who most often used food to nail his characters to the masts of their particular fortunes. Festering oranges mouldered in the backstreets of Todgers' neighbourhood, the malevolent Quilp snapped off the heads of a plate of cheap prawns, Magwitch was driven to crime by hunger, and Oliver Twist's 'please sir, I want more' wrapped up his reckless misery and desperate hunger with the thin, grey gruel of the workhouse where boys had been suffering the 'tortures of slow starvation for three months'.

'Shocking Death From Starvation' was a constant headline in the local news rags, but it was Dickens's friend the journalist Henry Mayhew who first examined in detail the realities of life among London's invisible poor, exposing in the city's midst an extent of hunger that no amount of charity soup could hope to alleviate. Mayhew wrote of the clamour, steam and stench of the streets, the discordant din of the markets, the bootblacks and dog-collar and rat-poison sellers, and the vast array of costermongers, peddlers and hawkers from whom everything was available. Crammed into rotting tenements, men, women and children purchased their meals on the street, spending their pennies on ancient staples like oysters, sheep's trotters, pickled herring, hot eels, pea soup, meat puddings, muffins, baked apples or kidney puddings, or on tea, coffee and hot potatoes. The penny-pie sellers – despite the circulation of the gruesome myth of Sweeney Todd, the murderous barber of Fleet Street who slit the throats of his customers and used their flesh as pie meat – did a roaring trade, pouring in gravy from an oil can to make the lids rise.

Books like Alexis Soyer's well-intentioned *Shilling Cookery for the People* (1855) delivered recipes that could be made with a simple gridiron, frying pan or black pot, but their economical instructions for dressed sprats, hashes, chops, puddings and pies were no more likely to have eased the situation than Frederick Eden's suggestions for making salt-fish palatable with a butter sauce had half a century earlier. Though some sixty thousand copies sold in less than three weeks, it was not the poorest who bought Soyer's book but artisans and families headed by clerks in business. The poorest earned as little as 5s a week, and it was spent on a daily 4-pound loaf with almost nothing left over for rent, tea, cheese or bacon, let alone a book. In such a light, poor Mrs Cratchit's ability to cook a Christmas pudding 'with its smell like a washing day' in the midst of her family's poverty was not only heroic ('the greatest success achieved by Mrs Cratchit since their marriage') but rare.

By the middle of the century, with the railways delivering gluts of fish to London, the price dropped low enough for the working classes to benefit from fried fish at a penny or from the shellfish, kippers and sprats found on street barrows. But it was baked potatoes – sixty million of them a year – that were most popular on the street. A halfpenny each, hot and quick to eat, they were used by the poor to keep their hands warm in their pockets for as long as they could stave off the cravings of hunger.

The poorest of all ate the discarded heads of eels, but everyone bought food that was 'easily-swallowed and comfortable' rather than solid and filling, and almost everyone had strong tastes, being habituated to rank relishes and rancid butters. The penny pie shop in Tottenham Court Road used high seasonings to disguise the taste of tainted meat, adding treacle for richness and pounds of *critlings* – the refuse left after rendering lard – for colour. On a winter's evening, a single halfpenny dumpling from a copper boiling pan might be all the dinner a child could hope for, while the eight-year-old watercress girl selling her copper-coloured wares at four-bunches-a-penny to the cooks of the middle classes told Mayhew that she had no dinner: 'Mother gives me two slices of bread and butter and a cup of tea for breakfast, and then I go till tea and has the same. We has meat of a Sunday and, of course, I should like to have it every day.'

Street children spent their few coins on a penny-slice of plum pudding, boiled trotters and pickled tripe, on boiled sweets luridly coloured with lead, arsenic and mercury, or on rhubarb, currant and cherry pies – even a slice of over-ripe pineapple – all sold in the street from a bit of polished wood or piece of oil cloth. From the 1840s, the Wenham Lake Ice Company had begun to import ice to sell in blocks to fishmongers, confectioners and wealthy households. Quick to catch at an opportunity, Italian immigrants like Carlo Gatti set up in business in London in the summer of 1850, selling hard, luridly coloured ices made from often dirty milk mixed with cornstarch and luring customers for their 'penny licks' with cries of *'ecco un poco!'*, ensuring their nickname: the Hokey Pokey men. Most thought that such street luxuries would never take off, and others jibed that soon there would be jellies in the street 'and then mock turtle and then the real ticket sir!' The vain hope in the back alleys was that, come the Great Exhibition, penny glasses of champagne would be available to all.

Nowhere perhaps was the division between rich and poor so viscerally captured than in an article published in 1866 in Samuel Beeton's terribly modern monthly, the *Englishwoman's Domestic Magazine*. Surrounded by creature comforts, mothers whose daughters played in the nursery with pretty toy villas could read in the magazine's pages a gruesome account of 'bits and ears' – the 'hairy tips and the gory severed parts of the ears of oxen and calves' that many of the impoverished tried to turn to account for their families. As the makers of the dolls' houses all but starved, their children made their way to the heaps of skins piled up beside the markets at London Bridge in search of food. This was poverty's larder – crawling with knife-wielding boys 'hunting about the hides and flapping them over to get at their fleshy side', swooping down on a tag of meat 'like a carrion crow on a worm'.

21

The Flight to Gentility, or Living for Appearances

The choice of Acquaintances is very important to the
happiness of a mistress and her family . . . Society should
be formed of such a kind as will tend to the mutual
interchange of general and interesting information

— ISABELLA BEETON

'Oh! How much prettier our houses are . . . than they used to be!'
exalted the interior decorator and journalist Jane Panton in her *Hints*
for Young Householders (1888). Where earlier Victorians had lived
self-consciously in an age of transition, the striving 'self-help' generation of the 1860s onwards were reaping the profits of industrialisation
and free trade. Wages rose faster than prices; the lower middle classes
were on the move.

Away from the grubby reality of factories, business and the street
poor, middle-class women were left to stew, to bite their lips and pass
the gravy while their men got on with the business of doing. Most
found themselves living in flats in towns or in the new suburbs
conglomerating at the edges of cities, wildernesses of acquaintances
in which their homes had become impregnable castles – '. . . No one
may approach without previous notification,' wrote Thomas Peacock's
daughter Mary-Ellen Meredith; there was plenty of talk but little
conversation.

Swooning over deep red or green dining rooms brightened by
gaslights, choosing cheerful Japanese papers for the walls, Mrs Panton
was unremarkable in finding the running of the kitchen rather a
tiresome business, filled with 'prosaic and difficult details', but she
described how to choose new 'cocoa-nut' or oilcloth flooring and

glazed tiles for the kitchen walls, part of an ever-expanding market for advice on everything from modelling cities in wax to collecting seaweed, planning a party or burying a relative. This was the information-hungry generation at which the successful *Englishwoman's Domestic Magazine* was aimed.

Growing out of articles that she had written for her husband's magazine, Isabella Beeton's *Book of Household Management*, first published in 1861, was almost entirely plagiarised from other sources, including Mrs Raffald, Eliza Acton, Alexis Soyer and – for the sections on health – Florence Nightingale, the cutting and pasting of an astute young suburban wife and journalist with a keen eye for the market. Mrs Beeton aimed at lower-middle-class housewives with an annual family income of between £150 and £200 – messengers, clerks or artisans might earn between £80 and £150 – and at women who dreamed of multiple servants but who managed with a solitary maid-of-all-work. With its precise instructions on etiquette and brisk general household guidance, her book neatly caught the public mood, selling two million copies in its first seven years.*

As 'with the COMMANDER OF AN ARMY,' Mrs Beeton wrote, 'so is it with the mistress of a house'; only by ordering the day into a rigorous, planned system could the drudgery of housework and cookery be converted into competent productivity. Updating Acton's recipe layout by listing ingredients at the start instead of at the end and giving the per-head cost for each dish, with Mrs Beeton's help family dinners or grander parties could be precisely planned with an eye for both seasonality and thrift. In contrast to her sensible predecessors, she did not stress the quality of seasonal market goods but laid down the rule 'that the best articles are the cheapest'. Boiled meats and roasts were designed to last for several meals as leftovers – more delicately known as *rechauffés* – progressing through the week. For one week in April she suggested:

---

* By which time its young author had been several years dead. Far from being the elderly matron in black bombazine, Beeton died of puerperal fever following childbirth. The commercial force of her work, lasting almost a century, was to slip from the hands of her labile husband Sam to become the profitable possession of the publishers Ward-Lock.

Sunday: clear gravy soup, roast haunch of mutton, sea kale, potatoes, rhubarb tart and custards in glasses.

Monday: skate with caper sauce, a boiled knuckle of veal and the cold mutton with mashed potatoes.

Tuesday: vegetable soup and toad-in-the-hole made from the very last of the cold mutton with rhubarb and custard, again.

Wednesday:*   fried soles with anchovy sauce, a new piece of boiled beef with carrots and dumplings, lemon pudding.

Thursday: pea soup made from liquor that the beef was boiled in, cold beef, mashed potatoes, mutton cutlets and tomato sauce, macaroni.

Friday: bubble and squeak made with remains of cold beef, roast shoulder of veal stuffed, spinach, potatoes, boiled batter pudding and sweet sauce.

Saturday: a stew made from the remains of the shoulder and its vegetables.

Everyday food was thus plain and unfussy at best, boring and regimented at worst. Mincing machines that bolted on to the edge of the table, introduced in the 1870s, eased the transition of grey, gristly leftovers into shepherd's and cottage pies, but they would also give rissoles and croquettes their bad name and were never used to prepare food for entertaining.

Common sense and economy lay at the heart of Beeton's Bible, but fantasy was also a key ingredient in its success, and it was heavily seasoned with some of the first chromolithographs – colour plates of food gussied up into ambitious forms. Regular dinner parties were opportunities for social rivalry in a world where manners and style were the mark of the man (and woman), and they subsumed much of the weekly food budget. Appearances were so important that greengrocers moonlighted as sham butlers – 'the dirty grubby dusty man . . . transformed . . . into the Waiter,' as *Punch* put it – and, like the decorative arts, dinner-party food was becoming ever more ornate and recherché as ambitious families vied to outdo each other, often offering pretentious amounts of champagne well beyond their means.

---

* Oh! The relief of new ingredients!

Part of the problem was that when writers like Acton defended French cooking as economical, they had in mind slow-simmered stews which could be made with scraps and cheap cuts, favouring old favourites like haricot mutton and the pot-au-feu gently simmered for hours, using meat juices from the pan in preference to expensive gravies and creating unembellished fruit pies with the best fresh food from the local market. Others, fearful of that dreadful crime of waste and at the same time eager for admiration, tried to marry economy with fancy French culinary footwork, burdened by the desire to impress with fancy borders, heavy garnishes and the lisping folly of French names. The upshot was, as the anonymous author 'V G' decried, that these same, nervous cooks served up large turbot raw in the middle, unbearded oysters and 'a slop of water from the pot in which the vegetables were boiled by way of gravy'.

Since formal entertaining was the very bedrock of social life, there was no escaping it. As each class sought to distance itself from the layer below it, manners changed as fast as ever, becoming at the same time highly codified. Invitations went out a fortnight before, place cards and handwritten menus were set, eveningwear was donned and the progression of the guests, in pairs according to rank, agonisingly planned. In a university town, an unwitting slip could cause high dudgeon: Gwen Raverat, granddaughter of Charles Darwin, wrote of her Cambridge mother despairing at the relative superiority of Professorial Chairs and of the touchy self-importance of some of the grandees and their wives – not such a far cry from medieval anxiety over what to do with a Pope's parents.

Drawing birds, skinning hares and negotiating barrows of coal, the cook battled to get all the dinner dishes out in time, as shiny and as well presented as the guests. She had to keep an eye on the roast to make sure that it was done until the last trace of blood was gone, and keep sauces at a simmer, vegetables at a gallop and fried food scrupulously drained. Milk replaced cream in sauces as companies like Express Dairies transported country milk by rail into the cities – free from the filth associated with the old urban dairies. Eggs, still small but now imported in vast quantities from France, were giving way to cornflour and arrowroot as thickeners. Contrasting soups, often heavy with sherry, were given a final 'boil up' before serving, but despite Francatelli's 130 recipes for soup, Oscar Wilde derided the inability of British cooks 'to make a soup which is anything more than a combination of pepper and gravy'.

The vegetable kingdom was now hardly explored as most relied on carrots (still thick and woody if we are to believe Mrs Beeton's cooking time of two and a quarter hours) and potatoes, boiled in 'plenty of fast-boiling water', coating them with gravy or a white sauce. The large heads of cauliflower and broccoli were boiled upside down and served whole; asparagus was still scraped and simmered in bundles; haricot beans, cabbage, the new Brussels sprout and the quintessentially Victorian 'vegetable marrow', or courgette, were all boiled quite soft – generally fifteen to twenty minutes for a cauliflower, fourteen for sprouts, ten for French beans and twenty for large cabbages, quartered. Purées were fashionable, made using a wooden presser and a horsehair or tammy sieve. Lettuce was often braised, and salads were served as a savouries, dressed with sweet Lucca oil or an egg-and-cream emulsion, but old habits died hard – even conservative Mrs Beeton considered raw vegetables a health risk to any but the fittest.

While Catherine Dickens's collection of recipes had contained only one solitary, daring tomato – cannily paired with a veal cutlet – by the last third of the nineteenth century tomatoes had completed their journey from poison to pleasure, baked whole or in slices, stuffed with breadcrumbs, stewed into a sauce with shallots and cayenne, or sliced raw in salads. By the end of the century they would arrive tinned from America, be commonly served as a soup and munched like apples by the working poor when the harvest was in glut. But of all vegetables, the potato still reigned supreme. By the late 1850s they were being cut into strips and fried from raw – in the 'French fashion', according to Mrs Beeton – to accompany rump steak, and though some fried parboiled potatoes, everyone by the 1870s agreed that these delightful crispy strips were called 'chips'. Soon – as steamships plundered the teeming northern seas, returning with such quantities in their refrigerated holds that fried fish for a penny became working-class fare – chips would replace the baked potato.

Nonetheless, fish was still considered far less nutritious than meat, and most was boiled without vegetables and served with a béchamel sauce, though carp was also stuffed, egged, breaded and baked, and sole fried, fricasséed or made into balls with parsley, lemon peel and breadcrumbs. Recklessly harvested for centuries, oysters became a luxury, their price rising alarmingly from eightpence a bushel in 1840 to a shilling a dozen in 1860. Chicken – or 'poulet', as it was fashionably called – moved in the opposite direction. It was boiled, pattied, potted or curried, and 'Chicken Marengo'* was popular – small pieces of the meat browned, floured and simmered with mushrooms, stock, garlic and pepper, and served with the sauce reduced to a syrup. Fish and fowl also came into their own served cold in aspic, *chaudfroid*† or mayonnaise coloured with parsley juice or pounded lobster spawn – even a little curry powder; Mrs Beeton made mayonnaise with stock and cream rather than eggs and oil, an easy if bland fallback.

Bananas and avocados were all but unknown except on the richest estates, and grapefruit was still uncultivated in British gardens, but the oranges that had been as jewels in the sixteenth and seventeenth centuries were imported in their millions, four to a penny and sometimes cheaper than apples. Horticultural catalogues boasted more than a thousand types of apple, seventy varieties of gooseberry and a hundred and fifty different sorts of pear, all typically destined either to decorate the table or to be baked in a tart, such an important element of British entertaining that an American diplomatic wife at the end of the century described it as 'so big and strong and solid that it impresses the unfamiliar mind as having been built by government contract'.

Manufactured gelatin assisted the intricate moulding of gaudy jellies: no one had to fill their kitchen with the smell of calves' feet boiling for hours unless they really felt like it, and few did. Under the combined influence of gelatin and arrowroot, creams and custards became solidly uncompromising and blancmanges unremittingly starchy. Showy, moulded Regency favourites like charlottes and sweet soufflés were stalwarts of the high Victorian dessert course along with 'Nesselrode Pudding' and 'Prince Albert Pudding', a sticky-sweet orange custard in a pastry case.

---

* A dish supposedly created in honour of the battle won by Napoleon against the Austrians in 1800, redolent of aspiration to all things French.
† Traditionally, chaudfroid was a sauce made from stock with cream and aspic, though some cooks also added mayonnaise.

Canning offered a solution to the problem of urban supply and when cattle-plague hit in the 1860s, Australian tinned meat – coarse-grained, overdone lumps with a wad of fat – cost less than half the price of fresh meat and business boomed.* So unpopular that the navy called it 'Fanny Adams' after the eight-year-old whose murder had shocked the nation,† tinned meat was generally foul, but it was cheap and it came in handy for unexpected guests, titivated into soups, stews and rissoles. As the United States recovered from its Civil War, its canning factories went into overdrive: exports to Britain rose from seven tonnes in 1866 to about ten thousand tonnes five years later, while in Uruguay, the fortunes of the newly founded port city of Fray Bentos were about to be made.

In 1888 *The Girl's Own Indoor Book* listed oxtail, salmon, curried rabbit, plum pudding and pineapple in jelly among the new varieties of tinned goods available, all easily warmed in a pan of hot water and just as simply turned out on to a plate, made to look 'really appetising' with a garnish of bright-green parsley or a slice of lemon. 'If you wish to have what may be termed higher-class delicacies,' the book continued, 'there is pâté de foie gras as well as truffled woodcock, lark, snipe, plover, partridges and quail', each for about half a crown.

Tinned foods were the tip of the iceberg in a veritable food revolution. Roller mills removed so much of the germ that flour became, finally, really white, and commercial bakeries like the Aerated Bread Company (ABC) ensured the ongoing decline of home baking despite quick-acting packaged yeasts and self-raising flours like Florador and Rizine. In 1868 the first cheese factory opened in Derbyshire; by the 1860s Huntley and Palmers were producing more than 120 varieties of packaged biscuits, and the poor were clamouring for cheap

---

* Sixteen thousand pounds of Australian tinned meat were imported in 1866, compared to twenty-two million pounds only five years later.
† The scandals of earlier attempts at canning that produced putrid meat had been broadly forgotten. It is likely that the tinned meat supplied to Sir John Franklin's fated 1850 expedition to find the North-West Passage had been boiled in salt water to save fuel, remaining partially raw at its core, rotting and poisoning many of the crew. Others believe that lead found in the tinned containers weakened the men.

factory jams – more colouring and sugar than fruit. Margarine, made from chopped cows' udders or suet emulsified with butterfat or milk and initially called Butterine, was invented in France and began to be mass-produced in America and Holland: oily, unpalatable and un-nourishing.* In 1880 the SS *Strathleven* arrived from Australia with the first shipment of successfully refrigerated beef and mutton, which sold for only 5 to 6d a pound.

Terrified of adulteration, Mrs Beeton waxed rhapsodic about the mechanically produced and shop-bought foods that were beginning to alter the diet of the nation. The age of the grocer with his pre-packed teas, desiccated Symingtons soups, evaporated and condensed milk, corned beef, ready-shredded suet, bottled horseradish, egg-powder and Chelsea Jelly – just add water – had arrived. Unlike her Con-tinental counterpart, the late Victorian urban housewife no longer tested the quality and prices of specialist shops, barrows and markets but sent out orders and had her food delivered from the grocer: Fortnum & Mason for the richest, Army & Navy or Arding and Hobbs for the middling sort, and chain-store co-operatives for the working classes.

As gas lighting and office hours pushed dinner back towards eight or even ten in the evening, the language of mealtimes took on a marked social significance – the working classes taking their 'dinner' in the middle of the day and their 'tea' in the evening – and for those who dined late, breakfast, afternoon tea and lunch acquired such impor-tance that specialist books were devoted to each separate meal. Con-venience foods promised to lighten the load, but it seemed that the cook had more meals to organise than ever.

Beeton believed that a tablecloth at breakfast exercised 'a certain moral influence upon the inmates of the house', and she set out cold joints on the sideboard – 'nicely garnished' fish and cold game, collared or potted meats or pies. There might be bloaters, anchovies, grilled mackerel or haddock, mutton chops, muffins, toast and preserves –

---

* It is perhaps unsurprising that the very notion of a 'standard of living' dates from the late 1870s.

though there were warnings about hot buttered toast that could 'make the butter bill into a nightmare'. Curry loomed large, with curried kidneys, eggs and rice, tinned pilchards fried with a curry-and-corn-flour crust, or Gothic-sounding 'devilled bones' made from the seasoned legs and wings of cold poultry re-grilled. Victorian gentleman worshipped the ham, and Aleyis Soyer's spirit-filled Magic Stove might sit at one end of the table for each guest to 'frizzle' a slice of bacon or whip up an omelette. As eggs became cheaper, patent egg-boilers, egg-holders and egg-top cutters were marketed; the Great British Breakfast had come of age.

For servants and children, lunch remained the main meal of the day, while others viewed it as 'the ladies meal' or thought it an indulgence. Anything left over from breakfast or the previous day's dinner was paraded: steamed puddings, lightly curried kedgeree, curried rabbit or sliced cold meats with horseradish or hot gravy, or a sandwich and a glass of sherry taken either in the nursery or on a tray in the parlour. When company called, a galantine of layered pressed meat, bread, cheese and biscuits did the honours, while up in the nursery the 'dearest' children were given a stomach-numbing round of bland food, for anything rich or spicy was considered overstimulating; excess was indulged only in the lavish children's parties that became fashionable among the middle classes from mid-century onwards.

As a refined afternoon habit, the 'cosy, chatty affair' of tea with sandwiches, biscuits and cakes entered Beeton's *Book of Household Management* only in its 1880 edition. Walnut cake, chocolate rolls, time-consuming seed cakes, Savoy biscuits and wafer-thin slices of bread and butter were arranged on the best china and cake-stands for numberless corseted ladies visiting the housewife on her weekly 'afternoon'. Queen Victoria, who presumably visited nobody, pre-ferred bone marrow on toast and is unlikely to have ever tasted the sponge cake sandwiched with jam that was named after her – a nursery luxury. The labouring classes, the old-fashioned and particularly those in the north took what the Grossmiths' 'nobody' Pooter called a 'meat-tea' in the late afternoon: a substantial meal of meat, cakes, pies and bread that did instead of dinner.

Depending on your point of view, the entertainments called 'sup-pers' were either a welcome culinary challenge or a trial, consisting as they did of laboriously prepared cold meats, pies and confections laid out on a side table heavy with fruits and flowers. Mrs Beeton's menu for a ball supper for sixty guests – well beyond the means of most of her readers – suggested 'beef, ham and tongue sandwiches, lobster and oyster patties, sausage rolls, meat rolls, lobster salad' . . . and off she went. The buffet groaned with decorative mayonnaises, iced Savoy cake, turnips cut into flowers, pressed tongue, stuffed shoulder of lamb, pigeon pies and jellies, custards, and fancy pastries or biscuits. Champagne, iced punch, lemonade and ices all completed the swanky effect as the guests helped themselves between dances, juggling plates and glasses with conversation and gossip.

Once the factories began to close at two on Saturday afternoon in the early 1850s, and in the wake of the Bank Holiday Acts of the 1870s, the concept of the weekend was born along with a growing belief that leisure was the reward for hard graft. Epsom Racecourse's catering on Derby Day astonished Charles Dickens with its mountains of mutton, lobsters, tongue, pigeon pie and 'an incredible quantity of ham' for sandwiches, and in the 1880s 'Major L' took his own mulligatawny soup, braised beefsteaks, minced pies, cold meats and a pint of champagne per head. Champagne also eased train travel, drunk 'to while away the tediousness of the journey, oil the wheels of life and improve the temper'. Only the foolhardy travelled unprepared, for railway food was universally abhorred: 'lumps of delusive promise . . . little cubes of gristle and bad fat . . . the scalding infusion satirically called tea . . . [and] sawdusty sandwiches' according to the *Financial Times*.

Showing a recklessness in the face of the British weather, town-dwellers traipsed to the seaside, to stately homes and to the open fields, touting their food with them; on Saturdays and Sundays in summer, Paddington Station was said to be packed with a crowd 5,000 strong on the Maidenhead platform alone. Beeton's provisions for a picnic for forty were exhaustive, including several joints of cold roast and boiled beef and lamb, roast fowl, ham, tongue, pies, lobsters, collared calf's head, baskets of salad, stewed fruit, plain pastry biscuits, puddings and blancmanges in their moulds, jam puffs, cheese, butter, loaves and cakes for tea. 'Coffee is not suitable,' she wrote, 'being difficult to make.' She packed a stick of horseradish, a bottle of mint sauce (well corked), salad dressing, made mustard, pepper, salt, good oil and sugar – and, 'if it can be managed, take a little ice'. Plates, glasses, cutlery, teacups and saucers, teapots and more than ten dozen bottles of various wines and cordials were also hefted along, though on the issue of who was to carry it all she remained silent.

Alternatively, Fortnum & Mason provided the finest pre-packed hampers available, so successful that they began to displace the great Christmas pies of old as gifts for family and friends. As the ideal (German) family Christmas was held up for admiration by Victoria to her subjects, and as Christmas cards and decorated trees began to catch on, the festival – though still broadly solemn and religious – crystallised not on Twelfth Night but on Christmas Day itself. Plum puddings and mince pies, leftovers from a forgotten age, still contained minced beef and the best kidney suet – with fancy moulding their only concession to modernity – but beef was replaced by goose, the plump breasts carved for the family and the legs sent down to the kitchen.

In the closing decades of the nineteenth century, though his mother the Queen famously preferred plain food, the Prince of Wales's self-indulgent and risqué Marlborough House set cut a dash in their pursuit of amusement and novelty. At his dinners, two hundred pheasants were used for a single dish, quails were stuffed with foie gras, larks were baked into a billowing croustade, consommés and colourful desserts could famously take three days to prepare, and soufflés were commonly made from five dozen eggs.

New establishments like the Café Royal and the Criterion, where Prince Edward dined regularly with his mistress Lillie Langtry in a private room, allowed beautifully dressed ladies to meet in public amid magnificently appointed interiors. Flush with the success of the Savoy Theatre, in the 1880s Richard D'Oyly Carte opened the Savoy Hotel with electric light in all the rooms, luring from Paris the celebrated hotelier César Ritz and his *maître-chef* Auguste Escoffier – men who would redraw the notion of what a hotel dining room could offer, seating male and female diners at individual tables against a backdrop of showy luxury, offering both a 5-guinea à la carte and a 12s fixed-

price service. Dining out was an early step on the road to female
emancipation, but the British were still so buttoned up that Henry
James was astonished by the lack of café society in London and at the
cultural vacuum caused by the ingrained antipathy of the middle
classes to *mix*.

Escoffier's grand *Guide culinaire*, written in 1903 and translated into
English in 1907, provided the backlash to the pseudo haute cuisine of
the middle classes, searching for a lighter, less fattening, consciously
refined and standardised professional style. He relied on *fonds de
cuisine* sauces though he also popularised sauces like Cumberland, a
mix of mustard, oranges, redcurrant jelly, port, pepper and salt, and in
the mould of the great French chefs of the Regency he presented his
cooking as a highly evolved art, producing menus – all in French – like
theatrical programmes. 'Sole Veronique' linked arms with ingenious
little novelties: wafer-thin Melba toast,* light mousses, tiny profit-
eroles the size of a hazelnut stuffed with foie gras or vegetable purées,
endless ways with eggs and transparent soups that were 'veritable
wonders of delicacy and taste'. Potato croquettes and lightly steamed
vegetables were moulded into fancy shapes, breaded and fried for
garnishes. 'Pêche Melba', famously created (like the toast) for the
Australian soprano Dame Nellie, presented peaches and ice cream in a
silver dish topped with spun sugar, cradled between the wings of an
ice-carved swan. Inventive, perfectionist and gleaming, Escoffier's
would be the style that would dominate British restaurant cooking
and catering for much of the twentieth century.

His astute contemporary Agnes Bertha Marshall, on the other hand,
dominated the upmarket domestic culinary landscape with exactly the
kind of pseudo-French food that made Escoffier snort. Criticising
tinned food, railway restaurants and the lack of good tomatoes for
salads, the entrepreneurial Mrs Marshall published a voluminous
collection of recipes in 1888, ran her own London cookery school,
gave polished demonstrations to hundreds of ladies at a time, and
marketed her own kitchen gadgets and culinary preparations like
coralline pepper and Luxette – a blend of cooked fish paste sold in
little earthenware pots for sandwiches, picnics and luncheons.

---

* Toast that was split in half and re-toasted.

But the dishes in *Mrs A. B. Marshall's Cookery Book* were as primped as a fashion plate. Nothing was simple: breakfast cutlets were made from a thick paste of cooked chicken, tongue or ham with egg and onion, then floured, breaded, 'made cutlet shape with the hand and a palette knife' and fried 'to a pretty golden colour'. Mushrooms were pressed into buttered bombe moulds lined with parsley and filled with a beef farce, covered and cooked in a bain-marie, de-moulded on to a plate of piped mashed potato, a rose of cream piped on to the top of each one. Ingenious *millefiore* 'paperweights', or *balettes*, were created with a dome of aspic jelly filled artistically with cut flowers made from coloured jelly, foie gras or egg. Mrs Marshall's garnishes were crimped, cut and coloured, and the visual appeal of every dish was artfully flawless. She sensibly noted that in Catholic countries where Lent was still a force, vegetables received more respect, but – far from embracing simplicity – her dishes caught the tone of the times, florid imitations of the art of Escoffier.

Where Marshall shone was on the stage of ices, selling her own patent ice-making machines, storage ice-caves, refrigerators, moulds, colourings and bottled flavourings. Her machines were squatter and broader than earlier patents, freezing the mixtures faster, and she was a wizard at fancy ices, layering them in complicated decorative moulds to produce exquisite water ices, iced custards, soufflés and mousses fit for the large assemblies and ball suppers that drove the late Victorians crazy. She used highly refined sugars, garnishes of maidenhair fern, and even gold and silver leaf as decoration. Marshall fumed at the 'poisonous filth' and 'vile concoctions' of the street sellers and included one recipe for a 'common' custard using milk, sugar and cornflour, but she was more at home with egg- and cream-rich custards and moulds in the shapes of baskets, hens on nests, and even vegetables and fish. She was also probably the first cook in Britain to record putting ice cream into a wafer cornet, using a mouth-watering mix of ginger ice and apple cream.

Other delightful concoctions included banana with lemon and orange, brown bread with burnt almond, chestnut with cedrati (a flavouring made from citrons), and Silver Ray's white rum with tangerine, apple and melon. She made chilled soufflés of Parmesan or Gruyère with caster sugar and aspic jelly, and her Parmesan ice was

Mrs Marshall's patent ice breaker – just one of many new kitchen inventions
designed and patented during the heyday of the Victorian kitchen.

robustly flavoured with coralline pepper and Leibig's meat extract
– far more delicious than it sounds. But her quest for novelty could
be overreaching as she froze devilled chicken, chutneys, curries,
Worcestershire sauce, egg yolks and even anchovies in small cups
of aspic, all as titivated as the overblown upper-middle-class
interiors of 1890s, all requiring the patience and artistry of a
professional.

At the other end of the scale from flashy hotel restaurants and
Marshall's voguish ices, shoppers could now respectably be seen in
the teashops of the ABC, Express Dairy Co. or Lyon's Corner-
houses, all of whom vied for customers looking for a cheap lunch,
tea and a bun or – more practically – the lavatory. Clean, bright
and speedy, they dealt the old-fashioned chop house a crushing
blow.

The world was shrinking. Package tours and private foreign travel, imports and – in place of chop houses and taverns – restaurants serving French, Italian and German dishes all meant that by the last decade of the nineteenth century, rather mangled recipes for foreign foods were being widely presented to and embraced by the middle classes.* The 1888 edition of Beeton's *Book of Household Management* contained recipes for Australian, German and Jewish dishes and, amusingly, for roasted wallaby-and-parrot pie, perhaps inspired by a small chain of Australian restaurants in London that was noted, incidentally, for its 'attractive young women behind the counters'. In the same year, *The Girl's Own Indoor Book* presented Italian, American, Swedish, Egyptian and 'bush' recipes.

The domestic dishwasher took off in the United States as the Archimedean or rotary whisk banished tortuous beating, enamel-covered pans provided some of the latest cookware, and British cooks could flick through the first books devoted entirely to cooking by gas. Advertisements for gas cookers with their easy-clean coatings stressed their convenience, economy and labour-saving efficiency, and, as gas became more widely available, houses no longer needed to construct their own gas plants (like the one at Penrhyn in Cornwall) but could hire ovens fuelled by penny-in-the-slot meters. They were rarely airtight, their thin sides leached heat, and they already had electricity peering over their shoulder – electric ovens and the Electric School of Cookery in Gloucester Road, London were both launched in 1894, though the ovens would take fifty years to catch on.

For all the vaunted advantages of gas and electricity, the eventual loss of the open fire and the range would ensure that the warmth, literally and metaphorically, went out of the British kitchen. As the century and its grandmotherly Queen aged, the terribly 'Victorian' and not always entirely respectable journalist George Augustus Sala characterised British cookery, writing that

---

* Novelty could work both ways. In 1885 an odd – and surely ironic, though sometimes you just cannot tell with the Victorians – little book entitled *Why Not Eat Insects?* suggested that since no one could afford to be dainty in 'these days of agricultural depression', grasshoppers and garden pests could be eaten. Not only might fields thereby be usefully emptied, but housekeepers could breathe easy in the 'discovery of a new entrée to vary the monotony of the present round'.

for £25 or thirty pounds a year you can get a female cook who is able to make . . . about a dozen soups . . . [and] an equal number of plates of fish . . . she will be a good roaster and boiler and a tolerable adept with the gridiron and the frying pan; her pies, puddings and sweets will be as a rule irreproachable and she will be able to give you a few simple entrées such as hashed mutton, stewed rump steak, haricot mutton, veal cutlet and bacon, or minced veal. For £40 . . . you shall have a cook who will be able to make a bisque of lobster or cray fish who can curry tripe or eggs . . . twenty different entrées . . . and who will even be able to send up a truite au bleu, a saumon à la Chambord, or a dariole of oysters. But unless you have a cook at £50 . . . I will wager she will be wholly unsatisfactory as a preparer of vegetables for the table.

THE TWENTIETH CENTURY

The art of clearing up in a newly servantless household, from
Entertaining with Elizabeth Craig, 1933.

22

Raging Inequalities and the Taste of War

I was taking a meal once at a London restaurant . . . a young man enters of the working class whose dress betokened holiday . . . He was embarrassed by the display of knives and forks, by the arrangement of the dishes, by the sauce bottles and the cruet-stand, above all, no doubt, by the assembly of people not of his class, and the unwonted experience of being waited on by a man with a long shirt-front . . . Abashed into anger, the young man asked roughly what he had to pay. It ended with the waiter's bringing a newspaper, wherein he helped to wrap up meat and vegetables . . . It was a striking and unpleasant illustration of social differences

— GEORGE GISSING

In 1903, the American author Jack London wrote of a Britain in which 'millions of people, men, women, children, little babes . . . have not enough to eat'. In the twentieth century's first few years, a number of devastating reports would prove what many already knew: despite winning the war against cholera, Britain had spawned a new generation of rickety, stunted, toothless and anaemic children, and the health of the poorest classes was continuing to decline. Recruitment for the Boer War indicated that Britain was no longer fit to defend itself: 38 per cent of men were too physically unsound to fight, debilitated by a century of industrialisation and by cheap, nutritionally inferior processed foods like margarine, condensed milk and jam. The government's Interdepartmental Committee on Physical Deterioration concluded in addition that a third of all children were undernourished and that working-class boys of 12 were on average 5 inches shorter than those in private schools.

R. Seebohm Rowntree's study of poverty in the city of York at the turn of the century demonstrated conclusively that it was impossible for the poorest to procure an adequate diet on the average labouring wage of between 12 and 20s a week. Rowntree wrote of a tranche of society below the poverty line, of endemic semi-starvation and low disease resistance in families where a bit of meat was still, at best, a weekly event, and where clothes, shoes, rent and payments towards funeral expenses left hardly enough for bread, tea, potatoes, rice, cheap sausages, rashers of bacon or suet pudding if you could afford the fats. Even skilled artisans earning 40s a week merely hovered above the poverty line, though in the middle classes the diet was enormously more varied with its big breakfasts and dinners of haricot mutton with carrots, potatoes and cauliflower, custard blancmanges, bread puddings and chocolate moulds.

In the face of international industrial competition these findings were urgent, for the bulk of the muscular work fell precisely upon the shoulders of the labouring classes. George Ewart Evans remembered, in his *Ask the Fellows that Cut the Hay*, that, at high-employment times like harvest and shearing, the centuries-old traditions of 'pork dumplings, spring cabbage and new potatoes, followed by suet pudding . . . boiled in the same pot' did cling on; 'the men had home-brewed beer to drink, the children small or very weak beer'. But the reports found that during the rest of the year, agricultural workers were living on pearl barley and water. 'Six Million Hungry People', the political slogan of the decade, was a pressing reality.

The 'Indian summer' between the death of Victoria and the onset of war in Europe was one of raging inequality, of the scrabble to make ends meet set against the crystal glitter of an outrageously wealthy upper class with their Ford or Austin motors and luxurious new country houses. The cigar-puffing King Edward VII, known as Tum Tum and quite the Toad of Toad Hall, had quickly swapped his outmoded frock coat for a morning suit, cleared out his mother's clutter from Windsor Castle and starrily remodelled the façade of Buckingham Palace; Sandringham was turned into a shooting estate. In 1905 Moët et Chandon threw him a birthday party at the Savoy, flooding the forecourt and parading gondolas and swans on its glassy surface, while twelve courses were served to the guests inside, a baby elephant presented the birthday cake, and the great Caruso sang.

With income tax less than a shilling in the pound, affluent industrialists like the Whitbreads, Levers, Liptons and Tennants were also appointing their vast houses with the trappings of success and comfort, shifting out Victorian overelaboration in favour of bright, harmonious furnishings. As Blériot prepared to cross the Channel in his wooden aircraft, telephones and typewriters were hastening communication, while trains, cars and motorised taxis all sped the leisured class towards weekend house parties where tennis, cricket, picnics, boating and fishing in the summer, hunting and shooting in the winter, and horseracing all year round provided endless entertainment and sport.

In these light-filled houses, soigné ladies with tiny waists and wide hats changed into gorgeous tea gowns at five o'clock to gossip over dainty pieces of Madeira or rich, fruity Dundee cake topped with almonds, or *génoises* – delicate fancy sponges flavoured with liqueurs, whimsically coloured and iced. Then they changed again, clipping on their diamonds, arranging their hair, and fixing corsages of lilies and orchids to their bosoms, meeting briefly before eight- or twelve-course dinners for a cocktail of whisky and angostura bitters or champagne and maraschino.

These dinners generally began – though Escoffier disapproved – with tiny, tasty hors d'oeuvres: ice-cold caviar with brown bread, smoked salmon, olives, radishes or chilled cantaloupe melon. Then came soups like those in his *Guide culinaire*: clear, velouté (velvety, stock-based), creamed vegetable, Scotch hare or brown onion, all strained through muslin – and fish, generally sole, trout or whitebait. In place of large roasts came made dishes of quail with grapes, woodcock, duckling breasts with port wine and aspic, tiny poussins, Parmesan soufflés or frogs' legs, and sauces which rarely contained flour. French ortolans, bunting and wheatears from Kent and Sussex were drowned in brandy. Escoffier had given steaks names – 'Chateaubriand' from the thickest part of the fillet, 'tournedos' from kernels of the fillet cut into rounds. Pheasant breasts were braised gently with vegetables until the point of a knife could be thrust into them without meeting with any resistance whatsoever, tenderly compliant to diners' forks.

For dessert, champagne sorbets and jellies, compotes, mousses, parfaits and meringues were served, sweet pancakes became a new favourite, and petits fours, glacé or forced hothouse fruits were arranged on plain silver or glass dishes, complemented by arrangements of blowsy roses. Savouries, or *bouchées*, completed the meal, small plates of haddock, potted prawns or eggs en cocotte with shrimp, oysters wrapped in bacon and baked into 'angels on horseback', toasted Camembert with cayenne and even sandwiches. At its best, it would all be as Escoffier laid down: amusingly cosmopolitan, exquisitely tasty, rarefied and faultlessly presented.

With its bicycles, cars and punts, Edwardian Britain seemed to hail the age of the great outdoors, with the painterly informality of Gertrude Jekyll's gardens alongside the rousing vistas of Edward Elgar's *Land of Hope and Glory*. Hefty shooting lunches of mulligatawny, curries, game pies, Irish stews or game casseroles with solid English puddings were carted in padded hampers to the game-keeper's lodge, with bread and cheese for the beaters and loaders. At garden parties, tea, iced coffee, sandwiches, cakes, fruit and ices were served as the guests ranged over green lawns to play badminton, tennis or croquet. Families regularly set out with tea baskets and spirit stoves; the *Woman's Book* (1911) recommended greaseproof paper plates, and others took papier mâché, burning and burying it before they set off home. In Kenneth Grahame's *Wind in the Willows* (1908) Ratty packs for a picnic on the river 'coldtonguecoldhamcoldbeefpickledgherkins-saladfrenchrollscresssandwidgespottedmeatgingerbeerlemonadesoda-water. "O stop, stop," cried the Mole in ecstasies: "This is too much!"'

For 'bachelors, male and female, in chambers, lodgings, diggings and the like, in fact to all who "batch"; to young couples with a taste for theatres, concerts and homely late suppers . . . yachtsmen, shooting parties and picnickers', the writer Frank Schloesser recommended the chafing dish or spirit stove for preparing quick, light meals: available from Harrods for 12s 6d, they were 'clean, economical, speedy and rather simple'. He made it sound fun, independent and gay to be a bachelor in 1904, reheating cold meats and leftover potatoes with a spike of Worcestershire or Tabasco sauce, refrying cooked fish with breadcrumbs, mushrooms, parsley and lemon peel, and heating skinned sardines from the box to serve on buttered toast. Schloesser gave rump steak a good 'drubbing' with a mallet or the poker wrapped in a cloth before simmering it with butter, lemon and bouillon, and made a 'Prawn Wiggle' with a cupful of prawns and another of cooked green peas left to bubble gently in a white sauce of milk, butter and flour – though even he could see no wiggle in it.

Omelettes had become something of an obsession partly, perhaps, because the majority of British cooks had missed the point, cooking them on both sides for up to ten minutes: Schloesser, like Acton, who had cooked six-egg omelettes in five to seven minutes, cooked a beaten egg for less than one minute, 'light, frothy, ethereal, almost gossamer like in its impalpable fairyhood'. For eggs en cocotte he used 'those dear little fireproof china cups especially made for the purpose', simmering the pot filled with egg, cream and parsley in boiling water for a handful of minutes. He rebelled against the Victorian 'unholy cult of mayonnaise' but made no apology for Maggi preserved soups, adding a dash of paprika, a slurp of sherry and a raw egg beaten up. He followed suit with 'Turtle tablets' by Levgien and Sherlock of Kingston, Jamaica and stacked his larder with tins and jars of clam chowder, clam broth, chicken gumbo, and terrapin and vegetable soups bought from the Army & Navy.

Witty Schloesser was wary of too many herbs – the gentle tang of chives alone was enough to give 'a baby scent, a fiery titillation, an echo of the great Might Be' – or the temptation to muddle flavours by adding drops of this or that. Conscious of the 'quality of the food' over its quantity, Schloesser (one suspects) spent his weekends at country house parties before returning to his London rooms and to 'Chaffinda', his chafing-dish 'wife', setting his own table with 'delicate Venetian glass, beaten copper finger-bowls, perfectly plain silver, and the simplest of white china' rather than 'dreadful mid-Victorian table decorations . . . branching candelabra, hideous épergnes'. Everything had to be, he chimed, 'perfect of its kind' – so perfect that he thought it wise to have a complete dress rehearsal the evening before a proposed dinner so as not to make a mess of it all in front of the guests.

In the great houses, Victorian wired bells had given way to electric ones, to speaking tubes and whistles that summoned servants to the far quarters of the building. In more modest homes, the servant problem was less about insolence than unavailability – as Mary Davies complained in her tartly named *The Housewife's What's What* (1904): 'In the present day very many people complain that they can't get servants, and when they do come, they won't stay. Certainly more girls go to mills, factories etc for work because they have their evenings and Sundays free . . . Formerly a cottage girl was brought up to know she must go into service.'

Urban employers considerate enough to give their servants a second thought took to dining out at restaurants on Sundays in order to give the staff a break. In the more prosaic reality of middle-class homes, aluminium cooking pots, gas stoves and linoleum flooring were beginning to appear, rubbish was burned, and Borax detergent was poured down sinks and drains to combat smells. Cold cupboards with blocks of ice wrapped in sacking were becoming more common, or, for those who couldn't stretch to one, a teaspoon of bicarbonate of soda was stirred into the summer milk to keep it from turning. Throughout the week, old meat was still 'done up' and corned beef welcomed, mostly from tins but occasionally home-made by repeatedly rubbing the meat with saltpetre, lemons and sugar before dousing it in brine for four days. Sheep's hearts were stuffed, dry-hash minces were topped with boiled potatoes, toad in the hole and bubble and squeak were useful fallbacks, and for dessert arrowroot puddings and cornflour shapes were paraded – the final debased incarnation of the courtly blancmange. Foie gras could be faked with calf's liver and fat bacon, omelettes could use leftovers, and polenta appeared as a breakfast treat, left to cool, then cut and fried; old, dried-out jams were 'rescued with a little hot water'.

E. S. Poynter, author of *What and How?* (1904), served creamed-tomato soup whipped up with a little flour, sugar, tomatoes, parsley, mace and bay leaf. Her range of made dishes included fillets of pigeon or 'fritot de volaille' – pieces of chicken with oil and lemon, dipped in milk and fried golden, served with a parsley and white sauce. Small birds like quail were stuffed with turkey forcemeat and sprinkled with olives and an iced tartare sauce, and savouries to close the meal were less likely to be potted prawns than cheese straws, devilled tomatoes, anchovy toasts or sandwiches.

Writing for the British in India, Poynter was among the first to proffer a recipe for 'Jhal Frezee: cut up into small squares any cold meat. Add a good quantity of onions sliced, some chillies cut up and a teaspoon of salt. Warm 2 oz ghi, and throw into it all these, and allow to fry stirring all the time until the onions are tender.' In London, the adventurous might try out the Hindostanee Coffee House in Portman Square, from 1910 the first restaurant to serve Indian food in London. It was not long-lived, but by the outbreak of war in 1914 another foreign entrepreneur, Mr Choy, had opened his Chinese café in Oxford Street.

The first pioneering health-food shop to set up in opposition to the rash of convenience foods was opened by James Henry Cook in Birmingham in 1898, wholesaling 'cokernut, desiccated or whole', tapioca, lentils, macaroni, sago, semolina and even pine kernels to use in place of suet at 8s a pound. The health-food store Hill's price lists at the opening of the twentieth century were stuffed with American cereals: Charlie Post's Toasties, Henry Perky's Shredded Wheat and Kellogg cereal products such as Granose and Nuttose and even the first peanut butters. But if 'society' and the well-off had begun to consider bodily health as a goal worth the striving, despite the policies of the new Liberal government from 1906 to provide school meals and cheap milk for children and nursing mothers, by the eve of the First World War a group of women in the Fabian Society had found that among the poor women of Vauxhall in South London little had changed since Rowntree's report. Underfed women and children were, they said, 'a disgrace and a danger to the state'.

The Fabian Society's report was unusually sympathetic to the reasons behind poor diet – the single blackened frying pan and stew pot; the unavailability of a larder; the old-fashioned and broken ranges, which devoured coal; the expense of gas and cooking fats; and the non-existence of 'joy in cooking for its own sake'. To impress upon the poor the virtues of porridge was useless – the fire had to be lit early, milk and sugar to make it palatable were unaffordable, and the children ''eaved at it', redolent as it was with the taste of fish or 'stoo' from the previous night's dinner. When milk was available, only a few of the women saved up enough to bring home the luxury of Quaker Oats, making instant porridge in a little enamel cup so that it escaped the clinging flavours of the family saucepan.

Here, meat was the preserve of the breadwinner, and the family made do with what he left behind after a neck of mutton with potherbs on Sunday and a stew of 'pieces' on Wednesday, often eaten standing. These children were worse off than those in the workhouse, and the red-lettered warnings on penny tins of condensed milk – 'This milk is not recommended as food for infants' – were ignored wherever fresh milk cost 4d a quart. There was no school, the report concluded, that could teach anyone to manage on a pound a week; '. . . if the scientific and trained teacher cannot solve the problem, the untrained, over-burdened mother should not be criticised because she also fails.' For this undernourished section of society in which almost a third of all deaths were of children under five, wartime rations would ironically deliver a higher standard of diet than they had ever enjoyed before.

As the prospect of war hovered, May Byron was already lobbying widely for a return to kitchen common sense in her *Pot Luck, or the British Home Cookery Book* (1914), collecting farmhouse dishes of beef collops, galantine of beef, beef stews, curried or fricasséed tripe and stewed oxtails together with more than 150 cake recipes, curled ginger snaps and an enormous selection of steamed and boiled pud-dings. Sugar came in packets, bicarbonate of soda and tartaric acid helped the cakes to fluff, concentrated soluble chocolate came in jars (though it still had to be dissolved in milk in front of the fire), but Byron was already urging a return to the 'good plain cooking done by our mothers and grandmothers . . . the old home-cookery before tinned things and preservatives were invented'. Within a few months she, and many of her readers, would be forced to re-evaluate every-thing they took for granted in the kitchen.

At the outbreak of war, Britain was already the world's largest consumer of tinned goods, dependent on imports for more than 60 per cent of its national food supply and 80 per cent of its wheat. The government was stockpiling wheat and sugar, but as the international situation deteriorated, prices began to rise fast. Women with money and big larders hurried to stock up on provisions, their chauffeur-driven cars lining up outside the grocers, pushing prices still higher and fuelling ill-feeling. On 4 August 1914, Britain embarked on her bloodiest conflict ever, and, as if a pin had been stuck into the balloon of luxury trades, they crumpled. Within two days of the declaration of war, the price of granulated sugar had been fixed at 4½ d per pound, butter at 1s 6d, margarine at 8d, Colonial cheese at 9s 5d and bacon at 1s 6d. Newspapers gave up their fashion pages for columns headed 'What Women Can Do', and recipes for sole, lobsters, cream, eggs and butter were replaced with earnest advice on 'cheap brown soup' or *crowdie* made from the liquid in which mutton had been boiled with onions, oatmeal, salt and pepper.

During the winter of 1914, when the dream of a quick war still persisted, the royal family dined on turkey, goose, baron of beef, venison, boar's head, cygnet and flaming plum pudding while puddings tested by Escoffier were sent to the troops at the front and the Carlton Hotel offered tough minced venison with eggs, noodles and chestnut purée to its patrons. Up at Chatsworth, the Escoffier-trained cook Mrs Tanner made one Christmas pudding for the family using French plums, stoned raisins, brandy and half muscatels and another for the staff from suet, breadcrumbs, stout and milk. At the same time, despite the Royal Navy's initial ability to maintain supply lines, the Parliamentary War Saving's Committee's leaflet 'How to Save and Why' recommended the collection of acorns, horse chestnuts and beech mast, but it did not think to explain what to do with them. In an attempt to regulate the complicated business of food prices, distribution and conservation, the Food Department was established in October 1916, becoming by the end of the year the first Ministry of Food with Lord Davenport at its head.

Rationing was held off, but trying to keep a family fed on meagre provisions was tough. Coal was scarce so cinders were collected, and briquettes of clay, sawdust and tar were laboriously home-made as cooks struggled to learn economical ways with one-pot cooking and 'hay boxes' – wooden boxes insulated with hay, newspapers or blankets in which a stew, rice or suet pudding, brought to the boil on the stove, could then be left to 'cook'. With little sugar, treacle or honey to make jams, fruit rotted; eggs were all but unprocurable in the towns, and the price of a chicken rose to more than 12s. There were propaganda meetings, cookery demonstrations, food-economy shops, even a film made for the new cinemas that demonstrated how to keep an allotment. The gospel of 'use as little as you can' settled on the nation.

As soon as anything was recommended, the supply of it was exhausted, and the system of voluntary rationing meant that 'one day they were begged to eat potatoes and potato recipe leaflets flooded the country, and the next day they were begged not to eat potatoes . . . owing to potatoes disease'. There were shortages of cheese, meat and every kind of fat. Cooks pestered their butchers for liver, oxtails, sweetbreads, kidneys and tripe. In 1917 privations began to bite hard – feeding stray dogs and throwing rice at weddings were both proscribed. Some butchers opened for just one hour a day; there were food queues and a cry for rations. The dapper little King George V launched the 'Eat Less Bread' campaign by Royal Proclamation, along with a plea to abstain from the use of flour in pastry,* but by the time Lord Rhondda took over from Davenport at the Ministry towards the end of 1917, things were dire. People were advised to eat slowly and only when they were absolutely hungry; everyone talked about food.

Large houses were closed while their owners moved into hotels, and women who had never cooked or cleaned became their own cooks and housemaids. Everyone saved the last slice or crust of bread; every teaspoon of breadcrumbs was bottled. As one clergyman's wife in the country wrote, 'food becomes scarcer and all of us who have gardens or allotments grow vegetables and keep animals. For the first time I keep a pig . . . we make efforts to achieve palatable cakes with cocoa butter and make jam with glucose. The long and losing battle with "substitutes" almost wears me out'. Under Rhondda a system of registration and coupons was put in place, and sugar was restricted by order. Finally, in January 1918, compulsory rationing was instituted, starting with half a pound of sugar for each person per week; a

---

* In the face of possible riots and social instability, flour remained off ration throughout the war, though it was coarsened, standardised and subsidised by government order. Seventy-six-per-cent wheat extraction bulked with soya and potato, the bread was dark and widely despised – but, crucially, it was there.

month later meat and butter rationing began, and by April fat control had been extended to the whole country.

The pre-war paradise of extravagance was but a distant memory as housewives all tried to make the best of a very bad job. Meat coupons had a cash value so that the amount you got depended on its quality, though on average no one got more than about a pound of meat a week along with 8 ounces of highly salted, fatty American bacon. Meat was stretched with beans, pulses and root vegetables and by mincing scraps, boiling them in milk and water, and summarily baking them in a dish. Minced meats were also bulked out with oatmeal to make rissoles, crumbed and fried or baked in a greased tin. Mock sausages were made from a moulded paste of lentils, cheese, carrots, onions, breadcrumbs and marge; nuts were crushed into everything for extra protein, but no matter how hard you tried, no amount of skill could make baked haricots the least bit like the roast mutton they were pretending to be.

With an allowance of only 4 and then 5 ounces of butter or marge and 2 ounces of lard per person each week, every scrap of grease was saved from the boiling bacon for frying or baking, and substitute butter was made from cocoa butter, olive oil, a teaspoon of honey and a few drops of butter colouring. Omelettes were out of the question, pasta had disappeared, potatoes were substituted for pastry, and cakes were attempted with dried egg and hoarded sugar.

Where a little sweetening could be found – and there were substitutes like Cornsyp or saccharin Sypgar – sago was boiled with fruit to thicken it into a 'jam'. Nothing was thrown away as peelings, tops and tails, dish rinsings, the remains of puddings and even fruit cores were made into soups and every bit of bone and cartilage simmered for stock. But it wasn't just food that was scarce; the price of everything needed for the kitchen had doubled. Basic kitchen tables cost 40s, plate racks 7s, and, with all metals at a premium, enamel and iron pans were increasingly hard to come by.

As the dreary summer of 1918 dragged on, the government implored gardeners to action; town beds were planted with garden peas, beans and cabbages, and marrows replaced sweet williams. By September it was rumoured that there was only enough basic food in store to last the nation for a month. On 11 November, just as many households thought they could take no more, almost as quickly as the war had started came the announcement of peace. After initial disbelief, crowds of people left their homes, singing and dancing in the streets as everyone considered the impact of the news for which they had been longing. Lights flared, packed cafés and restaurants remained open. People stayed out celebrating long, long after all the food and drink had run out.

23

Fleeting Fortunes and Discontented Domestics

If you keep on giving them Irish stew and rice pudding, they get mean and grumpy but if, on the other hand, you can give them brighter food, there is no reason why they shouldn't buy you that pearl necklace after all

— ERIC WEIR

At the end of the war nine million soldiers were dead. Women were now wearing trousers or skirts that skimmed the ankle, mourning their men and hoping for a new dawn. Instead, raging influenza carried off tens of thousands, food shortages remained a trial, unemployment rose, and the shops were not miraculously re-stocked. Rationing continued until the books expired in 1919; only in 1921, to a sigh of communal relief, was the Ministry of Food dismantled.

The Director of the *Daily Mail* Domestic Bureau, Mrs Peel, wrote in 1919 that 'the era of the Labour Saving House is dawning . . . Women are so disinclined to become domestic servants . . . that householders find themselves obliged to adopt labour saving apparatus.' She foresaw a time when basement kitchens would disappear, when meals would be served through a buttery hatch designed to prevent kitchen smells from penetrating into the dining room, when there would be no scullery, and when all tables and cupboards would be on casters, leaving no room for dust or beetles in the corners. Instead of varnished woodwork and whitewashed larders, she dreamed of a kitchen world in which painted woodwork and anything grooved was banished, where grill burners would take over from salamanders, and where gas and electricity would make coal a thing of the past.

Mrs Peel's vision was already finding practical application in the Modernist kitchens designed for new social-housing projects in Germany. No longer the largest room in the house, the shockingly avant-garde 'Frankfurt' kitchen was a mass-produced galley in which work surfaces pulled out like drawers, draining boards on hinges could be stowed away in the wall, and every space was filled with gadgets like fold-down ironing boards or built-in spice racks. In the 'Frankfurt Kitchen', the housewife was the household engineer, and machines, recently the murderers of men, became the practical functionaries of the home.

Streamlined rectangularity did not quite fit with a British middle class unwilling to forsake ornament entirely, but the Ideal Home Exhibition of 1920 demonstrated dishwashers for the first time in Britain, and from 1922 new women's magazines like *Good Housekeeping* extolled the virtues of heat diffusers, multi-level steamers, whistling kettles and aluminium saucepans – lighter, easier to clean and more effective on gas stoves. The famous test kitchens of the Good Housekeeping Institute professed new fireproof earthenware and glass braising dishes 'delightful to use'; pressure cookers revolutionised vegetable cooking; ovens began to include temperature controls, and tammies were a thing of the past. By the end of the decade the Baby Belling, the Aga and Diamond Brand pots and pans had all been launched, and cooks were finding that the electric griller 'makes grilling a pleasure – as easy to work as a Kodak'.

Chain grocery stores continued to bring a world of seemingly limitless convenience into the kitchen, with Sainsbury's, Lipton, Home & Colonial, Meadow Dairy and Maypole all competing for custom in the brave new world of branded, factory-made goods aggressively marketed. Edwards desiccated soups helped 'to make both ends meet'; Bovril was 'British to the backbone'; Pierce Duff's Gold Medal Baking Powder claimed 'the proof of the pudding is in the eating'. There was Shredded Atora Suet, Paxo stuffing, Chivers jams, sliced Wonderbread, San Jose tinned Californian pears, peaches and apricots, and Campbell's luxury soups at 8d a tin. Processed foods became staples for busy households, and even those who liked to cook kept an 'emergency' corner filled with bottled olives and gherkins, bouillon cubes, bottled fish, meat and grated Parmesan in case of unexpected visitors.

There was butter again for cakes and dried fruits as well, though they still had to be picked over, stoned and shredded. But the reality of the early 1920s was that most cooks were still making the best of it in times that remained difficult. From Warrington to Wimbledon, the cry of the hour was 'How dear everything is!' Fuel was still scarce, taxation had increased, fortunes were fleeting, and domestics, if they were there at all, were discontented. Woman who had worked in munitions factories, farms and railways now had the images of the emancipated Emmeline Pankhurst and Nancy Astor in their minds, and most simply did not want to go back into service.

Housewives were exhorted not just to think for themselves but to do for themselves too, to lay the breakfast table the night before or to cover the kitchen table with zinc so that pastry could be rolled directly on to it without a board. Few of them felt safe enough to throw away their hay boxes, using them for overnight porridge or one-pot casseroles which would be ready at the end of the day's work. One-pot cooking – 'braises', 'ragouts' and 'daubes' sounded so much better than 'stew' – had several advantages. Coal was scarce and the miners were striking – 'I have been down a coal mine . . . and can understand the difficulties of getting it, but these strikes are very serious, and it is important to know how to do without coal', as the self-styled 'sensible' Elizabeth Silvester advised in 1920.

Casseroles were liberation incarnate. The mix of browned meat, garlic, wine and vegetables required no skimming and could happily be ignored, giving the housewife time to prepare her home and herself; served straight to the table, the food arrived hot and without a congealing skin while the cook remained cool and unblemished. With one-pot dinners there was hardly any washing up, and it could all be such fun. Catherine Ives, author of a book discreetly called *When the Cook Is Away* (1928), recommended 'impressive casseroles in deep blue, and I once had a lovely purple one to go with some cottage crockery', while the society hostess Ruth Lowinsky assured her readers that earthenware was becoming far more chic than silver. How comforting it all sounded to the beleaguered housewife, never mind the fact that Lowinsky's book was printed on exquisite art paper and probably never went anywhere near a kitchen.

Roasting made you hot, frying made you smell, but, it seems, braising was the answer to the modern housewife's problems. For Virginia Woolf, the daube was agonisingly redemptive:

> . . . an exquisite scent of olives and oil and juice rose from the great brown dish . . . with its . . . confusion of savoury brown and yellow meats and its bay leaves and its wine . . . It was rich; it was tender. It was perfectly cooked. How did she manage these things in the depths of the country? . . . [Mrs Banks] was a wonderful woman. All his love, all his reverence, had returned; and she knew it.

Of course, Mrs Banks, like Lowinsky, enjoyed the services of a cook, but the point was made.

Cooks like Jessie Conrad, still stuck in the gloom of Victorian cooking, stewing breakfast rissoles for an hour, drearily over-boiling greens, thickening everything with flour and double-boiling coffee,* might have taken heed and gone back to basics. Aiming at those who were concerned about how to maintain their hands, complexions and tempers in the face of this startling need to cook, Mrs Peel – in her *Daily Mail Cookery Book* (1919) – explained from scratch how to separate the white from the yolk of an egg, how to whip cream and how to blanch, and was a great believer in tasting food as it cooked, keeping a jug of hot water and a spoon by the stove expressly for the purpose – an instruction entirely overlooked by all previous cookery writers. Mindful of the need to save effort as well as fuel, she suggested setting a whole morning aside to prepare several dishes that could be reheated later: a casserole of vegetables or pulses, boiled-fowl galantines, curried lentils and rice, baked beans and tomatoes, steamed puddings and soups like 'Brown Windsor', as well as small cakes for keeping. Forethought was the answer to the cook's desire to remain serene and lovely for her husband and her guests; even vegetables could be pre-cooked and carefully warmed up with a little butter.

---

* As Jessie Conrad's cookbook was originally conceived in the early 1900s, this is slightly unfair. By the time it was published, her husband had achieved his fame, yet her cooking showed no real sign of dragging itself into the twentieth century. Much of it was what another cook, Hilda Leyel, called a music-hall joke. Joseph Conrad was known for toying with his food and throwing pellets of rolled-up bread at his children; it may be that his wife's cookbook provided the answer to his lapses in gustatory concentration.

As the economic boom of the 1920s got into its swing, men's trousers widened into Oxford bags and women's hems and waistlines moved in opposite directions; cloche hats, rayon stockings, bathing dresses and nail polish became the vogue. The new rich and the new poor were surrounded by crazes for the turkey-trot, the Charleston, nightclubs, cocktails and all things American, and they heard for the first time the clipped accents of the BBC on programmes like *Home, Health and the Garden* that touched on subjects from the planning of an ideal kitchen to national dishes of the West Indies. A different breed of cookery writers emerged, influenced by Mediterranean and provincial French styles, as intelligently witty and slightly mad as the stars of the silent screen. Wry, cultured and ineffably polite, their outlook was as light and refreshing as their soufflés, chaudfroids, iced coupes and chicken mousses; they loathed starch and delighted in discernment.

Lady Agnes Jekyll, sister-in-law of the famous gardener Gertrude, was one of these, her *Kitchen Essays* (1922) generously taking on the spirit of 'make do' with a light heart, a bit of imagination and a knowing eye for standards. 'Let us use our brains,' she wrote, not for the first time appealing for intelligence in the kitchen. She cooked 'friendly' rice pudding with marmalade and egg yolks and re-baptised roast leg of mutton the more alluring 'Gigot de six heures', a modern take on Eliza Acton's version with its cloves of garlic, vegetables, claret and brandy. She simmered tomatoes in consommé, straining and softening them with whipped cream into a soup, and she transformed mashed potato from stiff tastelessness into something 'not much thicker than a well-made apple sauce', thinned with butter, stock or boiling milk and mashed with a clove of garlic.

Jekyll introduced the food of her beloved Venice to British cooks: minestrone, gnocchi with cheese, pastas with simple tomato sauces and *fritto misto* of calf's liver, veal cutlet, sweetbreads and brains all sautéed with lemon. She used new ingredients like aubergines and peppers and slow-stirred risotto rice with a pinch of saffron and scraps of white chicken, fish or lean diced ham into a compact, creamy mass enriched with butter and Parmesan. Risotto was a risky business: though plenty of cooks understood that it was imperative to preserve the identity of every grain, there were others like Jessie Conrad who laboriously boiled and drained the wrong sort of rice, adding the cheese and putting it aside in moulds 'for later'.

Jekyll cooked her own home-cured hams with a bottle of Madeira, serving them sliced with a Cumberland sauce, and thought out appealing recipes for well-made dishes that could be watched by the kitchen maid while she dressed for dinner. 'Garbure à la lionnaise' melted together onions, Parmesan and Gruyère with consommé, egg yolks and cream; 'Lobster à la Newburg' stewed chopped cooked lobster, butter, Madeira, cream and egg yolks to be served in white china ramekins with gossamer slices of bread dried to a 'lacy crispness' in a slow oven. With dishes like these under control, there was time to take the advice of Catherine Ives and rid your hands of the scent of onions by washing them in cold water before you raised them to your mouth again, now holding a cigarette.

The ice box or refrigerator was not only socially impressive; it became a friend for storing chilled tinned consommés or julienne soups with just a dash of sherry, sliced Camembert on ice, frozen horseradish sauce, tomato ices, chaudfroids, mousselines, mayonnaises and hollandaises all ready to be served. For dessert, Jekyll prepared a 'Russian Ice' from blackcurrant-bush leaves and served a lemon ice with a 'luscious black currant compote and some home made Cat's Tongue biscuits or sponge rusk'. Easier still, she wrote, 'capture a stately pineapple', but eat it in style in a starlit garden, split in half and filled with cream ices or a compote of red cherries with home-made biscuits scented with vanilla.

Embellishment was judged a misdirection of energy; one should instead aim at simplicity and strive after perfection. Marcel Boulestin – erstwhile secretary to the novelist Colette, society decorator, *Evening Standard* journalist and set to be the first television chef – urged the readers of his *Simple French Cooking for English Homes* (1923) and the diners in his famous restaurant – Le Boulestin, off Leicester Square – not to be afraid of simplicity, offering a vision of bourgeois French cooking and foods flavoured not with substitutes and chemical essences but with vanilla and pure coffee, of the best olive oil and red wine vinegar, and of jellies made in the old-fashioned way without gelatin. If the majority of homes in Britain had consigned fish to Fridays, Boulestin tried to reawaken interest by flouring and frying it in butter with a squeeze of lemon, grilling tunny fish, simmering sole with fine herbs in white wine, and poaching turbot in a court bouillon or serving it au gratin with breadcrumbs and a béchamel sauce.

Boulestin, like most French chefs, had a hundred ways with eggs, which had begun to be graded for quality. He understood that office workers with limited incomes also wanted to eat well, making plain tomato salads with chopped parsley, beetroot, salt, pepper and vinegar, rubbing chicory with garlic and preparing French beans with a chervil vinaigrette. In just ten and a half short lines he could conjure up a lyrically perfect chicken daube, stuffing the bird with a mix of bread, bacon, its liver, parsley, shallots, garlic and egg, browning it and cooking it in a fireproof dish on a bed of bacon, onions and parsley for thirty minutes before adding a glass of consommé and leaving it to cook for three hours.

Careful and unfussy Hilda Leyel, the creator of the Culpeper shops, also wrote in her co-authored *Gentle Art of Cookery* (1925) for cooks who did not need exact quantities and minute instruction but who did need inspiration and guidance, celebrating seasonality, freshness, connoisseurship, fruit and vegetables ('for the tendency of to-day is to eat less meat') and olive oil over the monotonous generality of the boiling pot. Her recipes ranged from a bouillabaisse of fish with wine, garlic, parsley and saffron to a 'Mooloo of fish' using 'cocoanut', green chillies, onion, garlic, butter, vinegar and green ginger. She pushed nubs of garlic near the bone of roasting lamb* and mixed basil and thyme with oxtail; aubergines were pre-salted, rinsed and tossed in butter or oil with tomato, parsley and a clove of garlic; the smallest broad beans were cooked in an earthenware pot in their pods, and haricots were stewed with butter, nutmeg, celery and cream. In Leyel's hands, onions became dishes in their own right, variously stuffed, spiced, glazed, braised, gratinated and puréed.

This elegant new breed of cooks finished meals with simply made coffee unalloyed by complicated apparatus, or with refreshing tisanes

---

* Roasting had now quite definitely become baking as the old spits and dripping pans were consigned to the iron-men's carts.

of lime or violet flowers, lemon or mint. They assured those who only ever used a drop of sherry in their trifle that using wine in cooking was neither scandalous nor ruinous. Brandy flambés, champagne sauces and red-wine casseroles, they urged, were inestimably superior to great joints, boiled rabbit, badly made hash and the endless cold meat that drove 'even respectable husbands to take blonde girls to restaurants'. Their laconic perfectionism was seductive: the modest and gentlemanly Sir Francis Colchester Wemyss suggested in 1932 that a beef steak pudding could be transformed from a railway-dining-room Chablis into a 1911 Montrachet with 'snipe and fillet steak, truffles, small mushrooms [and] a glass of port' – a sure sign that wartime poverty and belt-tightening were really over.

In the early 1930s the American interior decorator and *Vogue* writer Elsie de Wolfe, swathed in bias-cut satin and suffused with Riviera elegance, wrote that 'good taste in food is just the reverse of lavish and is stamped with the same restraint and elimination as the dress worn at dinner in 1934 compared to the dress worn at dinner in 1900.' De Wolfe's cocktails were perfectly shaken and her table was set with a fetishistic concern for detail, featuring the plain lines of uncut glass, silver cigarette boxes, chromium-plated candlesticks and single gladioli. Colour, form, contrast and proportion were as vital as in a Mondrian painting, as pared down as that spider-thin, black-clad icon of the '30s, Wallis Simpson, a woman who appeared never to eat and who was more likely to feed the bone marrow so beloved of Queen Victoria ('ogre's food', wrote Agnes Jekyll) to her snuffling pugs.

Far less interested in bourgeois cooking than in artful simplicity, De Wolfe liked restraint and a maximum of four courses at dinner.* Small steaks, or noisettes, of lamb, vol-au-vents, grilled sole, roast chicken, soufflés, risotto and baby fishcakes elbowed aside heavier cuts of red meat: '. . . each dish tastes like what it is and is innocent of yellow

---

* In this context it is useful to know that the wedding breakfast of the Duke and Duchess of York in 1923 contained eight courses. Princess Elizabeth's wedding in 1947 would contain only four and last just twenty minutes.

sauces and pink and black stars.' Soups were clear and sweets (as they were now known) were served in glasses: ices, chilled cantaloupe melon with cherries in brandy, fruit bathed in champagne or light, frothy *sabaiones* of eggs, sugar, lemon and Marsala, all complemented by poached meringues and caramel creams. Jelly had begun to lose its legs, the packet variety collapsing back into its bowl rather than standing proud, but with a national campaign to 'Eat More Fruit' and the novelty of the beloved banana, fruit had once and for all shed the millstone of humoural suspicion. Pancakes added theatre: crêpes Suzette set alight with brandy and curaçao, or 'Pancakes Barbara' gorgeous with whipped cream, vanilla ice cream, blanched walnuts and hot chocolate sauce ('. . . this is not a joke,' wrote De Wolfe). Indeed hot chocolate sauce – dark, glossy and undeniably luxurious – was a regular accompaniment to ices and wine-poached fruit.

Despite such indulgences, British waistlines had reduced during the war and women liked the new look. Slim silhouettes chimed with the Modernist obsession with health and fitness, with sunbathing and sanatoria, and with the new theories of dietetics that sprang from the recent discovery of vitamins.* Smoking was the new vice – De Wolfe allotted three cigarettes (exactly) to each of her guests – but fresh salads were the new virtue, reaching a prominence unseen since the Restoration. Hilda Leyel put chrysanthemums with potatoes and nasturtiums with beetroot. Mourning the demise of purslane, goat's beard and rampion, she used samphire, nettle shoots and Indian capsicum, urging – like John Evelyn before her – discernment: well-washed and dried leaves torn and never cut, the best-quality olive oil from the wine merchant and flavoured French vinegars but never brown malt. Iced asparagus was accompanied by a thick mayonnaise, salad bowls were rubbed with garlic, apple was mixed with celery, and a simple French dressing was dripped over a mix of cooked scarlet runners, waxy potatoes and endive.

Avocados were becoming supremely popular, and Leyel also made a salad of oranges, onions, black olives and red peppers, and another

---

* Following the discovery of proteins, vitamins were first recognised by a Dutch biologist, Cornelius Adrianus Pekelharing, in 1912. This would lead to fevered discussions about balanced nutrition and health and a new understanding of the benefits, in particular, of fresh fruits and vegetables.

with banana and walnut – combinations which matched the ingenious American salads combining poultry and fish, tangerines and truffles, pimentos and asparagus, chestnuts and pineapple. America's salads were as flashy and inventive as its citizens: the Roosevelt with artichokes, apples, chopped nuts, cloves, nasturtium seeds and lettuce; the Waldorf with celery, apples, bananas, nuts and mayonnaise; cream-cheese salads with nuts; fruit salads of oranges, pineapple, grapes, and even marshmallows served on lettuce leaves garnished with parsley.

Lush as it all sounds, it would be another five decades before the British really took salads to their hearts. In the meantime their detractors were legion: '. . . there is one awful moment of doubt,' wrote Edward Bunyard in 1937, 'when the English salad appears . . . At the worst it will have been "made" an hour beforehand to "save time" . . . resembling a copy of *The Times* which has floated down from Hammersmith to Deptford. The English salad! True emblem of lost hope, drenching skies and "approaching depressions".' Suspicious of oil, cooks drowned their leaves instead in tart vinegar or with salad creams of egg yolk, Worcestershire sauce and mashed potato – even unsweetened condensed milk. As Heinz's Salad Cream became a best-seller, Marcel Boulestin professed himself baffled, wondering whether the English salad was the result of ignorance or the aim of a curiously perverted taste.

Despite the economic slump that hit at the end of the '20s and the hardship and Depression of the '30s, when high unemployment meant that the poorest still survived on a diet high in carbohydrates and tea, the fashion for masses of social activity flourished. Peppered with stinging class-consciousness, it held at its heart the notion of the assured 'hostess', young women in faceless suburbs and third-floor town flats 'who want to know more about Good Food, for their own and their friends' pleasure and possibly . . . with an eye to social advancement', as Ambrose Heath noted in 1932. By the end of the '30s, three-quarters of all British families would have a gas cooker, a quarter a refrigerator, and many more cake mixers and American pop-up toasters. Party food was as much to do with fitting in as with standing out, and everything had to be done without help or apparent effort. Women pored over magazine advice for dishes that eliminated the need for carving, producing thick mousses of meat, fish or chocolate, cooking in individual china dishes – or en cocotte – and planning food that could be made in separate portions, especially recipes that used up cold meat in new ways such as little *kromeskis* – combinations of chopped meat bound in egg and béchamel, cooled, shaped into rolls, battered and fried.

Tray wagons appeared to help with the dishes and to hold the percolated coffee, and ladies without maids were encouraged to turn to simpler ways of entertaining – to drinks after church on Sunday, teas or bridge parties where cheese straws (*alumettes*) could be served with tinned soup. Hors d'oeuvres and savouries were handy for small, light meals and for entertaining: stuffed eggs, small tomatoes or grilled mushrooms, or more fiddly anchovy-stuffed olives or cornets of smoked salmon and caviar. Anchovy biscuits and creams, angels on horseback, cheese choux, croûtes of fried bread topped with ham or tongue, prawns, sardines or herring roes, as well as miniature sausage rolls and tomato jellies, could all be offered from a tray with cocktails in the drawing room at luncheon parties or as pre-theatre snacks.

The redoubtably buoyant Elizabeth Craig advised that 'to be a successful hostess, no matter your means, no matter your staff, you must make entertaining a business as well as an art,' making 'a hit with the trimmings, not with elaborate sauces'. Using an electric plate for cooking bacon, sausages, mushrooms, chops and steaks at the table and crêpe-paper serviettes that required no laundering, colour-co-ordinating her 'sets' of tableware with the food she put on them, Craig kept up appearances at all costs, resiliently gay on the surface and just a little strained underneath it all. It was as though, if she persevered with her yellow colour-scheme at the breakfast table ('cruets in the shape of yellow ducklings . . . tiny yellow or orange egg cosies', grapefruits, lemon marmalades and pimento scramble) for long enough, the horrid servant-less world would revert to its pre-war elegance and the Depression turn out to be a bad dream.

Craig's *Standard Recipes* (1934) was one of the first cookery books to include black-and-white photographs aimed, like *Woman's Own* and other weekly women's magazines, at housewives eager to impress.

Her food was less the cutlets of the cosmopolitan upper class than dishes using a combination of fresh and canned food: a lunch of tinned prawn mayonnaise, baked custard and stewed fruit, biscuits, radishes and cheese, and a dinner of cream-of-tomato soup, roast lamb with mint sauce, new potatoes, green peas and orange fritters. Particularly keen on bought pastry and custard powder, Craig made sure everything was trimmed and garnished, the paper doilies, sandwich flags, cutlet frills and drinking straws mirrored by boiled eggs cut like daisies, fluted slices of cucumber, radish roses, sprigs of mint and sprinkled paprika.

Curries had dropped out of fashion for a while, but war had blasted the doors of the world off their hinges, encouraging everyone to look beyond the navel-gazing confines of the teetering Empire. Leyel felt the time was right to devote a beguilingly romantic section of her book to 'Dishes from the Arabian Nights', including kebabs of mutton with apple and ground ginger and delighting in the ability of raisins and almonds to turn a commonplace dish into a sensual delicacy. She offered recipes for Hungarian sweet-pepper stew, or goulash, and for chicken stuffed with minced apple, almonds, coriander, nuts, sugar, lemon peel and allspice, attempting to reawaken culinary appreciation of spices and aromatics with dishes remarkable for their difference from the world of Scotch eggs and grapefruit – sensitive, sensuous recipes which mainly slid over the heads of Middle England.

Countess Morphy's voluminous *Recipes of All Nations* (1935) included recipes for Creole, Russian, Polish, Portuguese, Dutch, Indian, Norwegian, Belgian, Danish, Spanish and Italian dishes; only China, she felt, remained 'remote from both our understanding and from our palates', the chop suey of urban repute a thing unknown in China itself. But it was America, redolent of Hollywood and energy, youth and novelty, that took Britain by storm, and 'Chicken Maryland' was its standard bearer: breaded, fried, served with sweet-corn patties, a sliced banana and sometimes a horseradish-cream sauce. Hamburgers – mostly known as beefburgers – were also sometimes served with bananas; Frankfurt sausages became hot dogs when piled into a long roll with mustard, and baked Alaska ticked all the boxes for surprise, emerging from the oven as a crunchy meringue encasing still-frozen ice cream.

With their ritzy branding and advertising campaigns, American breakfast cereals were transforming the British diet as fast as their tins, and Force, Grape-Nuts, Malta Vita, Puffed Barley, Rice Krispies and British Weetabix divested themselves of their health-food branding to become staples for anyone wedded to convenience and speed. Grapefruit was the darling of the slimmers; black coffee, orange juice and toast took over from kedgeree and cutlets. Most women could only dream of breakfasting in bed in the style of their celluloid sisters, but single girls *could* enjoy their breakfasts in bed and waft around their flats after work in 'a trailing negligee and frou-frou', making the most of their liberation.

'Extra women', as unmarried girls were called, were advised that tinned luxuries like fish roes and green-turtle soup come in *one-woman* sizes and that baked eggs with creamed mushrooms, eggs Benedict, calves' liver or corned-beef hash did not hang on as leftovers. Some possessed an 'Easiwork' kitchen designed for the single cook, but the majority were given stern instructions to 'Live Alone and Like It', to surmount self-pity and marshal courage, humour, guts and ingenuity in the face of the single gas ring, hunting out foreign grocers whose delicacies – Greek olives, avocados, Russian borscht, Swedish goat's cheese and Mexican tamale pie – would provide as much conversation as nourishment at dinner. In bedsits, kippers could be dangled over the flames, cans of soup heated up and double boilers used to keep things warm; nut brittle and tangerine fudge could take the place of boring leftover pies. As to the delicate business of how long a man should be allowed to stay, well, it depended on whether it was forever or merely for the occasion: '. . . you can always keep on standing which will eventually wear down any man (if you don't drop first).'*

Children were beginning to have a better time of it too, freed from bready paps and offered instead rosy-cheeked apples stewed liberally into pies, roly-polys spread thickly with damson jam, and perhaps the remains of the warm chocolate soufflés left over from dinner. Cooks

---

* On the subject of whether to have an affair ('Will you or won't you?') Hillis left things open – '. . . this is every woman's own special problem, which nobody else can settle' – though under no circumstances should it even be considered by anyone under thirty.

began to appreciate that children – a generation that would, anyway, simply *have* to learn to cook for itself – found magic in making bread, toffee and gingerbread and in scattering hundreds and thousands or grated chocolate over tapioca. Writers who rarely suggested seeking the direction of a grown-up began to engage children's interest in the adventure of cooking, in making pies for 'camps' and even in boiling up their own jam or fudge, whipping up hollandaise and perfecting an omelette.

As motor-car sales rose, luncheon baskets were dug out from the detritus of a richer age to be joined by new thermos flasks and unbreakable crockery. Sunday motor excursions spawned a generation of ladies in tweed skirts and gentlemen in trilbies who pulled happily on to the side of the road to sit on a Welsh blanket and share liver paste, boiled eggs, minced chicken and cream, sliced ham, shortbread, Cheddar, tinned fruit and Dundee cake. Hilda Leyel devoted an entire book to recipes for picnics for motorists, and the delightful Francis Colchester Wemyss, despairing of the impossibility of eating well in out-of-the-way places, recommended carrying a packed box in the car, including 'flour, oatmeal or Quaker Oats, baking powder, butter, cheese, vinegar, salt, pepper, mustard, sugar, jam, cocoa and tea, bacon, tins of milk, beef and tongue to fall back on if fish or game cannot be come by, and eggs and potatoes' plus a kettle and a frying pan, considering that it would make its owner 'very independent and self-contained' when requiring the occasional meal *sub jove*.

Where the Great War had begun a slow process of unpicking class distinctions, by the end of the '30s it was clear that processed goods were rapidly modifying the disparity of diet that had previously existed between the rich and the poor. Ravioli, mortadella, tongue and tripe all emerged from the Open Sesame of the metal container; by 1939 Wall's had become the largest ice-cream manufacturer in the world – its synthetic mixture a mere illusion of purity – and a limited and expensive repertoire from Birds Eye frozen foods had been sold for almost a decade.

Aboard C. S. Forester's *African Queen*, Rose and Allnut 'were of the generation and class which has been educated to think that all good food came out of tins, and their year in Africa had not undeceived them'. But in England, George Orwell raged at the loss of treacle tarts,

Devonshire cream and Yorkshire pudding, at the deadened palates of the working classes who preferred their green peas, baked beans and milk from tins and their cheese foil-wrapped. 'Wherever you look,' he wrote in *The Road to Wigan Pier*, 'you will see some slick machine-made article triumphing over the old-fashioned article that still tastes of something other than sawdust.' Rich and poor alike had embraced the convenience of the tin.

In 1936, as Spain descended into civil war, Wallis Simpson fled across France pursued by the world's press, and the Crystal Palace was reduced to ashes, George Bernard Shaw declared that Victoria was dead at last. Britain indeed appeared to be enjoying a resurgence of interest in cooking and in food that was light, fresh, seasonal, healthy and tasty. As middle-class diners turned towards asparagus-cream soups and braised chicken with spring vegetables, campaigners like Florence White tried to recapture the best of Britain's disappearing traditional recipes: small raised mutton pies, lamb's-tail stews, clotted and scalded creams, regional bread and buns, frumenty, cock-a-leekie, caudles, cured hams and kidney puddings – a crusade that would be continued by Dorothy Hartley in the early '50s. And in towns, milk bars with chrome interiors, high stools and milkshakes, Lyons, ABC and other cafés were making it not just affordable but fashionable to eat out.

The average 1930s housewife had never bought a baron of beef, sticking instead to small shoulders of lamb and mutton. She may have relied on tinned salmon and sardines and still have had only four recipes for eggs, but vegetables were beginning to achieve a respect that turned on its head nearly 2,000 years of food snobbery, and raw fruit occasioned no murmur. Less well-off families boiled potatoes and greens and made blancmange or moulded cornflour shapes with tinned apricots, but, as a national food survey of 1938 reported, '. . . in recent years there has been a slight but nevertheless definite tendency towards the revival of home cooking.' Jaded appetites were beginning to be re-stimulated. The time was ripe, urged the report, for a National Home Cooking Campaign.

Waste the Food and Help the Hun!

When war was again declared in 1939, 60 per cent of all British food was still being imported. This time there was no delay: within days, the Ministry of Food was re-established, and by January 1940 rationing had begun with bacon, sugar and butter. By March all meat was rationed by price, followed in the summer by margarine and tea; over the following year cheese, eggs, rice and dried fruit, tinned tomatoes and peas, sweets and chocolate, biscuits, flour, jams, treacle and most other canned goods would follow, along with clothing, coal, soap, gas and electricity. The average adult weekly ration included 2 ounces of butter, cheese and tea; 2 ounces of cooking fat; 3 pints of milk and 8 ounces of sugar; there was an egg each week or fortnight, a pound of preserves every two months and about 16 points a month for foods that remained off ration.

Just as cooks were getting used to bananas, aubergines, peppers and avocados, to wine, olive oil, hot chocolate sauce, exotic fruits and fresh vegetables, they disappeared. The British housewife had to make it to the grocer early or queue round the block, and she had to rack her brains to produce meals with almost no fats or eggs. Onions were so rare that most wartime recipes included them with the caveat 'if possible' – low in nutrition they may have been, but without them the taste went out of stews and soups. The kitchen was now witness to an elongated struggle with tins of sulphurous powdered eggs, dry skimmed milk and basic 'utility' cheese, bringing the war into the heart of the home, turning it into its own joyless front. Had most housewives known that shortages would continue for fifteen years they might have untied their pinnies and given up.

Instead, there was urgency in the air and every housewife was keen to learn how to make something out of nothing. The Association of Teachers of Domestic Subjects was among the first to publish a wartime cookery book – *Hard Time Cookery* (1940) – concentrating not on taste but on the principles of diet and the roles of vitamins, minerals, proteins and fats, emphasising the need to keep healthy despite meagre supplies. Phlegmatic British housewives were exhorted to rise to the challenge by newspaper columns, magazine articles, government food leaflets and bracing cookery demonstrations from home economists with fairground voices who had before the war worked for the gas and electricity companies. They were galvanised by *The Kitchen Front* on the BBC, five minutes after the eight-o'clock news, where popular cooks like Ambrose Heath and, later, Marguerite Patten tried their best to make cooks believe that there were blessings in disguise: the good old pot roast, the potato cake, mealy stuffings which made meat go further, and meat, bean or lentil loaf. But, as Virginia Woolf wrote in her diary early in 1941, '. . . food becomes an obsession. I grudge giving away even a spice bun.'

Unceasing propaganda instilled into every family the national importance of thrift and the patriotism of survival; to the beat of poster slogans warning 'Food wasted is another ship lost', 'Waste the food and help the hun!' and 'A sailor's blood is on your head if you waste a scrap of bread!' cooks became kitchen warriors. Butter-papers were hoarded to grease tins; fat was rendered in cold water brought to the boil, then scummed, drained, left to set and the top and bottom scraped, and it was skimmed from soups and stews to be beaten into a cream for cakes or rubbed around the frying pan. Sour milk was used for scones; bones, scraps, giblets, gristle and the boiling liquid from vegetables went into the stockpot; breadcrumbs were once more palmed from the table and stored in jars; sugar was stretched with saccharine tablets. The importance of shortcuts and economy was ingrained into a generation of stoical women who 'lived through the Duration', who could never thereafter bring themselves to throw away a wrapper or a rind of bacon.

In the country, adolescent boys roamed the fields with shotguns after the harvest, seeking rabbits and pigeons to sell at the WI markets for a shilling or three, while houses with gardens dug up the flower-beds to grow vegetables and tomatoes rare as precious gems, bottling everything they could in Kilner jars, keeping chickens and preserving their eggs in zinc buckets filled with isinglass. Some won a pig at the local fete but became too fond of it to eat it, sending half its slaughtered flesh to the government and giving the rest away. But it was people in the towns who suffered the most, less able to grow or raise their own food and in constant danger of powdered glass from bomb-blasted windows ruining what they had. Ambrose Heath admonished that 'you've no idea how happy go lucky people are!' and warned his listeners to keep food away from windows.

The National Loaf was launched in 1942, made with wholemeal flour: 'nourishing . . . not as dark as brown and not as white as white, but very good for you'. Legally adulterated with chalk to bolster calcium deficiencies in the national diet, dry and grey, it was so hated that it was quickly dubbed 'Hitler's secret weapon'; in any case, there was little enough butter, marge or jam to make eating it anything like fun. Concentrated orange juice and rose-hip syrup high in vitamin C were distributed for nursing mothers and children, and, as part of their Lend Lease Agreement, America sent canned fish, Spam, biscuits and large tins of sausage meat. Yet with an all but meatless, fatless, fruitless, cheeseless larder and limited fuel, no matter how inventive the cook, meals were bound to be monotonous, dull and often beastly.

Hay boxes returned, along with the need to use the oven as little as possible and to cram it full whenever it was on. The kettle was left standing over the grill to warm, a single gas burner could be made to hold two pots with a sheet of iron, and the residual heat from electric elements could be used long after they were switched off. Cooks aimed constantly at stretching meat with stuffings or minced it, mixed it with flour and cut it into 'shapes' to be fried. Offal, off the ration, came into its own again: *Hard Time Cookery* extolled the virtues of tripe in a hotpot or with cheese, heart with roots, and breadcrumb stuffing. Where there was no stock for soup, vegetable soups were made with tinned or dried milk instead, bulked with rice, beans or macaroni.

Instead of shoulders of lamb and buttocks of bacon, there were tens of irredeemably un-alluring things to do with a can of corned beef or Spam, moulding it into cutlets or rissoles or dipping it into a flour-and-water batter for frying. Ambrose Heath gave a recipe for a meatloaf of mince, breadcrumbs, one egg, a little bacon and stock or milk, all rolled into a cloth and boiled for up to three hours: 'just the thing for Sunday supper, with a bit over for dinner on wash day!' Horsemeat, still forbidden flesh to most, was passed off as mutton, venison or salami, though the black market was more a dream of gin and Altars (filched Communion wine), nylons or chewing gum. People made do. Cakes were the hardest of all, made crumbly by powdered egg and relying on grated carrots or scarce dates for sweetness. Some splurged on a good cake by saving up their eggs and fat for a week, and others learned how to counteract the dryness by steeping the cake in tea. Icing was illegal, wedding cakes were more often cardboard than edible, and, as Christmas Day dawned, 'Austerity Pudding' was likely to be made with potato, grated carrot and apple, as much dried fruit as you could get your hands on, dried egg, flour, breadcrumbs, cooking fat and a scraping of precious golden syrup or marmalade.

Recipes like squirrel soup and rook pie from the Ministry of Food were often greeted with amazement and ridicule, but it was 'Woolton Pie', named after Churchill's Minister of Food, that attracted a derision bordering on hysteria. With rolled oats and mashed potato replacing fat-rich pastry and a filling of root vegetables or cauliflower mixed with a little beef extract, 'Woolton Pie' offended something visceral and elemental in the national psyche. Pastry was the backbone of British domestic cooking; it came with meat and gravy – or, at the very least, fruit and custard; this was an aberration.

Faking it was also a bleak fact of life. Mock cream was made with marge, sugar, dried milk powder and milk; mock mayonnaise with a tin of sweetened milk, vinegar, salad oil and a teaspoon of mustard; sausage meat and root vegetables were shaped into an unlikely model of a duck. Mock crab with its dried eggs, marge, cheese, salad cream and vinegar contained no whiff of the sea, and mock fish was made with ground rice and anchovy essence. 'Chops' were moulded from grated raw potato, soy flour and a rare onion and fried, and mashed potato did instead of pastry for 'apricot flans' which were filled with grated carrot and a spoonful of jam. Nuts, beans and lentils were all served in place of meat, and coffee-drinkers habituated themselves to substitutes made from beans, roasted chicory or even acorns.

'Afters' suffered terribly without the eggs, sugar, cream and fats on which they depended so that such treats consisted only of baked rice puddings or claggy sago – known to schoolchildren as fish eyes and goo. A stale tea bun could be made up into an approximation of a trifle with a little bottled fruit juice or a thin apple sauce, topped with a dollop of custard made with powder or, worse, mocked with potato flour and flavouring. Cooks did learn to bake without fats and there were windfalls: in Norfolk after a shipwreck, one man remembered 'there was that many oranges coming ashore . . . the sea was all orange . . . All the women from the country were . . . biking down with the kids and filling their sacks full.' There were also some for whom rationing was the spur to invention, like the young Elizabeth David, who made an ice cream as sensuous and priceless as its original seventeenth-century forebear, reducing the confectioner Jarrin's eight-egg custard to suit the single egg of the weekly ration and using milk in which she had left a single coffee bean to infuse.

In towns, restaurants had a 5s limit per customer and could serve only one course containing fish, meat, eggs or cheese. Claridge's was festooned with the flags of all the exiled royalty who made it their home, and anyone else could eat there too, for 5s – so long as they had another 15s for the bandsmen, 12 for the taxi and 5 for the coat-check. Communal Feeding Centres – soon happily renamed British Restaurants – were established by local authorities in school and church halls, serving three-course lunches for 1s 6d and no coupons, attracting long queues for cottage or fish pie, corned beef and beetroot, Spam, sponge with custard or bread puddings – food that kept the workforce going and bonded communities.

Britain's first cookbook devoted to Chinese food – *Chinese Cookery* (1943) – emerged from one of the bleakest years of the war, promising to use vegetables and tiny amounts of meat in new and palatable ways. With only a teaspoon of oil and very little fuel, Chinese cookery did indeed offer a partial solution to the monotony of wartime food, and its authors assured their readers that Oxo, Marmite or Bovril could be substituted for soy. But no letters, memoirs, diaries or novels suggest the existence of a family managing to escape the dreary grey food of wartime Britain with a hot, healthy dish of sweet-and-sour pork or vegetables with garlic.

After the war, when people could again walk home at night without looking at the sky, few were really interested in the fact that rations had levelled the dietary playing field, nor that they had generally left children taller, with better teeth and in more robust health. What people wanted was to pick up the pieces and get back to normal, but as the street parties, streamers and goodwill receded, austerity stretched out into infinity. For a while things actually seemed to be getting worse: in 1946 the sweet ration was halved, chickens cost 5s a pound, and the National Loaf got smaller and was rationed along with flour for the first time, causing queues at the bakers and the formation of a league of angry British housewives. To replace American tinned fish, greasy, rancid-smelling whale meat – Moby Dick – appeared. Most cooks loathed it, including Marguerite Patten, now demonstrating on the first-ever women's-magazine television show, *Designed for Women*.

The year 1947 brought a freakishly hot summer and a bone-freezing winter, the launch of Dior's New Look with its feminine, wide skirts, tiny waists and rounded shoulders – and the halving of the bacon ration. Potatoes were rationed for the first time, and ten million half-pound tins of snoek were imported from South Africa. As repellent as it sounded absurd – Marguerite Patten remembers it, simply, as 'awful' – snoek cost only 1½s or a point a tin, and it promised to make up for the loss of tinned sardines and salmon. But no matter how cooks longed for something new, Ministry recipes for snoek piquant (onions, vinegar, syrup), snoek pasties or snoek salads tickled no one's fancy. Two years later, more than a third of the tins remained unsold, most turning up on grocery shelves as cheap catfood.

For most children, bananas, oranges, pineapples, lemons and sweets remained strange and miraculous, and if housewives towards the end of the 1940s began to attempt anything close to a dinner or cocktail party, they were likely to gaze ruefully at their meagre stocks of food and serve baked beans and cauliflower soup rather than iced Camembert. During the 1948 Olympics in London, the government encouraged foreign teams to bring their own food with them. The year 1951 may have brought the Festival of Britain, but the meat ration was at an all-time low, food was still strictly regulated, and British cooks were sick of bracing themselves against the grind of shortages, sick of the nervous headache of enforced ingenuity.

Yet the Festival, with its modern exhibits, its crowds, fantasy and amusement, did mark the beginning of recovery. The following year tea was de-rationed, and in 1953, as Britain celebrated the conquest of Everest and the coronation of its young Queen, eggs and cream were too. In 1954, butter, marge, cooking fats and cheese were the last to go.

24

Learning to Walk, Loving to Run

We must once more learn to walk . . . before we can run
and now, I believe, is the time for encouragement
— AMBROSE HEATH

The gastronomic despair of 'the Duration' was waning, and it was time to throw off the shackles of substitutes and subterfuges. Sour cream was still hard to come by (and most British cooks would have thought it was 'off' anyway), buttery hollandaise and béchamel remained a fantasy, but, as they pinned up the temperature charts that came with their new thermostatically controlled gas and electric ovens, cooks were beginning to dream again. Ambrose Heath stimulated their imagination with chilli con carne, chicken gumbo, the paprika and goulash made popular by Polish airmen, and with salads and sweets made with lashings of cream, spoonfuls of sugar and great glugs of alcohol. In the same year, Raymond Postgate founded the Good Food Club and Guide, both aiming to reward high standards and denigrate the shoddy in pubs, hotels and restaurants. The first Guide congratulated a restaurant outside Aberdeen for the best mushroom soup and vol-au-vents outside France, another in Manchester for its creamed turbot and a third in Dorset for its jugged hare, but Postgate demanded from his readers that 'if the food and service is vile, refuse to eat it, and refuse to pay!'

That same year, Elizabeth David burst into the grey post-war world describing the kind of food that made one happy to be alive. With shortages still pinching, olive oil still sold in vials by chemists, and most people thinking of foreign food as alien, oily and horrid, work on David's *Mediterranean Food* was begun in the bleak winter of 1947 in defiance of the cold, the queues and grocers who asked you *who* basil and tarragon were. Hers was a fantasy of Parmesan and herbs, of lovingly prepared southern French, Greek, Italian and Egyptian foods, a slim volume with elegant illustrations by John Minton that was to be read as much for pleasure as for instruction. It evoked the vibrant colours, touch and smell of the French market; the piquant, earthy and aromatic flavours of garlic, anchovies, olives, marjoram, saffron and thyme, lemons, apricots and figs; and a spirit of cooking that was more about adventure, devotion and satisfaction than martyrdom and boast.

Less rissoles, gelatin, soup with flour or cold meat with mayonnaise than bouillabaisse and scallopine of calf's liver with pimentos, David's book had to wait for paperback publication in 1954 to achieve widespread notice. But it stirred the memory and the imagination, in many ways not a solitary epiphany but a return to a pre-war feeling for food where recipes took second place to the sight, smell and feel of the ingredients. David's was a writerly style, and her cultured voice, respect for history and regionality, and disdain for artificiality or for making do as well as the spirit with which she encouraged instinct over the slavish following of meticulous instruction, was, for its time in Britain, utterly unique.

In common with Escoffier and Boulestin, David adored the simple elegance of egg dishes, of omelettes, of melting eggs en cocotte and of mayonnaises slowly stirred with a spoon rather than bruised with a whisk. Her vision was of seasonal food freshly cooked, of pink meat and of meze on the beach in Greece, eaten while dabbling your feet in the Aegean. Steaming vegetable-and-pasta soup was made heady with a paste of uncooked garlic pounded with sweet basil and a tomato. *Avgolemono*, a chicken broth with rice, eggs and the fragrance of lemon, was matched with iced beetroot in jelly, the roots baked for hours in the oven until they bore 'no resemblance to the bloodless things sold ready cooked by the greengrocers', served in spoonfuls over a poached egg, not 'in a set piece or it looks like a nursery jelly'. Sliced ox tongue, Corsican ragouts, kid on skewers, moussaka and *osso buco* were all carefully explained while *pissaladina* provided the simplest of pizzas: a bread dough covered with slow-cooked onions, stoned black olives and anchovy fillets with a tomato sauce of garlic, oil and basil. David stuffed chicken with rice, raisins, almonds, onion, parsley, liver and basil, with green pimentos and orange, and threw down the gauntlet to her readers with 'Gigot à la provençale', an old French recipe quoted at length, untranslated.

David's writing was delightful, and, as foreign travel became easier, as vegetables were again imported and as delicatessens appeared on high streets, it was also a potential reality – something to reach for. But however much her arch, feline, chain-smoking, spirited preju- dices appealed to certain men and women of the educated middle classes in the mid-'50s (and sales of garlic presses did soar, much as she loathed them), there were still many who were not ready for the erudite or the brazenly foreign even when she told them exactly which shops stocked the goods. *Italian Food* (1954), *Summer Cook- ing* (1955) and *French Provincial Cooking* (1960) were propped on many kitchen shelves and would influence a whole generation of cooks in the '60s and '70s, but at David's side stood a society florist, Constance Spry, and her friend the proficient cook Rosemary Hume. Well-heeled girls from their finishing school at Winkfield Place or their cordon-bleu cookery school in London, uncomfortable with quiche lorraine or coq au vin and loathing aubergines, flicked instead through the magenta-covered, 3-inch-thick 1,246 pages of Spry's cookery bible with its pointers on whether to add milk to the empty or full teacup. Spry and Hume, after all, had authority; they had invented the dish of the decade: coronation chicken, with its curried, creamy mayonnaise and apricot purée, served to the Queen's guests on that day of days in 1953.

The *Constance Spry Cookery Book* (1956) toppled the endlessly updated Mrs Beeton from the head of the wedding list for upper- middle-class girls, providing polished, safely recognisable English and pseudo-French recipes in meticulous detail, emphasising proper method and measurement and demanding absolute precision. Soufflés required 'a clear mental picture of what you are doing and why you are doing it', and, since there was pride to be gained in a perfect outcome, you 'will perhaps have patience with these details if they seem unduly emphasised'. A rather daunting compendium, Spry's book covered recipes for every possible social occasion, dependably setting out the exact measurement for a potato chip while venturing into the realms of professional cookery – the kind of patisserie that should have been bought at the confectioner's, the kind of garnish more at home at the Savoy. 'It is one thing to choose a recipe and try it,' she wrote, 'another to know the whys and wherefores of its method and ingredients'; the word *suitable* cropped up on almost every page.

The fact that Spry and Hume chose to begin with recipes for cocktail parties and hors d'oeuvres (soon to be known as canapés) was telling, for they wrote for the notional daughters of Elizabeth Craig, non-working girls whose lives would be devoted to social engagement. They cajoled their readers to read the recipe, to spoon and not to slosh, to pay attention and to avoid touching silver serving dishes without a cloth or it would leave a print. They loved little things on sticks, stuffed celery with Stilton and choux buns with chicken and, while cautioning against over-adornment, neatly arranged their cutlets *en couronne*. They went into detail about the grain and colour of fresh meat, the brightness of fishes' eyes, the glories of home-made ice cream and the practicality of new emulsifying machines, or blenders. They showed how to put 'just the right amount' of cream into a stroganoff, and how to tie tournedos with string to keep their shape. Exacting and ambitious, Spry and Hume produced a straight-backed, foot-splayed ballet teacher of a book with a no-nonsense, confident air. Within five years many of their readers would rush out to buy the first English translation of *Larousse gastronomique*, a book 'not designed to help the lazy cook', a vast tome of over a million words arranged like an encyclopedia and generally kept at the back of the cupboard for use *in extremis*.

When her book appeared in 1956, Spry herself was already seventy years old and dizzied, perhaps, by the rapid spin of a world in which the secret of DNA was being unravelled, the four-minute mile had been run and the street smelled of Brylcreem and garlic. Against the background of the Coronation, coffee bars boasting Gaggia machines offered exotic liberation to urgent teenagers in slacks while architects declared the cafés to be a confirmation of 'the greatest social revolution since the laundrette'. To the background beat of the washing machine, the flicker of commercial television bounced off colour-coordinated walls while magazines offered a world of apparently limitless consumer choice, fuelling the fires of ambitious materialism.

With full employment and wage rises the shops were over-flowing, and the patrician Prime Minister Harold Macmillan declared that prosperous Britons had 'never had it so good'. Affluence brought embroidered bedlinens and table napkins, va-cuum cleaners, mixers and liquidisers, fridges, pressure cookers and Formica in every colour imaginable. Mrs Peel's premonition of hatches between the kitchen and dining room had become a reality, and American streamline design was marketed as Every-woman's dream, its sleek surfaces and functional efficiency trailing the breath of the American diner. *Homes and Gardens* declared that the 'Wrighton California' kitchen offered 'a lifetime of joy', and the 'English Rose' kitchen was precision-engineered from colour-coated, high-grade aluminium left over from the production of Spitfire nose cones and propellers.

New kitchens, dinette sets, kitchenette dressers with storage units and fold-down work surfaces, Formica tables and vinyl chairs were marketed with images of slim, well-coiffed cooks sporting useless pinnies and very high heels, apparently able to produce effortless soufflés at the flick of a wrist. Electrical sockets peppered the walls, kitchen steps folded out to reach cupboards which rose to the ceiling, and – goodness! – some housewives even hung pictures on the walls. By the mid-1960s waste-disposal units in sinks promised no more smelly bins or carrying the garbage pail to the street; cookers provided grills at eye level; non-stick pans were well established; electric spit-roasters for tiny joints echoed the glory days of the open fire, and electric frying pans had dials on the handles for temperature control. By the end of the decade almost 70 per cent of homes owned their own fridge. Alexis Soyer would have cheered to see the wall-mounted spice racks.

Yet, remote from the skiffle and the rock and roll, from the protesting sexuality of James Dean, Elvis Presley and Marlon Brando, the sort of loneliness seen in the 1860s and '70s was mushrooming among suburban women. Hand in hand with dynamic domestic design and incipient women's lib went the mild hysteria, depression and discontented neurosis of the suburban cook shackled to her appliances, surrounded by socially competitive neighbours. As Flanders and Swann so memorably put it:

> We're terribly *House and Garden*,
>   The money that one spends.
> To make a place that won't disgrace
>   Our *House and Garden* friends . . . !

These were the housewives spurred on by television cooks: initially by Philip Harben, the dynamic, tubby, bearded 'foodie' in a butcher's apron with his French and foreign dishes, and by Fanny Craddock in evening dress and jewels, peddling an unhinged fantasy of class and keeping her viewers entranced as much by what she was about to do to that poor unfortunate Johnny as by what she did with food. The debonair Robert Carrier with his St Tropez glitz could be counted on to turn modesty to luxury. Graham Kerr – the 'galloping gourmet' – the mournful Clement Freud and the spontaneous, fizzing Keith Floyd all followed, enticing their viewers with pastry crescents, pâté de foie gras and lobster soufflés, with pheasant en cocotte and casseroles. Cooking and gardening had become proficient middle-class hobbies, and cooking was, for the first time, a spectator sport.

With so much choice it was in some ways surprising that modest Marguerite Patten, the home economist who taught the nation how to cook in black-and-white step-by-step photographs in the mid-'50s and against the grey curtains of the BBC, was the most successful cookery personality of them all. Her *Cookery in Colour* (1960) – lurid colour indeed, garnished with a fairground array of typefaces – popularised home cooking by showing how family dinners and party food could actually look. Here were prawn cocktail (with a sauce of salad cream and tomato ketchup and a bed of knife-cut lettuce), salmon cutlets with bluish mayonnaise and a sprig of parsley, frozen mixed vegetables, piped mashed potato, croquettes and vol-au-vents, chaudfroid chicken with aspic jelly from a packet, Hungarian bean stews and pork spare ribs, bread in a basket, rabbit in mustard sauce and rice presented in moulded rings. Selling in its millions, *Cookery in Colour* made its publisher, Hamlyn, a fortune.

The secret of Patten's success was that she felt she could say, 'You know, you and I together, we will get through it.' She set out to re-teach housewives how to get the crackling back on pork and to make a good cake, guiding her readers through fruit, vegetables and different cuts of meat as if for the first time. She looked for shortcuts and cut out nonsense, and at packed demonstrations at the London Palladium she wore an evening gown but 'hoped it looked like one that could go in the washing machine'. Patten was confident and comfortable, and she accepted that if you had a busy young family you were unlikely to get the perfect result, comforting her readers not to hang their heads in shame when it all went wrong. She understood that cooking could be 'frightening', giving plans of work and tips for disasters, admitting that lumpy sauces, burnt food and cakes in which the fruit sank to the bottom happened to everyone. She was neither fashionable nor erudite, but she communicated effectively with people who wanted to cook and did not quite know how.

The Marguerite Patten cook tried to do something new and different as well as trying her hand at traditional cakes, raised pies and puddings using Stork margarine in place of suet and the steamer rather than the boiling pan. Husbands might return from work to find sweet-and-sour meatballs with a sauce made from green peppers, cornflour, soy sauce, brown vinegar, stock, mustard and tinned pineapple – a zing of a dish after decades of grey meat and gravy – or a goulash of lean beef and veal, canned tomatoes, onions, potatoes and two teaspoons of paprika with peas and carrots on the side. Osso buco in Patten's hands was nothing more recherché (though it sounded so) than stewed veal knuckle. It was daring to make shepherd's pie in scallop shells and to offer guests a fondue of Gruyère cheese along with a bottle of Blue Nun to dull the smart of a burnt tongue.

Some of these cooks, with predictably disastrous results, believed the unlikely dream peddled by the makers of time-controlled cookers and loaded their ovens with a stew, a pie and a pudding in the hope that they would be able to return home to find it all waiting to be served or, more frighteningly, 'safely left for the children to help themselves'. Others bought Bee Nilson's *Penguin Cookery Book* (1952), a modestly pioneering collection that covered the gamut of traditional British recipes with standard, uncomplicated French and Italian highlights. Nilson's 850 recipes presented straightforward ideas for beginners and a comprehensive reference for initiates, building on 'the foundation of simple dishes perfectly cooked, seasoned and served', describing simply how to make madeleines and stuffed stewed apples, to use flour, to make food go further, to pot-roast and braise, and to make the best of tinned fish and a perfect two-minute omelette.

As pre-war cocktail parties gave ground to the cheese-and-wine gatherings of the 1960s, a swathe of hosts and hostesses found themselves nervously ignorant, relying on the cheese and wine producers for their recommendations, sticking to colours rather than regions and the received wisdom of white with fish or chicken unless it was coq au vin. To accompany gin, sherry, vermouth and Dubonnet, savouries were firmly implanted on cocktail sticks arranged on trays or themselves stuck into a big lettuce, cabbage or grapefruit. Chipolatas were cut on the slant; bread, butter and anchovy paste were rolled, cut into pinwheels and baked; small curried fishcakes and quiches and savoury choux puffs were all arranged on colourful plates. There were unlikely sandwiches with anchovy and nut, bacon and baked beans, salami and cheese or even kipper and, for the cognoscenti, Parma ham, figs and avocados.

For post-theatre entertainment, pizzas ('like a gigantic open sandwich covered with spicy tomato, anchovy fillets and cheese', wrote Rosemary Hume), chicken mayonnaise or spaghetti with tomato gratin – 'and don't stint on the garlic' – were quite the thing, followed perhaps by pineapple meringue. Wedding guests were offered grapefruit-and-grape salads, tarragon chicken, chicken-liver pâté, tomato jelly and shrimp cocktail, while at tennis parties the hippocras and metheglin of the distant past were replaced by wine or cider cups, fruit cocktails, mulled wines and fruit fizzes. The birthday-party tables of middle-class children were covered with violet- and apricot-coloured meringues, orange jellies, bread and butter with hundreds and thousands, milkshakes, sausages on sticks, bright ice creams, pineapple chunks and brandy snaps.

Barbecues began to take over from picnics with mini-spit kebabs, gammon slices, chops, beefburgers and chicken legs, and at dinner, steaks with names triumphed over chicken and fish: 'Steak Diane' with shallots, butter, parsley and Worcestershire sauce, dramatically flambéed in brandy to squeals from the guests, or 'Tournedos Rossini' with its slice of pâté on top. Lemon-meringue pies could be made well in advance from gluey packet fillers, peppers were stuffed with rice, carrots mashed and liver pâtés whizzed up in new mixers, leaving the cook to enjoy her port and lemon with her female guests while the husbands talked conference etiquette. Along with the fondue, spirit stoves and electric frying pans were used for finishing off food at the table, and, for the terribly adventurous, Philip Harben demonstrated how to fry ice cream in breadcrumbs.

As a new appreciation of the glories of fresh, seasonal foods settled over at least part of the nation's cooks, food technology raced ahead. In some homes fruit bottling was no longer the time-consuming production of the past as fruit was packed into jars, covered with sugar syrup and cooked in the pressure cooker. Elsewhere, convenience foods battered the seasons into submission, making fruit, vegetables and fish available all year round. Grocers began to have open-top freezers to hold Birds Eye fish fingers, frozen peas and Wall's ice cream; tea bags, coffee powder, tinned tuna and desiccated soups all brightly filled the aisles of the burgeoning self-service supermarkets along with packet cake mixes, instant potatoes and, from the '60s, whole frozen dishes like Vesta beef curry, coq au vin and chicken à la king. Frozen food bought on the way home became the resort of families seduced by the idea of the TV dinner and women eager to slough off the perceived drudgery of cooking. For just such women – those who preferred a dry martini to a wet flounder – the 12,000 supermarkets in Britain were awesome, their 'shelves brilliant and bulging with nearly everything you ever heard of, all ready for you to add water to, mix and bake'. Pre-packed replaced the servant, and Elizabeth David – scourge of the synthetic, the plastic-wrapped and the inferior – began to long 'for the day when it's going to be clever to serve some relaxed English dish like cauliflower cheese'.

At Sainsbury's Self-service shopping is EASY and QUICK

1—As you go in you are given a special wire basket for your purchases.

2—The prices and weight of all goods are clearly marked. You just take what you want.

Supermarket shopping introduced the concepts of 'self-service' and ready-prepared meals, promising to make the housewife's life a doddle.

From the early 1960s, novelty cookbooks combining the passion of David and the practically of Spry began to appear with an emphasis on making entertaining chic. One was Arabella Boxer's *First Slice Your Cookbook* (1964), spiral-bound and colour-coded, allowing the 'cook hostess' to flick each of three horizontal sections to arrive at the ideal blend of starter, main course and dessert. With deep-fried dishes banished because of the smell, Boxer offered an alternative to over-elaborate catering food with country recipes which were a distinct change of direction: lobster-and-melon-ball cocktail, stuffed tomatoes with crabmeat, chicken-and-cucumber salad with paprika and cay-enne. Her main courses were designed to make your neighbours sit up and take notice – the 'spectacular gigot d'agneau en croute', boeuf à la mode, chicken in curry sauce with peeled grapes – and poached pears and apple charlotte, all accompanied by plenty of advice on what to drink for a nation waking up to wine.

The thriller writer Len Deighton, on the other hand, as talented in the kitchen as Ian Fleming's James Bond was with guns and women, turned his attention to men with the *Action Cookbook* and *Où est le garlic?* (both 1965), the second a collection of his singular graphic 'cookstrips' in the *Observer*. Deighton's men – real men – forsook

Len Deighton's innovative cook strips encouraged even professional men to forsake frozen food and reacquaint themselves with the notion of cooking from scratch.

frozen food, armed themselves with the secret weapons of the kitchen – the blender, pepper mill and omelette pan – and whipped up inviting food that mixed traditional bourgeois French and Italian with old English, preparing cassoulet, chilli con carne, stroganoff, Persian kebabs or boiled mutton with capers. Deighton made baked Alaska and fresh lemon-meringue pie, used Tia Maria in trifles, and oiled paper or foil for baking fish en papillote; he was capable of making a korma with dhal, chutneys and pickles without compromising his virility, was inspired by freshness and was as capable of larding meat as knocking up a drinks bar. Written by an accomplished bon viveur, Deighton's typographically striking, step-by-step book crooned to its readers, was a seduction in itself.

Bee Nilson's approach was ideal for beginner cooks in bedsits. Her cooks were more likely to work at a perfect fillet steak – bloody now – and at ratatouille than to make an easy cheese sauce with processed cheese and evaporated milk. Less adventurous bedsitters, though, might throw chopped green onions on the top of a warmed tin of vichyssoise (for guests), and, since one woman in every group could be counted on to be on a diet, they could forget desserts. Even without limited resources, the difficulties were legion: the problem of 'finding somewhere to put down the fork while you take the lid off the saucepan, and then finding somewhere to put the lid . . . finding a place to keep the butter where it will not get mixed up with your razor or your hairpins . . . cooking at floor level, in a hurry, with nowhere to put the salad but the washing-up bowl, which in any case is full of socks', as the journalist and writer Katharine Whitehorn put it. There was no point in worrying about stockpots when simple chicken casseroles with browned chicken pieces and a tin each of mushrooms and artichokes worked well, and good wine and saffron (the influence of Elizabeth David) could lift a risotto properly stirred. The idea of a perfect risotto stirred to creamy smoothness while on bended knee was, however, still too much for some – the easy alternative was to boil up some rice with a packet of soup and chop in a hard-boiled egg at the last minute, and it gave you time to clear up. Everyone loved chilli con carne, made slowly and with care or chucked together with a tin of baked beans and a dash of spice. Whichever way you went at it, you might have to sleep with a clothes peg on your nose.

The working classes, better off nutritionally than they had been for centuries, did not, in the main, buy David, Spry or Patten but opted instead for product-driven recipe books that came with the oven or the mixer that had become, according to Kenwood, 'a must in the modern kitchen'. These books promised to save time, energy and money, to transform boring basic vegetables into cream soups, tins of tuna into mayonnaises and tinned pineapple into fools and milkshakes. At school, shepherd's pie, brown stew, meat pudding, mince with vegetables, baked fish in parsley sauce, minced beef in batter, Spam fritters, Scotch eggs and steak-and-kidney pie were served with a splosh of watery greens. There was little fresh fruit but plenty of Edifas custard powder for the steamed puddings, baked jam sponges or treacle tarts.

The Great British Breakfast of bacon and eggs had become a weekend treat as the workforce rushed to catch their early trains and children were scrambled to the school gates. Britain was waking up again to food, but the heartland of plain dishes was shifting only slowly, with few families yet inclined to ditch the Sunday roast and trimmings, the custard with stewed fruit, or the stews, hams and puddings to which six out of ten still returned at lunchtime. Increasing numbers snacked between meals on new ready-wrapped snacks like the Penguin, Munch Mallow and Bandit.

Tempting the young, the open-minded and those who disliked cooking at home, food from all over the world was slowly becoming available on the street corner, in Greek tavernas, bistros with paper napkins, trattorias with draped fishing nets and plastic grapes, and Indian restaurants with tandoor ovens. Couples who preferred plain and sensible food clicked on past them, shuddering at the thought of curries, garlic and oil and the fishy smell of taramasalata. Instead they stuck to meat and puddings, murdered vegetables, the once-a-year salad and tinned fruit, or trotted off to the new breed of restaurants and pubs that became, according to Egon Ronay, simply 'heating-up places', reliant on deep freezes and the first commercial microwave ovens, chance by-products of radar technology. From Southend to Stornoway deep-freeze scampi, Maryland chicken, frozen vegetables and the kind of synthetic ice cream that Elizabeth David derided as sweetened lard inflated with air were served by staff who, according to the 1967 *Bad Food Guide*, were slovenly, dirty, inexpert and apathetic. The picnic basket was again relegated to the garage as Wimpy franchises, motorway chefs and transport cafés beckoned passing traffic with their neon lights, fast service, unchanging menus and lollies on a stick.

By the time widespread malnutrition had become a thing of the past and slimming a profitable business with Twiggy as its icon, the '60s were well into their swing. The young were flaunting trouser suits and miniskirts, macrobiotics and muesli, yogurt, nuts, health foods and brown breads. Chickens were no longer a rarity and vegetarianism chimed with the Summer of Love. On the other hand, Rachel Carson's *Silent Spring* (1962) voiced vehement outrage at the power of agribusiness, the use of DDT and pesticides, poisons, hormones and antibiotics. The book's success signalled the start of the backlash against battery practices and the machinery of the food trades, and against denatured foods stuffed with emulsifiers, preservatives, colourants and flavourisers. Within a year of its publication in 1963, Ruth Harrison's book *The Animal Machines*, with its call for a new attitude to animal welfare, was adding its voice to a growing disillusionment with the factory system.

Change can move at an agonising pace. Britain was so enamoured of the liberation that more than a century of food industries had provided that it would take more than a decade before the cries from Elizabeth David and her like – the cries to go slowly and respect freshness and seasonality – would finally filter into the general consciousness, leading consumers to clamour for organic, non-GM and environmentally sustainable foods.

25

'What I Myself Have Learned . . .'

The arrival of the microwaved bird is imminent.
Maureen is unnerved by the lack of aroma, of roast
flesh; it must all be confined within the white box. The
humming sounds threatening. She checks the LCD clock
on top of the fridge. Everything is perhaps going to
plan

— TIM LOTT

By the late 1960s Britain was beginning to face up to the consequences of its rapid industrialisation. Rachel Carson's book would lead to the setting up of the Swann Committee in 1969 to investigate the use of antibiotics in farming. Eventually herbicides, antibiotics and the use of the pesticide DDT in food would be banned. The Pandora's Box of horror stories and ethical issues to do with the food chain had been opened.

Cooking in Britain was no longer just about the rich and the poor, nor about the relative merits of slow, economical, traditional food over wasteful extravagance and culinary ignorance, nor was it just about urbanisation over rural self-sufficiency. From the mid-'60s onwards, there were really only two technological advances in the kitchen – the microwave and the domestic freezer – but there were enough fracturing economic and cultural influences to send hemlines up and down, hairstyles flat or backcombed, and the cook in his or her kitchen reeling.*

During the depressed and decimalised '70s, as IRA bombs accom-

---

* By 1971, 69 per cent of homes owned a fridge, 91 per cent a TV and 38 per cent a telephone (*Social Trends* 3, ed. Muriel Nissel, London, 1972).

panied general industrial meltdown, there were several extremes of British cooking: the élitist French style of *nouvelle cuisine;** the self-sufficient ethic of Tom and Barbara in *The Good Life* with their Aga, chickens, vegetable patch and pig, and the snobbish suburban aspiration of both Margot, their next-door neighbour, and Beverley, the vulgarian at the heart of Mike Leigh's stinging satire of suburban bad taste, *Abigail's Party*. As Beverley laid into her Bacardi and coke, offering gin and tonic ('Ice and lemon?') to the guests sitting on her new three-piece leather suite, she admitted that she had never actually used the rotisserie in her gleaming new kitchen with its over-sink light, gorgeous tiles and fridge-freezer. She hated food shopping. Arriving at Sainsbury's or the Co-op in her yellow Ford Escort, she got her trolley 'and I whiz in and I grab anything I can see, and I bung it in the wheely . . . we bung it in the car, bring it home, and it's done for the week, d'you know what I mean?'

Rather than stocking the freezer with frozen pizzas, Bev's mousy neighbour, Angela, liked making curries of leftovers – 'Have you ever tried pilchard curry? . . . very economical' – and she hardly touched Beverley's 'little cheesy pineapple ones'. They were both a whole world away from the emerging philosophy of Paul Bocuse, the leading proponent of nouvelle cuisine, a man who pressed his readers to go to the market before deciding what they would eat, to be aware of the seasons, never to cut corners, to cook with love, take risks, avoid rich stocks and lengthy marinating, and to prepare and cook fish pink at the bone, French beans crunchy and pasta firm.

Bev could take advantage of Freddie Laker's cheap air travel and holidays in Malaga, but squabbles about the Common Market and Britain's Empire-less place in both Europe and the wider world would pass her by. Yet in the boiling pot labelled cultural identity was a generation of immigrants whose memories and identities were entwined with the national cuisines they had left behind. Food and cooking in the '70s were on one level indeed dominated by the affordability of new home freezers and the growing culture of eating out. On another they were infused with a wistful longing for the past

---

* A new style of enterprising and curious cooking that threw away the rulebook, recognised by Henri Gault in 1973 as fresh, simple, refined and adventurous.

with its traditional values and an impetus to remember identity through home cooking.

Back in the mid '50s, Buwei Yang Chao's *Cook and Eat Chinese* had followed the example of Mr Lee in the '40s in an attempt to initiate British cooks into the delights of Chinese cooking and away from low-end Chinese cafés; it had included diagrams showing how to hold chopsticks, explaining that hot soups should be slurped loudly and that guests were allowed to reach across the table. As if that wasn't novel enough, she had used rice wine, spring onions and ginger from Chinatown, hot peppers, coriander, Szechwan pepper, oyster sauce and sesame oil, discussing the concepts of Chinese domestic cookery without stinting on authenticity. It wasn't just about cooking, it was about eating the Chinese way, a slim little book without illustrations that sold poorly and quickly vanished from the bookshelves.

Jane Grigson's *Charcuterie and French Pork Cookery* (1967) tempted cooks more prepared to try something new. Consciously following in the footsteps of Elizabeth David, this was not just a book of recipes: it conjured up a proud French tradition, the integrity of recipes honed over decades, consistent standards and the enjoyment of doing things properly rather than perfunctorily – a philosophy of preparation so rare that we call it artisanal. Challenging Britain's increasingly urbanising market towns and high streets and its endless quest for novelty, convenience and speed, Grigson's first book offered as an alternative the habit of care and persistence, of using odd bits and extremities of meat – pork belly, head meat, ears, trotters, tails, tripe and entrails – to produce something beautiful, delicious and, above all, imbued with history. Peeping out between the recipes for salting your own ham, mixing your own sausage meat, stuffing and roasting the heart and rendering the lard was the sense that this kind of cooking put you back in touch with your past, with the rhythms of the centuries and the land. In the spirit of Rachel Carson, it did the opposite of harm; this was cooking that took responsibility for the lives of the animals it butchered and that bothered to eat their guts.

One could almost hear Grigson whispering, 'Good luck!' at the end of her book, for she was setting the bar high. Four years later, her *Good Things*, quickly followed by *English Food*, took up the cudgel against the dinner-party snobbery that still avoided good

English food. Grigson's was a personal statement of belief in seasonal ingredients, offering traditional recipes, some from the golden days of eighteenth-century cooking, weaving the same magic around our national foods as *Charcuterie* had done for France, knitting into her pages the image of happy, calm rural life – the cat on the rocking chair, the crock pot steaming, the hunter with his gun and brace of pheasants, the garlic in the rafters and lashings of good butter and cream. Her vision was of oak rather than pine or Formica, of self-sufficiency and conviviality, of sharing, thinking and talking rather than watching television, of developing foods with perfect taste rather than perfect looks, of capturing and holding on to skilful cooking before it lost the fight with the brutishness of packaged, plasticised and dyed foods. It was a vision easily appropriated by the middle classes in the country, by those revolting against the commercialisation of the food industries, and by the health and wholefoods movement. With her example to follow, urban cooks could also 'fight, and demand, and complain, and reject, and generally make [themselves] thoroughly unpopular' in order to preserve skills and standards for their grandchildren.

Hardly a hint of the bread strike, Germaine Greer or the faddy Römertopf* found their way into the combination of feature, essay and recipe that characterised Grigson's books. Instead, she urged her readers to rescue old-fashioned wooden pie moulds and to raise hot-water crusts, to rediscover the joy of making and eating pastry which had not been factory rolled and re-rolled into a greying blanket. Sweetbreads, usually served up in lumps by hospital cooks, were wrapped in bacon, skewered and grilled, then scattered with browned breadcumbs and eaten with bread sauce, or they were fried with a syrupy gravy of butter and Marsala, Italian style. Despite myxomatosis, rabbits were still cheap, and Grigson cooked them in old-fashioned stews, jugged them, used Hannah Glasse's recipe with Seville oranges or prepared them Italian-style with sultanas, pine kernels, candied peel, lemon juice and bitter chocolate. Brown-bread ice cream, Gunter's speciality, enjoyed a renaissance in Grigson's hands.

---

* A porous, lidded earthenware pot in which food could be cooked without fats or liquids, the Römertopf enjoyed brief popularity in the '70s until cooks discovered that they were not, after all, much different from the typical casserole dish.

In a Grigson world, cauliflower and broccoli were rare visitors, and chicory, haricot beans, leeks, mushrooms, parsnips, parsley, peas, spinach, tomatoes, celery, carrots and asparagus were welcomed. Limes, occasionally on sale in Sainsbury's, were used to make bright ices; chicken (even better, capon) was cooked with morels, and calf's head or stomach was patiently prepared for family and friends – 'guest' was a word one imagines Grigson rarely used. Her contemporary, the broadcaster and chef Michael Smith, also lobbied for a reappraisal of a distinctive British national cuisine, his *Fine English Cookery* (1973) seeking out the history of dishes, bravely reworking recipes from Glasse, Raffald, Blencowe, Rundell, Acton, John Evelyn, Patrick Lamb and more to get to the heart of an indigenous repertoire unencumbered by French chicanery. Smith reinvented clary omelettes, chicken with celery sauce, beef olives, tea ice cream and flummery, and served them at his fashionable but almost unique restaurant The Greenhouse in Curzon Street.*

The same spirit of recapturing and perpetuating tradition suffused Claudia Roden's *Middle Eastern Food* (1968) and, a decade later, Madhur Jaffrey's *Invitation to Indian Cooking*. Like David's wistfulness for the Mediterranean during the coldest winter of the '40s, Roden's recipes summoned the woodsmoke and spices of the bazaars of her Middle Eastern upbringing. Her book was 'the fruit of nostalgic longing for, and delighted savouring of, a food that was the constant joy of life in a world so different'. The intensely social aspect of Roden's cooking lay as much at its heart as its centuries-old use of pine nuts, cinnamon, cumin, coriander, ginger, crushed garlic, cloves, mint and saffron. Hers was food traditionally cooked slow in tagines, and her book reintroduced to British kitchens the Arabic flavours once so adored by our Norman ancestors, with savoury pastries scattered with sugar, pounded meat and plenty of allspice, pomegranates and scented water.

Less Wonder Bread and Maxwell House coffee than the emotion of food, there was nothing stiff-upper-lip about either Roden or Jaffrey's cooking. They both encouraged imaginative cooks to seek out unusual ingredients like couscous and filo pastry in speciality shops and to try out at home many of the tastes to which they were being introduced in

---

* The restaurant launched the careers of Gary Rhodes and Brian Turner.

restaurants. Roden's meze may not have appealed to Beverley as she listened to Donna Summer's 'Love to Love You Baby,' but her hot vine leaves stuffed with minced lamb, purées of aubergine, haricot bean or avocado, fried liver or brains, tahini, hummus, *baba ganoush*, tabbouleh made from bulgar or cracked wheat and abundant parsley, robust Syrian bread salad or *fattoush* were all seductive to the customers of Crank's Health Food store in Carnaby Street, to lovers of yogurt and to those who were already initiates into the nutmeggy silkiness of a fine moussaka and the pungency of garlic and mint.

The flavours of Roden's Middle East and of Jaffrey's India brought fish alive; red mullet stuffed with chopped parsley, lightly floured and fried, or sea bass in green chutney could rescue Fish Friday from the despair of watery halibut with a parsley sauce. Dates in syrup, fig jams, quince and raisin pastes and rose-petal jam – if you had imagination and time, if you wanted to nurture as well as impress – could boot cake and custard into infinity. Authentic (the word chimes through these books) Indian food, using home-ground spices, ghee and palm oil and even asafoetida, untasted in Britain since the departure of the Romans, could transform cauliflower with turmeric, ginger and fresh coriander. Chicken baked with whole cloves, black peppercorns, cinnamon sticks, bay leaves and cardamom pods was an adventure that transformed the smells of frying steaks or boiling vegetables into an intoxicating whirligig to set the mouth watering.

Middle Eastern and Indian food returned spice to the British kitchen, reawakening our sense of smell as well as taste. Roden's and Jaffrey's recipes were detailed, running over large pages, moving step by step and easily through unusual processes, always with a fashionably chatty paragraph that set the dish in its historical and ethnic context. They breathed life, energy and desire and dangled adventure before cooks rapidly turning away from factory farming, bored with endless cheap chicken, wary of mercury poisoning in farmed fish and craving ideas for vegetarians. They titillated with hard-to-find ingredients like okra, tamarind and black-eyed peas, luring cooks momentarily away from the gammon slice with tinned pineapple ring.

Kitchen life was not all, or even mostly, cardamoms and coriander, of course. Instant potato and Spam were facts of life along with Tetrapaks and McDonald's, and a legion of women cheered as the novelist Shirley Conran vowed that life was too short to stuff a mushroom. But freezers were not only the baneful resort of those fixated on ready-prepared Black Forest gateau or bread-filled sausages, and their sales were rising: by 1967, 10 per cent of households owned one, and within twenty years that figure would rise to 66 per cent. Frozen food was part of the fabric of society, and cheap, colourful books from the early 1970s showed how to fill these chests with home-prepared soups and sauces, stocks, shepherd's and fish pies, goulashes, casseroles and pastry, all made in bulk and separated into containers for future use. They gave instructions for how to quick-blanch garden peas, beans and carrots, and suggestions for freezing cakes, Swiss rolls and the newly fashionable roulades, and endlessly repeated the principles of thawing. There were disturbing ideas for freezing things like sandwiches filled with sardines, cottage cheese and pâtés which make the modern reader shudder, but, for all that, the freezer had returned millions of British housewives to something akin to the ancient practices of preservation.

Freezers and microwaves were bound together in an eternal love affair; domestic microwaves enjoyed the fastest-growing sales of any kitchen appliance. Amid stern warnings about the use of metal, plastic microwave dishes appeared, sales of cling-film escalated along with freezer bags and Tupperware, and all the stuffed foods of the 1930s returned as easily reheated bar foods – eggs and tomatoes, eggs en cocotte, croquettes and vol-au-vents filled with mushrooms – kept in a holding pattern that delivered them flaccid or leathery and always colourless. Microwaves could be useful for steaming vegetables and fish, and it was not impossible to get a good treacle sponge with a little care. They were useful for defrosting and reheating stews, but in the hands of the unimaginative, they were dispiriting, gambling flavour and texture in favour of speed and convenience.

The middle ground of British cooking in the '70s – and right through the '80s too – was occupied by a kind of solid dependability which combined new flavours with old favourites, encouraging housewives to leave the tomato soup, shrimp cocktail, steak, sprouts and trifle to one side, jollying them along to try something different. *The Cookery Year*, first published in 1973, was a phenomenon, a one-stop manual compiled by a panel of writers including Katie Stewart, Jane Grigson and Ken Hom, packed with quality colour photos, wrapping up everything you could possibly want to know about cooking in a modern and accessible way. It showed cooks not just where joints of meat came from on each animal but what they looked like in their butchered state; it detailed cooking methods with step-by-step illustrations, included sections on how to plan wine with food, how to hull a strawberry, prepare a pineapple or make a melon ball, and how to trim and decorate pastry or draw a lattice pattern in sugar on a cake. In the spirit of Alexis Soyer, it even gave plans for kitchens, but most importantly it divided recipes into months when the ingredients were at their seasonal best and standardised them all to include preparation times, chilling or cooking times, the amount a dish would serve, its ingredients and its method. Each recipe was also given a compact introduction – where it came from, what to watch for, the kind of chat that kept it all informal, reassuring and weirdly familiar.

Although *The Cookery Year* assumed that cooks had enough silver cutlery for five courses, starched linen napery and brightly polished crystal, and while it was clearly about dinner parties and showing off, it contained recipes that a growing band of cooks were aspiring to make, and to make well: chicken livers with peeled grapes, pork with pistachio nuts, shrimps baked in sour cream, pears in tarragon cream, and lamb-and-apple pie, along with Hom's sweet-and-sour pork, red-cooked chicken or toasted fish. It was the kind of food you might expect in the very best restaurant of a large market town – food still recognisable to your grandmother.

This was the territory on which a very young Delia Smith, bob-cut and shirt-waisted, drew for the BBC television series that began in the mid-'70s: 'interesting dishes which are neither too complicated nor time-consuming'. If Grigson's ideal home contained a rabbit-skinning wife in a vast family kitchen, Delia's was more a vision of semi-rural or suburban homeliness, a jar of wooden spoons in the kitchen corner. Her tone was that of the home-economics teacher with plenty of hesitations to make sure her viewers weren't being left behind and lots of collusion: 'we're going to continue cooking . . . we'll be visiting . . .

I'm going to take you with me . . . we'll be taking a peep into an Indian spice shop.' She was classless, chummy – 'How's that?' – and endlessly chatty – 'Now for the egg bit.' There was an element of 'I promise' about her scripts and a slightly gauche reliability to her appearance. Her success was staggering.

Marguerite Patten was still writing enormously successful books on freezing, microwave cooking, cooking for weddings and for Sunday lunches, and 'hostess' cooking, with good traditional recipes mixed with those for fried cheese in breadcrumbs with cranberry sauce, the glamorous crown roast and cheesecake. In her books, colour photos coordinated the new swathe of brown-suited men with hessian tray-mats, chutneys, earthenware, terracotta and parsley pots with the sprigs growing out of holes. Delia was absolutely of this mould, but she also introduced new ingredients like the pretty but almost-tasteless kiwi, fennel, sweet potatoes and basil, juniper berries, garlic and home-made mayonnaises for those habituated to salad dressing – 'quite frightening to beginners', but you will find it 'laughably easy', she encouraged. Delia made lamb baked with orange and mint, mustard-glazed ham, poached trout, kidneys in fresh tomato sauce, duck with morello cherries and rhubarb fool. Like the domestic cooks of the Enlightenment, she stressed the importance of serving quick and hot, of not panicking, and she delivered dependability – her recipes were all road-tested, and they never seemed to fail.

The genius of Delia's cooking was that it was not in the vanguard of change like David, Grigson, Roden and Jaffrey but swept along in its wake, always just one step behind. Her viewers had already tasted gaspacho and summer pudding; now they could make them themselves. She encouraged them to accept that 'nowadays' oil was no longer a greasy Continental habit but entirely respectable, steering them gently towards an avocado sauce, introducing quiche lorraine as a 'cream, bacon and onion tart', diffusing the grizzly, grey sound of offal with her 'spare parts' cooking and serving crusty bread with absolutely everything. Delia's cooking filtered into parts of the British culinary consciousness that her predecessors had not reached; she, like her successful contemporaries Mary Berry and Katie Stewart – and Martha Stewart in America – gave cooks confidence and prepared the ground for a renewal of interest in David, Roden and Grigson in the decades to come. She stood at the cook's elbow whispering 'all you do is . . . now take . . . now remove . . . while that's happening' reassuring as a mother hen.

At the other extreme, Paul Bocuse's approach was well suited to the British economy just emerging from its doldrums in 1979 to become a society ready to make money, to be impressive and to buy the best. Poaching at a bare simmer in liquid was as close as he ever came to boiling, and though he promised no rich sauce, his basic stock – in the tradition of eighteenth-century French chefs – took up an entire page and used up to 12 pounds of meat. Aiming for a new purity of flavour, his garlic soup used 20 cloves of garlic to 4 pints of water; panade soups with a base of bread, egg yolks and cream acted as vehicles for the single accents of lettuce, sorrel, spinach, watercress or celery. He boiled hams with hay, thyme and bay leaves and was scathing about modern freezers and electric ice-cream makers which chilled ices into hard blocks rather than soft emulsions.

Some recipes were simplicity itself – pork chops grilled with butter and breadcrumbs and served with a strong Sauce Robert – but the Bocuse nouvellle-cuisine method was at heart professional, labour-intensive and intricate, and it was perfectly ripe for translation into the kind of finicky '80s British restaurant that catered to the need for conspicuous consumption. Places like the Roux brothers' Gavroche and Anton Mosimann's Dorchester had the very rich and the very thin reaching for their wallets and everyone leaving only a little less hungry than when they had arrived.

The élitism of nouvellle cuisine came at the end of a decade during which cultural as well as social identity seemed more than ever embedded in what was produced in the kitchen. Perhaps it was only from the standpoint of the emerging '80s that writers like Harry Mathews in his short story 'Farce Double' could draw on all of this intense interest in home cooking to satirise what he saw as the smug piousness of the scholar cooks and conspicuous culinary competence. The recipe at the heart of his story – boned, stuffed, rolled and roasted shoulder of lamb – is complex, arcane, fragile and risky enough to make a normal cook weep with its impossibly precise requirements: even for such a small cut of meat, the pre-roasting process (in the

With the *à la russe* style of dining, food was served directly on to the guests' plates and courses progressed much as they do today. It required far more cutlery, but left space in the centre of the table for decorations of flowers and fruits.

By the late nineteenth century, menu cards helped guests to pace themselves by showing them exactly what to expect.

The Georgian House, Charlotte Square, Edinburgh, had an impressive flagstoned kitchen boasting a semi-enclosed range, separate bread oven and charcoal stoves. It was crammed with all the up-to-the minute culinary equipment available.

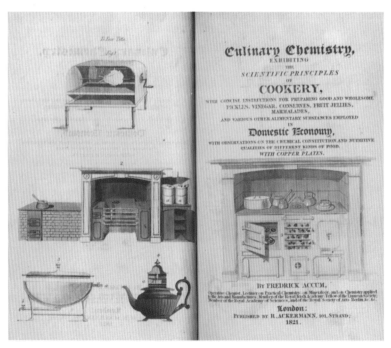

This frontispiece from Frederick Accum's *Culinary Chemistry*, 1821, demonstrates the evolution of the open fire into an early range, with charcoal burner to one side and hot cupboard on the other. On the right is a fully enclosed range with oven, boiler, hotplates and water-boiler.

The front kitchen at the Carlyles' house contained a simple, semi-enclosed range with a bottle jack for turning meat as it roasted and a small meat screen to the left; here there was clearly little culinary fanfare.

The kitchens of the Reform Club, London, 1841. Designed by the flamboyant chef Alexis Soyer and divided into separate offices for the different kitchen departments, the kitchens used gas ovens and were simply stuffed with Soyer's own ingenious inventions.

Mrs Marshall's 1885 *Book of Ices* contained lurid colour lithographs showing examples of the fancy creations that could apparently be made by anyone with access to her patent ice-cream makers, moulds, flavourings and colourings.

The restaurant at the Savoy, London, circa 1910, where men and women could dine together at small tables on the exquisitely tasty, light and sophisticated kind of cooking propounded by Escoffier.

BREAKFAST TIME.
Electric Coffee Percolator, Hot Plate, and Radiator.

Breakfast in the electric home, circa 1915. With electricity came new 'labour-saving' devices such as coffee percolators, hotplates and toasting machines.

Touted by advertisers as 'every woman's dream', functional, colour-coordinated 1950s kitchens relied on easy-clean Formica and Vitrolite, carrying echoes of the American diner.

An illustration from Elizabeth Craig's *Standard Recipes* of 1934, one of the earliest cookbooks to contain black and white photos.

The *Kenwood Recipe Book*, and other manufacturers' cookbooks from the mid-1960s, extolled the virtues of blenders, food mixers and mincers. Pâtés, purées and fancy baking were heavily promoted and doilies, food colouring and titivated presentation became all the rage.

During the 1970s, best-selling cookery writer Marguerite Patten offered recipes for dishes like Turkey Stroganoff, Turkey and Walnut Croquettes, Winter Salad and Crunchy Chicken Salad to 'hostesses' keen to make their mark.

The extraordinarily popular Delia Smith in her sunny kitchen – reliable tips and the promise of unpretentious success were her forte.

The original principles of Bocuse's *nouvelle cuisine* were, by the 1980s, often mangled by 'artistic' chefs catering to diners intent on overspending and undereating.

Hugh Fearnley-Whittingstall (*top left*), Nigella Lawson (*top right*) and Nigel Slater (*right*) have all caught the mood of the age with their various approaches: from ethical husbandry and 'nose to tail' eating to an ironic return to domesticity, all the while focusing on seasonal and regional produce and domestic proficiency. Interest in food and cooking has rarely been higher, despite growing debate about Britain's degenerating food culture.

Today formal dining has in the main been discarded in favour of the more reassuring and relaxed environment of the kitchen.

Auvergne) alone requires '4 senior cooks . . . standing on high step ladders and manipulating the poles . . . to . . . revolve [the meat] over the flames'. Thirty-eight pages of instruction cover days of urgent preparation, and behind the poetry of Mathews's writing is the obvious, gnawing truth that failure is inevitable.

What he adeptly exposed was the nerve at the centre of the British cook's life, a still-anxious place filled with the conflicting impulses to celebrate an ancient, strong national cuisine while being seduced by the cuisines of other cultures. But confidence was growing. To most European visitors, our kitchens were still broadly desultory places where ingrained skills appeared absent. But the success of Delia and the coterie of female 'farmhouse' cooks meant that there was an eagerness to improve. Restaurants showed what could be achieved with ingredients which did not come out of tins and packets and, as the '70s closed, cookery-book sales had never been more healthy. The less people needed to worry about where their food might actually come from, the more cookery programmes and articles flourished.

26

'Cuisine Poseur'

Foodies are the ones . . . salivating over restaurants, recipes, radicchio . . . 'I am a Foodie' is as proud a boast as the old Roman citizen's 'Civis Romanus sum'. . . What they both mean is, 'I am a winner'

— THE OFFICIAL FOODIE HANDBOOK

Three years after the wedding of Charles and Diana in 1981, and as ambition began to seep from the pores of the upwardly mobile with their aspirations for Gold Cards and Gucci bags, *Harpers and Queen* gave a name, 'foodyism', to the fierce and growing interest in food and cooking. Three years after that, Ann Barr and Paul Levy published the *Official Foodie Handbook*. More and more of us began to lap up food in restaurants reeking of status and boasting star chefs: Nico Ladenis, Alastair Little, Rowley Leigh, Marco Pierre White, Anton Mosimann and Raymond Blanc cooking at new restaurants like Kensington Place, Bibendum and the River Café. Innovation came not with gravy or sauce but with jus; almost no one was serving English food but what *Harpers and Queen* called 'Cuisine Poseur'.

The new generation who ate well in the trend-setting restaurants of the '80s soon began to clamour for books by celebrity chefs in an attempt to be as flashy in the kitchen as they were on the sales floor of the Stock Exchange or Next. Delia's Thatcherite mantra of *One Is Fun!* (1985) enjoined singletons to try out good food at home, and, with more cash in our pockets, ingredients went upmarket in the closing years of the decade: celeriac and mangetout, expensive Japanese sushi and tempura paid for on expenses, premium-priced ready meals from Marks & Spencer, herbs in packets, stuffed aubergine, banoffee pie and then grilled goats'-cheese salad, exotic mushrooms, vintage olive oils, flat-leaf parsley and loads of pasta. Iceberg was out, and rocket, radicchio and *mâche*, all packed in chemical-rich bags, were in.

Indian restaurants reinvented themselves with the balti and chilled Indian food arrived in Waitrose in 1987 as the taste for hot spice grew. By 1997 a Gallup poll was announcing that curry was the nation's favourite food, and in his 2001 general election speech Robin Cook tried to persuade us that chicken tikka masala had become our national dish. As long-haul travel became cheaper, the new Thai restaurants of the '90s were packed with diners seeking green chicken curry, satay and the coconut and lime flavours of the Land of Smiles. Pubs in cities and country lanes slowly began to throw out their microwaves, rebranding themselves as gastropubs. Originating at the Walnut Tree Inn in Wales, their moment came really in the '90s with David Eyre and Mike Belben's Eagle in East London, its open kitchen serving gutsy steak sandwiches to a clientele sitting at junk-shop tables on shabby-chic chairs.

At the other end of the scale, against the background of pot noodles and the proliferating golden arches of McDonald's, the new processes of compulsory tendering meant that private companies began to take over school catering, focusing less on nutrition than on profit and using pre-cooked, dried or extruded, nutrient-sparse convenience foods often prepared well in advance and rarely from fresh ingredients; school kitchens were in their death throes.

With the salmonella-in-eggs 'crisis' of 1988 that lost Edwina Currie her job as Health Minister, followed only six years later by the confirmation that BSE – caused by feeding the ground-up remains of ruminants to ruminants – had leapt the species barrier to emerge as nvCJD, confidence in the food being piled into super-market trolleys began to falter as fast as the animals were culled and burned and oxtail and brains became unavailable. In 1995 Jill Phipps, a thirty-one-year-old protestor, was crushed to death under the wheels of a veal-transporter, and in 2001, hard on the heels of the establishment of the new independent Food Standards Agency, the smell of roast mutton again rose into the countryside as sheep infected with foot-and-mouth were destroyed and immolated. Decades after Grigson, Margaret Visser in America and a legion of others first raised their concern about a loss of variety and flavour, genetic engineering, crop uniformity, degradation of fertile earth and the alarming reduction of wild fish stocks, food became a political hot potato.

Since the 1980s, cooks like Jeremy Round, author of *The Independent Cook* (1988), have urged their readers to be seasonally aware – though supermarket supremacy was not too far advanced for him to observe, in February, that '. . . chicken tends to be good value at this time of year.' Today, our need for reassurance is met by the likes of Nigel Slater, Jamie Oliver and Nigella Lawson – relaxed, messy cooks who savour the delight of domestic and family cooking, of roast (organic) chicken perfectly prepared, waxy potatoes, good sausages, boiled bacon, gooseberry pies and baking generally. Peasant dishes from Morocco and Basque Spain chime with a desire for unstuffy kitchen suppers rather than dinner parties. Hugh Fearnley-Whittingstall, Fergus Henderson and their ilk embrace the ideas of the Slow Food Movement that began in Italy in the late '80s, taking a vocal stand against intensively farmed and processed foods, encouraging rare breeds, regional speciality, resourceful self-sufficiency and nose-to-tail frugality which refuses to waste a scrap of the butchered animal.

But between 30 and 40 per cent of the food produced in Britain is never eaten, and the amount thrown away has risen 15 per cent in the last decade. Sales of convenience and takeaway food continue to increase – Britons eat three times more ready meals than the average European country – and new cookbooks never include sections on what to do with leftovers. Greedy for sugars, fats and salts, the nation suffers from high levels of nephritis, arteriosclerosis and hypertension; one in five children over twelve is overweight. Before the Second World War the process of raising a chicken to feed a family of five took around twenty weeks. It can now take only a handful to raise chickens that cannot walk – prime fodder for the junk-food industry – while storage and transportation times mean that even the fruits and vegetables in our supermarkets contain fewer nutrients than in the past.

In a society where more food is available to us than ever before, a lower proportion of income is spent on it than at any time in our history. It has become fashionable to focus on food with a social conscience, on Fair Trade and ethical production, on carbon footprints, food miles, organic food* and environmental responsibility. Three decades after Jane Grigson urged her readers to question the sources of their food, Britons are starting to care about pinpointing exactly where it comes from and what it went through to arrive on the shelves. Marks & Spencer know it – a honeyed voice croons over their television advertisements that 'This is not just food, this is M&S food'; even Starbucks know it, with their 'Commitment to Origins' scheme. These companies and many others market the tantalising illusion that we are increasingly in touch with the origins of what we put in our mouths, that our foods are 'hand picked', individual and unique, but it is still a pre-packed easy-meal, the answer to an atomised and servant-less society, and it is still competitive.

Perhaps the reality is that as a nation we like to be lectured and are happy to abrogate our food instincts for the short-term goals of speed and efficiency. The avalanche of newspaper and magazine articles, of radio and television programmes devoted to food and how we cook it, have conspired in part to turn a domestic reality into a leisure industry. Despite the fact that a recent survey told us that cooking is now more popular among under-thirty-fives in Britain than in France, we have yet to learn how to talk about food as memory (despite Nigel Slater showing us how) and history, to relax into it as part of the framework of our ordinary lives rather than as an issue, a programme, a new ingredient or a political promise.

Will we have been among the last to have had the privilege of seeing our mothers picking their own food or returning from the market with a basket overflowing, to watch them baking cakes, fluting pastry, larding beef or crisping bacon rind for us to crunch, whether in Shropshire or in Shepherds Bush? The last to witness a tribe of unfussy but skilful country cooks churning out hearty, delicious and untricksy

---

* In 2006 the Soil Association announced that while sales of organic food had risen from £105 million to £1.2 billion in the previous decade, three-quarters of organic fruit and vegetables sold by multiple retailers came from abroad, clocking up air miles as they quieted our concerns over food safety. As of March 2007 the Soil Association was about to rule on whether imported foods should be allowed to carry the 'organic' label.

seasonal food weighted with centuries of tradition – pies, puddings, fools, mousses, roasts of course, and endless things to do with apples?

The growing majority of us panic at mud, worms, beetles in the lettuce or the thought of gutting a fish, and we have forgotten how easy it is to make custard or ice cream that has a little goodness built in. It is not that we have stopped caring – *seasonality* and *sustainability* have become our watchwords – but few of us have their own smallholding on which to rear meat, and most of us haven't a clue how to go about getting back to the land.

Smoking fires, pungent gas, salamanders and toasting forks are behind us, but Britain is still a nation rich in produce. While cooking is no longer essential, our society continues to celebrate knowledge and expertise in cookery as it has for centuries. As we grope towards an understanding of what we have lost, we seem as a society to be unable to stop talking about food and the way we cook it. We have been obsessed as much by what was on the menu at Granita the night that Blair and Brown discussed their 'deal' as by the detail of the conversation itself. We continue to cook for sustenance, to impress, to woo, to show off, to comfort, nurture and compete. In almost any street in any town across Britain, there is cookery from Italy, China, India, Japan, Thailand, France and America, and Polish is the fastest growing ethnic cuisine; behind closed doors, millions of us are flicking through cookery books for inspiration, calling friends for advice on cooking times and seasonings.

There are eels in the Thames again, but few of would know how to begin to cook them. For a nation that loves its fish and chips, we are still broadly reluctant to deal with fish in the kitchen, yet we feed our children on omega-3 from a bottle. Mutton has disappeared; pestles are pushed to the back of the cupboard. When Jacques Chirac famously said that only Finland's food was worse than Britain's, were we really as shocked as we pretended to be? We buy green beans from Kenya and asparagus from Peru without considering its absurdity, and we unwrap pork pies heedless of their centuries of tradition. Still we shy away from entrails and, broadly, do not know what to do with vegetables.

In the course of our culinary history we have turned expectations on their head – now we know that brown bread is better for us, we relish dark muscovado sugars, we spend more on the slimming industry than we do on food aid for the starving, and £1 in every £7 is spent in Tesco supermarkets. Other things do not change: our foods – particularly bread – are still (but now legally) adulterated, and low-income families still eat more of it than do the rich. We still buy into the rules of dining, impressed by graceful manners and critical of belching, nose-picking and elbows on the table; by pretending that transgressions have not happened, we often show only how much we care. The flap of a white tablecloth makes many of us stand a little straighter. Food still sticks to the pan, the contents of moulds will not budge, custards still separate, the tension between chef and cook persists, fingers are sliced, wrists are burned, tempers fray, and bowls are licked.

Cooking is as much an art form, a commercial exchange, a social interaction and a symbol of class and nationhood now as ever it was in the previous two millennia. Our kitchen heritage is not just history; it represents traditions painstakingly acquired. Neither smug nor scornful, it lives in our present, showing us how much we have to applaud as well as to regain. It should be an essential and vibrant element of current culinary debate.

A Note on Measures

avoirdupois A system of weights based on the 16-ounce pound (or 7,000 grains). An Act of 1532 laid down that butchers should sell meat by *haver du pois* weight

bushel Johnson's *Dictionary*: 8 gallons, a 'strike' or any large quantity

firkin Generally a small wooden barrel or covered vessel which might be of several sizes, though it was sometimes defined as quarter of a barrel or 9 gallons (34 litres)

graine The smallest English unit of weight, originally a grain of corn or wheat

hogshead Johnson's *Dictionary*: In liquid, 63 gallons; any large barrel from its shape; from Dutch *ockshood*, 'measure'

peck The fourth part of a bushel; a dry measure of 8 quarts. In 1797 Frederick Eden quantified a half peck as 8 pounds 11 ounces

pipkin Johnson's *Dictionary*: A diminutive of Pipe (a large vessel) – a small earthen boiler. Elizabeth David defined a pipkin as a cooking pot usually thought of as small, though John Nott – in his *Cooks' and Confectioners' Dictionary* – specified the capacity as a gallon and a half

pottle A little pot or measure; a liquid measure equal to 2 quarts or half a gallon; a pot or vessel. Johnson's *Dictionary*: liquid measure containing 4 pints

quartern   A loaf usually about 4 pounds
scruple   A tiny measurement, equivalent to the apothecary's
                weight of 20 grains where an ounce was equal to
                480 grains and a pound was equal to 12 ounces

Sites and Houses

There are plenty of historic sites and houses open to the public and scattered the length and breadth of the British Isles, each offering intriguing glimpses into our kitchen past. Some exhibit the flash of a Roman mosaic, while others glory in their vast medieval halls. Whether preserved or reconstructed, there are kitchen courtyards; kitchens large or small, spartan or packed with the innovations of their day; ice houses; still houses or confectionaries; dairies; period dining-rooms; game larders and more. The following list, which includes all houses referred to in the text, represents only a taste of what is on offer, places where our past can almost be grasped by the hand . . .

PREHISTORIC
Culver Hole Cave, Llangennith, Gower
Danebury Iron Age Hill Fort, Stockbridge, Hampshire
Meare Lake, Glastonbury, Somerset
Museum of the Iron Age, Andover, Hampshire
Neolithic Village, Skara Brae, Bay of Skaill, Orkney

ROMAN
Binchester Roman Fort, Bishop Auckland, County Durham
Brading Roman Villa, Brading, Isle Of Wight
Chedworth Roman Villa, Yanworth, Nr Cheltenham, Gloucestershire
Fishbourne Roman Palace, Chichester, West Sussex
Housesteads Roman Fort (Hadrian's Wall) and Museum, Bardon Mill, Northumberland
Lockleys Roman Villa, Welwyn Garden City, Hertfordshire

The Roman Baths, Abbey Churchyard, Bath, Somerset
Segedunum Roman Fort, Baths and Museum, Wallsend, Newcastle
    upon Tyne
Verulamium Museum, St Albans, Hertfordshire

SAXON AND VIKING
Bede's World, Jarrow, Newcastle upon Tyne
Firsby Saxon Village Project, Saxby, Lincolnshire
Jorvic Viking Centre, York, North Yorkshire
Lindisfarne Priory, Holy Island, Berwick-upon-Tweed
Saxon Royal Palace, Yeavering, Northumberland

MEDIEVAL
Bodiam Castle, Bodiam, East Sussex
Durham Cathedral, Durham, County Durham
Glastonbury Abbey, Glastonbury, Somerset
The Medieval Hall, Cathedral Close, Salisbury, Wiltshire
Penshurst Place, Penshurst, Kent
Raby Castle, Darlington, County Durham
Stanton Harcourt Manor, Witney, Oxfordshire
Stirling Castle, Stirling
The Weald and Downland Museum, North Cray, Kent

TUDOR
Buckland Abbey, Yelverton, Devon
Canons Abbey, Northamptonshire
Compton Castle, Paignton, Devon
Durham Castle, Durham, County Durham
Eltham Place, London
Haddon Hall, Bakewell, Derbyshire
Hampton Court Palace, East Molesey, Surrey
Hardwick Hall, Chesterfield, Derbyshire
Ightham Mote, Sevenoaks, Kent
Ingatestone Hall, Ingatestone, Essex
Lacock Abbey, Nr Chippenham, Wiltshire
Longleat, Warminster, Wiltshire
The Vyne, Basingstoke, Hampshire

SEVENTEENTH CENTURY

Aston Hall, Birmingham, West Midlands
The Banqueting House, Whitehall, London
The Bishop's Palace at Abergwili, Camarthenshire
East Riddlestone Hall, Bingley, West Yorkshire
Ham House, Richmond-upon-Thames
Dyrham Park, Nr Bath, Gloucestershire
Muchalls Castle, Kinkardineshire, Grampian
Oakwell Hall, Batley, Huddersfield, Yorkshire
Oliver Cromwell's House, Ely, Cambridgeshire

EIGHTEENTH CENTURY

Calke Abbey, Derby, Derbyshire
Callendar House, Falkirk
Canons Ashby House, Daventry, Northamptonshire
Chatsworth, Bakewell, Derbyshire
The Georgian House, Charlotte Square, Edinburgh
Houghton Hall, Kings Lynn, Norfolk
Kedleston House, Derby, Derbyshire
Moseley Ice House, Birmingham, West Midlands
Osterley Park, Middlesex
Painshill Park, Cobham, Surrey
Paxton House, Berwick-upon-Tweed
Saltram House, Plymouth, Devon
Scotney Castle, Lamberhurst, Kent
Syon Park, Brentford, Middlesex
Tullynally Castle, Castlepollard
Uppark, Petersfield, West Sussex

REGENCY

Abbotsford House, Melrose
Brighton Royal Pavilion, Brighton, East Sussex
Jane Austen's House, Chawton, Alton, Hampshire
Normanby Hall, Scunthorpe, North Lincolnshire
Nynehead Court, Taunton, Somerset
Shugborough Park Farm House, Stafford, Staffordshire

VICTORIAN

Beaulieu Palace House, Brockenhurst, Hampshire
Carlyle's House, Chelsea, London
Cogges Manor Farm Museum, Witney, Oxfordshire
Cragside House, Morpeth, Northumberland
Erddig Hall, Wrexham
Glamis Castle, Angus
Glossop Heritage Centre, High Peak, Derbyshire
Harewood House, Leeds, West Yorkshire
The Judge's Lodging, Presteigne, Powys
Lanhydrock House, Cornwall
Penrhyn Castle, Gwynedd
Petworth House, Petworth, West Sussex
Saltram House, Plymouth, Devon
Wallington, Cambo, Northumberland
Wightwick Manor, Wolverhampton, West Midlands

EDWARDIAN

Castle Drogo, Drewsteignton, Devon
Duart Castle, Isle of Mull
Edwardian Kitchen at Milton Keynes Museum, Milton Keynes, Buckinghamshire
The Tenement House, Glasgow
Ulva Island Crofters Cottage, Ulva

OTHER

British Museum, London
Geffrye Museum of the Domestic Interior, London
London Canal Museum, Ice House, London
Museum of Domestic Design, Barnet, Hertfordshire
Museum of London, London
National Museum, Cardiff
National Museum of Ireland, Dublin
National Museum of Scotland, Edinburgh
Science Museum, London
Victoria and Albert Museum, London

Notes

7 **Dunaverney Flesh Hook** Along with the Battersea Cauldron, it is displayed in the Prehistory galleries of the British Museum in London.

8 **settlement** When settlement began to occur, the world's population altered radically, more than trebling at a growth rate that would remain unmatched until the Industrial Revolution.

10 **three and a half hours** See Wood 2001 and O'drisceoil 1993 for the results of a 1951 experiment in Ballybourney, County Cork.

11 **black butter** Seamus Heaney, 'Bogland', in *From Door into the Dark*, Faber & Faber, London, 1969.

11 **cheeses** According to Tacitus, who was writing of the Celts of Germany; Strabo's assessment that they made none was surely incorrect.

11 **fat-hen** *Chenopodium album*. Under the Tudors it would be known as Good King Henry.

12 **Songbirds, buzzards** Remains of all these have been found in the archaeological record though there is no absolute evidence that they were all actually cooked.

12 **kittiwake's bones** Cunliffe 1993, p. 86.

13 **thickly studded** Caesar 1951, Bk V, p.10.

13 **unbroken spirits** Tacitus 2003, p. 61.

17 **demoralising temptations** Tacitus 2003.

18 **screech owls** Plautus, *Plays*, trans. Paul Nixon, Heinemann, London, 1917, pp. 233–5.

18 **Asian spices** With the first-century Roman discovery of the monsoon winds, Arab control of the spice market was demolished. Rome could send ships direct rather than pursue the tortuous overland routes to Asia.

18 **Livy** *The Dawn of the Roman Empire*, trans. J. C. Yardley, Oxford University Press, Oxford, 2000, bks 31–40, p. 428.

18 **strange birds** Quoted in Barber 1973, p. 12.

18 Crispinus Juvenal, *Satires No 4 and 5*, trans. Peter Green, Penguin, London, 1998.

18 Shield of Minerva Suetonius, *Twelve Caesars*, trans. Robert Graves, Penguin, London, 1957, p. 277. Milt is fish sperm.

18 *Trimalchio's Feast* Petronius, *Satyricon*, 49 (the *Cena Trimalchionis*), trans. P. D. Walsh, Oxford University Press, Oxford, 1999.

19 graffito in Pompeii Quoted in Gowers 1993, p. 26.

19 a lettuce (each) Quoted in Grainger and Dalby, 1996, p. 100.

19 Martial Martial, *Epigrams*, trans. C. Ker, Heinemann, London, 1919, vol. I, bk V, no. 78. See also vol. II, bk XIV, no. 14 for references to guests preferring the mullet and boar to their host's company.

20 aromatic herbs Alcock 2001 believes that parsley was a common herb likely to have been grown here, despite its official introduction date of the sixth century. She also points out that our round-leafed mint is a native plant.

20 the vine Alcock 2001 tells us that there is evidence of vine trenches in Roman Britain, but that cultivation did not develop, in all likelihood hindered by the cold climate. Some villas also attempted vine cultivation, probably for home consumption.

20 dormice There is little evidence of dormice being bred for the kitchen in Britain, but it is not impossible, since this was such a particular delicacy, that the practice was pursued.

20 figs pre-chewed Columella, quoted in Giacosa 1992, chap. 7.

20 granary of the Empire Noted in David 1977, p. 9.

21 Vindolanda fragments The fullest account of the Vindolanda tablets is found in Bowman 1994. They date from a period just prior to the construction of Hadrian's Wall.

22 cookshops I have found Mary Walker Kelsey's essay on Roman baths in Walker 1991 very informative. Alcock 1996 is also particularly good on shops and markets in Roman towns.

22 breakfasts Known as *ientaculum*. The midday meal was known as *prandium*.

22 *promulsis* Also known as *gustatio*.

23 country villas Alcock 1996, Frere 1999 and Cunliffe 1971 are all important sources of information for the history of the Romano-British villa.

24 Orickwillow These and more can be seen at the British Museum.

24 napkins Tablecloths also appeared from the first century, according to Giacosa 1992, chap. 3.

24 glassmakers Alcock 2001, p. 130.

25 spoons Moore 2006.

25 *De re coquinaria* Known also as the *Artis magiricae libre X* or *Artis coquinariae liber*, this collection of recipes has caused endless speculation and academic argument, not least about its date of compilation, which process began some time during the first century and was continued by other hands.

25 pluck the flamingo Apicius, in Flower and Rosenbaum 1958, no. 6.1.

25 lack of quantities Elsewhere, a recipe for a sauce for chicken gives instructions to use exactly thirty-one peppercorns, but this is highly unusual. Kitchens did, however, rely on weights and measures, often in the shapes of gods' heads; they have been widely found in pound, ounce and scruple sizes.

26 bitter rue *Ruta graveolens*, a very strong herb recommended as an antidote to poisonous mushrooms or snakebites, or for indigestion or hangovers.

26 asafoetida By Apicius' time it had replaced the more ancient and powerful ingredient *silphium*, which came only from Cyrenaica or modern Libya. So eagerly was *silphium* desired that, as its supplies dwindled, it was for a while stored in the Roman Treasury before finally becoming extinct in the first century.

26 baked dormouse Apicius, in Flower and Rosenbaum 1958, no. 397.

26 mustard seeds Palladius also used honey in his recipe.

26 whatever good things Flower and Rosenbaum 1958, p. 101.

28 Sugar Dioscorides (first century AD) recommended sugar as a medicine for stomach, bowels, kidney and bladder in his *Materia medica*.

29 *Geoponica* Bk XX, chap. 46 is devoted to it. See Flower and Rosenbaum 1958, p. 22.

30 Pliny *Natural History*, 31.8.44, quoted in Flower and Rosenbaum 1958, p. 23.

30 cheap method Quoted in both Flower and Rosenbaum 1958 and Edwards 1984.

30 rank version Edwards 1984, pp. xxii–xxiii.

30 factory industry Grainger and Dalby 1996, p. 19.

31 Urbicius' factory Alcock 2001, p. 80.

35 *Beowulf* Alexander 1973, II. 147ff. (p. 55).

35 'The Groans of the Britons' Quoted in Frere 1999, p. 362.

36 birds flew in Bede 1969, chap. 13.

36 **Then in the beer hall:** *Beowulf: The Oldest English Epic*, trans. Charles W. Kennedy, Oxford University Press, Oxford, 1978, ll. 473ff.

36 **shared society** Alexander 1973, introduction.

37 **Taplow Barrow** In Berkshire, discovered in the 1880s.

37 **wild basil** Sempers 2004, p. 33.

37 **semi-permanent stock** For more detail on Anglo-Saxon foods, see Hagen 1992, Wilson 1973, and Wilson's essay on pottage in Wilson, *Liquid Nourishment*, 1993.

38 **Anglo-Saxon pottage.** Quoted by C. Anne Wilson in *Liquid Nourishment*, p. 10.

38 **quite refined** Ibid., p. 92.

38 **without my skill** Garmonsway 1978, p. 36.

38 **hlaford** Marjorie A. Brown in Carlin and Rosenthal 1988, pp. 1–13.

38 **floor-level hearth** The fourteenth-century chronicler Froissart attributed the strength and swiftness of the Scots army to their diet of 'underdone meat . . . cooked in the hides of the cattle it is taken from' and small cakes of oatmeal and water which they cooked 'rather like a wafer' on large, flat stones.

39 **Aelfric's vocabulary** Swanton 1975, p. 112.

40 **radish** Swanton 1975, p. 185.

40 *Sproutkele* Uglow 2004, p. 22.

40 **primitive peoples** See Wilson 2005, p. 61, and recorded as early as Homer's *Odyssey*. See also Hagen 1992, p. 70.

41 **Hywel Dda** See Bobby Freeman, *First Catch Your Peacock: A Book of Welsh Food*, Image Imprint, 1880, p. 31.

42 **walnuts** Uglow 2004, p. 22. Uglow notes that there are no documents for English monastic gardens in this period and that most evidence comes from the Continent, from monasteries like that at St Gall in Switzerland. Bede's World in Northumberland has a replica herb garden with raised beds.

42 **peach** Uglow 2004, p. 18.

42 **Ely** Wilson 1973, p. 328.

42 **Bede** Bede 1969, chap. 24.

42 **chicken spiced** Barber 1973, p. 40.

42 **fasting** Fast days were altered throughout this period, but, on balance, these were the days that were observed.

42 **before Michaelmas** Hagen 1992, p. 73.

43 **herring** With their ancient techniques of curing and salting oily fish, it was possibly the Vikings who bred in the Scottish their tradition of salting and smoking herrings to make kippers.

43 *craspois* A. J. Robertson, *Laws of the Kings of England from Edmund to Henry I* (1925), quoted in Wilson 1973, p. 28.

43 **Hunting** See Hagen 1992, pp. 177ff.

44 AD **1065** *The Anglo-Saxon Chronicle*, trans. G. N. Garmonsway, Dent, London, 1953. There is also an on-line version at http://britannia.com/history/docs/1066.html

47 **newe conceytes** I have found one of the most useful histories of this long period to be Dyer 1989. To explore medieval cooking in greater depth than I have space to do here, Henisch 1976 and Hammond 1993 are among the most comprehensive studies of the period.

49 *godisgoode* The Brewers Book, Norwich 1468–9, quoted in David 1997, p. 92.

49 **times of dearth** William Langland, *Piers Plowman*, Penguin, London, 1966, p. 90.

50 **300 pounds of grain** Tannahill 1998, p. 170.

50 **2 pounds of bread** Swabey 1999, p. 87. Alice's accounts show that they baked on average 230 white loaves and around 40 'black' at each baking. See, for example, the entry for Sunday, 2 October in *Alice's Household Book*, trans M. K. Dale, Paradigm, Bugnay, 1984.

50 **loosely regulated** See David 1977, p. 226.

50 **Assize of Bread** 51. Hen III.

50 **Alice de Bryene** Quantities are from Swabey's essay in Carlin and Rosenthal 1998, pp. 133–44.

51 **meagre store** Langland 1966, bk 5, 'Gluttony at the Ale House', p. 70.

51 **all I've got** Langland 1966, p. 89.

52 **an obsession** 'The Land of Cockaigne', quoted in Barber 1973, p. 61. See also 'The Vision of MacConglinne MacConglinne', in Mahon 1991.

52 **all hot** 'The Land of Cockaigne', quoted in Barber 1973, p. 61.

52 **poor country widow** Chaucer 1969, p. 232.

53 **Cabbage** This and the following examples are taken from the various *Tacuina sanitatis* edited in Arano 1976.

54 **Sauces** For an interesting discussion about the meaning of 'tempering' in medieval recipes and the importance of reducing everything to the smallest possible particles, see Scully's essay in Adamson 1995.

54 **as unnecessary to survival** Indeed Elizabeth David called medieval spices 'the jewels and furs and brocades of the kitchen and still room' (David 1970).

54 **three weeks' land labour** Tannahill's estimate in 1998, p. 167.

54 *cubebs* *Piper cubeba*, pepper berries from Indonesia; also called 'tail pepper'.

55 **mace, gromwell** Quoted in Barber 1973, p. 43. Gromwell is a *Lithospermum*, a herb from the borage family.

55 **thatcher might earn** Dyer 1989, p. 215.

55 **Far from treating** A regular suggestion found particularly clearly in the *Menagier de Paris* along with many other practical suggestions of a type rarely seen in British manuscripts of the period.

56 **thousands of pounds** We know that in 1288 the royal household used more than 6,000 pounds of variously flavoured sugars – violet and rose sugar being particularly prized. See Hammond 1993, pp. 10–11.

56 **feasts** See Warner 1791; also *The Chronicle of John Hardyng*, ed. Henry Ellis, London, 1812, p. 346: 'Came every daye for moost partie alwaye / Ten thousand folke, by his messis tould . . . / And in the kechin three hundred servitours . . .'

56 **earliest and most complete** There is in fact an earlier but much shorter Anglo-Norman work: Mss BL Royal 12 C.xii, containing some thirty recipes in French.

56 *The Forme of Cury* The full text is available on line at http://www.ibiblio.org/pub/docs/books/gutenberg/etext05/8cury 10.txt

58 **shivering mass** Jelly was particularly used for fish where warm spices were used to counteract their cold and humid properties. For more on medieval jellies, see Brears 1996. For a discussion of Martino's clarification with egg whites, see Santich's essay in Adamson 1995.

58 *sanders* The bark of the tree *Pterocarpus santalinus*.

58 **costly statement** The Countess of Leicester paid up to 14s a pound in 1265, when pepper cost only 2s 4d. See Wilson 1973, p. 283. Elizabeth I's mapmaker, John Norden, described the saffron fields in bloom as 'smiling'; see his *Speculum Britanniae*, London, 1683.

58 **Flowers** See Hieatt and Hosington 1998.

59 **efforts to be clean** All quoted in Henisch 1976, p. 91.

60 **population** Simon Schama, *History of Britain*, BBC Books, London, 2000, vol. I.

60 **streets were filled** From 'London Lyckpenny', a mid-fifteenth-century poem quoted in D. M. Low, ed., *London is London*, Chatto, London, 1949, pp. 29–32. 'Hot pies' from Langland 1966, B text, prologue, ll. 225–9.

60 **London's main thoroughfares** For more details, see Henisch 1976, Drummond and Wilbraham 1939, Dyer 1989 and Carlin and Rosenthal

1998; also, particularly, Henry Thomas Riley, ed., *Memorials of London 1276–1419*, London, 1868, p. 257.

61 filthy cookshop Chaucer 1969, General Prologue, ll. 379–87, and The Cook's Prologue.

61 flourishing establishment Fitzstephen was a clerk to Thomas à Becket. His survey of London was included in Stow's survey for Elizabeth in the 1590s and is the earliest British description of a cookshop. For details about the possessions of the urban poor found in wills, see Carlin and Rosenthal 1998.

62 charge of avarice Paris 1852, vol. 2, p. 340.

63 *Sir Gawain* An alliterative poem from the north-west Midlands, dated to around 1375. See Stone 1974.

63 Delicacies and dainties Stone 1974, 1.6, p. 25.

63 First course Walter of Bibbesworth 1990, ll. 1105ff., also quoted in Henisch and Butler 1985, pp. 2–3.

63 Ralph de Borne Bishop William Fleetwood, *Chronicon preciosum*, C. Harper, London, 1707, p. 83.

63 Archbishop Nevill Warner 1791, no. 5, p. 93.

65 curfews Paston Williams 1993, p. 45. Thurley 1993 also says that one Christmas feast at Eltham fed more than 2,000 people, and a visitor in 1466 described a banquet there as lasting three hours (p. 147).

65 King feasted From Hieatt and Butler 1985, Ms Cosin V.III.II, p. 39.

67 dish of peas 'This is the menu for the feast for the king at home' (Hieatt and Butler 1985, pp. 39ff.).

67 *comfits* The ancient origin of sugared almonds, which in France are still a traditional present for the guests at weddings and are not unlike the colourful sugared caraways served in Indian restaurants at the end of a meal. Wafering irons were taken to America by the Pilgrims in the early seventeenth century only to return five hundred years later in the form of American waffle-makers.

68 *nebula* According to Henisch 1976, p. 77.

68 compotes Mastercooks 1780, no. 100.

68 Ginger was preserved John Russell's recommendations to the Panter, or Butler, in the *Boke of Nurture*. Russell also notes that if anyone did suffer from extreme indigestion, they might eat a raw apple to cure their *fumosite* (wind).

68 Eleanor of Castile Quoted in Hieatt and Butler 1985, p. 12.

68 gingering up the guests David 1970 notes that the term *racy* may have come from the race, or root, of ginger and that all such ingredients 'added spice to your life'.

68 Bishop Grosseteste From Oschinsky 1971, Grosseteste's rules for the recently widowed Countess of Lincoln, rule 14.

69 Dogges grow leane Breton 1879.

69 port of Beccles Quoted in 'King Herring', in Walker 1995.

69 thou wyll not beleve W. Nelson, ed., *A Fifteenth Century Schoolbook*, Clarendon Press, Oxford, 1956, no. 30, p. 8, quoted in Henisch 1976.

69 Henry V's Queen Quoted in Austin 1888, 'banquets and bills of fare'. The feast took place on 24 February 1420.

70 Fish rissoles Lenten *ryshewys*; see Austin 1888, p. 43.

71 a day of much delightfulnesse Breton 1879.

71 Christmas is ended Hartley 1931, January.

72 *Boke of Nurture* Written in about 1460 from sources considered to be at least a century old. The most elaborate of all the manners books of the time, a complete manual for valet, butler, footman, carver, taster, usher and marshal, it was edited by F. J. Furnivall in 1868.

73 ate together in hall Oschinsky 1971, Household rules, 17th rule.

73 parlours From the French *parler*, 'to talk', originally the small rooms reserved in monasteries in which visitors were allowed to converse.

73 Woe is in the hall Langland 1935, p. 115.

73 Breakfast came after chapel Boorde 1870, p. 286; The Percys' breakfast is noted in Percy 1962.

74 *cowche* Henisch 1976 also suggests that starch was used and that warm stones might have been employed for 'ironing' the cloths flat. She says that the white cloth 'was the stage on which the drama of the meal was carried out' (p. 155).

74 Forks It is often suggested that Richard II introduced forks to England, but many disagree. The small forks in Gaveston's court inventory were more likely for sticky syrup preserves than for individual use. In 1463 the Will of John Baret of Bury St Edmunds bequeathed a single silver fork; Henry VII left a knife-and-fork set made of crystal, chalcedony and gold.

74 poorly fed lower servants Sneyd 1847, p. 25.

75 particularly courteous Froissart 1968, p. 402.

75 instruction manuals Erasmus, *De civilitate morum puerilium* (On Good Manners in Boys), 1530. See Sowards 1985, vol. 25.

76 to transgress Discussed by Goody 1982, p. 140.

76 no respect Froissart 1968, p. 414.

76 **Prioress** Chaucer 1969, ll. 128ff., p. 8.

76 **rules** All from Russell's *Boke of Nurture*, ll. 276ff.; see Russell 1868. Such rules were commonly listed; see also *The Boke of Curtasye*, R. Weste's *Boke of Demeanor* or Seager's *Schoole of Vertue*.

76 **Wynken de Woorde** This was the *Boke of Kervynge* (1508).

77 **Andrea Trevisano** Rye 1865, Embassy of Andrea Trevisano to Henry VII in 1497 (xliv).

77 **Costly wines** From Russell 1868, p. 9.

78 *clarrey* Wilson 2007, p.157.

78 **In 1412** See Swabey 1999. Alice's account books include a daybook kept in the Public Record Office (Chancery Misc Mss 4/8b) covering her expenses over that same year.

78 **waste** See Swabey 1999 for her estimate that the Bryene household was provided with about a pound of meat per day per head. The hiring of tableware is according to Dyer 1989, p. 90.

79 **monetary economy** For detailed discussions of the changes in the social order in the mid- to late fifteenth century, see Dyer 1989.

81 **taken for granted** There is a very rare recipe for pastry enriched with eggs and butter in the French *Viandier* and in a handful of European culinary manuscripts, but none of them are British. For a fuller discussion of late medieval and Tudor pies, see Santich's essay in Adamson 1995.

81 **short paest** From *A Propre New Booke of Cokery* (1545), found at http://www.godecookery.com/trscript.

81 **Leopold William's kitchen** The painting is by David Tenniers the Younger and is in The Hague.

82 **Frans Franken** The picture is *Lazarus and the Rich Man's Table*, c. 1605, The Bread Museum, Ulm.

82 **Bartolomeo Scappi** His guide, *Opera del'arte del cucinare*, 1570.

82 **short paste** This recipe is from *Platt Delightes for Ladies*, 1602, a24. There is also a recipe in Anon. 1588, p. 272.

83 **sweet potatoes** Markham 1631 (a compendium of his several titles), pp. 104ff.

83 **A W** 1594, p. 17.

88 **'dining parlour'** It has been argued that during the Middle Ages the communal dinner in hall held connotations of the Last Supper and the Mass while in Tudor times it returned to the atmosphere of the convivium, focus of civility and conversation. See Strong 2002.

88 **Paul Hentzner** Hentzner and Naunton 1797; the quoted passage is from

the 'Description of the Queen at Greenwich'. Hentzner also wrote, '[T]he Queen dines and sups alone with very few attendants and it is very seldom that anybody, foreigner or native, is admitted at that time, and then only at the intercession of somebody in power.' His text is also available online at http://etext.library.adelaide.edu.au/h/hentzner-travels/chapter1.html. See Weir 1998, p. 462 for information about Essex's rebellion in 1600.

89 *Dyetary of Helthe* Boorde 1870, chap. 4.

89 **meaty dishes** In 1532, en route to Calais, the King and his household ate 6 oxen, 40 sheep, 8 calves, 12 pigs, 132 capon, 20 storks, 34 pheasants, nearly 200 partridges (and the same each of cocks, plovers and teals), more than 700 larks and 24 peacocks. See Weir 2001, p. 62.

89 *acater* The 1522 household accounts of the Cliffords of Bolton Abbey are, characteristically for their time, arranged under the headings 'Pantry', 'Buttery', 'Ewery', 'Kitchen', 'Catery' and 'Strangers'. The exact number of messes served at breakfast, dinner and supper and the food supplied are all minutely detailed just as they had been in Alice de Bryene's household a century earlier. See the Bolton Abbey Mss, Chatsworth, 1522 & 1523.

89 **Cardinal Wolsey's Eltham Ordinances** Henry 8, 1526, cap. 43ff.

90 **in full blast** Quoted in Thurley 1993, p. 159.

90 **Dr John Caius** *Of Englishe Dogges. The Diversities and the Properties* (1576), trans. A. Fleming as *Caius' Dogs*, Theatrum Orbis, Amsterdam, 1880 p. 35.

90 **Scappi's kitchen** *Opera del'arte del cucinare.*

92 **attitudes to fish** In 1548 Saturday as a fish day was reintroduced by law, and in 1563 Wednesday joined it in an attempt to protect the British fishing fleets. After about 1585 these rules were abandoned. The Elizabethan Chronicler Holinshead wrote that the orders were made 'only to the end our numbers of cattle may be better increased and that abundance of fish which the sea yieldeth more generally received . . . for the preservation of the navy and maintenance of convenient numbers of seafaring men'.

92 **knockynge at paradyse gates** Boorde 1870, p. 82.

93 **serve him truly** *King Lear*, Act I, Sc. 4. In the poet Thomas Nash's *Lenten Stuff* (1599), the stalwart of the Yarmouth fishing industry, the kipper, is described as stinking and sweaty – welcome only in the Pope's court. Englishmen, Nash says, consider them but 'dogges turd'.

93 **we have as yet** Gerard 1597, p. 74.

93 **'great birds'** Songbirds were no longer baked into pies, on the whole, and only one cookery book, John Murrell's *New Booke of Cookerie* (1617), mentions owl in its bills of fare. The turkey taking over from medieval great birds is also noted by Wilson 1973, p. 129.

93 **Sir William Petre** The archive papers of Sir William Petre are found in Emmison 1970. The price of turkey at market in 1550 is from Paston Williams 1993, p. 95.

93 **'Virginia potatoes'** Originally, and confusingly, called the Virginia potato after the early colonial settlements where it was cultivated, but in fact from South America, the sweet potato had already arrived in England at the hands of John Hawkins in the early 1560s and via Francis Drake returning from his circumnavigation. Further details remain unclear. It may have arrived in England in the first instance via Ireland, where Sir Walter Raleigh certainly introduced it to his estates.

93 **oyle, vinegar and pepper** Gerard 1597, pp. 780–81 differentiates sweet potatoes, *Sisarum Peruvavanium*, from white potatoes, *Battata Virginiana*. Gerard also notes that sweet potatoes, as well as being candied and made into conserves, were generally 'eaten sopped in wine'. More information on plant introductions at this time can be found in Thacker 1994. Paston Williams 1993, p. 97 also notes that the Tudor pumpkin pie was taken to the new colonies. There is a recipe in Dawson 1596 for a sweet-potato pie.

94 **devoid of nourishment** Gerard 1597, p. 275, chap. 55, bk 2, *Poma Amoris*/Apples of Love.

94 *botargo* Anchovies first appear in print in Shakespeare's *Henry IV*, Pt 1, Act 2 (1596). They form part of a supper at an inn – with glasses of sack, they cost 2s 6d. While the English imported anchovies, they were exporting great heaps of salted smoked pilchards, pressed into wooden barrels and sent to Spain and Italy, where they were eaten with slices of orange. The Cornish pilchard industry, started in 1555, packed its last barrel in October 2005 (Oliver Duff, 'The End of the Cornish Pilchard Trade', *Independent*, 25 October 2005, p. 3).

94 **Thomas Muffett** Muffett 1655, p. 215.

95 *knops* Kent 1653, p. 35.

96 **Thomas Dawson** Dawson 1596, p. 10. Under Elizabeth, education boomed with over 130 endowed grammar schools founded. With Humanists like Francis Bacon, Thomas More and John Colet pressing for greater educational opportunities, literacy rates soared (see Pritchard 1999, pp. 200ff. for more on this).

96 **Anne Boleyn's coronation** From E. David, 'I'll Be With You in the Squeezing of a Lemon', *Wine and Food* (February/March 1969).

96 **ravishing bedfellows** Orange strainer according to Weir 2001, p. 72; Elyot 1539. Hieatt 1988, p. 12 notes A W's reliance on citrus as 'an indulgence rare before the Renaissance'.

97 **sign of wealth** Thomas Wyatt, also in love with Anne Boleyn, immortalised her in his sonnet 'Whoso list to hunt, I know where is an hynde'; Hentzer 1797; Boorde 1542.

97 **hart's flesh** Weir 2001, p. 276, taken from letters in the Vatican archives.

97 **Frenchmen cooking** William Harrison, 'Description of England', in Harrison 1877, bk III, chap. I.

97 **compound, artificial** Burton 1932, pp. 225ff.

97 **perfumed farce** Murrell 1617, p. 71.

98 **hooks and pricks** Markham 1615, pp. 100ff.

98 **dripping pans** The carbonado 'boats' from Platt 1948, a26; also for the capon and mallard recipes. Similar recipes in Murrell 1617. Mallard with cabbage from Dawson 1596, p. 10. 'To Farce a Legge of Lambe on the French fashion' also Murrell 1617, p. 71.

98 **pottage was not so much used** Boorde 1542, chap. 12.

98 **no art of cookery** Moryson 1617, vol. 4, chap. 4, 'Of Scotland', pp. 181ff.

98 **devouring his very guests** Moryson 1617, pp. 199–200.

99 **William Petre's Ingatestone household** William Petre's accounts, in Emmison 1970.

99 **40-shillings-a-year** His cook was paid the same as his gardener, both of them earning twice the salary of the part-time brewer.

99 **must all die for the great feast** Tusser 1557. Breton 1879, December, p. 11. Shred pies and blazing fire from Harrison 1577.

99 **Twelfth Night cake** A European tradition perpetuated in France with the *galette des rois*, a cake served at Epiphany, when the finder of the charm wears a paper crown for the remainder of the meal. On Friday, 6 January 1659 even Pepys bought one such 'brave cake'.

100 **large** The Howard Household Rolls, 1462–71, in Norfolk 1841. Harrison 1577 quoted in Pritchard 1999 in his discussion on inns.

100 **the world affords not** Moryson 1617, vol. 4, pp. 176ff.

100 **the general drink** Hentzner 1797, p. 62.

100 **survival and starvation** See Sim 1997, chap. 4 for a full exposition of Tudor ale and beer. Wine imports from Holinshed's *Chronicle*, on-line version, vol. 1, p. 167, col. 2.

100 **Elizabeth's England** Descriptions of dress from Stubbes 1583; other descriptions of the English from Frederick Duke of Wurtemburg (1592) in Rye 1865.

102 **'God help the wicked'** *Henry IV* (pt 1), Act 2, Sc. 4.

102 **about a shilling a pound** Muffett (1655, pp. 245ff.) wrote that the best sugar came in little loaves from Madeira and that Barbary and Canary sugar was next in quality – '. . . [it] were infinite to rehearse the necessary use of it in making of good gellies, cullises, mortises, white broths, and restorative pies and mixtures . . . Sugar never marred Sawce.'

103 **sugar balls** Platt 1948, opening epistle.

103 **a defect** As bloated, gouty Henry was the manifest embodiment of the lavish eating of his court, Elizabeth's teeth spoke volumes about hers. They are often discussed in the context of the Tudor love of sugar. However, Drummond and Wilbraham 1939 argue that it is in fact just as likely that a courtly lack of green, leafy vegetables and raw citrus fruits would have resulted in a scurvy-like lack of vitamin C, which would have made the gums bleed and teeth decay. Paul Hentzner certainly saw rotten teeth as an affliction of the rich. This quote is from his writings (Hentzner 1797, p. 34).

103 **translated from the Italian** *The Secrets of Alexis of Piedmont*, translated into English in 1558.

105 **hard, solid, light** Platt 1948, a54.

105 **musk** Platt 1948 suggests this in the list for handling sugar right at the start of his book. The description of musk is taken from David 1977.

105 **marchpane** Partridge 1584, Cap. 9 also gives a recipe using stale manchet, ginger, cinnamon, liquorice, aniseed, sugar and claret boiled to a stiff paste that could be moulded and dried. Closer to toffee than to modern gingerbread, this would evolve in the north of England into *parkin*, using oatcakes rather than breadcrumbs. Petre's cook information from Ayrton 1974, p. 24. Petre's is the oldest surviving account book documenting an Elizabethan progress.

105 **gum tragacanth** From the tree *Australagus gummifer*, still used by modern confectioners according to Davidson 1999. Partridge (1584) mixed it with lemon juice and egg whites, as did Dawson (1596), (who stipulated the bean-size piece to be used), while Platt (1948) used only egg whites.

105 **tapping the moulds** Platt 1948, a13.

106 **sixty varieties** Parkinson 1629.

106 **oranges** Cultivated for the first time in Britain by Sir Frances Carew at

Beddington in Surrey and by Lord Cecil at Burghley. Uglow, *Little History*. See also Thacker 1994, p. 78.

106 **soaked and boiled** Partridge 1595, 'How to dresse Orenges'; also Partridge 1584, Cap. 19.

106 **Venerie** Gerard 1597, pp. 60–62 on ginger.

107 **digestive comfort** Boorde 1870; Gerard 1597, p. 1458 on apples, pp. 1448ff. on apricots.

107 **'putrifie'** Elyot 1539, p. 21; Gerard 1597, p. 1458 on apples.

107 **place corrupted** Elyot 1539, p. 86.

107 **Lady Gardiner** Quoted in Platt 1948, p. xlviii.

107 **infinite patience** Candying flowers from Platt 1948, a.9.53.

107 **twisted sticks** Fifty years later, Rebecca Price would still be making sugar fancies to delight guests and children – miniature marzipans in the shapes of bacon and eggs, candied flowers and quinces – skills handed down from her grandmother's generation. See Fettiplace 1986, p. 107.

108 **in good temper** Platt 1948, a.54.

108 **done boiling** Platt 1948, a.35.

108 **rejoices the heart** Boorde 1870, chap. 13.

108 **never so dear** Holinshed's *Chronicles* (white meats), on-line version, bk III, chap. I

108 **the English Disease** Drummond and Wilbraham 1939, p. 151.

109 **'white leach'** Dawson 1596, pt II, p. 19. Eleanor Fettiplace's White Leach is discussed in Wilson 1987.

109 **Cream was thickened** Muffett 1655, p. 128.

109 **trifle** An essay on trifle by Helen Saberi, in Davidson and Saberi 2002, traces its evolution from here through the seventeenth and eighteenth centuries.

109 **paps** Breasts.

109 **'dish of snow'** *Proper Newe Booke of Cookerye* (c. 1545) – a vary rare book indeed – which is available on line at http://www.godecookery .com/trscript/trscript.html

109 **shape of castles** Venetian Calendar of State Papers, 7 July 1517, quoted in Brears 1996.

110 **French bisket** Platt 1948, a.19. To beat two hours from Dawson 1596, p. 13.

110 **Sarah Longe** Her receipt book is found in Caton 1999.

110 **do not burne** Dawson 1596, p. 12.

110 **intimate rooms** Smythson also added a great prospecting room to the roof of Hardwick Hall for Bess of Hardwick – the most powerful woman in England after the Queen.

111 **bowls** See Murrell 1621, following No. 74, 'A Bill of Service for a Banquet'.

111 **tissue of lines** Venice protected its lucrative glass-blowing industry by forbidding its artisans to work abroad, on pain of death. Realising the profit to be made from an appreciative British market, and taking his life into his hands, the first Venetian did establish a glass studio in London in 1572.

111 **broke 'the platters** Platt 1948, a.13. He also says that to make the paste really smooth and shiny like pottery, use a shiny rolling pin and smooth paper under the paste. Dawson 1596, pt 2, pp. 39–40.

111 **Elvetham** Related by John Lyly in his *Euphues: The Anatomy of Wit*, J. Boler, London, 1631.

112 **made his fire** All quotations in this paragraph are from Holinshed, on-line version, 'On The Manner Of Building And Furniture Of Our Houses', 1577, bk II, chap. 10.

113 **Merrie Wives** According to Brears 1984, female housekeepers were first noted in Shakespeare's *Merry Wives of Windsor* (1598).

113 **domestic factories** Noted by G. E. and K. R. Fussell in their edition of Platt's *Delightes for Ladies*, Crosby Lockwood and Son Ltd, London, 1948, p. xlii.

113 **kitchen table** For a long inventory of Elizabethan kitchen equipment, see Newbery 1563.

115 **voluminous herbals** Stuart housewives could also turn to Parkinson's *Paradisi in sole*, from which the gardening advice here is taken, as well as the list of culinary herbs that follows (pp. 461ff.).

115 **cornucopia** For more on this, see Fitzgibbon 1965, p. 146.

115 **tainted meat** *Delightes for Ladies*, quoted in Drummond and Wilbraham 1939, p. 36.

116 **Charmingly** Tusser 1557, 'May'.

116 **sallat** All of these salad suggestions are from Markham 1615. Dawson's flower salad from 1596, p. 26.

116 **melancholy** Burton 2001, discussion of properties of food beginning on p. 216.

116 **deintie dishes** Holinshed's *Chronicle*, on-line version.

117 **Chopped spinach** Tusser 1557.

117 **chine** A new word for a joint, particularly of beef or veal, including a part of the backbone, from *echiner*, 'to break the back of'.

117 **'Fricasees and quelquechoses'** Markham 1615, p. 69.

118 *olla podrida* The rather impractical *olla podrida* was characteristically adored by Sancho Panza, the puzzled gastronomical sidekick of Don

Quixote in Cervantes' work – one of the earliest of all European novels, published in 1605.

118 prunes, raisins Markham 1631, p. 81. The instructions on how to prepare roasts and season meats that follow are from the same source.

118 what eye Physiologus Philotheos 1688, p. 21.

119 marshal her sallets Markham 1615, p. 137.

119 Harrison Holinshed's *Chronicles, 1577*, on-line version, bk III, chap. I.

119 London bachelor Quoted in Fisher 1983, p. 61. Ben Jonson inviting a friend to dinner found in H.J.C. Grierson and G. Bullough, eds, *The Oxford Book of Seventeenth Century Verse*, Clarendon Press, Oxford, 1934, pp. 155–6.

120 Face creams Along with hair-dye recipes from Platt 1948. All other remedies here taken from Markham 1615, chap. 1, 'Of Physic'.

120 Ouch These practices, and the fact that the still and the alembic had long been associated with alchemy, conspired to ensure that witch persecution came to a head under James I, a fact noted by Hunter in her study of cookbooks in this period in Wilson 1991, p. 49.

120 neither 'swete Markham 1615, chap. 6 for a full discourse on all dairy products, including what time to milk the cows.

120 Holland, Italy and France Muffett 1655, p. 133.

120 The Scots Alexander Fenton, *Scottish Country Life*, Donald, Edinburgh, 1976.

121 lokkyd the dore Furnivall's 1868 editorial to Russell's *Boke of Nurture*.

121 cost of a chicken Reaching a peak of around 10d each in 1603.

121 ripe apple Elizabeth's death from J. Bruce, ed., *Diary of John Manningham of the Inner Temple 1602*, London, 1868, quoted in Weir 1998, p. 483.

122 BLESSED BE HE Misson 1719, p. 313.

123 earliest written record Wilson 1973, p. 316, notes this as the first English recipe for a pudding; the fact is generally accepted. It is also found in Murrell 1617, p. 57.

123 pudding before meat Yorkshire idiom noted in Brears 1984, p. 85. *Cranford*, ed. Elizabeth Porges Watson, Oxford University Press, Oxford, 1998, p. 33.

123 amber puddings See, for example, *Compleat Cook Expertly Prescribing the Most ready Wayes whether Italian, Spanish or French*, Nath. Brooke, London, 1662, p. 99.

123 boiled-rice pudding Murrell 1617, p. 59; Markham 1631, p. 76.

124 Pudding is so natural Ellis 1750, p. 51.

124 **boiled beef** Ellis 1750, p. 51.

124 **flummery** Wilson 1973, p. 213 notes that flummery was originally an almost solid dish made of oatmeal steeped in water and sometimes known as 'wash brew' in the West Country.

125 **new incarnation** Woolley 1670, p. 169.

125 **Countess of Kent** Kent 1653, p. 13.

125 **Lancashire pudding** Wilson 1973, p. 218.

126 **Yorkshire** Glasse 1747, p. 131 for the recipe for Yorkshire pudding, and p. 133 for the detailed description on how to boil a pudding and tie the cloth.

126 **very good dish** De Saussure 1995, p. 137.

130 **Sugar hath obtained** Parkinson, *Theatrum botanicum*, T. Coates, London, 1640, p. 1211. Estimate of sugar consumption from Hess 1995, p. 11.

130 **Physicall** In other words, medicinal. Parkinson, *Theatrum botanicum*, p. 1211.

130 **pigs of Westphalia** Westphalia hams were imported from Prussia during the seventeenth and eighteenth centuries. The pigs were fed on a diet of acorns and smoked over fine woods. The hams, like Bologna sausages (later called 'polonies', later still 'salamis', from the Italian for 'salt'), were sought-after luxuries.

130 **no part of the world** Moryson 1908, vol. 4, pt 3, chap. 3, 'England', pp. 142ff.

130 **Great Bee Hive** Anon., *Hell Upon Earth*, 1729, p. 1.

130 **Donald Lupton** Lupton 1632, 'Of London', p. 1.

131 **Leadenhall** Defoe 1927, vol. 1 discusses the state of Covent Garden about a century later, by which time it dominated all other markets of its kind.

131 **Mushrooms** In his treatise on salads, *Acetaria* (1699), Evelyn urges caution and skill in the selection of mushrooms; he boiled them for anything between fifteen minutes and an hour or grilled them to eat with fresh butter, pepper and salt. By then, he had decided that truffles were 'rank and provocative excrescences', but in this he was out of step with the majority of his gastronomical contemporaries. Evelyn 1996, pp. 42–3.

132 **Nicolas de Bonnefons** *The French Gardiner, Instructing How to Cultivate All Sorts of Fruit Trees*. By the time Evelyn translated and printed it in 1669, Bonnefons' book had run to six editions in France.

132 **William Coles** Coles 1656, p. 48.

133 **Art of Cookery** Moryson 1908, vol. 4, pt 3, chap. 3, 'England', pp. 142ff.

133 **Nicholas Breton** *Court and Country*, quoted in Hazlitt 1886, p. 28.

133 **dark-blue ribbon** For more on French and Italian professional cooks, see Braithwaite, *Rules and Orders for the Government of a Household of an Earl*, quoted in Hazlitt 1886, p. 39.

133 **Murrell's kickshaws** Murrell 1617, p. 67.

134 **Sarah Longe** Longe *c.* 1610, recipe 40; this manuscript is transcribed in Caton 1999.

134 **Forks** Coryat's *Crudities Hastily Gobbled up in Five Months Travels in France, Savoy, Italy etc*, first published in London in 1611, now unavailable; see W. Cater's 1776 edition. Ben Jonson initially mocked the use of forks in *Volpone* (1606), Act IV, Sc. I; this quotation is from *The Devil Is an Ass* (1616), Act V, Sc. IV.

134 **Merchant Taylors' Hall** *Frasers Magazine*, 44 (December 1851), p. 591. The essay on gastronomy and civilisation is by Mary Ellen Meredith, though some have suggested it was in fact written by her father, Thomas Love Peacock.

135 **globe-artichoke bottoms** Recipe from Kent 1653, p. 90. Potatoe pie recipe from Woolley 1664, p. 87. John Thacker, Dean of Durham Cathedral in the next century, filled the holes in his pastry lids with sweetmeats. See also Price 1974, p. 147.

135 **biscuits** In the north of England a tradition now developed of distributing sponge-finger, Naples or seed biscuits at funerals, wrapped in black-edged crêpe paper or fixed into papers with a black wax seal. For more on this see Brears's essay in *Petits Propos culinaires* 18, Prospect Books, Totnes, 1984.

135 **extreamely for an howre** Price 1974, p. 199.

136 **small yeasted cakes** Kent 1653, p. 37. The Shrewsbury cakes from Woolley 1670, p. 55. The regional varieties of spice cakes are all listed in Brears 1984, pp. 69ff.

136 **Lord Ruthven** Ruthven 1639, p. 3.

136 **thine in the bottome** Price 1974, p. 68.

137 **Other cooks** Digby 1669, p. 129.

141 **Puritan spoon** As detailed in Moore 2006.

142 **more than double** Thompson 1937, pp. 126–45. Food prices did rise after the Restoration; this would partly account for the increase in the Bedfords' bills at that time, but the increase was mostly due to an expansion in entertainment and a general increase in provisions ordered.

142 **pride, puritans, coaches** Lupton 1632, p. 101.

142 **sheep's head** Drummond and Wilbraham 1939, p. 100.

142 **and for her part** All quotes in the remainder of this paragraph are from Anon. 1664, p. 31.

143 **shoulder of mutton** Anon. 1664, p.117; for fricassée, see p. 81.

145 **obsession with news** Moritz, in Mavor 1768, p. 50.

145 **helpeth Digestion** Francis Bacon, *Natural History* (1627), quoted in Ellis 2004, p. 22.

146 **Puddle-water** *The Women's Petition* 1674.

146 **drowsiness** Caffeine was not identified until 1819 – and then only due to the scientific patronage of the poet Goethe – and it was not named until 1821, by French scientists.

146 **vested interest** Thomas Babington Macaulay argued in his *History of England* (Longman, London, 1858–62), that the coffee house was 'a most important political institution . . . the chief organ through which the pubic opinion of the metropolis vented itself' (vol. 1, pp. 366–70). The virtues of coffee were particularly vaunted in a pamphlet, 'The Properties of Chocolate, the Properties of Covee', printed in Oxford by Henry Hall in 1660, and in 'The Vertue of the Coffee Drink', published in London in 1670. For an in-depth history of the British coffee house, see Ellis 2004. By the way, the first coffee house to admit women was the Golden Lion in London, in 1717. There was also a room set aside for ladies to drink coffee in the Assembly Rooms in Bath, but letter-writing and conversation were the dominant activities.

146 **3s a pound** Thompson, 1937, p. 165.

146 **Triumvirate of new hot drinks** There was a fourth, drunk cold, but it was never as popular: salop. Salop was made from the root of a Turkish orchid mixed with water and sugar, and was supposed to have aphrodisiac qualities.

147 **Chocolate was more expensive** Both of these recipes are from Colminero 1652. The very earliest use of edible cocoa occurred in the form of medicinal comfits laced with cinnamon, citron and ambergris, known as Queen's Chocolates and sold by Richard Mortimer at a shop in East Smithfield in the 1660s.

148 **50s a pound** Price of tea from essay on breakfast by Eileen White in Wilson 1995 and from Hartley 1954.

148 **adulterated good leaves** Noted by Toussaint-Samat 1992, p. 598.

148 **Chinese recipe** Digby 1669, p. 155.

148 **Chiefly for novelty** Physiologus Philotheos [pseud. Thomas Tryon] 1685, p. 182.

149 **tea-table talk** Congreve, *The Way of the World*, 1700, Act 4.

153 clerk to the Navy Board Pepys 1983, vol. 1, p. 39, 3 February 1660.

153 thousands of rumps Beer 1955, 11 May 1660, vol. 3, p. 242.

153 those Golden Days May 1994.

154 'shampaigne' Thompson 1937, pp. 183ff.

155 do me hurt Pepys 1983, vol. 9, pp. 475ff., 9 March 1669.

155 a small green orange Pepys 1983, vol. 7, pp. 181–2, 25 June 1666.

156 pineapple Sir Matthew Decker's Dutch gardener Henry was the first to cultivate pineapples properly in England. His first did not appear until 1714, the same year as the first proper thermometer was invented – itself set to have an impact on Britain's kitchens. Evelyn's comments from his diary (Beer 1955, 14 August 1668, vol. 3, p. 513).

156 fruit is brought Misson 1719, p. 313.

156 salon or saloon Quoted in Hamlyn 1988, p. 23.

157 Digby's dining room From an inventory taken at his death: British Library ADD Ms 38, 175, fols 48r–50v.

157 professional folder See Rose 1682, especially the instructions for the butler or sommelier, p. 88.

158 landscape A term for table-setting famously used in Strong 2002. They become even more formalised in the eighteenth century.

159 'fifty angled custards' Jonson, *Staple of News*, Act 4, Sc. 2.

160 next hundred years White 2004, Day's essay on illustration in cookery books from Murrell to Jarrin.

160 a 'French House' Pepys 1983, vol. 2, p. 98, 12 May 1661.

161 two poached eggs Digby 1669, p. 134.

161 well-equipped kitchen The inventory is in British Library, ADD Ms 38, 175, fols 48–50. For easier reference, it is also printed as App. III in Digby 1997.

163 quantite of gravie Beer 1955, 12 April 1682, vol. 4, p. 278.

163 common meats Misson 1719, p. 314.

164 perfect courtier Pepys 1983, vol. 1, p. 269, 20 October 1660.

165 *fleur frite* It has become accepted wisdom that La Varenne introduced the flour-and-fat thickener later called a 'roux' – though the German Sabina Welserin's cookbook of 1553 (*Das Kochbuch deer Sabina Welserin*), a handwritten manuscript (ed. Hugo Stopp, Winter, Heidelberg, 1980) in fact describes the process more than a century earlier.

166 three pieces of Mutton May 1994, p. 8.

167 tortoises Massialot 1702, p. 254.

167 if it is well baked Lamb quoted in Aylett and Ordish 1965, p. 107.

167 Passe par tout Driver 1997, no. 53, p. 59.

168 **butter, three pound** May 1994, p. 4.

168 **old-fashioned sweet sauce** Conversely, the only recipe to appear in his pages is one for an old-fashioned and rather dull sauce of parsley, toast and vinegar, apparently the invention of the Duke of York – the future James II (which perhaps explains its inclusion, for Pepys was nothing if not a snob).

168 **it pleased me much** Pepys 1983, vol. 2, p. 207, 3 November 1661.

168 **dinner** The ingredients are from Pepys 1983, vol. 4, pp. 13–14, 13 January 1663; pp. 95–6, 4 April 1663.

169 **Calve's head** Blencowe 1925, p. 19.

170 **gentlewomen forced** Woolley 1670, p. 378.

170 **great negligence of parents** Hannah Woolley, *The Gentlewoman's Companion*, quoted in Parkiss 2006, p. 350.

170 **strangers to bisks** Sorbetière [pseud.], *A Journey to London in 1698*, quoted in Paston Williams 1993, p. 163.

170 **I must crave your pardon** Woolley 1673, p. 121.

171 **burnt-butter sauce** All from Price 1974 (fricassées pp. 92–5).

171 *delma* Noted in Barber 1973 p. 142.

171 **French and English styles** See recipes in Evelyn's manuscript collection, Eveyln 1997.

171 **'fricasie'** Woolley 1670, p. 226.

173 **disordered arrangement** It has been suggested that the confused arrangement of recipes in these early books – stretching right back to the earliest in the sixteenth century – resulted from the way in which food was served, as several courses containing both sweet and savoury dishes.

173 **fine, solid cook** All in this paragraph from Woolley 1670.

173 **milk the cow** Ivan Day has shown that this only results in a lump of separated curds; see 'Musings on Syllabub', in Brears 1996.

173 **lemon** Lemons were still adored, but they were expensive, a single fruit costing about the same as a basket of apples – from 2.5 to 7d each, according to Brears 1984.

173 **froth into glasses** Blencowe 1925, p. 28, lemon *sillibub*.

174 **'cabbage cream'** All taken from Woolley 1670.

174 **being Nasty** Woolley 1670, p. 43.

174 **sweat more** Woolley 1673, p. 65.

175 **neatly and cleanly drest** Woolley 1673, p. 136.

175 **we absolutely forbid** Evelyn 1996, p. 27.

176 **buttr stays hard** Digby 1997, p. 219. The Irish scientist and Fellow of the Royal Society Robert Boyle also experimented with new ways of

preserving meat, roasting it, cutting it up and packing it into a cask into which melted butter was poured.

176 **final recipe** Woolley 1670, p. 345.

178 **Chatsworth** The first of several garden ice-houses at Chatsworth was completed in 1715.

178 **first digge a pitte** Evelyn 1997, p. 61.

179 *Court and Country Cook* A conflation of his two French works originally entitled *Le Cuisinier royal* and *Nouvelle instruction*.

179 **Mary Eales** Eales 1718, p. 92.

181 **used in all desserts** Glasse, *The Compleat Confectioner*, 1760, p. 252.

181 **all the flaks** Borella 1770, p. 76.

186 **fair china plates** Anne 10.2.1702, quoted in Aylett and Ordish 1965, p. 105.

186 **china Mad** Quoted in Burton 1967, p. 156.

186 **envy game** Porter 1982, p. 240.

187 **instructions for mending** Glasse, *The Compleat Confectioner*, 1760, pp. 302–3.

187 **cream coloured Ware** Woodforde 1992, entry for 17 April 1777.

187 **shops** See Rochefoucauld 1995, p. 9.

188 **tea** In many houses, the stillroom was now used by the housekeeper for brewing tea, coffee and chocolate, as well as for her pickles, preserves and baking.

188 **drooled** Kalm 1892, p. 13.

188 **three in the afternoon** Swift 1963, start of second conversation, p. 121.

188 **Pea soup** Recipe from Kettilby 1714, p. 1. Kettilby has several for different occasions, using meat stock or not. This was one of the most popular soups of the day.

189 **soups** Along with the fricasées, these are taken from Howard 1708.

189 **at Lord Mountjoy's** Baillie 1911, vol. 1, p. 297, 'Dinner at Ld Mountjoy's, 15 March 1727'.

190 *Tatler* No. 148 (21 March 1709), quoted in Mennell 1985, p. 126. S. Djabri, ed., *Diaries of Sarah Hurst 1759–62*, Horsham Museum Society, Horsham, 2004.

190 **hailstones** Addison [pseud. Isaac Bickerstaff], *The Tatler* (1709), quoted in David's introduction to Nott 1980.

190 **chefs were still paid** From Jean Hecht, *The Domestic Servants in C18 England*, Routledge, London 1980, p. 142.

191 **develop in parallel** The most recent, scholarly and engrossing history of eighteenth-century British cooking, which surveys in detail the main

styles of the period – courtly, *nouvelle* and domestic – and the later tavern cooks, is Lehmann 2003.

193 **sumptuous Side Boards** Anon., *Hell Upon Earth*, 1729, p. 7.

193 **mania for pickling** See Freke.

193 **Matthew Bramble** Tobias Smollett, *Humphry Clinker* (1771), Oxford University Press, Oxford, 1998, p. 120.

194 **monthly gardening bulletins** Published monthly by Woodward from the early 1720s.

194 **Bradley's *Country Housewife*** Published separately from his *Ladies Director* in 1727 and 1732 and together for the first time in 1736.

194 **rotating plate** Richard Bradley, quoted in *The Whole Duty of a Woman*, by 'A Lady', 1737, chap. 24, on setting out dishes. Confusingly there were several books with the same title at this time.

195 **pineapple marmalade** Bradley 1732, pt II, pp. 94, 99 (also for tart).

195 **dinner is at one o'clock** Ellis 1750, introduction for 'ill Huswifery'; p. 71 for labourers' food.

196 **break the Gut** Ellis 1750, p. 81.

197 **no vegetables** De Saussure 1995, p. 137.

199 **'hot every night'** For example, see Tobias Smollett, *The Adventures of Roderick Random* (1748), Oxford University Press, Oxford, 1999, pp. 65, 374, both of which include meals taken by Roderick at ordinaries and taverns or ordered from a cookshop.

199 **most literate nation** Hay 1997, p. 9.

199 **hundreds of new works** It has been estimated that some 530 cookbooks were published in Britain during the eighteenth century against less than half that number in France (Lehmann 2003, p. 65).

199 **French cooks** Glasse 1747, 'To the Reader', pp. i–iv.

200 **stole recipes shamelessly** Stead 1983 offers a detailed study of Glasse's plagiarisms.

200 **wages** Mennell 1985, p. 97.

200 **in a 'quick oven'** Glasse 1747, p. 271.

202 **Yorkshire pudding** Wilson notes that the first recipe for Yorkshire pudding is in fact found in *Whole Duty of a Woman* (made under roasting mutton), published a decade earlier, in 1737 – though it is not called 'Yorkshire'.

202 **standard favourite** Glasse 1747, p. 17.

204 **be very careful** Glasse 1747, p. 5.

205 **swimming in butter** Turner 1985, entry for 17 October 1756.

205 **Martha Bradley** Bradley 1996, vol. 1, p. 654.

206 **market-gardening** Bradley, *A General Treatise of Husbandry and Gardening*, vol. II, T. Woodward, London, 1726, p. 273.

206 **2s a dozen** See Switzer 1728; also Malcolm Thick's essays on eighteenth-century vegetables in Walker 1995 and Mars 1993. The cost of forced vegetables from Bradley, *General Treatise*, pp. 41ff.

206 **as we cook turnips** Switzer, *The Practical Husbandman and Planner*, vol. I, Switzer, London, 1733, pp. 78–88; Kalm 1892, p. 15.

207 **sank to the bottom** Anon. 1744 and plenty of others.

208 **spoil garden Things** Glasse 1747, p. 18.

208 **never saw sugar** Kalm 1892, pp. 85–6.

208 **interconnecting bowls** Glasse 1747; pretty little side dishes, pp. 107, 117, 163; Thacker 1758; see Thacker 1985, p. 13.

208 **rabbits** Glasse 1747, p. 90.

209 **quantities of meat** Blencowe 1694, p. 23; Glasse 1747, p. 127.

209 **'pretty thick'** Glasse 1747, p. 101.

211 **Richard Bradley** Bradley 1732, pt II.

212 **killing 'your Turtle** Raffald 1769, pp. 12–15.

212 **Turtle a hundred weight** Raffald 1769, pp. 12–15.

212 **eggs as garnishes** 'A Lady' 1827, pp. 363ff.

212 **lie on a shilling** Marshall 1777, p. 96.

212 **good calf's head** Kitchiner 1817, no. 195, 'Mock Mutton Broth'.

212 **'supposed soup'** G. de la Reynière, *Almanach des gourmandes* (1803), quoted in MacDonogh 1987, p. 119.

213 **craftsman's weekly wage** Porter 1982, p. 235. Porter points out that this was a time of rising material comforts but that an entire family could just about survive for a week on 10s while craftsmen might earn between £2 and £3 in the same period.

213 **Edward Topham** Topham 1776, p. 129.

214 ***Evangelina*** Fanny Burney, *Evangelina* (1788), J. M. Dent, London, 1893, p. 122.

214 **draw out the jaw bones** Raffald 1769, p. 123.

215 **disagreeable Taste** Raffald 1769, p. 70.

215 **Taste must direct** Dalrymple 1781, p. 4. Dalrymple who was cook to Sir John Whiteford. Marshall used garlic in several of her broths; see 1777.

216 **Indian curries** Cole 1789, no. 191, 'Currey The Indian Way'.

216 **cattle** Drummond and Wilbraham 1939, p. 227.

216 **dinner without meat** Kalm 1748, p. 14.

216 **to leave off** Turner 1985, entry for 17 September 1757.

217 **rare in the middle** For more on the transfer of this culinary habit from

England to France, see Isabelle and Robert Tombs, *That Sweet Enemy*, Heinemann, London, 2006, p. 419.

217 **Lord Harvey** Quoted in Girouard 1980, p. 161.

217 **Stoutness** For more on the fascinating subject of the body and the self in eighteenth-century England, see the brilliant Porter 2003.

217 **toasting muffins** Quoted in Porter 1982, p. 324.

217 **John Penrose** Brigitte Mitchell and Hubert Penrose, eds, *Letters from Bath*, Sutton, Stroud, 1983, p. 177.

218 **gannet** See John Vidal, 'The Great Guga Hunt', *Guardian*, 31 July 2006, p. 13.

218 **could go no farther** Topham 1776, p. 156.

219 **frenchified** Woodforde 1992, 18 August 1873.

219 **For his own guests** Woodforde 1992, 19 April 1768, 20 April 1774, 24 September 1790 and 18 July 1786.

219 **Glasse** Glasse 1747, p. 309.

220 **extravagant** Raffald 1769, p. iii.

220 **Harvey** According to David 1970, p. 12.

220 **Lady Morgan** Quoted in Alice Thomas Ellis 2004, p. 354.

222 **Peruke** Misson 1719, p. 69.

222 **etiquette book** Trusler 1788.

222 **taverns** Porter 1982, p. 235.

222 **transparent as fine old wines** De Saussure 1995, p. 98.

223 **genever** For more on this, see Drummond and Wilbraham 1939, pp. 139ff. By 1621 there were already more than 200 liquor merchants in London selling the spirit. The Distillers Company was founded in 1638.

223 **smuggled** Statistics from Burton 1967, pp. 214–15.

223 **100 thousand people** Henry Fielding, *Inquiry into the Late Increase in Robbers*, Faulkner, Dublin, 1751.

224 **little money to spare** Turner 1985, entry for 15 July 1758.

224 **Sylas Neville** Porter 2003, p. 236.

224 **English virtue** Eden 1797, p. 535.

225 **obliged to despise** Topham 1776, p. 155.

225 **breakfast always at 10** Turberville 1993 p. 344.

225 **the Austens were dining** From Lehmann 2003.

225 **Maria Edgeworth** Quoted in Fowler and Cornforth 1974, p. 67.

226 **Duchess of Bedford** The first written account of afternoon tea is from Fanny Kemble, who was summoned to tea with the Duchess of Bedford at Belvoir in the mid-nineteenth century.

226 Thomas Twining Owned Tom's Coffee House in Devereux Court, expanding into the shop next door as his tea retail trade developed.

226 twenty million pounds Equating to about 2 pounds per head of population. Drummond and Wilbraham 1939, p. 242.

226 his kettle Samuel Johnson, *Works*, vol. 6, Jones & Co., London, 1825, p. 21.

226 lost their bloom Jonas Hanway, *An Essay on Tea by Mr Hxxxx*, London, 1757.

227 Russia took to tea Tannahill 1998, p. 127.

227 Alice Smith Quoted in *Petits Propos culinaires* 55, p. 55.

227 [pressing] you to eat Rochefoucauld 1995, p. 28.

227 etiquette The word *etiquette* was first used in print in the anonymous *True Gentleman's Etiquette* (1776). 'Promiscuous seating' from Trusler 1788.

228 smell of the victuals Adam and Adam 1788, vol. 1, pl. 5.

228 one big, permanent table Expanding tables were often called 'sets of tables' because they had so many leaves.

228 filling up the room Jane Austen, *Mansfield Park*, Walter Scott, London, 1894, p. 204.

228 bought at the confectioners Glasse 1765, p. 255.

228 Walpole For Walpole's grumbles, see Letter 1746, quoted in Pullar 1970, p. 163.

229 King of Prussia Woodforde 1992, entry for 24 August 1793.

229 culinary back seat Wilson 1973 and Paston Williams 1993 both make a point of this.

229 'Floating Island' Glasse 1747, p. 290.

230 'hedgehogs' One of the earliest hedgehogs from Howard 1708; Glasse 1747, p. 288.

231 'twinned' For twinned meringues, see Massialot 1702, p. 154.

231 cochineal Originally made from the dried and crushed bodies of the American beetle *Dactoylopius coccus*, this dye also was used to colour army officers' coats.

231 Moulded foods I am indebted to a stunning talk given by the most inspirational of all food historians, Peter Brears, at the Leeds Food Symposium in York (2006) for this insight.

231 landscape appearing Quoted in Brears's essay in Brears 1996, the fullest discussion of Georgian jellies available.

232 Cedrati and Bergamot Chips From Negri's trade card, printed in Fairfax House 1998, p. 44.

232 **women of taste** Porter 1982, p. 44.

233 **lump of soot** Swift 1745, 'Directions for the Cook'.

233 **through all ranks** Moritz, in Mavor 1768, p. 97.

234 **as black as my hat** Verral 1759, preface.

234 **Uppark** Sambrook and Brears 1997, essay by Brears, pp. 30ff.

239 **running mad** Quoted in Porter 1982, p 291.

239 **eight million** Drummond and Wilbraham 1939, p. 172.

240 **source of disease** Porter 1982, p. 355.

240 **no kind of pastry** Quoted in Day 2000, p. 74.

240 **vile concoction** Cobbett 1822, p. 13; also Buchan 1797, pp. 17ff.

241 **teach 'them to make** Quoted in Porter 1982, p. 373.

242 **weak concoctions** See, for example, Rundell 1809 and Kitchiner 1817.

242 **prison hulks** William Smith, *State of the Gaols in London*, 1776.

242 **Christ's Hospital School** Charles Lamb, *Recollections of Christ's Hospital Five and Thirty Years Ago* (1813), London, 1835.

242 **Nash's new kitchen** Quotes that follow are from Kelly 2003, p. 129.

244 **Lady Morgan wrote** From 'In France' (1829), quoted in E. Suddaby and P. Yarrow, eds, *Lady Morgan in France*, Oriel Press, Newcastle upon Tyne, 1971, p. 237.

244 **titillate** Sturgeon 1822, p. 80; Lamb 1823, pp. 132ff.

245 **emulsification** Carême 1836, p. 324, 'Sauce Magnonnaise'.

245 **bad cookery** Ude 1813, 'Advice to Cooks'.

246 **late eighteenth century** See Davidson 1999, p. 735; also Ude 1813.

247 *au gratin* The basic description from Davidson 1999, p. 350.

247 **Lord Alvanley's chefs** Murray 1998, p. 35.

249 *pouding* Carême 1836, p. 420.

249 **lack of ice** Quoted in David 1994, p. 328.

250 **journeyman gilder** Gunter 1830, p. 96. The Gunter family took over the shop of the celebrated Domenico Negri.

251 **Maria Rundell** Rundell 1821, p. 322.

252 **recognising that this** Dods 1826, p. 44.

252 **fastidious age** Dods 1826, p. 45.

252 **Harry began to redden** Charles and Frances Brookfield, *Mrs Brookfield and Her Circle*, Pitman, London, 1905, p. 290.

252 **Jane Carlyle** Writing to Jeannie Welsh on 5 April 1849; quoted in Rossi Wilcox 2005, p. 184.

253 **half as many candles** Quoted in Davies 1993, p. 37.

253 **Covent Garden bouquets** 'A Lady' 1827, p. 30.

253 flower-arranging One of the first books was written by Miss Malling, in 1862.

253 names were in the papers Henry James, *In the Cage*, Herbert Stone and Co., New York, 1898, chap. 8.

253 finger bowls Originally known as finger glasses.

253 Francatelli Francatelli 1846 includes à la russe bills of fare; see preface.

253 English comfort Tickletooth 1860, p. 151.

254 opportunity for the display *Hints for the Table*, Kent & Co., London, 1859, p. 25.

254 Beeton For her menu, see Beeton 1861, pp. 908ff., 'Dinner for six in January'.

255 Countess Onslow Her menu quoted in Paston Williams 1993, p. 331.

256 Wyvern Kenney-Herbert 1878, pp. 5–7.

256 Mrs Pendler-Cudlip Originally written under the name Annie Thomas, *The Modern Housewife*, Ward Lock & Co. London, 1883, p. 13.

257 No. 7 Charlotte Square Now a National Trust House known as The Georgian House.

260 done to a popple Dods 1826, p. 23.

260 genteel Dods 1826, preface.

261 When a girl Rundell 1809, preface, p. iii.

261 Cobbett Cobbett 1830, Evening 20 October 1825, pp. 93ff.

261 roast a mutton Aylett and Ordish 1965, p. 147.

263 mock All recipes from Kitchiner 1817.

263 Instead of hors d'oeuvres Rundell 1821.

264 tire the stomach Gunter 1830, p. 139. For more on Gunter, see David 1994, pp. 313ff.

264 domestic happiness Jane Austen, *Works*, ed. John Bailey, Nash & Grayson, London, 1927, pp. 424–5. Jane's friend Martha Lloyd lived with the Austen family and, in the tradition of Sarah Longe, kept a recipe book filled with details of how to make haricot mutton and stuffed cabbage. See her recipes in Black and Le Faye 1995.

264 'served upon a napkin' 'A Lady' 1827, pp. 206ff.

265 'Mullga-tawny' Recipe from Dods 1826, p. 61.

266 'Poor Man's' Kitchiner 1817, no. 310.

266 to buy the thing Cobbett 1830, Western Grove, 18 October 1826.

266 ZEST Kitchiner 1817, no. 255.

267 Anonymous author All these recipes taken from 'A Lady' 1827, for example 'Menu for a Seraglio Dinner', p. 59.

267 **tremendously indigestible** Kitchiner 1817, general observations on vegetables preceding no. 1032.

269 **Appert** See Appert 1811.

271 **wipe the slightly off joint** See, for example, Cobbett 1835, p. 41.

271 **will not keep** Austen, *Mansfield Park*, p. 197.

276 **stained green** Mayhew 1851, p. 82.

276 **murmering hum** Mayhew 1851, p. 82.

276 **Worcester, or 'Indian', sauce** The returning Governor was Lord Marcus Sandys. For sales, see Goody 1982, p. 164.

277 **easiness of access** Beeton 1861, chap. 3.

277 **coffee pot** George Dodds, 'Pot and Kettle Philosophy', in Dickens, *Household Words*, no. 8 (1854), p. 334.

278 **native cooks** Kenney-Herbert 1878, pp. 8–12.

279 **tested the heat** *Mrs Black's Household Cookery and Laundry* (1882), quoted in Paston Williams 1993, p. 298.

279 **perfect kitchens** Soyer 1846, pp. 611ff.

279 **Eugene Wrayburn** Charles Dickens, *Our Mutual Friend*, Chapman & Hall, London, 1907, p. 268.

280 **result happiness** Charles Dickens, *David Copperfield*, Bradbury & Evans, London, chap. 12.

282 **water!** William Thackeray, *Vanity Fair* (1848), Oxford University Press, Oxford, 1998, pp. 29–30.

283 **Grander dinners** Clutterbuck 1852. For the full text and notes, see Rossi Wilcox 2005.

283 **kippers** See Walker 1995, p. 41.

284 **Mrs Todgers** Charles Dickens, *Martin Chuzzlewit*, Oxford University Press, Oxford, 1998, p. 116.

285 **Soyer's first book** For the latest and best biography of Soyer, see Brandon 2004.

286 **the same dinner** *Punch*, no. 17 (1849), p. 1, 'Mr Brown's Letters to a Young Man About Town, Great and Little Dinners'.

286 **[rubber]** All from Dickens, *Household Words*, no. 1 (1851), p. 272, 'A Good Plain Cook'.

286 **cookery schools** Acton 1845, preface.

287 **toes cocked** Mayhew 1847, p. 214.

287 ***Old Curiosity Shop*** Dickens, J. M. Dent, London, 1907, p. 133.

287 **nowhere for ladies** There were of course exceptions. Wilson in Walker 1991 notes that Simpsons in the Strand had an upstairs room for ladies.

288 **small bit of bacon** Engels 1993.

289 Samuel Oldknow Burnett 1966, p. 47.

289 *Mary Barton* Mrs Gaskell, *Mary Barton* (1848), Edinburgh University Press, Edinburgh, 1993, p. 78.

290 Mayhew wrote This and the remainder of unattributed quotes in this chapter are from Mayhew 1851.

290 *Shilling Cookery* Sales from Tannahill 1998, p. 326.

291 like a washing day Charles Dickens, *A Christmas Carol* (1843), Rand McNally, Chicago, 1912, p. 82.

292 champagne Mayhew 1851, p. 206.

292 hunting about the hides *Englishwoman's Domestic Magazine*, no. 2 (1866), p. 61, 'The Depths of Poverty III, James Greenwood, Poverty's Larder'.

293 Wages rose faster In 1888 Mrs Panton wrote that prices had never been as low as in the previous seventeen years, during which sugar had dropped from 6d to 2d a pound, bread from 9d to 5d or so, and prime cod to 4d a pound. Panton 1888, p. 18.

293 little conversation Mary-Ellen Meredith, in *Frasers Magazine*, 44 (December 1851), p. 591.

293 difficult details Panton 1888, p. 9.

294 £80 and £150 White 2007, p. 171, quoting Booth's report of the 1890s.

294 best articles Beeton 1861, chap. 1, 'The Mistress, Virtue No 15'.

295 sham butlers *Punch*, 18 (1850), p. 72, 'The Greengrocer Who Waits at Parties'.

296 slop of water 'V G' 1862, pp. 38ff.

296 Gwen Raverat Raverat 1960, p. 78.

297 Oscar Wilde See Hamlyn 1988, p. 2.

297 fast-boiling water Beeton 1861, p. 246.

297 harvest was in glut Sala 1895, p. 24.

298 shilling a dozen Paston Williams 1993, p. 276.

298 government contract Krout 1899, p. 41.

299 Australian tinned meat Drummond and Wilbraham 1939, p. 381.

299 came in handy Drummond and Wilbraham 1939, p. 365.

299 to about ten thousand tonnes Drummond and Wilbraham 1939, p. 317.

299 *Girl's Own Indoor Book* Peters 1888, p. 418.

299 Huntley and Palmers Oddy and Miller 1976, p. 19.

300 age of the grocer Davies 1989, p 109.

301 butter bill Panton 1888, p. 26; for devilled bones, see Hill 1865; and for tinned fish curried, see Peters 1888.

301 'cosy, chatty affair' Beeton 1880, p. 1242.

301 'meat-tea' See also Arnold Bennett's description of 'meat-tea' in *Anna of the Five Towns*, Methuen Shilling Books, London, 1912, chap. 12, p. 259.

302 ball supper for sixty Beeton 1861, p. 956.

302 incredible quantity Quoted in Hughes 2005, p. 540.

302 improve the temper L. 1887, p. 51.

302 *Financial Times* 16 November 1879.

302 Maidenhead platform White 2007, p. 263.

302 Beeton's provisions Beeton 1861, p. 960.

303 Christmas Day And Boxing Day was made a public holiday in 1870.

304 veritable wonders Escoffier 1907, p. 97.

304 'Pêche Melba' The raspberry purée was a later improvement.

305 'poisonous filth' *Table*, 26 January 1895.

306 all of whom vied For a précis of growth in London during the last decades of the century, see White 2007, pp. 286–7.

307 attractive young women White 2007, p. 130.

307 gas See Cookson's essay in *Petits Propos culinaires* 3, Propect Books, Totnes, 1979.

307 George Augustus Sala Sala 1895, p. xii, 'To the Lady'.

311 millions of people Jack London, *People of the Abyss*, Isbister & Co., London, 1903, chap. 25.

312 Rowntree's study Rowntree 1901.

312 *Ask the Fellows* George Ewart Evans's reminiscences about Suffolk farmers, published by Faber & Faber, London, in 1962.

314 game-keeper's lodge Plenty of fine houses installed game larders at this time, such as that at Chatsworth.

314 greaseproof paper Jack 1911, p. 344.

314 *Wind in the Willows*, London, 1908, chap. 1, 'The River Bank'.

314 Schloesser Schloesser 1904, p. 2.

315 'perfect of its kind' Schloesser 1904, p. 194.

316 Mary Davies Davies 1904, pp. 75, 276.

316 bicarbonate of soda Sykes 1914, p. 150.

316 *What and How?* Pynter 1904.

317 Jhal Frezee Poynter, 1904, Recipe 148.

317 a disgrace and a danger Reeves 1913, p. 229.

318 children under five Twenty-eight per cent of deaths in 1913 were of children under five.

318 higher standard of diet Burnett 1966, p. 243.

318 good plain cooking Byron 1914, preface, p. v.

318 **outbreak of war** Burnett 1966, p. xiv.
319 **hurried to stock up** The Anti-hoarding Act of 10 August 1914 was broadly unenforced, though it did diminish the spontaneous panic of the first weeks of war; see Burnett 1966, pp. 35–6.
319 **price of granulated sugar** Peel 1929, p. 54.
319 **Escoffier** Shaw 1994, p. 62.
319 **Mrs Tanner** Deborah Devonshire, 'Christmas at Chatsworth', *Spectator* (18 December 2004).
320 **begged to eat** Peel 1929, p. 90.
320 **food becomes scarcer** Peel 1929, p. 101.
323 **labour saving apparatus** Peel 1919, p. 1.
324 **easy . . . as a Kodak** Colchester Wemyss 1931, p. 23.
325 **coal mine** Silvester 1920, p. 179.
325 ***When the Cook*** Ives 1928, p. 143.
325 **more chic than silver** Lowinsky 1931, p. 6.
326 **Virginia Woolf** *To the Lighthouse* (1927), Harcourt Brace, New York, 1955, p. 150.
326 **Jessie Conrad** Conrad 1923.
327 **Lady Agnes Jekyll** Jekyll 1922, pp. 12ff.
329 **chicken daube** Boulestin 1923, p. 64.
329 **tendency of to-day** Leyel 1925, introduction, p. vi.
330 **blonde girls** Weir 1931, p. 18.
330 **beef steak pudding** Colchester Wemyss 1931, p. 159.
330 **dress worn at dinner** De Wolfe 1934, p. 4.
330 **innocent of yellow sauces** De Wolfe 1934, p. 3.
331 **Hilda Leyel** See Leyel 1925, index, for her salads.
332 **The English salad!** Bunyard 1937.
332 **social advancement** Heath 1932, p. 15.
332 **refrigerator** Patten 1999, pp. 30–39; gas cookers from *Petits Propos culinaires* 3 (1979); gadgets from Craig 1933, p. 14.
333 **successful hostess** Craig 1933, introduction.
335 **negligee and frou-frou** Hillis 1936, p. 117.
335 **'Live Alone and Like It'** The title of Hillis 1936.
336 **adventure of cooking** See especially Meighn 1937, for boys and girls from nine to fourteen.
336 **packed box in the car** Colchester Wemyss 1931, pp. 227–8.
336 **Open Sesame** The title of Heath 1939.
336 **illusion of purity** See David 1994, p. 305.
336 ***African Queen*** Heinemann, London, 1935, p. 170.

336 **George Orwell** *The Road to Wigan Pier* (1937); Berkley, New York, 1961, p. 170.

337 **Bernard Shaw** *The Daily Sketch* (December 1936), responses to the burning of the Crystal Palace.

337 **Florence White** White 1932 – a masterpiece of research and collation – and Morphy 1935.

337 **milk bars** By the late 1920s, large companies were starting not only to bottle milk but to pasteurise it. By 1925 practically all London milk was pasteurised, though many thought it raised the price and affected the taste, and so opposed it. With the advent of Milk Marketing Boards and improved transport, milk began for the first time in modern history to be massconsumed, regional cheese producers suffered, and dairies began to close.

337 **food survey of 1938** Crawford and Broadley 1938, p. 109: the survey was driven by increasing information about nutrition and diet, the vast new food market and by a growing preoccupation with general health.

339 **I grudge** Anne Olivier Bell, ed., *Diary of Virginia Woolf*, Hogarth, London, 1982, vol. 5 (1936–41), entry for 26 February 1941.

340 **happy go lucky** Heath 1941, pp. 81ff.

340 **National Loaf** Ministry of Food, quoted in David 1997, p. 84.

341 **extolled the virtues** Association of Teachers 1940, pp. 25, 27.

341 **meatloaf** Heath 1941; these were extracts from his early-morning BBC broadcasts.

342 **oranges** Bella Bathurst, *Wreckers*, HarperCollins, London, 2005, p. 279.

343 **snoek** Marguerite Patten interview with the author, 2006.

344 **gaze ruefully** *Vogue* (1947), quoted in Sissons and French 1963, p. 137.

345 **vile** Postgate 1951–2, p. 20.

347 **patience with these details** Spry 1956, p. 320.

348 **greatest social revolution** *Architectural Design*, no. 24 (6 June 1954), pp. 1765–77.

349 **'never had it so good'** At a Tory rally in Bedford on 20 July 1957.

349 **'a lifetime of joy'** *Homes and Gardens* (1957), quoted by Lesley Gillian in *Financial Times*, 16 April 2005.

349 **their own fridge** Oddy 2003, p. 186.

350 **terribly *House and Garden*** Flanders and Swann, from 'Design for Living', *At the Drop of a Hat*.

351 **get through it** Marguerite Patten interview with the author, 2005.

351 **in the washing machine** Ibid.

351 **children to help themselves** Patten 1964, no. 954.

352 **foundation of simple dishes** Nilson 1952, introduction to chap. 3.

352 **unlikely sandwiches** See Beer 1953.

353 **shelves brilliant and bulging** Bracken 1961, p. 91.

353 **relaxed English dish** David 1984, p. 39, originally from *Punch* (6 November 1961).

356 **put down the fork** Whitehorn 1961, p. 13.

356 **worrying about stockpots** Bracken 1961.

356 **'a must in the modern kitchen'** *Kenwood Recipe Book* 1967.

356 **At school** 'Meals for School Children', Westminster County Hall, London, *c.* 1957.

356 **heartland of plain dishes** Warren 1958.

357 **Instead they stuck** A fuller evocation of unimaginative 'English' cookery of the time is hilariously found in Alice Thomas Ellis, *The 27th Kingdom*, Duckworth, London, 1982.

357 **sweetened lard** David 1994, p. 305.

357 **inexpert and apathetic** Cooper 1967, introduction.

360 **d'you know what I mean?** Mike Leigh, *Abigail's Party*; French, London, 1979.

362 **fight, and demand** Grigson 1971, introduction.

363 **fruit of nostalgic longing** Roden 1968, introduction.

364 **red mullet** First fish recipe from Roden 1968; second from Jaffrey 1976.

365 **freezers** Oddy 2003, p. 186.

366 **interesting dishes** Smith 1975.

370 *Official Foodie Handbook* Article from *Harpers and Queen* (August 1982); *The Foodie Handbook*, Ebury, London, 1984.

371 **chicken tikka masala** For more, see Basu 2003.

372 **chicken tends** Jeremy Round, *The Independent Cook*, Barrie & Jenkins, London, 1988, p. 53.

372 **more ready meals** *Telegraph*, 26 February 2006 and 19 August 2006 'Weekend' section; also 'Costing the Earth', Radio 4, 14 April 2005.

372 **fewer nutrients** Andrew Purves, *Observer Food Monthly* (May 2005). In the last fifty years, potatoes have lost 100 per cent of vitamin A, 45 per cent of their iron and 35 per cent of their calcium; oranges have six times less vitamin A than they did.

372 **more food is available** But much of it is thrown away, according to Lord Haskins's Report, 2005. Also 'Today Programme', Radio 4, 14 April 2005, and 'Costing the Earth' on the same day.

373 **under-thirty-fives** *Observer*, 17 September 2006; Rob Sharpe, News, p. 13.

374 **Granita** Tellingly, it took the redoubtable Ben Schott finally to discover what was actually on the menu.

Bibliography

PRIMARY SOURCES

Accum, Frederick, *Culinary Chemistry*, R. Ackermann, London, 1821

Acton, Eliza, *Modern Cookery for Private Families*, Longmans & Co., London, 1845, 1855

—, *The English Bread Book*, Longman Brown Green, London, 1857

Adam, Robert and James, *Works in Architecture*, 3 vols, The Authors, London, 1788–1822

Adams, S. and S., *The Complete Servant*, Knight & Lacey, London, 1825

'A Lady', *Domestic Economy and Cookery for Rich and Poor*, John Murray, London, 1827

—, *The Whole Duty of a Woman*, fourth edn, T. Read, London, 1737

Alexander, Michael, trans., *Beowulf*, Penguin, London, 1973

Anon., — *The Good Hous-wives Treasurie*, Edward Allde, London, 1588

—, *Coach and Sedan Chair Pleasantly Disputing for Place and Precedent*, London, 1636

—, *The Compleat Cook*, Nathan Brooke, London, 1662

—, *The Court and Kitchen of Elizabeth Commonly Called Joan Cromwell, the Wife of the Late Usurper*, Tho. Milbourne for Randal Taylor, London, 1664

—, *The Genteel Housekeeper's Pastime, of the Mode of Carving at the Table*, J. Moxon, London, 1693

—, *The Complete servant-Maid*, *c.* 1670; ninth edn, Edw. Midwinter, London, 1729

—, *Hell upon Earth or the Town in an Uproar*, J. Roberts, London, 1729

—, *Adam's Luxury and Eve's Cookery*, R. Dodsley & M. Cooper, London, 1744

—, *The School for Good Living, or a Literary and Historical Essay on the European Kitchen*, Henry Colburn & Co., London, 1822

—, *Hints for the Table*, Kent and Co., London, 1859

—, *A Book of Simples*, Sampson, Low & Marston, London, 1910

Appert, Nicolas, *The Art of Preserving*, Black & Co., London, 1811

Arano, Luisa Cogliati, and Oscar Rath, trans., *The Medieval Health Handbooks Tacuina sanitatis*, Barrie & Jenkins, London, 1976

Association of Teachers of Domestic Subjects, *Hard Time Cookery*, London, 1940

Athenaeus, *Deipnosohistae*, Heinemann, London, 1927

Austin, T., ed., *Two Fifteenth Century Cookery Books*, Early English Text Society, O. S. 91, Trubner, London, 1888

A W, *A Boke of Cookrye with Serving in of the Table, or, God Huswife's Handmaid for Cookerie in her Kitchin*, Edward Allde, London, 1594

Bailey, Nathan, *Dictionarium domesticum*, T. Cox, London, 1736

Bailey, Walter, *A Short Discourse of the Three Kinds of Pepper in Common Use*, London, 1588

Baillie, Lady Grisell, *The Household Book of Lady Grisell Baillie 1692–1733*, Scottish History Society, Edinburgh, 1911

Beaty-Pownall, S., *The Queen Cookery Books No 8: Breakfast and Lunch Dishes*, Horace Cox, London, 1901

Bede, *The Ecclesiastical History of England*, ed. B. Colgrave and R. Mynors, Clarendon Press, Oxford, 1969

Beer, E. S., ed., *The Diary of John Evelyn*, Clarendon Press, Oxford, 1955

Beer, Gretel, *Sandwiches for Parties and Picnics and How to Make Them*, Herbert Jenkins, London, 1953

Beeton, Isabella, *Beeton's Book of Household Management*, S. O. Beeton, London, 1861

Beeton, Samuel, ed., *Englishwoman's Domestic Magazine*, 1852–81, Early English Text Society, E. S. 10, London, 1870

Bennett, Arnold, *Anna of the Five Towns*, Methuen, London, 1912

Bibbesworth, Walter of, *Tretis*, ed. W. Rothwell, Anglo Norman Text Society, London, 1990, from MS. Cambridge University Library MS. GG.1.1 fols 279va–294rb.

Blencowe, Mrs Ann, *The Receipt Book of Mrs Ann Blencowe AD 1694*, Guy Chapman, London, 1925

Bocuse, Paul, *The Cuisine of Paul Bocuse*, trans. Collette Rossant and Lorraine Davis, Grafton, London, 1979

Bonnefons, Nicolas de, *The French Gardiner – Instructing How to Cultivate All Sorts of Fruit Trees*, London, 1658

Boorde, Andrew, *A Dyetary of Health or Compendyous Regyment* (1542), ed. F. J. Furnivall, Early English Text Society, E. S. 10, London, 1870

Borella, *The Court and Country Confectioner*, G. Riley & A. Cooke, London, 1770

Boswell, James, *Journal of a Tour to the Hebrides with Samuel Johnson*, Charles Dilly, London, 1786

Boulestin, Marcel, *Simple French Cooking for English Homes*, Heinemann, London, 1923

—, *Myself, Two Countries*, Cassell, London, 1936

Bowman, Alan K., *Life and Letters on the Roman Frontier: Vindolanda and Its People*, British Museum Press, London, 1994

Boxer, Arabella, *First Slice Your Cookbook*, Nelson, London, 1964, 1979

—, *English Food*, Hodder & Stoughton, London, 1991

Bracken, Peg, *The 'I Hate To Cook Book'*, Arlington, London, 1961

Bradley, Martha, *The British Housewife*, S. Crowder, London, *c.* 1760; facsimile edn, vols 1–6, Prospect Books, Totnes, 1996

Bradley, Richard, *The Country Housewife and Ladies Director Parts I and II*, Woodman & Lyon, London, 1727; Browne & T. Woodman, London, 1732

Brereton, Georgine, ed., *Menagier de Paris*, Clarendon Press, Oxford, 1981

Breton, Nicholas, *Works of Nicholas Breton*, ed. A. B. Grosart, Edinburgh, 1879

Brillat-Savarin, Jean-Anthelme, *The Physiology of Taste*, trans. Anne Drayton, Penguin, London, 1994

Buchan, William, *Domestic Medicine*, fourteenth edn, A. Strahan, Edinburgh, 1794

—, *Observations Concerning the Diet of the Common People*, A. Strahan, London, 1797

Buckmaster, John Charles, *Buckmaster's Cookery: Being an Abridgement of Some of the Lectures Delivered in the Cookery School at the International Exhibition for 1873 and 1874*, G. Routledge & Sons, London, 1874

Bunyard, Edward, *The Epicure's Companion*, Dent, London, 1937

Burke, Helen, *Kippers to Caviar: Cooking for All Occasions*, Evans Brothers, London, 1965

Burnet, Regula, *Ann Cook and Friend*, Oxford University Press, London, 1936

Burnett, John, *Plenty and Want: A Social History of Diet in England from 1815 to the Present*, Penguin, London, 1966

Burton, Robert, *Anatomy of Melancholy*, ed. Holbrook Jackson, Dent, London, 1932

Buttes, Henry, *Dyets Dry Dinner*, Tho. Creede for William Wood, London, 1599

Byron, May, *May Byron's Pot Luck, or the British Home Cookery Book*, Hodder & Stoughton Ltd, London, 1914

—, *May Byron's Rations Book*, Hodder & Stoughton, London, 1918

Caesar, Caius Julius, *The Conquest of Gaul*, trans. S. A. Handford, Penguin, Harmondsworth, 1951

Caius, J., *Of Englishe Dogges*, trans. A. Fleming, A. Bradley, London, 1880

Carême, Antonin, *French Cookery*, John Murray, London, 1836

Carter, Charles, *The Practical Cook*, W. Meadows, London, 1730

—, *The Complete City and Country Cook*, A. Bettesworth, London, 1732

Carter, Susannah, *The Frugal Housewife or Complete Woman Cook*, E. Newbery, London, 1790?

Cato, *De agricultura*, trans. Andrew Dalby, Heinemann, London, 1934; Prospect Books, Totnes, 1998

Chao, Buwei Yang, *How to Cook and Eat in Chinese*, Faber & Faber, London, 1956

Chaucer, G., *The Canterbury Tales*, trans. N. Coghill, Penguin, London, 1969

Clutterbuck, Lady Maria [pseud.], *What Shall We Have for Dinner?*, Bradbury and Evans, London, 1852

Cobbett, Anne, *The English Housekeeper*, Cobbett, London, 1835

Cobbett, William, *Cottage Economy*, C. Clement, London, 1822

—, *Rural Rides*, London, 1830

Colchester Wemyss, Sir Francis, *The Pleasures of the Table*, J. Nisbet & Co., London, 1931

Cole, Mary, *The Lady's Complete Guide*, G. Kearsley, London, 1789

Coles, William, *The Art of Simpling*, J. G. for Nath. Brooke, London, 1656

—, *Adam in Eden*, J. Streather for Nath. Brooke, London, 1657

Collingwood, Francis, *The Universal Cook and City and Country Housekeeper*, J. Scatcherd, London, 1801

Colminero, Antonio, *Chocolate or An Indian Drink, by the Wise and Moderate Use Whereov Halth is Preserved, Sicknesse Diverted and Cured, Especially the Plague of the Guts*, trans. Capt James Wadsworth, John Dakins, London, 1652

Columella, *De re rustica*, Heinemann, London, 1948

Conrad, Jessie, *A Handbook of Cookery for a Small House*, Heinemann, London, 1923

Cooper, Derek, *The Bad Food Guide*, Routledge, London, 1967

Cooper, Joseph, *The Art of Cookery Refin'd*, R. Lowndes, London, 1654

Copley, Esther, *Housekeeper's Guide*, Jackson & Walford, London, 1834

Craig, Elizabeth, *Entertaining with Elizabeth Craig*, Collins, London, 1933

—, *Elizabeth Craig's Standard Recipes*, Collins, London, 1934

Cre-fydd, *Cre-fydd's Family Fare*, Simpkin and Marshall, London, 1864

Culpeper, Nicholas, *The English Physician*, Peter Cole, London, 1653

Dallas, Eneas Sweetland, *Kettner's Book of the Table*, Dulau, London, 1877

Dalrymple, George, *The Practice of Modern Cookery*, Edinburgh, 1781

David, Elizabeth, *A Book of Mediterranean Food*, John Lehmann Ltd, London, 1950

—, *Syllabubs and Fruit Fools*, Elizabeth David Ltd, London, 1969

—, *Spices, Salt and Aromatics in the English Kitchen*, Penguin, London, 1970

—, *English Bread and Yeast Cookery*, Allen Lane, London, 1977

—, *An Omelette and a Glass of Wine*, Robert Hale, London, 1984

—, *Harvest of the Cold Months*, ed. Jill Norman, Viking, London, 1994

Davidson, Caroline, ed., *Richard Bradley's Country Housewife and Lady's Director*, Prospect, London, 1980

Davies, Elspeth, *Dr Kitchiner and the Cook's Oracle*, Pentland Press, Durham, 1993

Davies, Mary, *The Housewife's What's What: A Holdall of Useful Information for the House*, T. Fisher Unwin, London, 1904

Dawson, Thomas, *The Good Huswifes Jewell*, E. White, London, 1596

Day, Mabel, and Robert Steele, eds, *Mum and the Sothsegger*, Early English Text Series, O. S. 199, Oxford University Press, Oxford, 1936

Defoe, Daniel, *The Behaviour of Servants in England*, H. Whittridge, London, 1726

—, *A Tour through the Whole Island of Great Britain 1724–5*, 2 vols, Peter Davies, London, 1927

Deighton, Len, *Action Cookbook*, Cape, London, 1965

—, *Ou est le Garlic?*, Penguin, London, 1965

Dickens, Charles, ed., *Household Words*, London, 1850–59 (weekly)

—, *All the Year Round*, London, 1859–93 (weekly)

Digby, Sir Kenelm, *The Closet of the Eminently Learned Sir Kenelm Digby* (1669), ed. Jane Stevenson and Peter Davidson, Prospect, Totnes, 1997

Dods, Meg [pseud. Christian Isobel Johnstone], *The Cook and Housewife's Manual*, Edinburgh, 1826

Dumas, Alexandre, *Le Grand Dictionnaire de cuisine* (1844), Grobel, Paris, 1958

Eales, Mrs Mary, *Mrs Mary Eales's Receipts, Confectioner to Her Late Majesty, Queen Anne*, London, 1718

Eden, Sir Frederick, *The State of the Poor*, J. Davis, London, 1797

Edlin, Abraham, *A Treatise on the Art of Bread Making*, London, 1805

Elliot, Alistair, ed., *Roman Food Poems*, Prospect, Totnes, 2003

Ellis, Audrey, *Easy Freeze Cooking*, Corgi, London, 1973

Ellis, William, *The Country Housewife's Family Companion*, James Hodges, London, 1750

Elyot, Sir Thomas, *The Castel of Helth*, Thomae Bertheleti, London, 1539

Emmison, F. G., *Tudor Secretary: Sir William Petre at Court and Home* (1961), Phillimore, London, 1970

Emy, Oficier, *L'Art de bien faire les glaces d'office*, Paris, 1768

Engels, Friedrich, *The Condition of the Working Class in England*, Oxford World's Classics, Oxford, 1993

Englishwomans' Domestic Magazine, The, Chatto & Windus, London, 1983

Escoffier, Auguste, with Phileas Gilbert and Emile Fetu, *Le Guide culinaire*, Flammarion, Paris, 1903; fourth edn, 1921; first English trans., Heinemann, London, 1907

Evelyn, John, *Acetaria: A Discourse of Sallets*, ed. Christopher Driver, 1699; facsimile edn, Prospect, Totnes, 1996

Farley, John, *The London Art of Cookery*, J. Scatcherd, London, 1784

Fettiplace, Elinor, *Elizabethan Country House Cooking*, ed. Hilary Spurling, Viking Salamander, London, 1986

Fin-Bec [pseud. William Blanchard Jerrold], *The Dinner Bell*, William Mullan & Son, London, 1878

Fleetwood, Bishop William, *Chronicon preciosum*, C. Harper, London, 1707

Flower, Barbara, and Elizabeth Rosenbaum, trans. and ed., *The Roman Cookery Book of Apicius: A Critical Translation and the Art of Cooking by Apicius*, British Book Centre, New York, 1958

Francatelli, Charles Elme, *The Modern Cook*, London, 1846

—, *Plain Cookery for the Working Classes*, second edn, Bosworth & Harrison, London, 1862

Fraser's Magazine (London), 1830–c. 1840

Freke, Elizabeth, Mss Book begun 1684, British Library, London, Add Ms 45718

Froissart, Jean, *Chronicles*, ed. and trans. Geoffrey Brereton, Penguin, Harmondsworth, 1968

Furnivall, F. L., ed, *Early English Meals and Manners (Babee's Book)*, Early English Text Society, original series, 32, London, 1868

Galen, *Galen on Food and Diet*, trans. and ed. Mark Grant, Routledge, London, 2000

Gardner, Jane, ed., *Caesar's Conquest of Gaul*, Penguin, London, 1982

Garmonsway, G. N., ed., *Aelfrie's Colloquy*, London, Methuen, 1939

Garrett, Theodore, *Encyclopaedia of Practical Cookery*, 8 vols, L. Upcott Gill, London, 1892–4

Gerard, John, *Herbal or General Historie of Plantes*, John Norton, London, 1597

Gille, B., *Comment vivre chez les Anglais*, Gigord, Paris, 1981

Gilliers, *Le Cannameliste françois*, Nancy and Paris, 1768

Glasse, Hannah, *The Art of Cookery Made Plain and Easy (by A Lady)*, London, 1747; fifth edn, 1755

—, *The Compleat Confectioner*, London, 1760; see also 1765 edn

—, *The Servant's Directory or Housekeeper's Companion*, London, 1760

Greenway, Diana, trans., *Henry of Huntingdon's The History of the English People 100–1145*, Oxford University Press, Oxford, 2002

Grigson, Jane, *Charcuterie and French Pork Cookery*, Michael Joseph, London, 1967

—, *Good Things*, Michael Joseph, London, 1971

—, *Dishes from the Mediterranean*, Sainsbury's, London, 1984

—, *English Food*, Ebury, London, 1992

Grimod de la Reynière, Laurent-Alexandre-Balthazar, *Almanach des gourmands*, vol. 3, Maradan, Paris, 1805

Gunter, William, *The Confectioner's Oracle*, Alfred Miller, London, 1830

Gwara, Scott, ed., *Anglo Saxon Conversations: The Colloquies of Aelfric Bata*, Boydell Press, Woodbridge, 1997

Hall, William, trans., *French Cookery, by Carême*, John Murray, London, 1836

Haly, Ann, ed., *William Verral's Cookbooks 1759*, Southover Press, 1988

Hamlyn, Matthew, *Recipes of Hannah Woolley*, Heinemann, London, 1988

Harrison, William, *Description of England in Shakespeare's Youth* (edited from the first two edns of Holinshed's *Chronicles 1577, 1587*), ed. F. J. Furnivall, New Shakespeare Society, London, 1908; on-line version at http://www.fordham.edu/halsall/mod/1577harrison-england.html

Hartley, Dorothy, *Food in England*, Macdonald, London, 1954

—, ed., *Thomas Tusser's Good Points of Husbandry*, Country Life, London, 1931

Hayward, Abraham, *The Art of Dining*, John Murray, London, 1852

Hazlitt, William, *Old Cookery Books and Ancient Cuisine*, Elliot Stock, 1886

Heath, Ambrose, *Good Food*, Faber & Faber, London, 1932

—, *Open Sesame: The Way of a Cook with a Can*, Nicholson & Watson, London, 1939

—, *Kitchen Front Recipes and Hints/How to Cook in Wartime*, Adam and Charles Black, London, 1941

—, *Good Food Again*, Faber & Faber, London, 1950

Hentzner, Paul, and Sir Robert Naunton, *Travels in England during the Reign of Queen Elizabeth*, trans. R. Bentley and ed. Horace Walpole, London, 1797

Herrick, Robert, *Selected Poems*, ed. David Jesson Dibley, Carcanet, Manchester, 1989

Hervey, Lord H., *Lord Hervey and His Friends 1726–38*, ed. Earl of Ilchester, John Murray, London, 1950

Hess, Karen, ed., *Martha Washington's Booke of Cokery and Booke of Sweetmeats*, Columbia University Press, New York, 1995

Hickman, Peggy, ed., *A Jane Austen Household Book: The Recipes of Martha Lloyd*, David and Charles, London, 1977

Hill, Benson, *The Epicure's Almanac*, London, 1841–3

Hill, G., *The Breakfast Book*, Richard Bentley, London, 1865

Hillis, Marjorie, *Live Alone and Like It: A Guide for the Extra Woman*, Duckworth, London, 1936

Holland, Mary, *The Complete British Cook*, London, 1800

Holt, Vincent M., *Why Not Eat Insects*, E. W. Classey, London, 1885

Hopkinson, Simon, *Roast Chicken and Other Stories*, Ebury, London, 1994

—, and Lindsay Bareham, *The Prawn Cocktail Years*, Macmillan, London, 1997

Howard, Henry, *England's Newest Way in All Sorts of Cookery, Pastry and All Pickles* etc., Chr. Coningsby, London, 1708

Hughes, Anne, *Diary of a Farmer's Wife 1796–7*, Penguin, London, 1981

Hume, Rosemary, *Party Food and Drink*, Chatto & Windus, London, 1957

Ives, Catherine, *When the Cook Is Away*, Duckworth, London, 1928

Jaffrey, Madhur, *An Invitation to Indian Cooking*, Cape, London, 1976

Jarrin, G. A., *Italian Confectioner*, John Harding, London, 1820

Jekyll, Lady Agnes, *Kitchen Essays*, Nelson, London, 1922

Jerrold, William, *The Epicure's Yearbook and Table Companion*, Bradbury & Evans, London, 1868

Jewry, Mary, *Warne's Model Cookery and Housekeeping Book 1868*, Frederick Warne and Co., London, 1868

Kalm, Per, *Account of His Visit to England . . . in 1748*, trans. J. Lucas, Macmillan & Co., London, 1892

Kenney-Herbert, Col. A. ('Wyvern'), *Culinary Jottings for Madras*, Higginbotham, Madras, 1878

—, *Common Sense Cookery for English Households*, Edward Arnold, London, 1894

—, *Fifty Breakfasts*, Edward Arnold, London, 1894

—, *Fifty Dinners*, Edward Arnold, London, 1895

Kent, Elizabeth, Countess of, *True Gentlewoman's Delight*, W. J. Ghent, London, 1653

Kenwood Recipe Book, The, fifth edn, Victory Press, Leicester and London, 1967

Ker, W.C.A., trans., *Martial Epigrams*, Heinemann Loeb Classical Library, London, 1968

Kettilby, Mary, comp., *A Collection of above 300 Receipts in Cookery, Physick and Surgery*, Richard Wilkin, London, 1714

Kidder, Edward, *Kidder's Receipts of Pastry and Cookery*, ed. Jane Jakeman, Ashmolean Museum, Oxford, 2001

Killen, John, ed., *The Famine Decade: Contemporary Accounts 1841–1851*, Blackstaff, Belfast, 1995

Kitchiner, William, *Apicius Redivivus or the Cook's Oracle*, Samuel Bagster, London, 1817

Krout, Mary, *A Looker-on in London*, Stevens and Brown, London, 1899

L., Major, *Breakfasts, Luncheons and Ball Suppers*, Chapman & Hall, London, 1887

La Chapelle, Vincent, *The Modern Cook*, 3 vols, Thomas Osborne, London, 1733

Lamb, Charles, *Letters of Elia*, London, 1823

Lamb, Patrick, *Royal Cookery*, Maurice Atkins, London, 1710

Langland, William, *Piers the Plowman*, trans. Henry W. Wells, Sheed & Ward, London, 1935

Lawson, Nigella, *How to Be a Domestic Goddess*, Chatto & Windus, London, 2000

Lawson, William, *A New Orchard and Garden*, London, 1623

Lee, M. P., *Chinese Cookery: A Hundred Practical Recipes*, Faber & Faber, London, 1943

Leigh, Mike, *Abigail's Party*, Samuel French, London, 1979

Levi-Strauss, C., 'The Culinary Triangle', *Partisan Review*, 33 (1966), pp. 586–95

—, *The Origin of Table Manners*, trans. John and Doreen Weightman, Cape, London, 1968

Leyel, Hilda, *Green Salads and Fruit Salads*, Routledge, London, 1925

—, *Picnics for Motorists*, Routledge, London, 1936

—, and Olga Hartley, *The Gentle Art of Cookery*, Chatto & Windus, London, 1925

Lindsay, Jessie, *Manual of Modern Cookery*, University of London Press, London, 1927

Low, D. M., ed., *London is London*, Chatto & Windus, London, 1949

Lowinsky, Ruth, *Lovely Food*, Nonesuch Press, London, 1931

Lupton, Donald, *London and the Country Carbonadoed*, Nicholas Okes, London, 1632

Magazine of Domestic Economy, The, 1836–44

Markham, Gervase, *The English Huswife*, London, 1615

—, *Ways to Get Wealth*, London, 1631

Marnette, Monsieur, *The Perfect Cook Being the Most Exact Directions for Making All Kinds of Pastes . . . Pies . . . (Pastes and Pies)*, London, 1656

Marshall, Agnes Bertha, *Mrs A. B. Marshall's Cookery Book*, Simpkin, Marshall, London, 1888

—, *Mrs A. B. Marshall's Larger Cookery Book of Extra Recipes*, Simpkin, Marshall, Hamilton, Kent & Co. Ltd, London, 1891

—, *Fancy Ices*, Marshall, Simpkin, London, 1894

—, *The Book of Ices*, Robert Hayes, London, 1898?

Marshall, Elizabeth, *The Young Ladies' Guide in the Art of Cookery*, Newcastle, 1777

Massialot, M., *Le Cuisinier royal et bourgeois / The Court and Country Cook*, trans. J. K., J. Churchill, London, 1702

Mastercooks of King Richard II, *The Forme of Cury*, ed. Samuel Pegge, J. Nichols, London, 1780

Mattingly, H., trans. and ed., *Tacitus' Agricola*, Penguin, London, 1948

Maundeville, Sir John, *The Voiage and Travayle of Syr John Maundeuile, Knight*, ed. John Ashton, Pickering and Chatto, London, 1887

Mavor, W., *The British Tourists 1798–1860*, 6 vols, London, 1768

May, Robert, *The Accomplisht Cook* (1660), facsimile edn with intro and glossary, ed. Alan Davidson, Prospect, Totnes, 1994

Mayhew, Henry and Augustus, *The Greatest Plague of Life: Or the Adventures of a Lady in Search of a Good Servant. By One Who Has Been 'almost Worried to Death'*, G. Routledge & Sons, London, 1847

—, *London Labour and the London Poor*, Woodfall, London, 1851

Meighn, Moira, *Moira Meighn's Adventure Book of Cookery for Boys and Girls and for Anyone Interested in Cooking*, Oxford University Press, Oxford, 1937

Meyer, Kunro, ed., *Vision of MacCoglinne*, Nut, London, 1892

Middleton, John, *Five Hundred New Receipts in Cookery, Confectionery, Pastry, Preserving Etc*, rev. Henry Howard, London, 1734

Misson, Henri, *Memoirs and Observations in His Travels over England*, trans. J. Ozell, D. Browne etc., London, 1719

Montagne, Prosper, *Larousse gastronomique*, ed. Nina Froud and Charlotte Turgeon, Hamlyn, London, 1961

Morgan, Lady Sydney, *France*, Henry Colburn, London, 1817

Morphy, Countess [pseud. Marcelle Aza Forbes], *English Recipes including the Traditional Dishes of Scotland, Ireland and Wales*, Published for Selfridge & Co. by Herbert Joseph, London, 1935

—, *Recipes of All Nations*, Published for Selfridge & Co. by Herbert Joseph, London, 1935

Morris, Richard, ed., *Liber cure cocorum*, Philological Society, London, 1862

Moryson, Fynes, *An Itinerary Containing His Ten Years Travel* (1617), J. MacLeHose and Sons, Glasgow, 1908

Moxon, Elizabeth, *English Housewifery Exhibited in above 450 Receipts*, James Lister, Leeds, *c.* 1749

Muffett, Thomas, *Health's Improvement or Rules Comprising Discovering the Nature, Method and Manner of Preparing All Sorts of Food Used in this Nation* (written *c.* 1595), Samuel Thomson, London, 1655

Murrell, John, *A New Booke of Cookerie*, John Browne, London, 1617

—, *A Delightful Daily Exercise for Ladies and Gentlewomen*, T. Devve, London, 1621

—, *Two Books of Cookerie and Carving*, fifth edn, J. Marriot, London, 1641

Napleton, Lewis, *A Guide to Microwave Catering*, Northwood, London, 1967

—, *Microwave Recipe Book*, Northwood, London, 1977

Nashe, Thomas, *Lenten Stuffe, or the Praise of the Red Herring*, N L & C B, London, 1599

Newbery, Thomas, *Dives pragmaticus* (1563), Manchester University Press, Manchester, 1910

Nichols, John, *Progresses and Public Processions of Queen Elizabeth (etc)*, 3 vols, John Nichols and Son, London, 1823

Nilson, Bee, *The Penguin Cookery Book*, Penguin, London, 1952

Norfolk, John Howard Duke of, *Accounts and Memoranda if Sr J Howard 1462–1471*, Roxburghe Club London, 1841

Nott, John, *The Cook's and Confectioner's Dictionary*, London, 1723; facsimile edn, ed. Elizabeth David, Lawrence Rivington, London, 1980

Nutt, Frederick, *The Complete Confectioner*, London, 1789

Ordinances of the Households of Edward III—William and Mary: Proceedings of the Society of Antiquaries of London, London, 1790

Orwell, George, *The English People*, Collins, London, 1947

Oschinsky, Dorothea, ed., *Walter of Henley and Other Treatise on Estate Management and Accounting*, Clarendon Press, Oxford, 1971

Panton, Mrs Jane Ellen, *From Kitchen to Garret: Hints for Young Householders*, Ward & Downey, London, 1888

Papin, Denys, *A New Digester*, London, 1681

Paris, Matthew, *English History*, trans. J. A. Giles, Bohn, London, 1852

—, *Chronicles*, ed. Richard Vaughan, Alan Sutton, Gloucester, 1984

Parkinson, John, *Paradisi in sole*, H. Lownes & R. Young, London, 1629

Partridge, John, *Treasurie of Commodious Conceits Commonly Called the Good Huswife's Closet*, Richard Ihones, London, 1584

—, *A Widdowes Treasure*, I. Roberts for E. White, London, 1595

Patten, Marguerite, *Learning to Cook with Marguerite Patten*, Phoenix House, London, 1955

—, *Step by Step Cookery*, Hamlyn, London, 1962

—, *500 Recipes: Canned and Frozen Food*, Hamlyn, London, 1963

—, *Cookery in Colour 1960*, The Complete Guide to Gardening and Cooking, Hamlyn, London, 1964

—, *Marguerite Patten's Pressure Cookery*, Collins Glasgow, 1977

—, *We'll Eat Again, London*, Hamlyn, London, 1985

—, *Microwave for One*, Hamlyn, London, 1987

—, *Post War Kitchen: Nostalgic Food and Facts from 1945–1954*, Hamlyn, London, 1998

—, *Century of British Cooking*, Grub Street, London, 1999

Payne, A. G., ed., *Cassell's Popular Cookery*, Cassell and Co., London, 1889

Peel, Mrs C. S., ed., *The Daily Mail Cookery Book*, third edn, Associated Newspapers, London, 1919

Peel, Dorothy Constance, *How We Lived Then – 1914–18*, John Lane, London, 1929

Pepys, Samuel, *Diaries*, ed. Robert Latham, Bell & Hyman, London, 1983

Percy, Thomas, ed,. *The Household Papers of Henry Percy, 9th Earl of Northumberland (1564–1632)*, Royal Historical Society, London, 1962

Peters, Charles, ed., *The Girl's Own Indoor Book*, Religious Tract Society, London, 1888

Petty, Florence, *The 'Pudding Lady's' Recipe Book*, sixth edn, G. Bell, London, 1920

Philp, Robert Kemp, *Enquire Within upon Everything*, Houlston and Stoneman, London, 1856, edns to 1909

—, *The Dictionary of Daily Wants*, vols 1–3, Houlston & Wright, London, 1859

Physiologus Philotheos [pseud. Thomas Tryon], *The Good Housewife Made a Doctor – An Appendix to the Book A Way to Health*, Andrew Sowle, London, 1685

—, *Monthly Observations for the Preserving of Health*, A. Sowle, London, 1688

Platt, Sir Hugh, *Delightes for Ladies*, P. Short, London, 1602; ed. G. E. and K. R. Fussell, Crosby Lockwood and Son Ltd, London, 1948

Postgate, Raymond, ed., *The Good Food Guide 1951–2*, Cassell and Co., London, 1951–2 and other edns

Poynter, Miss E. S. [ESP], *What and How?*, Thacker, Spink, London, 1904

Price, Rebecca, *The Compleat Cook: The Secrets of a Seventeenth Century Housewife*, ed. Madeleine Masson, Routledge & Kegan Paul, London, 1974

Pritchard, R. E., *Shakespeare's England: Life in Elizabethan and Jacobean Times*, Sutton, Stroud, 1999

Propre New Boke of Cokery c 1545, Richard Lants and Richard Banks, c. 1557–8

Punch, or the London Charivari, London, 1841–1992, weekly

Quaglino, *The Complete Hostess*, ed. Charles Graves, Hamish Hamilton, London, 1935

Rabisha, Will, *The Whole Body of Cookery Dissected*, R W for Giles Calvert, London, 1661, 1682

The Radiation Cookery Book, thirty-second edn, New World Cookery, London, 1947

Raffald, Elizabeth, *The Experienced English Housekeeper*, Manchester, 1769

Raverat, Gwen, *Period Piece: A Cambridge Childhood*, Faber & Faber, London, 1960

Redgrave, Vincent, ed., *The Household Book of Alice de Bryene*, Paradigm Press, Bungay, 1984

Reeves, Mrs Magdalen S. P., *Round about a Pound a Week*, G. Bell and Sons, London, 1913

Richardson, Samuel, *Pamela*, Penguin, London, 1980

Rhodes, Sir Hugh, *Boke of Nurture*, H. Jackson, London, 1577

Riley, H. T., *Memorials of London 1276–1419*, Longmans, London, 1868

Rochefoucauld, François de la, *A Frenchman in England, being the Mélanges sur l'Angleterre . . .*, trans. S. C. Roberts, Caliban Books, London, 1995

Roden, Claudia, *A Book of Middle Eastern Food*, Nelson, London, 1968

Rose, Giles, *A Perfect School of Instruction for the Officers of the Mouth*, London, 1682

Rowntree, B. S., *Poverty: A Study of Town Life*, Macmillan & Co., London, 1901

Rumpolt, Max, *Ein neues Kochbuch*, Frankfurt, 1581

Rundell, Maria Eliza [A Lady], *A New System of Domestic Cookery*, John Murray, London, 1809, 1819, 1821, 1827, 1831, 1849, 1852, 1861

Ruscelli, Girolomo, *The Secretes of Master Alexis of Piedmont*, London, 1558

Russell, John, *Boke of Nurture*, 1577; ed. from the Harleian MS. 4011 in the British Museum by F. J. Furnivall, Bungay, 1868

Ruthven, Patrick Lord, *The Ladies' Cabinet Opened*, London, 1639, 1654

Rye, William B., *England as Seen by Foreigners*, John Russell Smith, London, 1865

Sala, George Augustus, *The Thorough Good Cook*, Cassell, London, 1895

de Saussure, Caesar, *A Foreign View of England 1725–1729*, trans. Mme van Muyden, Caliban Books, London, 1995

Scappi, Bartolomeo, *Opera del'arte del cucinare*, Venice, 1570

Schloesser, Frank, *The Cult of the Chafing Dish*, Gay and Bird, London, 1904

Scully, Terrence, ed., *Le Viandier of Taillevent*, Ottawa University Press, Ottawa, 1988

—, *The Vivendier—A Fifteenth-Century French Cookery Manuscript*, Devon Prospect Books, Totnes 1997

—, trans. and ed., *Chiquart's On Cookery: A Fifteenth-Century Savoyard Culinary Treatise*, Peter Lang, New York, 1986

Short [pseud.], *Dinners at Home: How to Order, Cook and Serve Them*, Kerby & Endean, London, 1878

Silvester, Elizabeth, *Silvester's Sensible Cookery*, Herbert Jenkins, London, 1920

Sisam, Kenneth and Celia, eds, *The Oxford Book of Medieval English Verse*, Clarendon Press, Oxford, 1970

Skelton, John, *The Poetical Works of John Skelton*, ed. Alexander Dyce, Thomas Rodd, London, 1843

Smith, Delia, *Family Fare Series*, BBC, London, 1974–5

—, *One Is Fun!*, Hodder, London, 1985

—, *How to Cook*, 3 vols, BBC, London, 1998

Smith, E.C. [taken to be Eliza], *The Compleat Housewife*, Williamsburg, 1734; Arlon House, Kings Langley, 1983

Smith, Henry, *The Master Book of Soups*, Practical Press, London, 1949

Sneyd, C. A., trans., *A Relation of the Island of England, about the Year 1500*, Camden Society, London, 1847

Sorbière, Samuel, *A Journey to London in the Year 1698*, A. Baldwin, London, 1698

Sowards, J. K., *Collected Works of Erasmus*, University of Toronto Press, Toronto, 1985

Soyer, Alexis, *The Gastronomic Regenerator*, Simpkin & Marshall, London, 1846

—, *The Modern Housewife or Menagère*, Simpkin, Marshall & Co., London, 1849

—, *Shilling Cookery for the People*, Routledge, London, 1855

—, *A Culinary Campaign (1857)*, intro Michael Barthorp and Elizabeth Ray, Southover, Lewes, 1995

Sprat, Thomas, *Observations on M de Sorbier's Voyage into England*, J. Martyn & J. Allestry, London, 1665

Spry, Constance, and Rosemary Hume, *The Constance Spry Cookery Book*, Michael Joseph, London, 1956

Stone, Ian, ed., *Sir Gawain and the Green Knight*, Penguin, London, 1974

Stow, John, *A Survey of London (1598)*, ed. Henry Morley, Allan Sutton, Stroud, 1994

Stubbes, Philip, *The Anatomie of Abuses*, second edn, J. R. Jones, London, 1583

Sturgeon, Launcelot, *Essays Moral, Philosophical and Stomachical on the Important Science of Good Living* (known also as *Essays on Good Living*), London, 1822

Sugg, Marie Jenny, *The Art of Cooking by Gas*, Cassell and Co., London, 1890

Swanton, Michael, ed., *Anglo-Saxon Prose*, J. M. Dent, London, 1975

Swift, J., *Polite Conversations*, London, 1738; ed. E Partridge, Deutsch, London, 1963

—, *Directions to Servants*, G. Faulkner, Dublin, 1745

Switzer, S., *A Particular Method . . . for the Raising Italian Broccoli, Spanish Cardoon, Celeriac Fenochi . . .*, London, 1728

Sykes L., *An Olio of Proved Recipes and Domestic Wrinkles*, Abel Heywood, Manchester 1914

Tacitus, Cornelius, *The Agricola*, Penguin, London, 2003

Tegetmeier, William Bernhard, *A Manual of Domestic Economy: With Hints on Domestic Medicine and Surgery*, Home & Colonial School Society, Hamilton, Adams and Co., London, 1880

Thacker, John, *The Art of Cookery*, I. Thompson & Co., Newcastle, 1758

Thompson, Gladys Scott, *Life in a Noble Household 1641–1700*, Jonathan Cape, London, 1937

Tickletooth, Tabitha, *The Dinner Question*, Routledge, Warne, London, 1860

Topham, Edward, *Letters from Edinburgh 1774–1775*, Edinburgh, 1776

Trusler, J., *The Honours of the Table*, Literary Press, London, 1788

Tryon, Thomas, *A Treatise of Cleanness in Meats and Drinks, of the Preparation of Food etc*, London, 1682

Tschumi, Gabriel, *Royal Chef—Recollections*, William Kimber, London, 1954

Turberville, A. S., ed., *Johnson's England*, Clarendon, Oxford, 1993

Turbeville, George, *The Booke of Hunting (1576)*, Clarendon, Oxford, 1908

Turner, Thomas, *The Diary of Thomas Turner 1754–1765*, ed. D. Vaisey, Oxford University Press, Oxford, 1985

Tusser, Thomas, *A Hundreth Pointes of Good Husbandrie* (1557), ed. D Hartley, Country Life, London, 1931

Ude, Louis Eustache, *The French Cook*, Cox & Baylis, 1813

Varenne, François Pierre de la, *Le Cuisinier françois*, La Haye, 1656

Verral, William, *Complete System of Cookery*, London, 1759

'V G', *Dinners and Dinner-parties, or the Absurdities of Artificial Life*, second edn, Chapman & Hall, London, 1862

Warner, Richard, *Antiquitas culinarae or Curious Tracts*, London, 1791

Webster, Thomas, and Mrs William Parkes, *An Encyclopedia of Domestic Economy*, Longman, London, 1844

Weir, Eric, *When Madame Cooks*, Philip Allan, London, 1931

Westminster City Council, *Meals for School Children*, ed. Mrs E. Earle, London, 1957 (pamphlet for schools)

Weston, J. L., ed., 'The Debate of the Body and Soul', in *The Chief Middle English Poets*, G. C. Harrap, London, 1913

White, Eileen, ed., *The English Cookery Book*, Totnes, Prospect Books, 2004

White, Florence, *Good Things in England*, Jonathan Cape, London, 1932

The Whole Duty of a Woman—(Later Reprinted as the Ladies' Companion), T. Read, London, 1737

Whitehorn, Katharine, *Kitchen in the Corner: A Complete Guide to Bedsitter Cookery*, Macgibbon & Kee, London, 1961

Whiting, Sydney, *Memoirs of a Stomach*, London, 1853

W. M., *The Queen's Closet Opened 4e. Including also The Queen's Delight and The Compleat Cook*, Nathaniel Brooks, London, 1658

Wolfe, Elsie de, *The House in Good Taste*, Century, New York, 1913

—, *Recipes for Successful Dining*, Heinemann, London, 1934

Women's Petition against Coffee, The, London, 1674

Wood-Legh, K. L., ed., *A Small Household of the C15: Account Book of Munden's Chantry, Bridport*, Manchester University Press, Manchester, 1956

Woodforde, Revd James, *The Diary of A Country Parson 1758–1802*, selected by David Hughes, Folio Society, London, 1992

Woolley, Hannah, *The Ladies Directory*, T. Milbourn, London, 1661

—, *The Cook's Guide*, London, 1664

—, *The Queen Like Closet*, London, 1670

—, *The Ladies Delight*, London, 1672

—, *The Gentlewoman's Companion*, London, 1673

— [T P], *The Accomplish't Ladies Delight*, London, 1675

—, *The Compleat Servant Maid*, ninth edn, London, 1729

Woorde, Wynken de, *Boke of Kervynge*, London, 1508

Wright, Thomas, *A Volume of Vocabularies*, 2 vols, 1857–73

SECONDARY SOURCES

Adamson, Melitta Weiss, *Food in the Middle Ages: A Book of Essays*, Garland, London, 1995

Albano, Caterina, ed., *Gentlewoman's Companion – A Guide to the Fairer Sex*, Prospect Books, Totnes, 2001

Alcock, Joan P., *Life in Roman Britain*, Batsford, London, 1996

—, *Food in Roman Britain*, Tempus, Stroud, 2001

Allen, Darina, *Irish Traditional Cooking*, Kyle Cathie, London, 1995

Arnold, Walter, *The Life and Death of the Sublime Society of Beefsteaks*, Bradbury and Evans, London, 1871

Attenborough, F. L., *Laws of the Earliest English Kings*, Cambridge University Press, Cambridge, 1922

Aylett, Mary, and Olive Ordish, *First Catch Your Hare – A History of the Recipe Makers*, Macdonald, London, 1965

Ayrton, Elizabeth, *The Cookery of England, Being a Collection of Recipes for Traditional Dishes of All Kinds from C15 – Present*, Deutsch, London, 1974

Barber, Richard, *Cooking and Recipes from Rome to the Renaissance*, Allen Lane, London, 1973

Baren, Maurice, *How It All Began in the Pantry*, Michael O'Mara, London, 2000

Barnes, Julian, *The Pedant in the Kitchen*, Atlantic, London, 2003

Barnett, L. Margaret, *British Food Policy in the First World War*, Allen & Unwin, London, 1985

Basu, Shrabani, *Curry: The Story of the Nation's Favourite Dish*, Sutton, Stroud, 2003

Bateman, Michael, *Cooking People*, Leslie Frewin, London, 1966

Battiscombe, Georgina, *English Picnics*, Harvill Press, London, 1949

Beauman, Fran, *Pineapple, the King of Fruits*, Chatto & Windus, London, 2005

Birley, A., *The People of Roman Britain*, Batsford, London, 1979

Bitting, A. W., *Appertizing or the Art of Canning*, Trade Pressroom, San Francisco, 1937

Black, Maggie, and D. le Faye, eds, *The Jane Austen Cookbook*, British Museum Press, London, 1995

Boon, George C., 'A Roman Pastry Cook's Mould from Silchester', *Antiquaries Journal*, 38 (1958), pp. 237–40

Bradfield, Nancy, *900 Years of English Costume*, Peerage Books, London, 1987

Brandon, Ruth, *People's Chef – A Life in Seven Courses*, Wiley, Chichester, 2004

Brears, Peter, *The Gentlewoman's Kitchen: Great Food in Yorkshire 1650–1750*, Historical Publications, Wakefield, 1984

—, 'Transparent Pleasures: The Story of the Jelly', pts I–II, in *Petits Propos culinaires* 53, 54, Prospect Books, London, 1996

—, *Compleat Housekeeper*, Historical Publications, Wakefield, 2000

Bridge, Tom, and Colin Cooper English, *Dr William Kitchiner, Regency Eccentric, Author of the Cook's Oracle*, Southover Press, Lewes, 1992

Brothwell, Don and Patricia, *Food in Antiquity*, Thames & Hudson, London, 1969

Burton, Elizabeth, *The Georgians at Home*, Arrow, London, 1967

Byrne, M. St Clare, *Elizabethan Life in Town and Country*, Methuen, London, 1954

Campbell-Culver, Maggie, *The Origin of Plants*, Headline, London, 2001

Camporesi, Piero, *Bread of Dreams: Food and Fantasy in Early Modern Europe*, trans. David Gentilcore, Polity Press, Cambridge, 1989

Carlin, M., and J. T. Rosenthal, eds, *Food and Eating in Medieval Europe*, Hambledon Press, London, 1998

Carr, Alf, *When It's Time to Make a Choice: 50 Years of Frozen Food in Britain*, British Frozen Food Federation, Grantham, 1998

Caton, Mary Anne, *Fooles and Fricassees: Food in Shakespeare's England*, Folger Shakespeare Library, Washington, DC, 1999

Cookson, Caroline, *Technology of Cooking in the British Isles 1600–1900*, pt 1, Prospect Books, Totnes, 1979

Cooper, Artemis, *Writing at the Kitchen Table*, Penguin, Harmondsworth, 2000

Cooper, Charles, *The English Table in History and Literature*, S. Low, Marston, 1929

Cosman, M. P., *Fabulous Feasts: Medieval Cookery and Ceremony*, George Braziller, New York, 1976

Coxhead, Elizabeth, *Writing at the Kitchen Table*, William Luscombe, London, 1975

Crawford, Sir William, and H. Broadley, *The People's Food*, Heinemann, London, 1938

Cunliffe, Barry, *Fishbourne, Roman Palace*, Society of Antiquaries, London, 1971

—, *Iron Age Communities*, Routledge, London, 1991

—, *Danebury*, B. T. Batsford for English Heritage, London, 1993

Dalby, Andrew, *Food in the Ancient World from A–Z*, Routledge, London, 2003

Davidson, Alan, *The Oxford Companion to Food*, Oxford University Press, Oxford, 1999

—, and Helen Saberi, *The English Kitchen – Trifle*, Prospect Books, Totnes, 2001

Davies, Jennifer, *The Victorian Kitchen*, BBC Books, London, 1989

Day, Ivan, 'Further Musings on Syllabub', in *Petits Propos culinaires* 53, Prospect Books, Totnes, 1996

—, ed., *Eat, Drink and be Merry: The British at Table 1600–2000*, Philip Wilson, London, 2000

—, and H. Saberi, eds, *The Wilder Shores of Gastronomy*, Ten Speed Press, Berkeley, 2002

Derbyshire Records Office, *Taste of Old England: Early History of Traditional English Food*, Archives First Series, Derbyshire Records Office, Derby, 1994

Driver, Christopher, *The British At Table 1940–1980*, Chatto & Windus, London, 1983

—, ed., *John Evelyn, Cook*, Prospect Books, Totnes, 1997

—, and Michelle Berriedale-Johnson, *Pepys at Table*, Unwin Hyman, London, 1984

Drummond, J. C., and Anne Wilbraham, *The Englishman's Food*, Jonathan Cape, London, 1939

Drury, Susan, 'Flowers in English Cookery in the C17 and C18', in *Petits Propos culinaires* 20, Prospect Books, Totnes, 1985

Dyer, Christopher, *Standards of Living in the Later Middle Ages: Social Change in England c 1200–1520*, Cambridge University Press, Cambridge, 1989

Edwards, J., *The Roman Cookery of Apicius*, Rider and Co., London, 1984

Ellis, Alice Thomas, *Fish, Flesh and Good Red Herring*, Virago, London, 2004

Ellis, Markman, *The Coffee House: A Cultural History*, Weidenfeld & Nicolson, London, 2004

Emmison, F. G., *Tudor Food and Pastimes*, Benn Ltd, London, 1964

Fairfax House, York, *Pleasures of the Table: An Exhibition 1600–1900*, York Civic Trust, York, 1998

Fisher, M.F.K., *The Art of Eating*, Pan Books, London, 1983

Fitzgibbon, Theodora, *The Art of British Cookery*, Phoenix House, London, 1965

—, *Traditional Scottish Cookery*, Cookery Book Club, London, 1967

Flanders, Judith, *The Victorian House*, Harper Collins, London, 2003

Flandrin, Jean-Louis, and Massimo Montanari, *Food: A Culinary History from Antiquity to the Present*, Columbia University Press, New York, 1999

Fowler, John, and John Cornforth, eds. *English Decoration in the Eighteenth Century*, Barrie & Jenkins, London, 1974

Freeman, Sarah, *Mutton and Oysters: The Victorians and Their Food*, Gollancz, London, 1989

Frere, S. S., *Britannia: A History of Roman Britain*, Folio Society, London, 1999

Garnsey, Peter, *Food and Society in Classical Antiquity*, Cambridge University Press, Cambridge, 1999

Giacosa, I. G., *A Taste of Ancient Rome*, trans. A. Herklotz, University of Chicago Press, Chicago, 1992

Girouard, Mark, *Life in the English Country House*, Penguin, London, 1980

Gold, M., *Assault and Battery*, Pluto Press, London, 1983

Golding, Louis, and Andre Simon, eds, *We Shall Eat and Drink Again*, Hutchinson, London, 1944

Goody, Jack, *Cooking, Cuisine and Class*, Cambridge University Press, Cambridge, 1982

Gowers, Emily, *The Loaded Table: Representations of Food in Roman Literature*, Clarendon Press, Oxford, 1993

Grainger, Sally, and Andrew Dalby, *The Classical Cookbook*, British Museum Press, London, 1996

Hagen, Ann, *A Handbook of Anglo-Saxon Food*, Anglo-Saxon Books, Pinner, 1992

Hammond, P. W., *Food and Feast in Medieval England*, Sutton, Stroud, 1993

Hardyment, Christina, *Slice of Life: The British Way of Eating Since 1945*, BBC Books, London, 1995

Harvey, John, 'Vegetables in the Middle Ages', *Garden History*, 12 (1984), pp. 89–99

Harvie, Christopher, *Nineteenth-Century Britain*, Oxford University Press, Oxford, 2000

Hay, Douglas, *Eighteenth-Century English Society*, Oxford University Press, Oxford, 1997

Henisch, B. A., *Fast and Feast: Food in Medieval Society*, Pennsylvania State University Press, London, 1976

—, 'Benson E Hill, The Epicure's Almanac of 1841', in *Petits Propos culinaires* 24, Prospect Books, Totnes, 1986

Herbodeau, Eugene, and Paul Thalamas, *George Auguste Escoffier*, Practical Press Ltd, London, 1955

Hieatt, Constance B., *An Ordinance of Pottage: An Edition of the Fifteenth Century Culinary Recipes in York University's MS Beinecke 163*, Prospect Books, London, 1988

—, and Sharon Butler, eds, *Curye on Inglysch: English Culinary Manuscripts of the Fifteenth Century*, Special Series 8, Oxford University Press and Early English Text Society, Oxford, 1985

—, and B. Hosington, 'From Espinee to Sambocade: Flowers in the Recipes of Medieval England', in *Petits Propos culinaires* 59, Prospect Books, Totnes, 1998

Hill, Ray, *The Health Food Store*, Nuhelth Books, Stroud, 1998

Hole, Christina, *The English Housewife in the Seventeenth Century, Containing the Manuscript Collection of Sarah Loveland*, Chatto & Windus, London, 1953

Hone, Nathaniel, *The Manor and Manorial Records*, Methuen & Co., London, 1906

Hughes, Kathryn, *The Short Life and Long Times of Mrs Beeton*, 4th Estate, London, 2005

Jack, Florence, *The Woman's Book*, T. C. & E. C. Jack, London, 1911

Johnston, James P., *A Hundred Years' Eating: Food, Drink and the Daily Diet in Britain*, Gill & Macmillan, Dublin, 1977

Kelly, Ian, *Cooking for Kings: The Life of Antonin Carême*, Short Books, London, 2003

Kummer, C., 'Roast Chicken', *Atlantic Monthly* (November 1985), pp. 122–4

Labarge, Margaret, *A Baronial Household of the Thirteenth Century*, Harvester Press, Brighton, 1980

Lehmann, Gilly, 'Food and Drink at the Restoration as Seen through the Diary 1660–1669 of Samuel Pepys', in *Petits Propos culinaires* 59, Prospect Books, Totnes, 1998

—, *The British Housewife: Cookery Books, Cooking and Society in C18th Britain*, Prospect Books, Totnes, 2003

Lucraft, Fiona, 'The London Art of Plagiarism', in *Petits Propos culinaires* 42, Prospect Books, Totnes, 1992

—, 'A Study of the Compleat Confectioner by Hannah Glasse', in *Petits Propos culinaires* 56–8, Prospect Books, Totnes, 1997–8

MacDonogh, Giles, *A Palate in Revolution: Grimod de la Reynière and the Almanach des Gourmands*, Robin Clark, New York, 1987

—, *Brillat-Savarin: The Judge and His Stomach*, John Murray, London, 1992

Maclean, Virginia, *Short Title Catalogue of Household and Cookery Books Published in the English Tongue 1701–1800*, Prospect Books, London, 1981

Mahon, Brid, *Land of Milk and Honey: The Story of Traditional Irish Food and Drink*, Poolbeg, Dublin, 1991

Mars, Valerie, *Food Culture and History*, vol. 1, London Food Seminar, London, 1993

Mennell, Stephen, *All Manners of Food: Eating and Taste in Britain and France from the Middle Ages to the Present*, Blackwell, Oxford, 1985

Moore, Simon, *Spoons 1650–2000*, Shire, Aylesbury, 2006

Murray, Venetia, *High Society: A Social History of the Regency 1788–1830*, Viking, London, 1998

Oddy, D., and D. Miller, eds, *The Making of the Modern British Diet*, Croom Helm, London, 1976

Oddy, Derek, *From Plain Fare to Fusion Food: British Diet from the 1890s to the 1990s*, Boydell Press, Woodbridge, 2003

O'drisceoil, Diarmuid, 'An Experiment in Bronze Age Cooking', in *Petits Propos culinaires* 45, Prospect Books, Totnes, 1993

Oxford, A. W., *English Cookery Books to the Year 1850*, Oxford University Press, Oxford, 1913

Parkiss, D., *The English Civil War*, HarperCollins, London, 2006

Parissien, Steven, *The Georgian House*, Aurum, London, 1995

—, *George IV: The Grand Entertainment*, John Murray, London, 2001

Paston Williams, Sarah, *The Art of Dining*, National Trust, London, 1993

Peterson, Toby, 'Arab Influence on Western European Cooking', *Journal of Medieval History*, 6 (1980), pp. 317–41

Petrie, G., 'Notice of Ruins of Ancient Dwellings at Skara Brae', *Proc. Soc. Antiq. Scotland*, 7 (1869), pp. 201–21

Porter, Roy, *English Society in the Eighteenth Century*, Allen Lane, London, 1982

—, *Flesh in the Age of Reason*, Allen Lane, London, 2003

Prochaska, Alice and Frank, *Margaretta Acworth's Georgian Cookery Book*, Pavilion, London, 1987

Pullar, Philippa, *Consuming Passions: A History of English Food and Appetite*, Hamish Hamilton, London, 1970

Purkiss, Diane, *The English Civil War: A People's History*, Harper Collins, London, 2006

Rossi Wilcox, Susan, *Dinner for Dickens*, Prospect Books, Totnes, 2005

Salway, P., *Roman Britain*, Oxford University Press, Oxford, 1982

Sambrook, Pamela, and Peter Brears, *The Country House Kitchen 1650–1900*, Sutton, Stroud, 1997

Scola, Roger, *Feeding the Victorian City*, Manchester University Press, Manchester, 1992

Scully, Terrence, *The Art of Cookery in the Middle Ages*, Boydell, Woodbridge, 1995

Sempers, Chris, *Anglo Saxon Magic, Medicine and Wisdom*, Corvus Books, Ferriby, 2004

Shaw, Timothy, *The World of Escoffier*, Zwemmer, London, 1994

Sim, Alison, *Food and Feast in Tudor England*, Sutton, London, 1997

Sissons, Michael, and Philip French, eds, *The Age of Austerity, 1945–51*, Hodder, London, 1963

Smith, Joan, ed., *Hungry for You*, Chatto & Windus, London, 1996

Smith, Michael, *Fine English Cookery*, Faber & Faber, London, 1973

Spencer, Colin, *British Food: An Extraordinary Thousand Years of History*, Grub Street, London, 2002

Stead, Jennifer, 'Greensauce', in *Petits Propos culinaires* 3, Prospect Books, Totnes, 1979

—, 'Quizzing Glasse: or Hannah Scrutinised', in *Petits Propos culinaires* 13–14, Prospect Books, Totnes, 1983

—, 'Viper Soup, Viper Broth, Viper Wine', in *Petits Propos culinaires* 51, Prospect Books, Totnes, 1995

Strong, Roy, *Feast: A History of Grand Eating*, Jonathan Cape, London, 2002

—, and Julia Trevelyan Oman, *Elizabeth R*, Secker & Warburg, London, 1971

Swabey, Ffiona, *Medieval Gentlewoman: Life in a Widow's Household in the Later Middle Ages*, Sutton, Stroud, 1999

Symons, Michael, *History of Cooks and Cooking*, Prospect Books, Totnes, 2001

Tannahill, Reay, *Food in History*, Penguin, London, 1998

Thacker, Christopher, *The Genius of Gardening*, Weidenfeld & Nicolson, London, 1994

Thacker, John, *Cathedral Cookery*, Durham University Library, Durham, 1985

Thomas, Annie, *The Modern Housewife or How We Live Now*, Ward, Lock & Co., London, 1883

Thurley, Simon, *The Royal Palaces of Tudor England: Architecture and Court Life 1460–1547*, Yale University Press, London, 1993

Tims, Barbara, ed., *Food in 'Vogue': Six Decades of Cooking and Entertaining*, Pyramid Books, London, 1976

Toussaint-Samat, M., *A History of Food*, trans. Anthea Bell, Blackwell, Oxford, 1992

Toynbee, J.M.C., *Art in Roman Britain*, Phaidon, London, 1982

Trease, G. E., 'Spicers and Apothecaries of the Royal Household in the Reign of Henry III, Edward I and Edward II', *Nottingham Medieval Studies*, 3 (1959), pp. 19–52

Trigg, Stephanie, *Wynnere and Wastoure*, Early English Text Society 297, Oxford University Press, London, 1990

Turner, H. T., ed., *Manners and Household Expenses of England in the C13 and C15*, Roxburgh Club, vol. 57, 1841

Turner, Jack, *Spice: The History of a Temptation*, HarperCollins, London, 2004

Uglow, Jenny, A *Little History of British Gardening*, Chatto & Windus, 2004

Urban, Tigner Holmes, Jr, *Daily Living in the C12: Based on Observations of Alexander Neckam in London and Paris*, University of Wisconsin Press, Madison, 1952

Varey, Simon, 'Hell on Earth, or the Joys of Viper Soup', in *Petits Propos culinaires* 50, Prospect Books, Totnes, 1995

Visser, Margaret, *Much Depends on Dinner: The Extraordinary History and Mythology, Allure and Obsessions, Perils and Taboos of an Ordinary Meal*, Penguin, London, 1989

—, *The Rituals of Dinner: The Origins, Evolution, Eccentricities and the Meaning of Table Manners*, Penguin, London, 1993

Walker, Harlan, ed., *Oxford Symposium on Food and Cookery 1990: Feasting and Fasting*, Prospect Books, Totnes, 1990

—, ed., *Public Eating – Proceedings of the Oxford Symposium on Food and Cookery, 1991*, Prospect Books, Totnes, 1991

— ed., *Oxford Symposium: Disappearing Foods*, Prospect Books, Totnes, 1995

—, ed., *Cooks and Other People: Proceedings of the Oxford Symposium on Food and Cookery, 1995*, Prospect Books, Totnes, 1996

—, ed., *Oxford Symposium on Food and Cookery – Food in the Arts*, Prospect Books, Totnes, 1998

—, ed., *Milk: Beyond the Dairy: Oxford Symposium of Food 1999*, Prospect Books, Totnes, 2000

Warren, Geoffrey C., ed., *The Foods We Eat*, Cassell, London, 1958

Weir, Alison, *Elizabeth the Queen*, Jonathan Cape, London, 1998

—, *Henry VIII, King and Court*, Jonathan Cape, London, 2001

Weir, Robin, and Peter Brears, *Mrs Marshall, the Greatest Victorian Ice Cream Maker*, For Syon House by Smith Settle, Ltd, Otley, 1998

White, J., *London in the Nineteenth Century*, Jonathan Cape, London, 2007

White, R. J., *The Age of George III*, Heinemann, London, 1968

Wilkins, John, et al., eds, *Food in Antiquity*, Exeter University Press, Exeter, 1995

Wilson, A. N., *After the Victorians 1901–53*, Hutchinson, London, 2005

Wilson, C. Anne, *Food and Drink in Britain, from the Stone Age to Recent Time*, Constable, London, 1973

—, 'A Cookery Book and Its Context: Elizabethan Cookery and Lady Fettiplace', in *Petits Propos culinaires* 25, Prospect Books, Totnes, 1987

—, 'Meals and Mealtimes, Then and Now', in *Petits Propos culinaires* 45, Prospect Books, Totnes, 1993

—, *Luncheon, Nuncheon and Other Meals: Eating with the Victorians*, Sutton, Stroud, 1995

—, *Water of Life: A History of Wine Distilling and Spirits 500 BC to AD 2000*, Prospect Books, Totnes, 2007

—, ed., *Banqueting Stuffe: The Fare and Social Background of the Tudor and Stuart Banquet*, Leeds Symposium on Food History and Traditions, Edinburgh University Press, Edinburgh, 1991

—, ed., *Liquid Nourishment*, Edinburgh University Press, Edinburgh, 1993

Woman, A, *Young Woman's Companion or Frugal Housewife*, Russell & Allen, Manchester, 1811

Wood, Jacqui, *Prehistoric Cooking*, Tempus, Stroud, 2001

Wood-Legh, Kathleen, *Small Household of the Fifteenth Century*, Manchester University Press, Manchester, 1956

Wright, Thomas, *History of Domestic Manners and Sentiments in England during the Middle Ages*, Chapman and Hall, London, 1862

Youings, Joyce, *Sixteenth Century England*, Allen Lane, London, 1984

WEBSITES

www.foodtimeline.org
www.thousandeggs.com

Acknowledgements

'I must frankly own,' wrote Mrs Beeton in the preface to her monumental work, 'that if I had known, beforehand, that this book would have cost me the labour which it has, I should never have been courageous enough to commence it.' I know how she felt. But while Isabella cut and pasted her recipes and household instructions in isolation at the parlour table, I've been supported by the learning and wisdom of an army of kind people. With the oft-repeated and obvious caveat that all failures, omissions, inconsistencies and errors are my own, I would therefore like publicly to thank:

my kind, clever and inspiring friends, including Paul Bailey, Rodney Bolt, Jane and Ken Cox, Kirsty Gunn, Ravi Mirchandani, George Morley, Lawrence Norfolk, Jeremy Trevathan, George Walden, Frank Wynne and Andrea Wulf, for all their particular insights;

all the staff at the British Library Rare Books Room and at the London Library; Stella Coomb at Hammersmith and Fulham Council; Audrey Hammond; The Leeds Food Symposium, in particular its organiser and author of one of the first outstanding histories of food and drink in Britain, C. Anne Wilson; Madeleine Marsh; Diane Naylor and Andrew Peppit at Chatsworth; Dr Peter Morris, Head of Research Science at the Science Museum, London; Marguerite Patten; Alan Slade at the British Museum; David Smith at the New York Public Library; Harriet O'Brien; Lynne Olver at foodtimeline.org; and Simon Winder at the Penguin Press, who very kindly supplied me with many of the classics on his redoubtable list;

and the ones who really made it happen: Caroline Dawnay at PFD; Stephanie Cabot, formerly at the William Morris Agency, London;

Bill Swainson, Emily Sweet, Nick Humphrey, Kate Tindal-Robertson, Rosie Hardman, Sarah Morris, Minna Fry, Andrea Belloli, Sarah Barlow, Alan Rutter, and the whole gorgeous team at Bloomsbury in London; Margot Weale at Midas; Karen Rinaldi, Sara Mercurio and Amanda Katz at Bloomsbury in America; and David Cross and the Arts Council of Great Britain, without whose support this book would have turned out to be quite a different thing.

Taste is dedicated to our children and to my parents: the loving buffers of my world. Yet at its heart lies the innate generosity and blinding intelligence of my husband, David Miller; without the cushion of his support and his stoic ability to bear and to forgive the spikes of my ball-juggling anxieties, it could neither have been researched nor written. To him, above all, my most loving thanks.

Index

Due to the detailed nature of this book, indexed references to particular foods and culinary styles/techniques are limited to pages on which particular information about them is given, omitting their appearance in, for example, ingredients lists.

NB – Figures in **bold** refer to illustrations

A Note on the Author

Kate Colquhoun is the author of *A Thing in Disguise: The Visionary Life of Joseph Paxton* (2003), which was short-listed for the Duff Cooper Prize 2004 and long-listed for the Samuel Johnson Prize 2003. She reviews regularly for the *Daily Telegraph* and has written for *The Times*, the *Financial Times*, *BBC History Magazine*, *Saga Magazine*, *The Garden* and *Country Life*. She lives in London with her husband and two children.

A Note on the Type

The text of this book is set in Linotype Stempel Garamond, a version of Garamond adapted and first used by the Stempel foundry in 1924. It's one of several versions of Garamond based on the designs of Claude Garamond. It is thought that Garamond based his font on Bembo, cut in 1495 by Francesco Griffo in collaboration with the Italian printer Aldus Manutius. Garamond types were first used in books printed in Paris around 1532. Many of the present-day versions of this type are based on the *Typi Academiae* of Jean Jannon cut in Sedan in 1615.

Claude Garamond was born in Paris in 1480. He learned how to cut type from his father and by the age of fifteen he was able to fashion steel punches the size of a pica with great precision. At the age of sixty he was commissioned by King Francis I to design a Greek alphabet; for this he was given the honourable title of royal type founder. He died in 1561.